DAVID BOYLE:
FROM ARTISAN TO ARCHAEOLOGIST

David Boyle (1842–1911), a Scot by birth and a blacksmith by training, rose to international prominence as Canada's premier archaeologist before the First World War. His contemporaries honoured him for his enormous contributions to the emergence of modern archaeology and anthropology, and to the museum and historic preservation movements in central Canada. Subsequent generations, however, lost sight of his significance. This biography rescues Boyle from obscurity and reinstates him in his proper place in Canadian history.

Boyle's transformation from artisan to archaeologist is a remarkable story. His odyssey begins within the vibrant and earnest British artisan culture which extolled the self-improvement ethic and believed in the proposition that knowledge is power and the key to respectability. Initially, the commitment to the acquisition and imparting of knowledge led Boyle into school teaching in rural Ontario. This well-documented phase of his career is of no little importance to educational historians since Boyle was an early practitioner of the radical child-centred theories and methods of the controversial Swiss educator Johann Heinrich Pestalozzi. Boyle emerges from the pages of this book as a truly innovative and superior nineteenth-century teacher.

Gerald Killan also vividly shows how in the 1870s Boyle's ideas about self-culture and child-centred education fused with his passions for Darwinian biology, geology, and archaeology. As a consequence he stimulated an 'intellectual awakening' in Elora, Ontario, and brought the villagers face to face with the unsettling scientific concepts and debates of the mid-nineteenth century.

Subsequently, Boyle found his place in the world of scholarship in Toronto as curator-archaeologist of the Canadian Institute Museum (1884–96) and the Ontario Provincial Museum (1896–1911). During this phase of his career, Boyle conceptualized, launched, and to a large extent completed the program that laid the groundwork for the development of Ontario archaeology as a systematic and scientific discipline.

For those interested in the beginnings of Canadian archaeology and anthropology this is an indispensable reference. It will also be of considerable interest to general readers and to specialists in Ontario social and educational history, museum development, and heritage preservation.

GERALD KILLAN is a member of the Department of Social Sciences, King's College, affiliated with the University of Western Ontario.

D1382773

GERALD KILLAN

To Bill Donaldson
On the occasion of the
10th OAS symposium
29 Oct '83

Cheers
Gerald Killan

David Boyle: From Artisan to Archaeologist

FOREWORD BY WILLIAM C. NOBLE

PUBLISHED IN ASSOCIATION WITH
THE ONTARIO HERITAGE FOUNDATION BY
UNIVERSITY OF TORONTO PRESS
Toronto Buffalo London

© University of Toronto Press 1983
Toronto Buffalo London
Printed in Canada
ISBN 0-8020-2475-0 (cloth)
ISBN 0-8020-6496-5 (paper)

Canadian Cataloguing in Publication Data

Killan, Gerald, 1945–
    David Boyle: from artisan to archaeologist
    Includes index.
    ISBN 0-8020-2475-0 (bound). – ISBN 0-8020-6496-5 (pbk.)
    1. Boyle, David, 1842–1911. 2. Archaeologists – Ontario – Biography. I. Ontario
Heritage Foundation. II. Title.
    FC3072.1.B69K54   971.3'03'0924   C83-094164-9
    F1058.B69K54

This book has been published with the help of a grant from the Social Science Federation of
Canada, using funds provided by the Social Sciences and Humanities Research Council of
Canada, and a grant to the University of Toronto Press from the Ontario Heritage Foundation,
Ministry of Citizenship and Culture.

To Robert G. Bowes and Jacques R. Goutor, friends and advisors

Contents

Foreword

David Boyle (1842–1911), as this excellent biography relates, is the founding father of modern archaeology in Ontario and, indeed, in eastern Canada. His contributions to the theory and practice of Canadian archaeology were enormous; this book essentially documents the early history of the Ontario archaeological tradition. Strangely, however, despite his immensely innovative and impressive contributions as an archaeologist and his noteworthy work as an educator, ethnologist, and museum curator, Boyle remains a shadowy or unknown figure to most Canadians. He is truly one of the forgotten men of Canada's past. For this reason Dr Killan's biography is important and timely; it rescues Boyle from obscurity and reinstates him in his proper position in Canadian history. Both the general reader and the specialist will find *From Artisan to Archaeologist* a smoothly integrated work that provides compelling insights into the emergence of modern archaeology-anthropology and the museum and historic preservation movements in central Canada.

But what of David Boyle himself? What kind of a man was he? How did he rise to achieve international renown as the most important single figure in Canadian archaeology prior to the First World War? This book answers all of these questions, and begins by tracing his origins. We learn that David Boyle was born in Greenock, Scotland, on 1 May 1842, the son of a blacksmith who emigrated to Canada West in 1856 when David was fourteen years old. David himself apprenticed as a blacksmith in Eden Mills, Wellington County (1857–60). His subsequent transformation from artisan to archaeologist is a remarkable story; it is the odyssey of a self-taught individual who rejected the prevailing materialist values of his day and dedicated himself instead to the ideal of self-culture and to the acquisition and imparting of knowledge. Boyle acquired his attitudes to life and learning in growing up within a vibrant and earnest artisan community that extolled the self-improvement ethic and believed in the proposition that 'knowledge is power and the key to respectability.' To the end of his life, he remained the 'quintessential product of the British autodidact artisan culture out of which he sprang.'

Initially, the quest for knowledge led him into school teaching, first as the master of a one-room schoolhouse in Upper Pilkington Township, Wellington County (1865–71), and later as the principal of the Elora Public School (1871–81). This well-documented phase of his career is of no little significance for students of Ontario's educational history, since Boyle was an early practitioner of the radical child-centred theories and methods of the controversial Swiss educator Johann Heinrich Pestalozzi (1746–1827). Boyle emerges from the pages of this book as a truly innovative and superior nineteenth-century teacher. It was during this period that David Boyle, a caring man of patience and persistence, undertook the poignant task of teaching a deaf mute girl how to read and write.

During the 1870s in Elora, Boyle's self-improvement ethic and child-centred educational philosophy fused with his passions for Darwinian biology, geology, and archaeology. The result was the formation of three significant cultural institutions: the Elora Mechanics' Institute, the third largest of its kind in Ontario by 1881; the Elora School Museum, which housed one of the best natural science collections in Ontario; and the Elora Natural History Society, which promoted all lines of scientific enquiry and brought the villagers face to face with the unsettling complex of ideas raised by the Darwinian revolution of thought. Dr Killan vividly portrays how these institutions stimulated an 'intellectual awakening' in the once parochial village, and in so doing provides us with a better understanding of the process by which the scientific concepts and debates of the mid-nineteenth century percolated down to the Ontario countryside by the 1870s.

Following brief and unsuccessful stints as a textbook promoter (1882–3) and a proprietor of Ye Olde Booke Shoppe and Natural Science Exchange (1883–8) in Toronto, David Boyle found his place in the world of scholarship as curator-archaeologist of the Canadian Institute Museum (1884–96) and later the Ontario Provincial Museum (1896–1911). The latter was housed in the Toronto Normal School and its important collections were eventually transferred in 1933 to the David Boyle Room of the Royal Ontario Museum. From 1884 until he was permanently incapacitated by a stroke in 1909, Boyle conceptualized, launched, and to a large extent completed a program that laid the groundwork for the development of Ontario archaeology as a systematic and scientific discipline.

Little is known about Boyle's private life, although it is evident that he was rarely free from financial worries as an underpaid, overworked teacher and museum curator. In the year of Confederation, 1867, he married Martha Frankland and over their forty-four years of marriage they raised five children. Susanna, the eldest, studied medicine at Trinity Medical College and upon graduation joined the faculty of Women's Medical College, an accomplishment that greatly pleased her father who firmly believed in the equal treatment and education of the sexes. Son John became a druggist and James a medical doctor; both eventually moved west, the former to Vancouver, the latter to Edmonton where he was elected to the Alberta legislature. William flourished in the dry goods business, while the youngest daughter, Anne, became an ardent feminist spokesperson and a journalist.

It is remembered that David Boyle enjoyed his pipe and whiskey and was renowned as a raconteur; he had a phenomenal memory for humorous stories and anecdotes. He frequently regaled people with his tales at public gatherings and Burns night celebrations. His Scottish humour, published in the *Scottish American Journal* for many years under the pseudonym of 'Andrew McSpurtle' and written in 'broad Scots' vernacular, attracted a loyal readership. Although an ardent Scottish patriot, Boyle was also keenly aware of the need to stimulate a Canadian national sentiment. To that end he also wrote a book for children entitled *Uncle Jim's Canadian Nursery Rhymes for Family and Kindergarten Use* (1908), illustrated by the young upcoming artist Charles W. Jefferys. It was a lively, delightful volume of nonsense and humour, the first of its kind in Canadian children's literature.

Of his published writings, though, it is the *Annual Archaeological Reports for Ontario* that stand as the most visible testimony to David Boyle's importance. He established this journal in 1887 and continued to edit and illustrate it until 1908. It represents the first periodical published in Canada devoted primarily to archaeology, but also includes valuable anthropological and ethnographic articles of the day. The series was continued under Boyle's successor as provincial archaeologist, Dr Rowland B. Orr (1852–1933), until it lapsed in 1928.

Boyle's interest in the past Indian occupations of Ontario essentially crystallized in the 1870s, a consequence of his studies into natural science and geology and his explorations of the fields and river valleys of Wellington County. He made one of his first artifact finds, a worked deer phalange, some time during the 1860s on his uncle's farm, 'Braeside,' near Richmond Hill north of Toronto. But it was only after his move to Toronto that he took up relic collecting with fervour. His first major excavation occurred on 5 October 1885 when he reinvestigated the historic Neutral Dwyer ossuaries north-west of Hamilton, Ontario. These burials had previously been examined by the Rev. Charles Dade in 1836, and by Henry R. Schoolcraft in 1843–5. Boyle obtained enough skulls and other specimens to put together an exhibit in the front window of his Toronto bookstore. Thus began his zealous collection of artifacts for the Canadian Institute Museum.

While much of David Boyle's work involved sometimes tedious administrative and curatorial duties such as cataloguing new specimens or preparing public exhibits, he resorted to the field as often as possible. Indeed, it is as a field man that Boyle is probably best known among the modern Ontario archaeological fraternity. Many of the sites he visited are now classic: Serpent Mounds near Peterborough; the Clearville, Lawson, Parker, Southwold, and Solid Comfort sites in south-western Ontario; Ste Marie and Christian Island on Georgian Bay; the Bon Echo pictographs and Beckstead sites in eastern Ontario; and the Nipigon Bay rock paintings north of Superior. This indefatigable field worker also produced in 1906 the first archaeological map of Ontario. Boyle's work in the field culminated in 1908 with salvage excavations at the St David's historic Neutral Iroquois cemetery in the Niagara Peninsula. This site was being looted by Canadian and American relic hunters, a situation that greatly offended Boyle's scientific and patriotic sensibilities. Ironically, Boyle, the teacher, *par excellence*, did not train any archaeological successors, an unhappy consequence perhaps of financial constraints. Nevertheless he did extend opportunities and considerable encouragement to a number of willing volunteers, including such notables as Andrew F. Hunter, George E. Laidlaw, and William J. Wintemberg.

By the end of his career, David Boyle, the self-taught ex-blacksmith, had become one of Canada's foremost scientists, an honoured member of both the American and British Associations for the Advancement of Science, the International Congress of Americanists, and a founding member of the American Anthropological Association. On a more local level, he was a recognized leader of the province's burgeoning heritage preservation movement. He wrote the *History of Scarboro* (1896), an outstanding example of local history, and served nine years as secretary of the Ontario Historical Society (1898–1907). Formal honours accrued to him. In 1908 he was awarded the prestigious Cornplanter Medal for Iroquois Research by the Cayuga County Historical Society of New York State. And while bedridden in June 1909, 'as the shades of night were fast closing around him in his sick room,' the University of Toronto Senate called a special meeting to confer upon Boyle the degree of LLD. He died on 14 February 1911, and was buried in Mount Pleasant Cemetery, Toronto.

Today, David Boyle is being rediscovered and remembered. It was most fortunate that in 1948 the late Professor Thomas F. McIlwraith (1899–1964), who established the first department of anthropology in Canada at the University of Toronto in 1926, managed to acquire many of Boyle's letters and papers. These he housed at the Royal Ontario Museum in the ethnology department. Having the privilege of examining these documents in 1969 and believing them to be a veritable treasure, I resolved that something should be done to recognize David Boyle for the important Ontario and Canadian figure that he was. Opportunities presented themselves in 1975 through the Ontario Heritage Foundation. In October of that year, the foundation established a David Boyle Scholarship for Archaeology. Dr Gerald Killan became the first recipient of this blue-ribbon award in 1977 for his proposal to write a full-scale biography of Boyle. The publication of his book marks a second concrete measure to honour the man. A third step towards restoring David Boyle to modern public recognition occurred with the erection of a historical and archaeological plaque by the Ontario Heritage Foundation. This distinctive marker was unveiled with full ceremonial dignity in front of the Elora Public Library on 28 November 1976, a blustery and overcast Grey Cup day. David Boyle is also remembered within the Royal Ontario Museum where a room is named after him in the archaeology division. While many of Boyle's archaeological specimens have disappeared over the years, his original catalogue cards and descriptions survive in that museum which he helped to found.

It gives me deep pleasure to thank and congratulate Dr Killan on behalf of the Ontario Heritage Foundation, the Ontario Ministry of Citizenship and Culture (originally the Ontario Ministry of Culture and Recreation), and everyone involved in the realization of this biography. All persons interested in the beginnings of Canadian archaeology will find this volume to be a primary, indispensable reference work.

WILLIAM C. NOBLE

Preface

The private papers and manuscript collections upon which this biography is based are to be found in a variety of repositories. The most substantial collection of Boyle papers is stored in the department of ethnology and the library-archives of the Royal Ontario Museum. These documents shed much light on Boyle's career as an educator in Wellington County (1865–81), and later as an archaeologist-curator in Toronto. They include the original copies of most of his public speeches and minor publications as well as a complete set of Boyle's *Archaeological Reports* (1887–1908). The department of ethnology also houses the invaluable George Laidlaw scrapbooks, the Andrew F. Hunter correspondence and field notes, and many of the records of the Ontario Provincial Museum. The extensive Andrew F. Hunter papers at the Simcoe County Museum and Archives in Minesing, Ontario, were also of much benefit in the preparation of this work. Considerable Boyle material is to be found at the Ontario Archives, particularly in the education department records, the Ontario Historical Society collection, and the Charles Clarke papers. The small amount of Clarke papers and the Elora Mechanics' Institute records at the Wellington County Museum were also helpful sources. In the Baldwin Room of the Metropolitan Toronto Central Library, one may peruse the Boyle scrapbooks, and the records of his ill-fated business venture, Ye Olde Booke Shoppe and Natural Science Exchange (1883–8). This study was also facilitated by the modest collections of Boyle papers at the Smithsonian Institution Archives in Washington, DC, the National Anthropological Archives of the National Museum of Natural History, Washington, DC, and the Peabody Museum of American Archaeology and Ethnology at Harvard University, Cambridge, Massachusetts. Finally, the 'epistles' of Andrew McSpurtle (Boyle's *nom de plume*) in the *Scottish American Journal* from 1875 to 1908 proved indispensable. A great many archivists and curators helped me during the research of this book. I am grateful to every one of them.

Perhaps the greatest frustration in researching this volume was the paucity of sources relating to Boyle's early years in Britain, not a surprising development when studying a working-class family, and the lack of documentation pertaining to his private life. For providing me with what little data do exist on these matters, I am especially indebted to Mrs Helen Boyd of Ottawa, the Boyle family genealogist, and to the late Mrs Adelle Harris of Toronto, Boyle's granddaughter. I am pleased to acknowledge that Mr W.R.S. McIntyre of Birkenhead, England, a retired headmaster and local historian, and J.L. Hamilton, chief librarian of the Central Library, Greenock, Scotland, undertook research on my behalf. Mr John Millar, managing director, Heap and Partners Ltd, Merseyside, England, also provided me with information about the old Canada Works of Birkenhead.

A number of archaeologists have guided me through my personal fog of confusion about the development of archaeological method and theory and the current state of their profession. Thanks are due to Kenneth Kidd, James Pendergast, William Russell, and William Fox for patiently answering my often uninformed queries. Mima Kapches at the ROM kindly assisted in selecting the archaeological illustrations for this book. Bruce Trigger has been a source of inspiration; his careful assessment of an early draft of this manuscript saved me from many embarrassing errors and questionable interpretations. But most of all, I wish to acknowledge the considerable efforts of William Noble, who more than anyone else was determined to rescue David Boyle from oblivion. It was Dr Noble, as chairperson of the Archaeological Committee of the Ontario Heritage Foundation, who launched the David Boyle Scholarship for Archaeology and in his own inimitable fashion declared me the first recipient of that prestigious award. Dr Noble commented at great length on the early draft of this manuscript, and he honours me again by writing the foreword to this work.

Several of Ontario's fine civil servants have been of no little assistance. David Roberts gave me full access to the files he compiled when researching for the Ontario Heritage Foundation plaque erected in Elora (1976) to commemorate Boyle. Allen Tyyska and Phil Baker have been the long-suffering middlemen between myself, the foundation, and the University of Toronto Press.

The financial assistance that permitted the research for this volume came in the form of the David Boyle scholarship. The Hon. John White, current chairman of the OHF, and Professor Syd Wise, past chairman, have both strongly supported this project and for that I am grateful. King's College (London, Ontario) provided generous annual research grants and typing assistance, but most importantly, a partial study leave during which time the manuscript was written.

To my parents, who indirectly subsidized my research in Toronto by providing food and shelter, and who buoyed my spirits during my regrettably long absences from my wife and children, I owe incalculable debts. Without complaint, those closest to me – Linda, Jeremy, Jared, and Jessica – have altered their pattern of life to suit my scholastic needs and priorities. Their rewards for so doing, I admit, have been negligible. Finally, it gives me great satisfaction to dedicate this work to my two friends and colleagues Robert G. Bowes and Jacques R. Goutor. In both their cases, the old cliché that this book (at least in its present form) would not have been possible without their guidance is most certainly appropriate.

G K

PARTIAL GENEALOGY OF THE BOYLE FAMILY

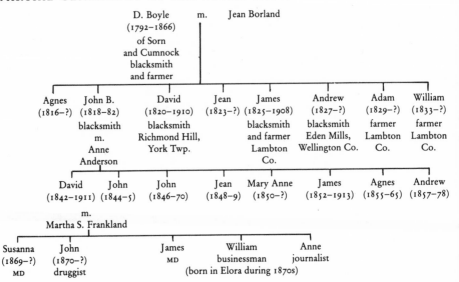

Old David Boyle of Cumnock, ca. 1853 (Helen Boyd, Ottawa)

John Borland Boyle, ca. 1853 (Helen Boyd, Ottawa)

Martha Frankland Boyle, ca. 1870 (Helen Boyd, Ottawa)

The Public School in Elora, Ontario, where David Boyle was principal, 1871–81 (Helen Boyd, Ottawa)

David Boyle and the students of the Elora Public School, ca. 1872 (Helen Boyd, Ottawa)

David Boyle at his desk, Ontario Provincial Museum, 1900 (Ontario Archives)

David Boyle, ca. 1905 (Adelle Harris, Toronto)

David Boyle with his first grandchild, Adelle, ca. 1908 (Adelle Harris, Toronto)

DAVID BOYLE: FROM ARTISAN TO ARCHAEOLOGIST

1

Son of Vulcan, 1842–60

'My father was born in Sorn, where his father was the village blacksmith,' reminisced David Boyle towards the end of his life.[1] Sorn, a compact string of unremarkable one-storey, red sandstone houses, dominated by an imposing ancient castle and seventeenth-century church, nestled on the bank of the River Ayr just a few miles north of Cumnock in Ayrshire, Scotland. The Boyles, in fact, had flourished as blacksmiths in the area for at least four generations. They were 'sons of Vulcan,' the independent and indispensable master craftsmen, workers of wrought iron who shoed the horses and made and repaired the implements required on the farms and in the mines and forests of the surrounding district. Within the framework of the British occupational structure, sons of artisans normally followed their fathers into the trades, while the sons of the unskilled and semi-skilled followed their fathers into labouring work. Well-to-do artisans could afford the luxury of sending their children to school and of supporting their sons during the years of apprenticeship; and so it was with the Boyles of Sorn.

David Boyle's grandfather, another David by name, who for the sake of clarity will be identified as D. Boyle (1792–1866), fared exceedingly well in Sorn. Married to a local girl, Jean Borland, he sired a large family, six boys and two girls. Convinced as were most artisans that knowledge is power, D. Boyle saw to it that his offspring received some formal elementary education, at least to the point that they could all read and write. The youngest son, William (b. 1833), was fortunate enough to acquire some secondary schooling in Ayr and later at Glasgow. The other children, with their father's example to inspire them, taught themselves other elements of useful knowledge.[2] In common with so many of their class, they made their way through grammar texts and volumes on political philosophy, natural science, and Scottish history and literature, particularly the works of Robert Burns, Scotland's national poet. Burns had been born some twenty miles distant at Alloway and much of his inspiration had come from the Ayrshire landscape. The Boyles of Sorn typified those 'earnest and reputable people' of the British nineteenth-century autodidact artisan culture.[3]

For the four eldest sons of D. Boyle,[4] practical education came in the village blacksmith's shop. Here, during their years of apprenticeship under master craftsmen and journeymen, the occupational skills, customs, and attitudes – the so-called mystery or secrets of the trade – were indelibly impressed on the boys by precept and example. Perhaps the most important legacy of the apprenticeship period was the set of attitudes that served to distinguish the craftsman from the unskilled labourer. In the shop they developed a sense of the dignity of craft status and of the privileged position held by craftsmen in the community. They were made keenly aware that their special skills and trade were exclusively their own. This feeling was heightened by the anticipation of the economic rewards, security, and upward mobility that their craft had brought to their family in the past.[5]

D. Boyle of Sorn had much in common with the lower strata of the British middle class. Certainly his ideals and goals in life were cast in a bourgeois mould. His social aspirations went beyond the normal expectations of his trade, and by the mid-1830s he had acquired the financial means to realize them. Having divested himself of his business in Sorn, D. Boyle moved his family near Cumnock, a mining town a few miles south on the Lugar Water, and took up a lease on some two hundred acres of land on one of the large estates. Again the elder Boyle succeeded, this time as a commercial farmer. Assisted by his sons, sub-tenants, and hired help, he cultivated cash crops of wheat, oats, and turnips, and raised livestock for the expanding urban centres in Ayrshire. There was little the family lacked in a material sense; theirs was a comfortable life. Yet, notwithstanding his own good fortune, D. Boyle was not free of anxiety, particularly about the economic prospects of his offspring. As one son after another completed his apprenticeship in the late thirties and early forties, they faced a limited range of opportunities within which to practise their craft in the Ayrshire countryside. As they weighed their options, conversation turned frequently to the prospect of emigrating to North America where land was reputedly cheap and skilled artisans scarce. Eventually, in 1849, four of D. Boyle's sons and their families emigrated as a group to Canada West.

Meanwhile, the eldest son, John Borland Boyle (1818–82), the father of the subject of this biography, had already left Cumnock some time during the late 1830s. He had 'tramped' to Greenock, a bustling commercial and industrial port on the south bank of the Clyde River in Renfrewshire, some twenty-two miles downstream from Glasgow. Since the turn of the century Greenock had flourished largely from the shipping trade with the Americas and her population had doubled to about 36,000 inhabitants. 'Greenock for Sugar and Ships' adequately summed up the town's main industrial activities. Her sugar refineries were the largest outside London, while her shipbuilding industries earned international recognition, particularly after Henry Bell's *Comet*, launched in 1812, demonstrated the commercial potential of steamships.[6] Greenock and other west Scotland ports had a singular advantage in the growing expertise of their marine engineers, who by mid-century began to specialize in the building of high-speed and reliable passenger steamships.[7] Once Greenockians had dreamed of rivalling mighty Liverpool itself as a centre of trade and commerce: however, by the time John Boyle arrived in the port seeking employment, Glasgow was laying that dream to rest. Glasgow increasingly dominated the shipping, trade, and commerce on the Clyde as steam tugs and steam dredgers opened the river so that large ocean-going vessels could penetrate to the very heart of the metropolis. By the 1850s, then, Greenock's economic future hinged more than ever on the development of the shipbuilding and engineering industries.[8]

In the engineering shops of Greenock, John Boyle found permanent work at the forge. He was hired by the long-lived family firm of Caird and Company. During the 1840s, the company was one of the first on the Upper Clyde to build iron ships while most other yards continued to construct only wooden sailing vessels for the merchant trade. Earlier, in the mid-1820s, the firm had expanded into the business of general and marine engineering, where it quickly became known as an 'honourable rival' of the family of Napier, Britain's leading marine engineers. In 1846 the gifted designers at Caird and Company introduced the inverted vertical direct-acting engine, which became standard for screw steamers later in the century. The firm also entered the locomotive market and began in the 1840s to build steam engines for the Scottish railway companies of the period.[9] The healthy competition between Caird and its larger rivals, such as Napier and the renowned Scotts of Greenock, kept the company on the cutting edge of west Scotland's industrial expansion.

It was quite normal for a company like Caird to engage rural 'jobbing' smiths such as John Boyle, craftsmen accustomed to turning their hands to every kind of smithy work. This practice enabled the company to avoid the costly apprenticeship system. Apprentices required training by master craftsmen or journeymen; they wasted fuel up the chimney and ruined iron as they learned. Better, the company reasoned, to take the skilled country smith and introduce him to the highly specialized and restricted range of work to be found in their shipyards and engineering factories. After working some years in the Caird shipyards, John Boyle found a place in the company's new locomotive shop. It must have been a bewildering world at first, with so many artisans and labourers, each with a defined task, lined up beside the forges and anvils, and all under a single roof. The noise was mind-numbing and the air foul. Sweating artisans, moving from the heat of the forge to the cold draughts behind, fell victim to chronic pleurisy, pneumonia, and consumption. Not to be found in these works was that romantic figure of the robust and independent village smith happily pounding iron in 'the shade of the spreading chestnut tree.' In the new factories the wage-earning blacksmith had little opportunity of gaining the independence of the old master craftsman. No one of them could hope to claim ownership of the new technology, the complicated machine tools such as the giant trip-hammers and the steam hammers, the new type of furnaces, fuels, and forges, and the huge physical plant that housed them.[10]

Despite the surroundings, John Boyle must have taken consolation in the fact that he had avoided the fate of many traditional craftsmen such as the hatters and shoemakers who had lost purpose and status in the evolving industrial order, their skills made redundant by the winds of technological change. As a village smith with a wide range of experience, he easily adapted his general skills to the requirements of the factory and became a specialist in the forging of locomotive wheels. In so doing, he made the transition from the old elite in the guild tradition to the more recent factory elite, the so-called aristocracy of labour. That all-important status of craft remained his, for in the social scale of things, this new labour aristocracy held 'the knowledge that they occupied a firm and accepted position just below the employers, but very far above the rest.'[11] At Caird and Company, John Boyle received a wage befitting his station and skills in the range of 20s–25s weekly,[12] enough to afford a reasonably furnished home outside the appalling dockside slums of old Greenock, and a life-style several notches above the hard and brutal existence of the vast majority of the working masses. He could also count on regular employment even during periodic recessions, since firms like Caird and Company did not normally disperse their workers during slumps; instead, employees, fearing the spectre of unemployment and the Poor Law, usually negotiated wage reductions with company officials on a district and industry basis.[13]

In 1842 such things as wages and job security probably weighed more than usual on John Boyle's mind. It was a year of severe depression, one of the worst economic slumps to hit the industrial districts of Britain in the nineteenth century. The year before John Boyle had married Anne Anderson, a Highland lass with roots in Perthshire and Argyllshire. On the first day of May 1842, Anne gave birth to their first child, a boy. They named him David, after his grandfather in Cumnock.

The odds did not favour young David surviving his childhood, so high was the infant mortality rate in British industrial centres. Over 50 per cent of all children in the industrial cities died before reaching the age of five,[14] and the child mortality rate in Greenock, the most unhealthy town in nineteenth-century Scotland, was undoubtedly one of the worst in Britain. Housing conditions in Greenock had deteriorated badly since the 1830s when waves of destitute Irish arrived to join the many displaced Highlanders forced to the urban centres during the late eighteenth century by proprietors seeking to convert farmland to pasturage. In the unpaved streets, lanes, and built-over courts off Dalrymple Street, which ran parallel to the river, these working poor found shelter in the jumble of decayed tenements, cellar dwellings, and jerry-built shacks in the shadow of quayside factories and warehouses. It was a place of unspeakable filth, stench, and human degradation. Since Greenock lacked adequate supplies of water, the teeming thousands obtained their water from a dozen wells of questionable safety. Understandably, epidemics of typhus, cholera, smallpox, and other infectious diseases occasionally swept the town.

Greenock also lacked sewage facilities. Only the wealthy enjoyed the luxury of privies connected to their homes; in the great majority of dwellings the lack of such conveniences created a night-soil problem of staggering proportions.[15] From the parliamentary enquiry into the Sanitary Conditions of the Working Classes (1842) came this horror story from Greenock: 'In one part of the street,' Market Street, 'a narrow back street, ... there is a dunghill – yet it is too large to be called a dunghill. I do not mistake its size when I say it contains a hundred cubic yards of impure filth ... It is the stock-in-trade of a person who deals in dung; he retails it by the cartful. To please his customers, he always keeps a nucleus, as the older the filth is the higher the price.'[16] To compound the difficulties of life in Greenock, the burgh was proverbially wet – the wettest large town in all of Britain. The moist atmosphere usually kept a dense cloud of smoke hovering over the place. 'The wall of hills behind,' remarked one ex-resident, 'presses this dark curtain like a pall close to the water front, and holds it there.'[17]

While the Boyle family may have avoided the worst of Greenock's slums by living in the less crowded artisan section of town to the east – on East Quay Lane – they could not escape the effects of their unsanitary surroundings.[18] Young David lost a brother in 1845 and a sister in 1849, both only a year old at the time of their deaths. Two other brothers and a sister born in Greenock managed to survive their childhood. On the whole, life for the Boyle children was relatively comfortable. Along with the benefits of their mother's daily care (she did not have to seek employment outside the home), they enjoyed tolerable living quarters, warm homespun clothes, a solid diet, and occasional sojourns to their grandfather's farm. Their Ayrshire father and Highland mother, accustomed since their youth to the beauty of the countryside, also took advantage of holidays and summer Sundays to set out for the long lanes and rural roads up the hills and beyond to the south. From the higher elevations, on those rare days when the winds dispersed the smog below, the view of the Clyde was spectacular. All in all, the seamier side of Greenock made little impression on the young David Boyle; he fondly remembered only the excitement, the pride in Greenock's ships in direct contact with every port of commerce; the hum of activity on the steamship quay with the noises of escaping steam, the ringing of bells, and shouts of sailors casting off lines. The memory of local characters that formed part of his childhood never left him – 'Heather Jock,' the minstrel; 'Dung Sawney,' a 'scavenger' known for his strange habit of attending funerals; and 'Preachin' Mary,' a 'daft' old religious fanatic who provided no end of amusement for the insensitive street urchins.[19]

II

Reflecting on his development through childhood and adolescence, David Boyle acknowledged the powerful and positive influence of his father. 'Almost my complete teacher in my young days' were the words he chose to describe his father's role.[20] John Boyle's legacy to his son consisted essentially of the social attitudes, beliefs, and modes of behaviour of his own artisan experience. At the heart of John Boyle's personal creed was a commitment to self-improvement. This was an approach to life learned initially in his own father's home, and later powerfully reinforced by the artisan culture of Greenock. Unlike John Boyle, who entered the new stratum of skilled workers in industrial Scotland from the older ranks of master craftsmen, many of the factory artisans first learned their skills in the iron, engineering, and manufacturing industries that sprang up after 1800. They were entirely the creation of the industrial revolution with no lineage to the older and respected elite of craftsmen. This new group of skilled factory labour craved similar social acceptance and respect, and to satisfy that need focused on the goal of 'self-improvement.' In so doing many adopted the values of the capitalist system and emulated the style of life and the rules of behaviour set by the middle class.[21]

A man of firm purpose, John Boyle set a worthy example for his eldest son by virtue of his commitment to the artisan program for self-improvement. Family and home were the focus of his leisure activities. He adhered faithfully to the ideals of moral rectitude, sobriety, and thrift, determined as he was not only to safeguard his living standard, but to fulfil his aspirations for a better home, perhaps even to own his own lot and house. He indulged mainly in 'rational' amusements, whether in the form of suburban excursions to pursue his interest in natural science, home study, or attending the Greenock Mechanics' Institute. Established in 1839 to promote the ideals of self-help, education, and sobriety, the institute boasted a good circulating library, a well-rounded program of lectures, concerts, and classes in literature, the sciences, and the arts, and by 1851, swimming and bathing facilities.[22] John Boyle may have also subscribed to the Watt Library, which housed among other things a scientific collection established in 1816 by James Watt himself, a native Greenockian and one of the inventors of the steam engine.

John Boyle placed a heavy emphasis on the value and advantages of learning. He took great pride in his own literacy and wanted his children to acquire a sound education. To this end, he chose to enrol young David, when he was about seven years old, in the Mason's Hall School, operated in rooms leased from the local Masonic Lodge on Charles Street. The institution was supported both by local parish council funds and the 2d–3d per week tuition fees. The Mason's Hall School sought to provide a basic education in English grammar, writing, arithmetic, geography, and scriptural knowledge – history and composition were added in 1853 – for a nominal number of boys and girls under no compulsion to attend. Even by the standards of the time, the school was primitive and small. Scotland's system of parochial elementary education, once a model for the rest of Europe, had deteriorated badly in the early nineteenth century, especially in the rapidly expanding urban-industrial centres. Fortunately for David Boyle, he came under the tutelage of an able teacher, the Rev. Mr Kay, a classical scholar who evidently succeeded in stimulating his young charges.[23] It can be reasonably surmised that the Rev. Mr Kay found young David Boyle an intelligent lad with an active imagination, a little too mischievous and fun-loving perhaps, but extremely eager to learn.

The Mason's Hall School came under the control of the Established Church of Scotland, although such parochial schools were open to all denominations. Actually, the Boyles had little sympathy for the concept of an established church following the Great Disruption of 1843 which saw the formation of the secessionist Free Kirk of Scotland dedicated to the principle of the separation of church and state. While of firm opinion on certain religious issues, John Boyle was neither a dogmatic Presbyterian nor a zealous church-goer; he does not seem to have been caught up in the upsurge of evangelism associated with the Free Kirk Movement. Following the example of his own upbringing in Sorn, he encouraged his children to believe in a higher authority and an afterlife, but without subjecting them to a sternly religious domestic home environment. Moreover, John Boyle was not inclined to mix religion with every aspect of his daily life, or to depend upon his faith as a means of coping with everyday difficulties. In this respect he was at one with his brothers and father, as indicated by what remains of their personal correspondence which is devoid of scriptural references, or invocations to the divine, so commonplace in the letters of the mid-Victorian era. The absence of dogmatism, and the lack of intense religiosity in the home, was bound to influence young David. He would grow up to be a nominal Presbyterian, remarkably independent in his thinking on religious matters, and willing to question conventional beliefs and practices upon encountering the Darwinian revolution of thought. Eventually he would turn his back on organized religion altogether.

At school, among his peers, mainly the sons and daughters of artisans, shopkeepers, and tradesmen, and in his parents' home, David Boyle learned certain attitudes about class, race, and religion. He came to know his place in the social order. As most historians of the working class are wont to state, 'the artisan creed with regard to labourers is that the latter are an inferior class and that they should be made to know and kept in their place.'[24] The boy, when nine or ten years old, would not have been conscious of having ties with the labouring class; as an artisan's son he was different from that group in terms of life-style and status. Rather, he would have probably identified himself with his *petit bourgeois* class-mates, and their goals and values. So, too, young David learned to rank race and religion. To be a Scot and a Presbyterian would be cause for rejoicing in his estimation. At the other end of his scale would come the Irish Catholics, to him a decidedly inferior breed, mostly labourers, who filled the slums of Greenock. He watched them arrive in droves in 1847 and 1848 after the tragic famine. On the streets, as many youngsters were prone to do, David and his school chums made the Irish Catholics targets of derision. 'Preachin' Mary' often suffered their taunts. 'I can well remember,' confessed David, 'teasing her by making some Scriptural allusion, and then seeing her scowl terribly as she proceeded to talk at us with all her might, generally from the top of a cask or bale ...; but whether our allusions were simply religious ones or of an anti-Catholic kind I cannot say. My idea is that they were the latter, and that "Preachin' Mary" was Irish.'[25] David Boyle did not entirely outgrow these youthful racial and religious prejudices.

A fervent Scottish patriotism also took firm root early in David's intellectual development. It was a patriotism that emerged out of a romanticized view of Scotland's history, literature, and folklore. John Boyle, who traced his ancestry back to the twelfth century, raised his children on stories of Scottish accomplishment. He delighted them with tales of Wallace and Bruce, and interspersed the heroic stories and legends with occasional visits to historic sites. David thrilled to the memory of a steamboat trip to Dumbarton and the 'auld fortress o' Clutha' with its associations with the legendary Wallace. 'Man, I uise to see the rock ilka day o' my life when I was a laddie,' wrote David in later years, 'an' ance I min' gaun wi' my father to the verra bit. Wallace's sword was there then.'[26] The cult of Burns also flourished in the Boyle home. At an early age David knew many of Burns's poems by heart. Burnsian folklore – the witches, warlocks, spunkies, elves, fairies, and ghosts – enormously tickled the fancy of all the Boyle children. Their father added the legends, stories, and poems about St Clement, or 'Old Clem,' the patron saint of blacksmiths. This childhood love for folklore would blossom into serious study many decades in the future when David Boyle took up archaeology and ethnology.

During the late forties and early fifties, both in Greenock and later in Birkenhead, events in the Near East sparked a first interest in archaeology in the young Boyle. The excavations and discoveries in Mesopotamia made by the Frenchman Paul-Emile Botta at Nineveh and Khorsabad, and by the Englishman Austen Henry Layard in Nimrud, apparently left their impress on the mind of the boy.[27] In fact, the British public was swept up by the romance of these early archaeological excavations which verified the existence of Biblical Assyria. David would have learned of Layard's accomplishments at home through the press, and at school from the Rev. Kay, who like most clerics was probably excited by the archaeological confirmation of Scripture. All Britain marvelled as priceless Assyrian treasures came into the possession of the British Museum. David may have even perused a copy of Layard's *Nineveh and Its Remains* (1848–9), a volume that became almost mandatory reading for the informed British public. The book sold a then impressive eight thousand copies in its first year alone, and rivalled the sales of another runaway best seller, *Mrs. Rundell's Cookery*. Shortly after, a condensed version of *Nineveh*, published for wide popular consumption, appeared in the railway station bookstalls under the title of *A Popular Account of Discoveries at Nineveh* (1851).[28]

When David Boyle experienced the first stirrings of a political awareness as an adolescent, his father again served as mentor. Before departing the British Isles at age fourteen, David had probably formed the basis of his liberal-radical political philosophy, including opinions on the issues of universal suffrage and the ballot, free trade, and the value of associations of working men. John Boyle, of course, had been witness to some of the most exciting events in British political and social history: the great reform agitation of 1830–2; the development of political unions and trade unions as important features of Scottish political life; and the Anti-Corn Law League and Chartist movements in the 1830s and 1840s. The artisans in the shipyards and engineering shops were a politically active lot. Customarily they met during their lunches in the parlours of the public houses, where one of their numbers would read the newspaper aloud as a prelude to intense discussions.[29] Blacksmiths in every community formed small compact local trade unions, friendly societies or workingmen's associations: their motto – 'Numbers without Union are Powerless; and Union without Knowledge is Useless.'[30] John Boyle would have certainly belonged to one of these groups and could not have avoided the debates during the late thirties and forties on Chartist demands and methods, on the role of trade unions, and on the corn laws.[31]

Well-to-do artisans like John Boyle, particularly the iron founders, engineers, and machine builders, all beneficiaries of the industrial revolution, were often quite moderate in their politics and trade union activities. Few such labour aristocrats in the iron and engineering industries took a prominent role in the Chartist drive for political reform.[32] After the disastrous outcome of the Chartist-inspired general strike of 1842, the Friendly United Smiths actually expunged the right to strike from their rules in 1845 and determined instead to settle disputes by peaceful negotiation. While they might have rejected radical tactics, this stance did not mean that artisans like John Boyle lacked sympathy with some or all Chartist demands for universal suffrage, equal representation, vote by ballot, abolition of property qualifications for members of parliament, and wage payments for MPs. For John Boyle, and later his son David, there was no political principle for which they had greater respect than suffrage extension, and free trade ran a close second. David maintained a careful watch on the Scottish political scene throughout his life. Some thirty years after leaving his native land, he still became excited when thinking of liberal reform in Britain. 'The time's comin',' he wrote, 'whan they'll no' hae a single Conservative checkin' frae Johnny Groat's to Lan's En'. We'll ding doon Estaibled Kirks; we'll gie the crofters their ain lan'; ... we'll dae awa wi' a' sinecure offishes: ... an' ... play the deevil genrally wi' a' the relics o' feudalism an' shupersteetion.'[33]

Here, then, in British artisan culture of the mid-nineteenth century, are to be found many of the influences that shaped the pattern of David Boyle's life, and his values, beliefs, and goals. His artisan family provided an environment that nurtured the ideals of self-discipline and self-improvement, education and intellectual inquiry, earnestness and thrift, hard work and social ambition. By adhering to these ideals, his father, uncles, and grandfather showed him the way by making the most of their opportunities. Like them, David would dedicate himself to a program of self-improvement, and when the time came, first as a teacher in rural Ontario, and later as a professional archaeologist and museum curator in Toronto, he would realize the full potential of his artisan philosophy.

III

'We had a visit of Brother John about the New Year,' wrote Adam Boyle from Cumnock in April 1853 to his younger brother William, then in Canada West. 'He speaks too of trying America but I do not think he will come this year yet, and we had word from him since that. He is left Caird and gone to the Railway to make wheels by piece work for 32/ a week. Little David is here on a visit till we go away. I dare say he has been here a month already.'[34] As this letter suggests, the year 1853 was one of dramatic change for John Boyle's family. During the winter they moved to Birkenhead, England, a small shipping, shipbuilding, and industrial centre on the south bank of the Mersey River directly opposite Liverpool. The locomotive industry in Greenock was on the wane. The private firms like Caird and Company, unable to compete successfully with the locomotive shops of the larger British railway companies to the south, concentrated on marine engineering as orders for locomotives declined. Eventually the firm retired from the field altogether. Seeing the writing on the wall, and having heard through the artisan network of the splendid opportunities for blacksmiths in Birkenhead, John Boyle made the decision to change jobs. He immediately found employment at the Canada Works, the large and sophisticated engineering complex erected in 1853 by the firm of Peto, Brassey and Betts after it received the contract to build the Grand Trunk Railway across the Canadas. John Boyle's weekly pay packet of 32s placed him in one of the top wage brackets for an artisan in Britain at the time.

Had John Boyle not found such a lucrative position in the locomotive shops of Birkenhead, he would probably have gone to Canada West to join his brothers and parents. In 1853, his father, old David Boyle of Cumnock, still strong and healthy in his sixty-first year, had chosen to join his sons who had emigrated four years earlier. 'Markets has [sic] not been so good this six or seven years,' explained Adam Boyle, reflecting his father's unease about the economic prospects in rural Ayrshire.[35] But from Canada West came assurances that the elder Boyle would certainly prosper and become a fully independent man of property and consequence instead of remaining a tenant farmer, albeit a relatively successful one. His boys had done remarkably well for themselves in the colony. One son (yet another David), already carried on a blacksmith business in York Township, just north of Toronto; Andrew worked at his trade in the village of Eden Mills near Guelph; while James had purchased a hundred-acre farm in Sarnia Township, Lambton County, and intended to open a blacksmith shop at the earliest opportunity. With their example as his inspiration, old David Boyle had liquidated his assets in Cumnock during the spring and summer of 1853 and set sail for the St Lawrence. He took with him a substantial sum of money, considerable family possessions, and a variety of farm implements, including a plough and the castings of a cheese press.

'I have great hopes that ... father will buy us ... a piece of land each,' Adam confided to William before departing Cumnock, 'as the rest of the family is all provided for already, we being the youngest of the family.'[36] Their father fulfilled those hopes. He took his two youngest sons to the village of Mandaumin in Sarnia Township. There he purchased the already established farm belonging to his son James and then saw to it that his three offspring took possession of one-hundred-acre farms next to each other, several concessions to the south of his property.[37] Doubtless news of their good fortune and the descriptions of the excellent prospects for blacksmiths in the booming colony were read eagerly back in Birkenhead in the home of John Boyle.

Birkenhead, in the early 1850s, was a thriving and healthy community in which to work and live. The population had trebled to 24,300 between 1844 and 1847 when a great dock construction scheme commenced to compete with the congested dockage facilities available to Liverpool shipping. Houses and shops sprang up at a surprising rate in these years. Much of the new building, while hurriedly erected, adhered in general to a praiseworthy town plan adopted by the local government prior to the expansion. In the late forties, the docks construction companies, plagued by mismanagement and engineering incompetence, fell into financial difficulties and suspended work. There followed a great exodus of working people from the town, leaving a considerable number of vacant houses. By the time the Boyles arrived, work on the remainder of the docking scheme had been resumed, though not on as grand a scale as the original conception.[38] On the quayside of one of the new docks could be found the Canada Works. Not far away was located Birkenhead's other major industry, the renowned iron shipbuilding yard of the Laird family, originally from Greenock.

At the Canada Works, John Boyle once again found himself in the vanguard of British technology. The awesome new engineering complex included brass and iron foundries, machine and bridge fabrication shops, boiler works, two fully equipped blacksmith shops, the largest of which housed forty furnaces, and a fitting plant capable of building ten locomotives simultaneously. At peak production, the firm required 1200 men to produce the locomotives, rails, plates, and girders for the 540-mile Grand Trunk Railway and the nearly 2-mile-long Victoria Bridge, an engineering wonder in its time, which spanned the St Lawrence at Montreal. A vast amount of parts and equipment had to be shipped to the Canadas to be laid, fitted together, riveted, and transformed into the famous rail highway. By December 1854, the 'Lady Elgin,' the first of the locomotives, and 9 other engines, along with a 155-foot span for the bridge and much other material, had arrived in Montreal.[39]

The Boyle family enjoyed the amenities and surroundings of their new town. They had little difficulty finding suitable accommodation since many small but comfortable artisans' cottages remained vacant after the exodus of the late forties. There were few factories and foundries with tall chimneys to pollute the air. A short distance away, country lanes and paths, the river front, and remnants of the great Wirral forest invited picnics and hiking excursions where David and his father could pursue their interest in wild flowers and insects. They may well have visited Storeton, a place where amateur palaeontologists searched for fossil species in the extensive freestone quarries.[40] Thanks to the ferry service across the Mersey, the Boyles also made frequent trips to Liverpool to enjoy the many cultural attractions available to the artisan community. David recalled with awe the exhilaration and excitement of the bustle and congestion of this major seaport.

On arriving in Birkenhead, the Boyles at once entered David, then eleven, at St Andrew's School, one of the best elementary institutions of learning in town. It was situated alongside St Andrew's Church, an imposing Gothic building in Conway Street. David adapted quickly to his new surroundings since the institution was 'conducted on the Scotch parochial system' and offered the same range of subjects that he had known at the Mason's Hall School in Greenock.[41] Many of the students were also Scottish and all were the children of literate, regularly employed artisans, shopkeepers, office workers, minor officials, and the like. The faculty consisted of a principal and a certified teacher, assisted in the class-rooms by several monitors, older male students who taught the younger groups by way of the rote method. It may be that in his last year at the school David Boyle served as a monitor, or played out the role at home for his brothers and sisters; perhaps here the seeds of his later ambition to become a teacher were sown. In any event, judging from the entries in the school log book, which recorded homework assigned and the encouragement given to personal appearance and good behaviour, St Andrew's supported John Boyle's efforts in the home to inculcate the values of self-discipline and self-improvement.

As John Boyle had probably foreseen, with the completion of the Montreal-Toronto section of the Grand Trunk in 1856, the labour force at the Canada Works was reduced until other engineering contracts were obtained. Even then, the shops would not require nearly so many artisans as during the heyday of the Grand Trunk. Now, he concluded, the time was right to join his brothers and parents in the Canadas before he faced a period of unemployment. When John Boyle decided to emigrate, he could hardly be described as a fugitive from impoverishment. His decision had been made largely on the basis of economic considerations.[42] Wages in the Canadas for skilled workers were known to be about twice the standard wages in Britain. Food was cheaper and ownership of property within reach of the artisan. His children would have enhanced opportunities for schooling and for learning a trade. David, now fourteen years of age, would be apprenticed as a blacksmith as soon as possible. All accounts of Canada West, whether from relatives or the emigrant grapevine, told of a vigorous economy stimulated by a railway mania, immigration, reciprocity with the United States, and a high demand in Britain during the Crimean War for Canadian lumber and wheat. The advertising of the steamship and railway companies with agents in Liverpool reinforced this promising picture. In the work place, even the trade unions promoted emigration to British North America by providing advice and information, and in some cases, monetary aid. Trade union leaders, enamoured with 'popular strength-through-scarcity and wage-fund theories' looked upon emigration of skilled artisans as a cure for unemployment and low wages in Britain.[43]

Pushed and pulled to the New World by all these factors, John and Anne Boyle, with their five children,[44] embarked from Liverpool some time during 1856. Trans-Atlantic travelling conditions, once fraught with disease, extreme discomfort, and the very real possibility of death, no longer deterred immigrants now that the British parliament had enacted stringent passenger legislation. The ocean crossing, even for steerage passengers, had become relatively safe and comfortable. After about six weeks at sea, the Boyles arrived at Quebec. They booked on a steamboat to Montreal, from which point they were whisked to Toronto in a mere thirteen hours on the Grand Trunk Railway by a locomotive that John Boyle might well have helped to build. After a brief and happy reunion with John's brother David and his family in York Township, the new arrivals made their way to Eden Mills in

Wellington County. Here John learned from his brother Andrew of an opening for a blacksmith in Salem, a hamlet in Nichol Township, some twenty miles away to the north-west.

IV

To John Boyle, a superior workman accustomed to the advanced methods and technology of industrial Britain, the village blacksmith shop in tiny Salem must have seemed a step backward in time to the days of his youth and apprenticeship in Sorn. Nevertheless, he gratefully accepted the job since an immediate source of income was of prime importance before the costs of boarding and setting up a home ate away his small cash reserves. Salem would only be a temporary phase of John Boyle's life; he anticipated changing jobs and location as soon as more congenial and remunerative employment, preferably as a wheelwright in one of the new Canadian locomotive factories, became available.

In 1856 Salem had reached what was destined to be the height of its prosperity as a gateway and supply centre for the tract of land being opened to the north and west along the new road to Saugeen (now Southampton) on Lake Huron. The village would thrive for another decade until bypassed by the railway. A Pennsylvania Dutchman, Sem Wissler, had carved Salem out of the bush in 1845. Being a practical and imaginative businessman, Wissler had immediately seen the possibilities of the village site for mills and a tannery: the Irvine River flowed fast there; ample supplies of tanning bark could be obtained in the surrounding forest; and settlement in the immediate hinterland promised to grow apace. Within a year, Wissler had constructed a dam and a flume, a sawmill, and a building that housed a tannery, general store, and shoeshop that employed up to twenty shoemakers. Ten years later, the other standard pioneer industries and businesses had appeared – flour mills, a brewery, taverns, and the blacksmith shop where John Boyle worked for a short time.[45]

Salem's growth was typical of the development taking place across Canada West. Massive road and railway construction during the 1850s contributed in large part to the settlement of the remaining agricultural land below the Shield, to the development of constellations of villages, towns, and cities, and to concomitant integration and industrial growth.[46] Canada West, in short, was in the process of being transformed from a colonial backwater into a bustling, intensively developed community of about a million inhabitants with a distinct regional character of its own.

At some time during 1857, the Boyles left Salem. John found the position he desired in London, a town situated at the forks of the Thames River in Middlesex County in the heart of the south-west peninsula of Canada West. Here, in the new locomotive shops of the Great Western Railway Company, he resumed his highly skilled career as a wheelwright, and subsequently forged and set the wheels for some of the first locomotives built in London by that company. Satisfied with his wages and working conditions, he remained with the Great Western for the remainder of his working days. Over the years he saved diligently and invested wisely. When he died in 1882, his estate included a home in one of the better working-class districts of London, and five other properties besides.[47]

David Boyle did not accompany his parents to London in 1857; instead, he was sent to apprentice as a blacksmith under his uncle Andrew in Eden Mills, a small village situated about five miles from Guelph, in the south end of Eramosa Township at the eastern edge of Wellington County. Like Salem, Eden Mills had sprung up during the 1840s as a saw and grist mill site, and eventually attracted most of the essential small businesses and service industries required by the surrounding agricultural population.[48] Eden Mills, in common with many of the villages and towns in Wellington County, had a pronounced Scottish character. The ranks of the businessmen and artisans invariably contained the names of the Scottish born, while the architecture reflected the influence of the Scottish mason. There were, in fact, more Scots by birth in Wellington County than in any other part of Canada West.[49]

Living and working with his uncle and his family, within a close-knit Scottish community, made David Boyle's adjustment to the new society, and to the separation from his parents, relatively easy.[50] David's cultural interests, his appetite for reading and general scientific knowledge, also served to assuage the loneliness. When tired of educational pastimes, the forests, fields, and streams around Eden Mills provided endless recreational pleasures for the new Canadian. He also took up outdoor curling in the winter-time, a sport that became one of his passions. Curling rivalry prevailed between the villages and towns in the county, a rivalry generated to a significant extent by exuberant Scottish athletes and their local supporters. While young David took his job, his learning, and his sports seriously, he did evince a strong sense of humour and a teenager's propensity for playing practical jokes. John R. Connon, the historian of Elora who interviewed people acquainted with Boyle in these years, recorded that David's 'resourcefulness in contriving ridiculous situations seemed to be without limit and continued until late in life.'[51]

Almost from the beginning of his apprenticeship, David Boyle doubted that he would be satisfied with his place at the anvil; indeed, he said as much towards the end of 1857, on the occasion of the visit to Guelph by Elihu Burritt, New England's so-called Learned Blacksmith.[52] A self-taught and brilliant linguist, a proponent of temperance and self-culture, Burritt had achieved international fame as a consequence of his fight in the United States for the abolition of slavery, and for peace and world brotherhood.[53] Greatly impressed by what education and knowledge had done for his fellow blacksmith, David is purported to have said at the time: 'If he could do it, I can.'[54] With Burritt's example in mind, he eventually resolved that as soon as he had completed his apprenticeship, he would resume his formal studies; he would then work at his trade to support himself through grammar school. Even before he left Eden Mills, he had determined that secondary schooling would lead to a career as an educator. The Burritt visit to Guelph was not, as local tradition would have it,[55] the sole cause of David Boyle's determination to acquire an education and become a teacher. What seems more likely is that Burritt accelerated Boyle's journey down a path he would have followed in any case. Given his background in British artisan culture, his commitment to the code of self-improvement, and the example of the various members of his family who had improved their social position, it was as natural for David Boyle to attempt to advance socially and intellectually beyond the status of village smithy as it had been to become a blacksmith in the first place.

2

A Pestalozzian in all things educational, 1860–71

I

In 1860, at eighteen years of age, David Boyle completed his apprenticeship in Eden Mills. The time had arrived to leave the home of his uncle, to strike out on his own, and to acquire the formal education he so eagerly desired. Through the Scottish artisan network of Wellington County, he sought a specific kind of employment situation where he could practise his trade near a grammar school, under an employer who would permit him to work irregular hours so that he could attend classes. Eventually he found such a position in Elora, in Hugh Hamilton's blacksmith shop on Carlton Street, a firm that undertook 'Blacksmithing in all its Branches' including the production of wagons, carriages, and 'Dobbins Patent one-horse Cultivator.'[1] Hamilton placed David under the supervision of a sympathetic master craftsman, Sandy Cuthbert, and provided lodgings for his new journeyman in his own home. During the four years that he lived with them, the Hamiltons grew quite attached to their ambitious young boarder who was so dependable at work, so serious in his studies, yet so remarkably full of good humour.[2]

Situated some thirteen miles to the north of Guelph, at the confluence of the Grand and Irvine rivers, Elora owed its existence to the mill potential of the Grand River Falls. As a village site there were few more charming and scenic settings to be found in the province. The precipitous walls of the river gorges, carved out of limestone, had been shaped and reshaped for centuries by the eroding action of water and frost. The result was an idyllic few miles of natural grandeur, of rocky recesses and caves and forested river banks. The village of about one thousand inhabitants had grown steadily since the 1830s with the influx of settlers into the surrounding townships. To serve the fertile agricultural hinterland, various businessmen had exploited the water power to build a variety of mills to grind grain, to saw and plane lumber, and to card and full wool. Others had established a foundry and agricultural implement works, distilleries, general stores, taverns and hotels, a bank, and an assortment of artisans' shops. The businessmen, professional people, and artisans of Elora, together with farmers in the vicinity of the village, already supported several churches; a mechanics' institute, established in 1857; a newspaper, the Elora *Observer*, which first appeared in 1859; a public and grammar school; and a variety of voluntary associations.[3] Notwithstanding its size and location, Elora was a vibrant community where David Boyle would find many kindred spirits in the search for knowledge.

During the next four years (1860–4), Boyle came under the influence of the headmaster of the Elora Grammar School, the Rev. John G. MacGregor, a graduate in arts of Glasgow University and in theology of Edinburgh Divinity College.[4] Not all village grammar schools attracted such a qualified and competent teacher. MacGregor saw to it that his students received a thorough grounding in the standard and classical subjects: Greek, Latin, French, English literature and composition, history, geography, and mathematics. Not all of these courses appealed to Boyle; he barely endured mathematics and struggled through the languages. He especially enjoyed history, literature, and geography, and excelled at writing. In fact, he obtained the top prize in English composition in his final year of school.[5]

As he sharpened his writing skills under MacGregor, Boyle was also encouraged to improve his command of the spoken word – not an easy task for a man accustomed to speaking 'broad Scots' vernacular and hearing daily the colourfully vulgar speech of his fellow blacksmiths. He recognized that the effort had to be made to smooth out the rough edges of his tongue, since he could be denied a teaching certificate should he demonstrate ignorance of the rules of grammar and good pronunciation. Furthermore, he could not lay claim to the respectability and status he associated with education and the teaching profession if he spoke like a common labourer. 'The moment a person begins to speak in our presence,' he wrote later with his own experience in mind, 'we begin to form our opinion, either as to his knowledge of the topic under discussion, or as to his general culture ... Even when he is a clear thinker and can express himself felicitously, the value of his utterances may be very materially lessened to educated listeners by the perpetration of ... blunders' of grammar and pronunciation.[6]

Conscious of his own deficiencies, Boyle overcame what he considered to be his verbal handicap by 'persistent consultation of a dictionary,' by 'close attention to good speakers,' and by mutual improvement sessions with others. As a spokesman for professionalism in the teaching ranks in the 1870s and 1880s, he would demand that all educators do as he had done, and live up to the highest standards of diction and grammar. Those who took 'a foolish pride' in the retention of a peculiar 'twang or brogue,' he argued, 'should never attempt to teach English ... Every word we utter in the school room ought to be a model for imitation by the pupils.' These ideas associating correct and fluent speech with higher status and respectability had been voiced frequently at mid-century by middle-class school promoters concerned with encouraging individual upward mobility, class betterment, and the 'civilizing' of the lower classes so as to foster social harmony. Boyle had evidently taken to heart the message of such as Egerton Ryerson, the chief superintendent of schools, who emphasized that incorrect or vulgar speech would 'constitute an impassable gulf between the mechanic's sons and those rewards and positions of power and usefulness' to which they might aspire.[7]

David Boyle graduated from the Elora Grammar School in July 1864, a noteworthy accomplishment for a twenty-two-year-old artisan, considering that only a small minority of the population in the Canadas had acquired any secondary schooling at all. That same year he obtained a second-class teacher's certificate after passing the examinations set by the Wellington County Board of Education. Armed only with this middle-level certificate, lacking both teacher training and experience, he could at best expect an initial appointment in one of the county's rural elementary schools. He found such a post by January 1865 in a one-room schoolhouse in Pilkington Township, just a few miles west of Elora.

On the surface at least, Boyle had entered a strange occupation to realize his ambition for advancement, since elementary teaching in Canada West scarcely qualified as a 'profession.' The sad truth was that the preponderance of rural teachers had not attended normal or model schools to receive basic training in pedagogical methods and theory. Most held their positions by virtue of passing an examination set by county boards of education, designed to test their knowledge of the subject matter they were expected to impart to their pupils. Even those that failed these tests were often issued temporary third-class teaching permits by local boards of trustees keen to hire them at the lowest possible level of remuneration. Moreover, school boards were often prone to engage female teachers simply because their services could be obtained relatively cheaply, this circumstance being a key factor in the feminization of teaching in Ontario in these years.[8] Rural teachers' salaries, complained spokesmen for teachers' associations at the time, approximated 'the wages of the ploughman, farm servant or hodman,'* and fell short of the

---

* From the 1870s to the early 1900s wages and prices in Ontario remained relatively constant. A common wage for labourers was $1.00 per day, for artisans $2.00 to $3.50. In 1865 a male teacher holding a second-class certificate could expect an annual salary of about $260 in his first year of teaching.

wages paid to 'mechanics, artisans, clerks and clergymen.'[9] Isolated, neglected, poorly paid and unappreciated, the rural teacher also quite often lacked self-respect. What, then, had possessed David Boyle to abandon a highly regarded trade with substantial earning potential for a 'profession' of questionable status in which there was every indication that he would have to struggle to make ends meet?

Had Boyle subscribed to prevailing social and economic attitudes that extolled the pursuit of wealth, his decision to change careers would have made little sense. It could not be said of Boyle that he had little regard for monetary considerations; he was too much the practical, thrifty Scot for that. But he did hold to a set of priorities that placed intellectual and cultural values above purely economic concerns. The pursuit and the imparting of knowledge possessed an overwhelming mystique for Boyle, not surprising for a young man influenced all his life by the artisan self-improvement ethic, and taught by the blacksmith fraternity that knowledge is power and the key to respectability. He believed strongly in the idea that there existed an integral relationship between the school system and the welfare and progress of society. Teaching also promised to provide ample opportunity for self-culture, for reading and study and reflection, particularly in the sciences, the arts, and great literature.

Furthermore, from the point of view of the skilled artisan entering the teaching profession, it seemed reasonable that he would not initially receive a princely salary. Was he not, after all, in the position of an 'apprentice' teacher, who in common with every apprentice in every trade perforce must learn the 'secrets and mysteries' of his particular craft? Teaching, like blacksmithing, seemed to him part science, part art; its mechanics and purposes had to be broken down and methodically studied. After mastering the skills of the educator's craft, the teacher would acquire the respect of the community, and the status that in Boyle's scale of values was associated with the profession. He was quite prepared to start near the bottom with a second-class certificate and at a lower pay scale than he could earn as a skilled craftsman. Through continued self-improvement, however, he expected to acquire his first-class certificate and advance through the ranks of the teaching profession in much the same way as an apprentice blacksmith achieves the rank and wage of a master craftsman.

Boyle's youthful idealism and ambition, while commendable, were to be tempered by the realities of teaching in a one-room schoolhouse on a lonely back concession. He would understand soon enough that the life of a teacher and learned man was not all that he had thought it to be. As a teacher, and later as an underpaid, overworked curator of an archaeological museum, he would complain bitterly and regularly about a system that demonstrated such a low regard for its educators and scholars by paying them salaries barely sufficient to provide a comfortable home for their families, or to educate their children. In the years to come, David Boyle would rarely enjoy freedom from financial worries. It was the price to be paid for the pursuit of his intellectual and cultural goals. Being one's own man, he would discover, could almost be overwhelming.

All this, of course, lay in the future, for in January 1865 Boyle, a bachelor with few responsibilities, could hardly wait to step in front of a class-room, motivated as he was by the zeal of a recent convert to progressive educational theories. Doubtless, a basic source of his initial enthusiasm for teaching was his discovery, through methodical study, of a philosophy of education that differed radically from anything he had himself experienced. Since the 1850s, when as an apprentice blacksmith in Eden Mills he had resolved to become a teacher, Boyle had read deep into literature on educational theory and method. He collected all the information he could find, and began as early as 1859 to compile a collection of scrapbooks – a habit he continued for over twenty years. [10] He filled the scrapbooks with clippings from a variety of local county newspapers, and from Egerton Ryerson's *Journal of Education* which contained articles from an impressive array of international periodical sources. The clippings covered every conceivable pedagogical topic and were pasted chronologically into the scrapbooks with no attempt at classification. While attending the Elora Grammar School, Boyle rounded out his self-imposed teacher training programme by familiarizing himself with as many teaching manuals as he could acquire or borrow from the mechanics' institute library. Before long, a definite pattern emerged in the material chosen for inclusion in the scrapbooks; the clippings indicated that David Boyle was becoming a convert to many of the philosophical assumptions, instructional methods, and psychological principles espoused by the North American and British disciples of the controversial Swiss educator, Johann Heinrich Pestalozzi (1746–1827).

II

A product of the eighteenth-century Enlightenment, an advocate of Rousseau's theories on human nature and education, Pestalozzi was one of the first to introduce into the schoolroom the Enlightenment concerns for equality of opportunity, liberty, and respect for individual personality. During his career, he challenged educators to re-examine many of their ideas on teaching aims and methods. Instead of seeing the child as an object to be moulded into a shape determined by the schoolmaster, Pestalozzi proclaimed that every individual's personality was sacred, that each child had inherited a unique potential that must be respected in the class-room; indeed, the teacher's function should be to discover and to foster each student's 'potential.'[11] In short, education was, for Pestalozzi, child-centred; education was to be shaped for the child, not the child for education. He also argued that if the child's potential was to be developed to the full, learning must take place in a class-room environment conducive to emotional stability, an environment roughly parallel to the climate created in the home by the kind, loving mother. Thus, it followed logically that corporal punishment as a method of encouraging learning through fear must be banished; if required as a last resort to control a recalcitrant pupil, the rod was only to be administered as a parent would punish his own child, that is, as an expression of love.[12]

Radically different teaching methods were also deemed essential by Pestalozzi to develop the talents and potential of each child. He abhorred the rote method of learning, the mechanical memorization of facts without providing the pupils with an adequate understanding of the principles involved in the subject under study. As an alternative, he sought to develop his students' intellect and powers of reasoning, his concern being not so much what was learned, as how to learn.[13] To accomplish this goal, Pestalozzi developed an 'experience curriculum' based on the assumption that direct concrete observation, often inadequately called 'sense perception,' was the primary means of acquiring knowledge. His best-known innovation, novel at the time, was the 'object lesson' method, designed to use everyday materials and things familiar to the child and involving discussion and oral presentation in place of memorization and book work.[14] Field trips, for instance, became mandatory to study science and nature. After a thing was observed in the concrete and understood, then the teacher – always through activity and sense perception – could move on from the known to the unknown, from the simple to the complex, from the concrete to the abstract.

Finally, for Pestalozzi, an education involved more than the training of intellect; a person's moral and physical faculties must also be activated if the full potential of that human being was to be realized. His followers turned to games, martial drills, and gymnastic exercises of increasing difficulty 'to bring back,' as Pestalozzi put it, 'the body of the child into the full unity and harmony with his intellect and heart which originally existed.'[15] As for moral education, this posed the problem of greatest importance. He recognized that religious concepts and the virtues of love, faith, trust, and obedience could not be taught by word of mouth to elementary school children. Morality, like all knowledge, had to be first experienced, felt, and taught by example, primarily in the home and then supported in the family-like atmosphere of the class-room. 'Practice, not preaching, was the basis of moral education.'[16] Religious instruction in the school, Pestalozzi argued, should not begin with Bible study, but by drawing the attention of the students to the presence of the divine in nature and in their surroundings.

In the 1860s, across predominantly rural Canada West, widespread understanding and use of Pestalozzian theory and method lay some time in the future.[17] Without training, most rural teachers had only the slightest acquaintance with the advances made during the first half of the nineteenth century in pedagogical theory and practice. Typically, they applied the traditional rote system, and reinforced it with a liberal use of the cane in the belief that the behaviour and intellect of their students would thereby be improved under the threat of a sound thrashing. This state of affairs would exist in Ontario until formal teacher training became widespread with the opening of more normal schools and the establishment of county model schools in 1877.[18]

Yet some teachers who, like David Boyle, made the effort broke free from traditional approaches. By reading widely, Boyle came into contact with Pestalozzian-inspired literature from a variety of sources, one of which was indigenous to Canada West. Egerton Ryerson, the well-travelled Chief Superintendent of Common Schools for the Canadas since 1846, had promoted Pestalozzianism in his monthly *Journal of Education* (established 1848), which was by law required reading for all teachers, trustees, and superintendents in the province. With the founding of Ryerson's Educational Museum in 1855 in the Toronto Normal School, the object lesson approach was brought to the attention of teachers such as Boyle who cared to visit and learn. Moreover, through the Educational Depository, teachers and school-boards could purchase at cost a variety of charts, maps, apparatus, and specimens for class-room use. Ryerson also established links with the English Home and Colonial Infant and Juvenile School Society, and acquired from this source quantities of instructional aids that could be purchased by teachers. The society had been founded by such people as Charles and Elizabeth Mayo and James Greaves who were largely responsible for introducing Pestalozzianism to England.[19] Their aim was to propagate these new principles both at home and in the colonies.

When Edward A. Sheldon, superintendent of schools in Oswego, New York, visited Toronto's normal and public schools in 1859, he discovered materials that he said he 'did not know existed anywhere – collections of objects, pictures, charts of colors, forms, reading charts, books for teachers giving full directions as to the use of this material. They were mostly the products of the Home and Colonial Training Institution, London.'[20] An inspired Sheldon returned to New York, contacted the Mayos at the English Home and Colonial Society, hired one of their instructors, and launched what became known in North American educational circles as the 'Oswego Movement.' By 1871, Sheldon had introduced the English brand of Pestalozzianism into all eight normal schools in the state, and subsequently 'saturated New York schools with teachers indoctrinated with object-lesson teaching.'[21]

David Boyle read about all these developments before he taught his first class. Since at least 1859 he had perused Ryerson's *Journal of Education*, and the occasional issue of the *American Journal of Education*, edited by Henry Barnard (1811–1900), who popularized Pestalozzi's ideas among American educators.[22] Boyle's scrapbooks for the period 1859 to 1865 are full of clippings pertaining to the philosophy and methods of the Mayos in England, Sheldon in Oswego, and other British and American devotees of Pestalozzi. Furthermore, in the educational section of the Elora Mechanic's Institute library could be found volumes by Charles Mayo and Edward Sheldon, and David P. Page's widely read, Pestalozzian-inspired *Theory and Practice of Teaching* (1847).[23]

In abandoning the blacksmith shop and embracing a philosophy of education fundamentally different from the one prevalent in the rural schoolhouses of Canada West, Boyle revealed a side of his character that refused to follow generally accepted social behaviour and ways of thinking. As his knowledge broadened, his attitudes would become increasingly unconventional, even iconoclastic in so far as he enjoyed attacking traditional and venerated ideas and institutions. His views on such topics as religion and the role of churches in society, on evolution, and on women's rights, when eventually articulated in public – always in a blunt, no-nonsense fashion – would scandalize some people, and on occasion even endanger his career. To some extent, this part of his character may be ascribed to family influences. Independent thinking, the absence of dogmatism, especially in matters of religion, and a willingness to give new ideas a hearing, were traits characteristic of the Boyles.

Yet the tendency to defy convention was probably more typical of the self-taught man forced to find his own intellectual way. Boyle discovered Pestalozzianism himself, through laboured self-education, not in a controlled, formal setting where his enthusiasm and idealism might have been modified and shaped by some mature and experienced educator's scepticism and balanced sense of proportion. Lacking the restraints of the formal educational process, Boyle easily became a convert to Pestalozzianism. The reformist, humanitarian implications of the Swiss educator's theories probably hastened the conversion by appealing to Boyle's liberal-radical political ideals formed back in Britain. Pestalozzian theories seemed appropriate to a man who was by nature kind and gentle, and concerned about providing opportunities for the improvement of the intellectual and social condition of the working classes. For all these reasons, Boyle devoured books and periodicals pertaining to the Pestalozzian approach so that from the start of his career as a teacher this normally self-effacing individual could truthfully say that he was 'well-read in the science of education, and held many views contrary to those in general acceptance.'[24]

III

Middlebrook Public School, in school section no. 2 of Pilkington Township, Wellington County, stood in a tranquil setting between two small trout streams, along the road to Elmira about three miles west of Elora. When David Boyle took over as schoolmaster in January 1865 there was, apart from the location, not much to say of a complimentary nature about this rural centre of learning. The school building, a low-roofed, unplastered log structure, about 20 × 22 feet in size, was poorly ventilated, dirty, badly furnished, and ill-equipped. An attendance rate of 38 per cent suggested that for most parents in the section, schooling came second to the struggle for economic survival – the children's services were deemed essential in the fields and around the home.[25] Parents permitted their children to attend school on a seasonal basis determined by the routine of the farm. The rural community did not demand much of the educational system. 'The ends were clear and the means were limited. Schooling would enable a child to read his Bible and get on in the world; the three RS were sufficient to enable him to do this.'[26] Even with low attendance, Middlebrook was very crowded, since the names of 160 pupils were to be found on the register.[27]

Worse still for the new schoolmaster, Middlebrook also had a history of serious discipline problems, a factor which had contributed to the resignation of Boyle's predecessor. A few of the older male pupils – there were sixty-four students on the register over sixteen years of age – seemed to attend classes for the single purpose of making the schoolmaster's life miserable. When the trustees of the section hired David Boyle, they cared little about his lack of experience. They probably thought that his blacksmith's brawn and personal ambition would compensate for any other deficiencies. Their main concern was that as a beginner, he could not command a high salary – at an annual starting wage of $260, he was the lowest paid male teacher in the township; the trustees could thereby hold down the local education tax rates.[28] Under these less than favourable circumstances, Boyle began his new career.

Charles T. Currelly (1876–1957), the first curator of the Royal Ontario Museum of Archaeology, and an accomplished raconteur, often told the following anecdote about David Boyle's first day in front of a class. 'The young ruffians started almost at once to be troublesome, so Boyle ordered the one he thought was the ring leader to come up to his desk. The young man came up ready for a fight, and squared off for a blow. There was a flash and he lay on the ground. Boyle had brought an axe handle to school with him. There was no more trouble in the school.'[29] While this story undoubtedly titillated the literary luminaries of the Senior Common Room in Victoria College, Toronto, where Currelly lunched during the early 1950s, the anecdote had little basis in fact. David Boyle eschewed the use of force in the class-room as a matter of principle, and in any case, he would certainly not have risked his career by unlawfully assaulting a pupil his first day on the job!

A more reliable version of Boyle's inauguration at Middlebrook School is to be found in John Connon's *History of Elora*. According to Connon, Boyle survived his first day as a teacher precisely because he did not resort to violence. Instead of bludgeoning his pupils with an axe handle, he evidently nonplussed the potential recalcitrants by appealing to their sense of honour and acting as if he believed they possessed one. Boyle asked them to sign 'a pledge stating that while in the school or on the school property they, on their honour as gentlemen, would behave themselves.' This expedient, suggests Connon, solved the discipline problem, for 'if those young men were to be considered gentlemen, they could not break their word of honour.'[30] Since Connon was personally acquainted with some of the students in that first class at Middlebrook, and had himself studied under Boyle in the 1870s, he knew well that his old teacher had treated his pupils with kindness, dignity, and respect.

That David Boyle was an extraordinarily gifted teacher soon became apparent to the residents of Pilkington. In September 1865 the local superintendent reported that Boyle had 'conducted the school so as to secure general confidence, and materially advance the scholars.'[31] A few months later, after the public examinations in December, his efforts were again acclaimed in the Elora *Observer*. 'Mr. Boyle certainly deserves great credit,' the editor concluded, 'for having brought the school out of a state of lethargy into one of competitive healthfulness and activity.' In spite of the cramped conditions of the old log schoolhouse, 'the order was all that could be desired, and much superior to what could have been expected.'[32]

David Boyle seems to have succeeded at Middlebrook by a judicious application of the Pestalozzian principles he had learned through self-study. One of the first tasks he had set for himself involved brightening up the school building and grounds. As he put it: 'A little paint, a little whitewash, a little taste, a few dollars, a happy face, a determined will, and the thing [was] done.'[33] He covered the walls of the room with maps, pictures, and illuminated texts, the window sills with potted plants, and he laid out a portion of the playground for a flower bed. 'Our happiness is in a great measure under our own control, and if we are not happy we have ourselves to blame,' he would later tell other teachers complaining of their wretched working conditions. One of the 'amenities' of a teacher's life, he argued, occurred when pupils remarked that 'they would rather be in school than at home, because it was so much "nicer".'

Boyle's kindly, patient, and humorous personality enabled him to establish an immediate rapport with his pupils, and to create the desired home-like atmosphere in the class-room. Rarely did he resort to corporal punishment, and only administered it, 'in flagrant cases of bullying, obscenity, and contumacy.'[34] The 'lick 'em and they'll learn school,' he felt, could only produce 'a generation of coarse bullies and cruel tyrants – unfeeling parents and hard task masters.'[35] To abolish all forms of corporal punishment was no solution either, for the end product would be 'a race of mawkish, tender-hearted sentamentalists' [sic] who would rear 'families of petulant, self-willed children.' He urged as a middle way, a 'kindly, common-sense discipline' that relied on 'gentleness and public opinion, and above all ... the prohibition of speech' which gave the transgressor 'due time for reflection, and to repent of his error.'[36] When inflicting punishment, he 'seldom hurried beyond the sacred law of love; after punishing, he had no rest till he had quite made it up with the poor delinquent.' Punishment through ridicule he abhorred. 'No boy can possibly do anything but hate a teacher that mocks at his fall, instead of flying to lift him up again with outstretched hands.' He abolished what he considered 'barbarously stupid forms' of punishment then quite commonly used, which required students 'to assume constrained positions' such as holding books or slates over their heads, standing on one foot, or placing a finger on the head of a nail in the floor.[37] He laid down few rules and granted many privileges so long as they were not abused. His pupils were permitted to retire or take a drink when they pleased, to sit and converse quietly together when they could be mutually helpful, and to stand rather than sit if it suited them. Such freedoms and absence of stern authority were not often found in early Ontario schoolhouses, when even at the relatively enlightened 'official' level, educators virtually equated 'education with restraint.'[38]

Boyle understood that the temperament and behaviour of the teacher in and out of the class-room was important in establishing an atmosphere of emotional stability wherein learning could best take place. 'Nothing is more repulsive,' he wrote, 'to children, or indeed to old people, than the frowning, fault-finding pedagogue.'³⁹ Praise of the attempts and attainments of his students came naturally to him, and he endeavoured not to lose his temper. 'If you are a chronically short-tempered person,' he concluded in his later years, 'quit teaching at once. Your presence in the school room will only worry the children.'⁴⁰ He evidently enjoyed the company of young people, and if his own account is to be believed, attempted to cultivate the image of a father-figure by joining them at play in the schoolyard, and by taking pains to recognize them out of school, 'whether by smile, nod, word, playful touch, or kindly look.' He did not pretend to know everything, or to be incapable of making a mistake; 'he felt himself equally free to confess occasional ignorance and to tender an apology.'⁴¹ Sensitive to youthful fears and anxieties, Boyle tried to eliminate competition in the class-room, especially at examination time. He did not favour the policy of the chief superintendent, who expected teachers to urge their pupils to compete for prizes. To that end, Ryerson had created a system of rewards through provincial subsidies to schools that purchased prizes from the education office in Toronto. If awards had to be given at the semi-annual public examinations, Boyle insisted that they should go to everyone who 'had conscientiously tried to do their duty that half-year.' To reward on the basis of grades alone, he argued, could only contribute to the 'spiritual stunting of the whole school.'⁴² The climate Boyle created at Middlebrook certainly impressed visitors. 'We have seldom been at an examination,' reported the Elora *Observer* in March 1869, 'where we noticed so much good feeling and kindness between teacher and pupil.'⁴³

On the question of actual teaching methods, David Boyle proved to be as advanced in his ideas as he was on other subjects. In keeping with Pestalozzian theory, he rejected the rote method of teaching. He saw little use in forcing children to memorize definitions, grammar rules, historical dates, or arithmetical tables if they did not first understand the meaning of what they were committing to memory. 'Copying' he denounced as 'the principal deadly sin of the schoolroom,' a useless practice, because, like memory work, it did not teach pupils 'how to think.'⁴⁴ The primary purpose of teaching for Boyle was to encourage 'the growth and development of intellect.' The model teacher, he believed, would refuse to press books 'into the unwilling hand' or stimulate a child's 'brain into maddening exertions;' rather, 'he will watch for indications of a natural inclination' to a special vocation in life and 'encourage and direct it as may seem discreet.'⁴⁵

From the start of his teaching career, Boyle adopted the object lesson method and applied it to all subjects. In mathematics, he avoided books altogether when teaching the youngest pupils. Instead, he appealed to their senses by constructing arithmetic lessons around 'things and places familiar to the pupils, such as rails or wires in a fence, boards in a barn, bricks and windows in a house, sheaves in a field.'[46] For lessons on fractions he used 'apples, turnips, blocks, strips of paper, string, foot rules,' or anything else that would illustrate division and sub-divisions. In geography classes, his students built rough relief maps out of sand, clay, water, and wood blocks in order to comprehend the basic principles of the subject. No matter what the topic, Boyle tried to find a unique and interesting way of illustrating his points by sense perception. Monotonous routine, which too often characterized the schoolrooms of Canada West, gave way to 'surprises in every lesson' at Middlebrook, and later at the Elora Public School. Living up to his own ideals of teaching was no easy task. A conscientious rural teacher, Boyle explained, had to spend up to sixteen grueling hours a day 'devising schemes for teaching a dull little boy the difference between "b" and "d", or between "p" and "q"; thinking out how to elucidate the mysteries of the multiplication table for the benefit of some ten or twelve-year old ...; cudgeling [his] brains for easy methods of teaching "parts of speech," or the geographical defini-tions; ... studying the various methods of fixing pupils' attention; of gaining their confidence and teaching them to think, and in the preparation of the next day's work.'[47] At least there was one advantage to this rural one-room school experience; with little supervision, Boyle had the opportunity to give full rein to his individuality and originality.

Outside the class-room, in the fields, woodlots, and river valleys of Upper Pilkington, David Boyle found the widest scope for his methods. Since his own boyhood ramblings with his father in rural Britain, he had been 'passionately fond of botany and entomology,' and now tried to interest his students in these subjects by taking them on regular field trips, and having them notice such things as wayside weeds, wild flowers, and common insects which they normally took for granted.[48] He was convinced that by teaching children to observe on such walks, the teacher could add immeasurably to the value of his pupils' school experience. 'Children are almost invariably keen-eyed by nature,' he argued. 'They are always eager to see things, and a very little stimulus, applied early enough, will arouse this faculty to most rigorous action.'[49]

The stimulation of a pupil's intellect, in Boyle's view, did not constitute a teacher's sole responsibility; the educator also had a duty to foster the moral development of his students. Boyle thought of the public schools as primarily agencies 'for the inculcation of everything that relates to citizenship,' and this objective in turn required doing all that was possible, both 'intellectually and morally,' for the children. Should the public schools fail in that responsibility, he concluded, 'they are only excrescences.'[50] The aim of the teacher, he explained to the North Wellington Teachers' Association, was to supply the country with 'first-class citizens.' To accomplish that goal, teachers must foster 'a love for the truly good – uprightness and integrity of purpose; loyalty to home, to country and to religion; respect for parents, old age and authority; for temperance, industry and thrift, for self-denial and if need be self-sacrifice, and generally to be guided by the teaching of the Golden Rule.'[51] Inherent in this statement lay one of the tenets of the North American Pestalozzian school promoters – that society could be reformed and reshaped through the public educational system. By creating 'citizens' with the aforementioned virtues, Boyle assumed that the schools could do much to rid society of crime, poverty, vice, and ignorance, and to re-establish human relations on the principles of 'co-operation' and the 'spirit of robust Christianity.'[52]

Interestingly enough, this rather commonplace assumption had been foremost in the minds of the school promoters such as Egerton Ryerson when they established the tax-supported, publicly controlled provincial elementary school system from 1846 to 1850. Although Canada West was a predominantly rural and agricultural province – only 15 per cent being urban dwellers in 1851 – the school system had been deliberately created largely in the interests of the growing urban middle 'class' (defined occupationally in the range from artisan to professional).[53] This 'class' feared the consequences of the rapid growth that their province was undergoing, in particular, the violence, delinquency, crime, drunkenness, and vice that had accompanied the social and economic development of their expanding commercial towns and cities, especially Toronto, the provincial metropolis. The influx of the 'famine Irish' and the emergence of a nascent proletariat, led many in this middle class to conclude that a common school system was a vital necessity. These people equated 'ignorance and vice, schooling and virtue.' Motivated by such concerns, urban educators and politicians advocated the education of the poorer classes, believing this would facilitate social cohesion and harmony between the classes, lead to less deviant behaviour, and encourage a more productive labour force.

First as an artisan and then as a teacher, Boyle was in attitude very much a member of this middle class and endorsed these goals of the public school system. As a boy in the industrial districts of Greenock and Birkenhead, he had witnessed many of the social problems the future likely held in store for an increasingly urban and industrial Ontario, unless something was done to check class tensions and inequalities. The importance of the school system as an agency to inculcate the young with the spirit of social co-operation and

Christian morality grew in his estimation as he came to doubt the capacity of organized religion to deal with society's ills. 'Drones, conservative to a degree ..., clogged in the March of Intellect, by dogmas and reposing in ruts along the way,' were terms he used indiscriminately to describe most clerics.[54] 'The arduous task of educating the people' to the practical application of Christian precepts, he argued, had fallen upon others. Humanitarian laymen, Boyle claimed in partial violation of the facts, had initiated and guided the movements for Negro emancipation, religious toleration, prison reform, Sunday school work, temperance, labour movements, social reconstruction, the political franchise and other major social issues. 'Doing absolutely nothing for a time in favor of these projects, (if indeed they have not actually created obstructions), as soon as the first gleam of success appears on the horizon, the reverend gentlemen catch up one by one, and fall quietly into line.' For the sake of his teaching career, Boyle wisely kept many of these stridently anti-clerical thoughts to himself, until after he left the profession in 1881. Such statements again reflect the intense, independent, anti-authoritarian mind of the self-taught man.

Philosophizing about the social importance of the moral development of school children was far easier than actually accomplishing the task. Many Ontarians about the time of Confederation expected the schools to support the home and church through daily religious instruction based on Christian principles acceptable to all denominations. On this question David Boyle also had strong opinions, and followed the dictates of his own conscience, even at the risk of offending some of the devout church-goers in Upper Pilkington. At Middlebrook he followed provincial regulations that prescribed daily religious opening and closing exercises, but beyond that, he resisted all pressure from local ministers to use the Bible as a 'text book' to teach the principles of Christianity. Each year the school inspector noted that the teacher in school section no. 2 continued to be the only schoolmaster in the township who did not use 'the Bible or Testament for any purpose' other than required by law.[55]

'Never,' Boyle asserted some fifteen years later in reference to this period, 'was a cry indicative of more imbecility on the part of the bawlers than that of those who [shouted] "the Bible in the Public Schools".'[56] From his Pestalozzian standpoint, he could not conceive how Bible reading or formal religious instruction would serve to teach young pupils the difficult, abstract principles of Christian morality and good citizenship. Observation and sense perception were as basic to teaching morality as they were to teaching arithmetic. Children learned a code of morals by watching and emulating the actions and behaviour of their parents and teachers. To those who advocated the Bible in the class-room, Boyle answered that 'without sermonizing or any assumption of sanctimoniousness,' he was better able to inculcate 'the principles of Christian morality ... in some practical shape many times daily' in the happy, family-like atmosphere of his class-room. Even then, Boyle admitted that 'no school, no teacher, or no system' of learning could eradicate 'the evil effects of bad home training,' or the negative influences of 'trashy five and ten cent sensation novels; ... the vile articles in newspapers giving the details of suicides, murders, abortions, seductions and divorces, to say nothing about the suggestive advertisements; and the glaring inconsistencies in the "walk and conversation" of Sunday School Teachers and others to whom children naturally look for example.'[57]

David Boyle also considered love of country to be a vitally important element of a child's moral development. In these years immediately before and after Confederation, as British North Americans attempted to create and consolidate the new Dominion of Canada, he saw the public school as an agency of nation building. Raised as an ardent Scottish nationalist, Boyle could scarcely believe the lack of patriotic and national sentiment in his adopted country. It was a concern shared by a few other Canadian, or more precisely Ontario, nationalists who called themselves 'Canada First.'[58] Boyle, who undoubtedly was familiar with their ideas, may well have been echoing their thoughts. 'What boy now-a-days,' he queried, 'ever so much as hears the mere name of patriotism in all the weary wasted years of his senseless schooling? I love my [adopted] land,' he added, but he was 'self-taught to do so.'[59] To rectify what seemed to him an intolerable situation, he tried in his class-room constantly to impress upon his pupils the concept of Canada 'as one of the most highly favored lands, ... its people ... enjoying the best kinds of parliamentary government, the foremost school system, the most invigorating climate, and the highest condition of general comfort and prosperity.'[60] Patriotic indoctrination would become a central theme in Boyle's life. In the years ahead he would become a scholar of Canadian history and pre-history; and as provincial archaeologist and secretary of the Ontario Historical Society, he would justify his research, his writing, and his heritage preservation activities on the basis of their patriotic value.

IV

David Boyle remained six and a half years at Middlebrook Public School, about twice the average length of time spent there by his four predecessors. Several factors induced him to stay, not the least of which was the recognition he received in monetary terms from his board of trustees. As he grew in self-confidence, Boyle had demanded and received from the penny-wise trustees substantial annual increments, until by 1870 he was the highest-paid teacher in the township, receiving a respectable salary of four hundred dollars.[61] Dramatically improved working conditions also influenced his decision to remain. In the spring of 1866, the old log school burned to the ground. 'There was no doubt the fire was incendiary,' reported the Elora *Observer*.[62] The trustees replaced the log structure with a stone building, the largest in the township, and equipped it with new seats and desks, maps, and equipment.

A changed domestic situation also restricted Boyle's mobility in these years. In 1867 he married Martha S. Frankland, who had immigrated with her widowed mother to Pilkington from Yorkshire, England, in 1855. Prior to her marriage, Martha had lived near Middlebrook School on the farm of her brother, Thomas, who later edited the Elora *News* (1872–3) before emigrating to Manitoba. Martha's mother, Susanna Frankland, resided with the Boyles until her death in 1880. David's responsibilities mounted rapidly when his two dependants became four with the birth of a daughter, Susanna, in 1869, and a son, John, in 1870. Except for the fond and uncritical recollections of her youngest daughter, Anne, virtually nothing is known about Martha Boyle, her character, interests, or relationship with her husband. Described as a shy, unassuming though cheerful woman of twenty-six when' she married, Martha seemed to provide a helpful stabilizing influence for her studious, intense, and forthright spouse. Their personalities, while dissimilar, complimented each other, and were united by a mutual regard for each other's talents and ideals. According to her daughter, Martha was by nature neither an intellectual nor a controversialist like her husband. If David wished intellectual stimulation at home, he was more likely to find it in discussion with his spry mother-in-law. '[Susanna Frankland's] recreation was reading,' reported the Elora *Lightning Express*, 'and her memory being good, she was able to take her share in the discussion of many questions that are thought to lie beyond the range of "woman's kingdom".'[63] Perhaps it was in deference to her more assertive and literary-inclined mother that Martha Boyle sought fulfilment as a homemaker. She conceived it to be the wife's function to look after her husband, her 'bairns' and her house – the patriarchal system of nineteenth-century Canadian households suited her. From start to finish of their forty-four years of marriage, Martha seems to have contributed to her husband's career by keeping his domestic life in order, making few demands, and causing him few unsettling domestic problems or anxieties.

While several favourable circumstances may have combined to hold David Boyle at Middlebrook School a few years longer than he might otherwise have stayed, they could not hold him there indefinitely. After six years there was little scope for advancement, either professionally or intellectually, in his isolated schoolhouse. In a rural district he could not reasonably expect a much higher salary than the one he was earning by 1870 – a sobering thought with a growing family to support. More worrisome, both the challenge of teaching and his enthusiasm seemed to be waning now that he had mastered the problems of the one-room school. The routines and the innumerable daily tasks had become more and more oppressive; he found himself becoming a 'slave' to his school work. Looking back on this period, he warned others 'against letting school-drudgery eat out one's life.'[64] Boyle sought relief and stimulation in the activities of the North Wellington Teachers' Association. This organization gave him an opportunity to share his experiences with others and to debate educational issues. The association meetings also allowed him to order, and to begin to write down, his thoughts on teaching methods and theories, thoughts now leavened by years of practice and experimentation. His informed contributions to the discussions so impressed his colleagues that they elected him their vice-president in 1869.[65] The mutuality of a teachers' association, however, could not satisfy Boyle's needs either. After six years of isolated country teaching, he required the challenge and stimulation of a larger school, and the cultural and intellectual environment of urban life.

Since he wished to remain in the teaching profession, there seemed only one sure way out of Middlebrook School, and that was to upgrade his qualifications by sitting the exams for a first-class teacher's certificate. With characteristic determination, he began to focus his reading towards achieving that objective, and in December 1870 attempted the county board examinations in Elora. Charles Clarke, the one-time journalist who had helped to draft the radical Clear Grit political platform in the early fifties, and who was then a part owner of a general store in Elora, wrote in his diary an account of the board of examiners' meeting at which the papers of the candidates for teachers' certificates were graded. 'I was struck with the general bad character of the writing, the numerous errors in spelling and the strange blunders in the historical and scientific papers,' he recorded. 'The best and only readable scientific paper was from David Boyle, who fails, however, in mathematics. He has got good hold of the most important matters for Common School teachers, however, and makes no mistakes in orthography.'[66] Boyle, in fact, had achieved first-class grades in most of the standard subjects – reading, spelling, etymology, grammar, composition, geography, education, and school law – and passing grades in writing, history, drawing, geometry, natural philosophy, chemistry, and human philosophy.[67] In addition, he successfully sat several optional examination papers in natural history, agricultural chemistry, and botany, and thus received permission to teach these subjects. But his lack of success in mathematics meant that he was denied his first-class teacher's certificate. It was small consolation to know that he was not alone in his predicament, since the failure rate at these county-wide examinations was remarkably high, sometimes over 80 per cent.[68]

After this humbling experience, the record of which would return to embarrass him in the future, Boyle could scarcely have anticipated that an opportunity for advancement would suddenly arise some eight months later when the principalship of the Elora Public School became vacant. At first he held little hope of obtaining the post. In fact, he had not been aware of the opening early enough to submit an application before an able and qualified candidate had been appointed to the headmastership at a sparsely attended meeting of the Elora school trustees on 3 July 1871. A week later, however, at a second fully attended meeting, the majority of the trustees, despite cries of outrage from several of their colleagues, rescinded the earlier decision, ostensibly because the position had not been advertised. Boyle subsequently tossed his hat into the ring on the invitation of one of the trustees unfriendly to the fallen candidate. At the next board meeting in August, the Elora *Observer* reported that after three ballots and heated debate – 'during which some not very complimentary phrases were used, giving indication that when the trustees went to school the ordinary rules of courtesy were not much in vogue' – David Boyle was chosen principal over the original choice and one other candidate.[69] 'The truth was,' alleged the *Observer* in a final editorial salvo in December, 'that the religious persuasion of the [original candidate] caused the action, though none of the Board had the manliness to assert it.'[70] In Elora, with its heavy concentration of Scots, being even a nominal Presbyterian was a distinct advantage.

David Boyle must have experienced mixed feelings about these events, all of which were described in detail in the local press. He was probably aware of the amount of back-room 'political' intrigue involved, and that religion played a pivotal role in the trustees' decision. As a civil servant towards the end of the century, Boyle would rail against the fact that political affiliations and religious opinions could hinder a person's advancement. Yet, at this stage of his life, when such considerations worked in his favour, ambition seemed to stifle whatever qualms or twinges of conscience he may have felt about the circumstances of his appointment. All the same, he must have cringed to read in the *Observer* that Thomas Connon, one of the trustees who operated a photography business in the village, had asserted publicly 'that the choice of the Board had fallen on the least qualified candidate.' In the same issue, another trustee questioned Boyle's credentials, and argued that 'at the Christmas examination Mr. Boyle should be required to take a first-class certificate.'[71] A stubborn man, especially when stung by the criticisms of school trustees, David Boyle determined to prove himself to his detractors. As they suggested, he did obtain his first-class certificate at the next examination in January 1872[72] and then went on to set in motion a number of activities from his base in the public school that were destined to inspire something of an 'intellectual awakening' in the village of Elora.

3

Elora's intellectual awakening
1871–81

I

Writing in his diary in February 1867, the Elora merchant Charles Clarke, soon to become MPP for Wellington Centre (1871–87),[1] bemoaned the lack of intellectual stimulation in his rural village setting. The villagers' 'worlds never go beyond Guelph,' complained Clarke, who longed for the ferment of ideas to be found in the cities. 'The great want of the country is conversation of an elevating, awakening character.'[2] Twelve years later, he proffered an entirely different opinion. 'We have a population of more than average intelligence,' he wrote in November 1879, 'and there is abroad in this community a spirit of enquiry, a desire for knowledge, an encouragement of educational means greater than is ordinarily found in a Canadian village.'[3] This was no idle statement. The Elorans whom Clarke once scorned now supported what was recognized as one of the finest mechanics' institute libraries in Ontario, one of the province's few museums, and a vigorous scientific and literary society. What and who had wrought the change?

Forces of urbanization helped make Elorans less insular, particularly since the village fell in the zone of intense competition where the hinterlands of Hamilton and Toronto overlapped. The arrival in 1870 of the Wellington, Grey and Bruce Railway, under construction from Guelph to Owen Sound, heralded the demise of Elora's 'backwoods' status. The W.G.B. Railway represented the city of Hamilton's response, belated and ultimately unsuccessful, to the challenge posed by the Toronto, Grey and Bruce line for control of the trade and commerce to the north and west of Guelph.[4] Eventually Elora would be drawn securely into the transportation nexus of the provincial metropolis when a second line, the Credit River Railway, terminated there in 1880. On the strength of its new rail connections the village developed as an important local shipping centre for grain and live-stock. Those parochial Elorans who once might have refused to venture to the cities beyond Guelph, now found the influences of these centres inexorably encroaching upon their existence. Improved communications, whether by rail or through the medium of the printing press, kept Elorans daily in touch with the political, commercial, and cultural happenings of the provincial capital and the world beyond.

Since the effects of urbanization touched most hamlets and towns across the southern portion of Ontario at mid-century, they do not sufficiently explain what made the 'desire for knowledge' so intense in Elora. This small community of about 1550 inhabitants in 1871 remained as typical in its social composition as scores of other villages in Wellington County. In the final analysis, the individual initiative and dedication of a handful of people set Elora apart from its neighbours; foremost among those injecting vitality into the cultural affairs of the place stood David Boyle, the principal of the public school.

When Boyle moved back to Elora in August 1871 he was twenty-nine years of age. In appearance, he looked almost too young to hold the position of school principal. Part of his problem was that he was quite short, or more precisely, his legs were short in proportion to the rest of his body – an inherited trait shared by others in the male line of his family. He tried to compensate for his size and boyish appearance by growing a long beard, styled in the fashion worn by federal Liberal leader Alexander Mackenzie – the upper lip bared. Yet while youthful in general bearing, Boyle's countenance commanded respect; he was a handsome man, with wide, penetrating but kind eyes, a studious gaze, and a straight, aristocratically proportioned nose. Flecks of gray at the temples anticipated the full head of snow-white hair that, by his middle forties, gave him a strikingly distinguished look.

The tension and anxiety associated with oppressive amounts of work and study may have helped turn his hair prematurely white. For a start, administering a school that bulged at the seams with pupils was no easy task. 'The rooms ... are in a very crowded state,' described one local paper in 1874. 'The inspector ... has already given notice that another teacher or two must be engaged as the numbers [of students] now taught are far beyond what the law allows.'[5] Initially, Boyle struggled along with three women assistants to handle the approximately four hundred pupils registered at the school. Fortunately for the teachers, the attendance rate did not go much beyond 60 per cent, while the congestion was slightly alleviated in 1876 with the expansion of the building and the addition of another instructor.[6] Adding to the principal's difficulties, however, was a high turnover of the teaching staff caused by the penny-pinching trustees who, with an eye on the next election, refused to pay decent salaries if that meant increasing the tax rate. In September 1876 Boyle's staff of four were all 'beginners,' each receiving a paltry annual salary of about $200, low even by the standards of the time.[7] The principal himself earned only $550 in 1875, not a great improvement on the $400 he had received in his last year at Middlebrook.

The task of breaking in his inexperienced colleagues, and of teaching in, and administering, a crowded school, paled in comparison to the onerous burden of extra-curricular and community activities that Boyle was to assume in Elora. His contributions to the cultural life of the village began quite by accident when he discovered several hundred books stacked in a hallway between the public school and the wing of the building that housed the high school. These volumes were the remains of the old mechanics' institute library that had ceased operation in 1869 owing to poor management and for want of subscribers. Struck with enthusiasm, Boyle soon fixed his sights on the task of resurrecting the institute and its library. Not the least of his motives was a determination to win the respect of those school trustees who had publicly opposed his appointment to the principalship.

Boyle had several other reasons for wanting a good library in the village. The autodidact ethic, ingrained by his upbringing, had become a part of his daily cycle; he found time on most days for study and self-improvement. The natural sciences, particularly biology, had absorbed his spare moments for many years so that he was quite familiar with the flora and fauna of the region. Now he wished to read deep into the thoroughly unsettling complex of ideas raised by the Darwinian 'revolution.' Since becoming a teacher, Boyle had also turned his attention to geology and palaeontology, his imagination excited by the rich variety of fossils to be found in the river valleys and gravel beds of Nichol and Pilkington townships. 'I can conceive of no more profitable and pleasing way ... to spend a few hours,' he confessed, than in the Elora gorge, 'where almost every few minutes the hammer exposes a gracefully formed shell.'[8] There was so much more that he wanted to learn about geological formations, systems, and fossil strata. Further, since he intended to introduce the pupils of both the public and high schools to the delights of rock and fossil hunting, he recognized the necessity of a basic library of the latest scientific texts and reference books.

Another emerging interest for Boyle was the field of New World archaeology. The curiosity he had felt as a youth, when told of Botta and Layard's discovery of the long lost remains of Biblical Assyria, was rekindled by archaeological finds of his own. Boyle quite literally stumbled into archaeology as he pursued his natural science interests in the fields and river valleys of North Wellington. Chance surface finds of small chipped flints, rough or unfinished chert tools, and potsherds, picked up while on nature hikes, especially after spring and fall ploughing, raised a host of questions in his mind. Who were the people who fashioned such strange objects? The blacksmith in him marvelled at the workmanship and perseverance of the primitive toolmakers and craftsmen. Where had they gone? When? Why? What lost cultures awaited the Ontario archaeologist? Everywhere, it seemed, traces of this past beckoned him. By a stroke of luck, while visiting his Uncle David's farm, 'Braemore,' in Richmond Hill in the late 1860s, he was able to take spade in hand and dig when told of the existence of ashbeds on the property. 'An old camp site marked the place,' he recalled, 'and from the beds of ashes several phalangal bones were taken,' one a 'somewhat remarkable specimen' having a turtle figure marked on it.[9] Boyle knew that to make sense of his findings would require a wide range of reading.

In promoting the mechanics' institute, Boyle considered more than his own and his students' intellectual well-being. Having achieved upward mobility as an educator, and having realized many of the middle-class aspirations of his artisan culture, he perceived it as a duty and a responsibility to encourage the self-improvement ethic among the labouring classes. A mechanics' institute, he wrote with a touch of condescension, should 'excite in the mind of the working man, a taste for that kind of literature, which is calculated to do him most good.'[10] Boyle did not assume that 'plain' mechanics and tradesmen would be the driving force behind the institute; that task should fall to those who occupied 'a much higher position in the social scale.' Hence, it was to 'clerks, bookkeepers, businessmen and members of the learned professions' that Boyle first appealed for support in his effort to revive the mechanics' institute in October 1871.

Assisted by John Smith, the editor of the Elora Observer, Charles Clarke, and others, David Boyle convinced many of the businessmen and professional people that an institute would survive if it complied with the regulations set by the Association of Mechanics' Institutes of Ontario to become eligible for an annual grant of up to $400.[11] The association had been created in 1868 by the Sandfield Macdonald government to exert a measure of control over the proliferating number of subsidized mechanics' institutes across the province.[12] Government assistance was made contingent upon an institute organizing a program of evening classes and operating a library on practical subjects such as 'Mechanics, Manufactures, Agriculture and Horticulture, Science, the Fine and Decorative Arts, History and Travels.' The provincial association also subscribed to the philosophy of the British movement and considered the libraries to be secondary and supportive to adult education classes and lectures of a useful and technical nature.

David Boyle guided the Elora Mechanics' Institute through its first decade, initially as librarian (1871–2), until the books were moved from the schoolhouse to the residence of one of the members able to provide a reading room service in the evenings. Subsequently, Boyle served two terms as president (1873 and 1880), and figured prominently on the managing, fund-raising, and book selection committees. He was particularly adept at persuading Elorans of all classes to join the institute. 'Few libraries are so well patronized in proportion to the population as our own,' reported the *Observer*.[13] Since its first year of operation some two hundred people had paid the annual dollar subscription fee to use the library.[14] These included employers, professionals, farmers, and some two dozen students, but more significantly, the major users of the library were labouring men, the artisans and their apprentices who, according to one newspaper report, took 'the chief interest in the prosperity of the institution' – an unusual phenomenon in these libraries which were most often frequented by middle-class patrons.[15]

The managing committee had made special efforts to entice working men; for a start, it had arranged that artisans were adequately represented on the various committees. Boyle, meanwhile, launched an innovative public relations campaign that reached into the factories and shops of the village. Special lists of library holdings and recent acquisitions pertinent to the work or interests of specific groups of craftsmen were posted in the appropriate places of employment. Advertisements and lists of holdings could be found all over the village, in banks, the post office, the railway station, warehouses, shops, and 'even the bar-rooms.' 'In the great struggle for the "almighty dollar",' Boyle wrote, 'literature and literary pursuits are likely to be lost sight of, so that it is just as much a necessity for Mechanics' Institutes to advertise themselves, as for the merchant to advertise his goods.'[16]

Doubtless Boyle raised a few eyebrows in his attempt to promote the institute when he supported the interests of working women, particularly the domestic servants, sewing girls, and shop women in the community whose welfare, he believed, was 'a matter of neglect, if not indifference' to most members of the managing committee.[17] Boyle attempted to canvass the women's workplaces and reach them through the press. 'We are requested to state,' the Elora *News* informed its readers, 'that ladies are admitted to [the night] classes precisely on the same footing as gentlemen, and are invited to attend. Go girls.'[18] When few working women responded to his initiatives, Boyle proposed what many must have considered to be quite a radical solution. Why not, Boyle dared ask, 'popularize our institutions, by electing a few ladies to act on the general committee' of the provincial association, and by admitting working women to membership in the local institutes at a reduced rate since they received such 'a low rate of remuneration.'[19] Regrettably, the all-male leaders of the mechanics' institute movement in Ontario lacked both the inclination and the courage to implement such ideas.

The belief that women should be afforded the same educational opportunities as men had been something the Boyle family had long taken for granted. Back in Scotland, David's aunts had been sent to the parish school to learn to read and to write, and later adhered to the self-improvement ethic of their men folk. As a boy visiting his grandfather's farm in Cumnock, David must have stood in awe of his strong-willed, assertive Aunt Agnes, his father's elder sister, who considered herself the equal of any man. For a time in the early 1850s, Agnes greatly amused her brothers by declaring an intention to purchase and to operate her own farm upon emigrating to Canada West.[20] Though she did not fully realize this aspiration – she did the next best thing and married a Lambton County farmer – her family did not question her capacity to accomplish whatever she set her mind upon doing. Family influences, and perhaps the experience of having attended co-educational schools in both Greenock and Birkenhead, laid the foundation for Boyle's belief in the equality of educational opportunity for both sexes. As he matured and came to understand the social and economic restrictions on Victorian women, he resolved to resist, in his own way, a system that denied them basic rights. His appeal on behalf of the working women of Elora in the mid-1870s was one of his first public declarations in favour of equal treatment of the sexes. From this initial statement he would become an ardent supporter of the emerging feminist movement in Ontario and advocate the right of women to attend the universities, to enter the professions, and to exercise the franchise.

Although the Elora Mechanics' Institute may not have attracted many working-class female members, it flourished all the same mainly because of its exceptionally fine collection of books. The managing committee, with Boyle at the centre of activity, sponsored a variety of events – concerts, social entertainments, art and science exhibitions – to raise money for book purchases and to qualify for matching government grants. As a consequence, the library expanded by some four to five hundred volumes annually, until by 1881 the collection comprised approximately five thousand volumes and required the publication of a catalogue for the members.[21] What may seem by modern standards a piddlingly small collection was an impressive achievement for a rural Ontario village in the 1870s, especially in the face of what the secretary aptly called 'a depression unequalled in Canada for many years.'[22] But more significantly, it was one of the largest mechanics' institute libraries in the province! In 1884, the Elora library with 5977 books had surpassed the London Mechanics' Institute with 3075 volumes, Guelph with 3729, Kingston with 4517, and St Catharines with 5346. The villagers could well boast that their library was 'the very largest and best in the Province, outside of Toronto [with 10,634 volumes in 1884], and Hamilton, and possibly one or two towns.'[23] The provincial inspector agreed with this assessment and reported in 1884 that '[Elorans] have one of the finest libraries in Ontario, not being over ten per cent of Fiction.'[24] The library users, moreover, seemed to be an unusually serious lot. The *Observer* marvelled at the fact that only 25 per cent of the approximately 4500 books borrowed from the library in 1876-7 were fiction – a remarkable figure when one considers that 79 per cent of all books borrowed from the Toronto Mechanics' Institute in 1875 were novels.[25] The Elora statistics were a testimonial to the quality of the library collection in the fields of biography, history, travel, the physical and natural sciences, agriculture, mechanics, theology and religion, education, folklore, and periodical literature in general. David Boyle and the few others responsible for selecting the books had evidently purchased with admirable discretion.

Much to Boyle's disappointment, the evening classes and lectures, which were supposed to be the primary focus of each local institute's adult education program, did not succeed in Elora. Classes were organized – Boyle himself instructed in grammar and writing – but the artisans of the community showed little inclination to attend. 'The committee appointed different nights to meet the young men,' the secretary reported in October 1873, 'but only 2 or 3 ever put in an appearance, so the classes were dropped for want of attendance.' Again, in 1876, he reported that because of past experiences, night classes were 'not even tried this year.' Interestingly, during the winter of 1876-7, 'classes for mensuration, arithmetic, writing, and bookkeeping were held for nearly thirty evenings ... with a good average attendance,' only to be dropped the following season because 'little or no disposition was evinced for [their] formation.'[26] Boyle attributed the failure of the classes and lectures to indifferent teachers and speakers. His solution to the problem was simple in the extreme – lecturers and class leaders should resort to Pestalozzian techniques. 'A working man desires something better than mere talk to attract him from his fireside,' Boyle argued. 'What we want to hear in a lecture is, in our day, quite of secondary importance to what we want to see. Object teaching is just as much a desideratum for adults as for juveniles, and if any course of lectures scientific or otherwise, can be arranged, that will introduce this method of instruction, there will be no lack of hearers.'[27] Purely oral explanations fail utterly, he argued, when levelled at a mechanic used to working from drawings and patterns.

Actually, the reason for the failure of the night classes was far more complicated than Boyle's pedagogical explanation. Not poor teaching methods, but an unattractive range of courses more likely explains the lack of attendance. Classes in arithmetic, grammar, composition, penmanship, and bookkeeping had little practical relevance to the small community of artisans and apprentices, some of whom might have attended technical courses designed to improve their understanding of their trades, had such been offered. To be fair, there were probably not enough people available, or capable, of teaching courses with a purely mechanical slant. As for unskilled male labourers, and female shopkeepers and domestics, forced by circumstances to work long hours simply to eke out an existence for themselves and their families, unexciting evening classes in elementary subjects would have had little attraction. Interestingly, what happened in Elora was consistent with a province-wide trend, as most local mechanics' institutes dropped out of adult education and became mere circulation libraries. The organization of technical and practical evening courses as in Britain, the model encouraged by the Association of Mechanics' Institutes of Ontario, apparently went beyond the limits and interests of the province's largely rural and small-town population.[28] The British example, appropriate for a highly urbanized society with a large, skilled industrial working class (especially the so-called aristocracy of labour that sought the respectability associated with learning and knowledge), seems to have been ill-suited for Ontario society in the 1870s.

When Dr S.P. May, the superintendent of the Educational Museum and Library in Toronto, conducted a survey of institutes across the province in 1880, he discovered that fewer than half of them organized evening courses, and that many improperly used their grants to purchase books of fiction. On the basis of May's report, the Liberal government of Oliver Mowat introduced the Free Libraries Act in 1882 which provided for the transfer of any mechanics' institute collection to municipal control as a free public library. In time this transfer occurred in Elora, and to this day the public library stands as Boyle's permanent legacy to the village.*

II

Over the course of the 1870s, the Elora Mechanics' Institute library afforded David Boyle his first real opportunity to pursue his abiding interest in the natural and physical sciences. These years of rigorous self-imposed study – a veritable orgy of self-education – were of critical importance in his intellectual

---

* Most appropriately, it was in front of the Elora library (built in 1910 with funding from the Carnegie Foundation) that the Ontario Heritage Foundation, in 1976, erected one of its handsome blue and gold historical plaques to commemorate Boyle's accomplishments.

growth and laid the foundation for his later career as an archaeologist. In Elora, Boyle immersed himself in the study of Darwinian biology, and geology (with special emphasis on palaeontology and mineralogy), and acquired a broad knowledge of contemporary scientific literature, and the new way of scientific thinking dominated by the twin doctrines of uniformitarianism and evolution. Through his interest in flora and fauna, Boyle was familiar with the main tenets of Charles Darwin's epochal *Origin of Species* (1859) before the move to Elora, and once there he devoured every volume he could find on the subject and filled the shelves of the mechanics' institute with all the Darwinian literature that came to his attention. His readings included: Darwin's *Descent of Man* (1871) and *Expression of the Emotion in Man and Animals* (1872) which confirmed the hypothesis that man was descended in body and brain from the apes; and *Man's Place in Nature* (1863) by T.H. Huxley, 'Darwin's Bulldog,' the professor of biology at the Royal School of Mines who popularized in respect of man the biological theory of evolution through natural selection by the survival of the fittest. In common with many North Americans, Boyle also found much to his liking in the writings of Herbert Spencer, particularly his *First Principles* (1864) in which Spencer sought to apply evolutionary theory in a systematic way to fields other than biology. These standard tomes on evolutionary theory soon led Boyle to lesser known volumes. These included: *The History of Creation* (1876) by the German biologist and social Darwinist, Ernst Haeckel; and the literature of 'New England Intellectualism,' the defenders of Darwin such as the Harvard botanist Asa Gray, Harvard philosopher and Spencerian popularizer John Fiske, and the Scottish-born president of Princeton, James McCosh, all of whom sought to reconcile science and religion for a concerned North American public. And for lighter reading, Boyle regularly perused the new popular magazines such as *Appleton's Journal* (est. 1867) and *Popular Science Monthly* (est. 1872) which ran large numbers of articles on Darwin and Spencer.[29]

All the while, Boyle enhanced his understanding of evolutionary theory by reading into geology and palaeontology. From Charles Lyell's *The Principles of Geology* (three volumes, 1830–3), a study that had paved the way for public acceptance of Darwin, Boyle grasped the geological doctrine of uniformitarianism.* Lyell demonstrated evolution through stratigraphical geology and the fossil record, and belied Archbishop Ussher's calculations, based on the

---

* In this theory, Lyell argued that the sedimentary deposits, or the stratification of the rocks, should not be seen as the product of either a single, divinely inspired act of creation, or a series of catastrophic convulsions and universal deluges; rather, they were the product of processes and agencies still active that had advanced without interruption at a uniform rate and in a uniform way over countless generations.

Old Testament, that 'creation' happened at some time during 4004 BC. Boyle, of course, did not confine his study to the library. He may have absorbed Lyell and dispensed with Ussher as an intellectual exercise in the comfort of an armchair, but he also confirmed his ideas systematically and scientifically in the field, by reading the rocks of Wellington County where evolution was a palaeontological fact. The fossil strata along the banks of the Grand and Irvine rivers demonstrated to him, as no book possibly could, the gradual change of organic forms from one another and the survival of the fittest through the millennia.

David Boyle learned, too, how the twin doctrines of uniformitarianism and evolution had helped to encourage the rapid development of scientific archaeology in the Old World. From his reading of such classics as Lyell's *The Geological Evidences of the Antiquity of Man* (1863) and John Lubbock's best-selling *Prehistoric Times* (1872), as well as the many journals in the mechanics' institute that featured articles on archaeological themes (*Blackwood's Magazine, The Canadian Journal, Chamber's Journal, Harper's Weekly, Leisure Hour, Popular Science Monthly*), he came to realize that geology, through stratigraphical and fossil evidence in Britain and Europe, had conclusively demonstrated the great antiquity of man. These and other publications described how, by the 1860s, informed opinion in Europe had finally accepted the implications of the doctrine of uniformitarianism, that human artifacts buried under thick strata of earth and gravel, or layers of stalagmites in caves, must have been left there eons ago. Boyle learned how pioneer archaeologists such as William Pengelly, excavating first in Kent's cavern near Torquay and later with Falconer at the Windmill Cave at Brixham in Devonshire, England, and the Frenchman, Boucher de Perthes, working in the Somme gravels near Abbeville since 1837, had proved man's great age by associating his early tools with animals long extinct. Boyle read, too, in such works as Daniel Wilson's *Archaeology and Prehistoric Annals of Scotland* (1851) and *Prehistoric Man: Researches into the Origin of Civilisation in the Old and New World* (1862), of Christian Jurgensen Thomsen, the curator of the Danish National Museum of Antiquities, who in 1819 was the first to begin classifying collections of archaeological specimens into the three technological ages of Stone, Bronze, and Iron, and of Thomsen's young protégé, J.J.A. Worsaae, who stratigraphically demonstrated the Three Age system in his excavations in the Danish peat bogs and shell mounds. Thus, by absorbing Lyell's theories of stratigraphical geology, the evolutionary views of the Darwinists, the idea of the antiquity of man, and the Danish concept of the Three Age system, Boyle's thought was being shaped by the same influences that had first given rise in Britain and Europe to systematic prehistoric archaeology.[30]

While David Boyle's chief sources of archaeological inspiration came from Europe, particularly Britain, he did not entirely neglect the American scene, although his reading in this area seems to have been limited and unsystematic during the Elora period. He kept up to date on the Mound Builder controversy then raging across the United States, and pondered the question of who built the mounds – a lost race or the ancestors of the American Indian. He read Caleb Atwater's pioneering essay 'Description of the Antiquities Discovered in the State of Ohio and Other Western States' (1820),[31] in which the author speculated that the Ohio earthworks had been built by a vanished race, probably Hindus who migrated from India via the Bering Straits and later moved to Mexico. For a synthesis of the literature pertaining to the Mound Builder question written since Atwater's study, Boyle consulted John D. Baldwin's popular *Ancient America, in Notes on American Archaeology* (1872). This study drew heavily on E.G. Squier and E.H. Davis's important *Ancient Monuments of the Mississippi Valley* (1848), the first issue of the Smithsonian Contributions to Knowledge series.

The Elora Mechanics' Institute also contained volumes that stimulated Boyle's thinking on the problem of 'Early Man' in the Americas, including J.W. Foster's *Prehistoric Races of the United States of America* (1873). Foster, the president of the Chicago Academy of Science and a former head of the American Association for the Advancement of Science, boldly asserted that the evidence existed for man's antiquity in America, and attempted to prove his hypothesis by pointing to instances where human bones had allegedly been discovered in association with those of the mastodon. Boyle also kept abreast of Charles C. Abbott's excavations in the Trenton gravels of New Jersey. In *The Report of the Peabody Museum of American Archaeology and Ethnology for 1877* – reviewed by Toronto professor Daniel Wilson in the *Canadian Journal* – Abbott, on the basis of argillite tools found in geological strata, argued that man in America dated back to glacial times.[32] The knowledge of Abbott's work in New Jersey, and also of the celebrated cave discoveries in the Old World that proved the existence of Pleistocene inhabitants, inspired Boyle to explore the caves of the Elora Gorge for evidence of 'Early Man' in Ontario. His excavations, barren of results, eventually forced him to conclude that 'labor devoted to the excavation of cavern floors in America will prove devoid of such results as have rewarded men of science in the Old World.'[33]

In Elora, then, an Ontario archaeologist was in the making. Boyle's interest in prehistory was growing through his geological and naturalist field-work, his reading, his chance surface finds, his 'digs' into the ash pits of 'Braemore' and the caves of Elora, and his awareness of the archaeological sites that dotted the landscape of southern Ontario, sites that cried out for explanation. All these factors served to activate Boyle's boyhood predisposition for the study of the past; a predisposition, it will be recalled, that had been shaped by his father's ardent Scottish patriotism, and by the 'romance of excavation' associated with Botta and Layard in Mesopotamia. In these Elora years, however, it would be wrong to describe archaeology as the all-consuming passion of Boyle's life; more accurately, it was just one dimension of his wide interest in natural science. As an archaeologist, he was still very much an amateur or antiquarian collector who did not consider himself knowledgeable enough to write, or to lecture, on archaeological themes as he did in geology and biology. But the intellectual interest was there, burning on; so, too, an almost child-like sense of wonder and excitement he felt for the subject.

In point of fact, during the 1870s Boyle gave first priority to another of his interests – the movement to introduce science into the public school curriculum. This question assumed the proportions of a personal crusade for Boyle, whose enthusiasm as a Pestalozzian educator was increased both by his reading of the works of the great nineteenth-century scientific thinkers and by the encouragement given to scientific studies by Egerton Ryerson, the chief superintendent of education. Throughout the 1860s in the *Journal of Education*, Ryerson had assiduously promoted the case for science in the curriculum. He relied to a large extent on the rationale provided by Herbert Spencer and T.H. Huxley, the most influential exponents of scientific studies in English-Canadian scientific and educational circles in the nineteenth century.[34] Excerpts from Spencer's *Education: Intellectual, Moral, and Physical* (1861) appeared in the *Journal* in 1864 and 1865, bolstered by multiple references to Huxley's pronouncements on the same subject.[35]

As the crowning legislative achievement of Ryerson's career, the Common School Act of 1871 is best remembered for entrenching the principle of free compulsory education for every child in Ontario from the age of seven to twelve years inclusive. The legislation also stands as a bench mark in the effort to have science taught in the school system since it called for the training of teachers in scientific subjects, the development of programs of studies, the selection of texts, and other regulations necessary to encourage the study of natural history, agriculture and agricultural chemistry, and mechanics. Ryerson, in common with most British and North American science promoters influenced by Spencer and Huxley, presented two main arguments, one practical, the other intellectual, to justify the teaching of science subjects. Admitting that the knowledge acquired in the common schools was 'very meagre, extending for practical purposes very little, and in many cases not at all, beyond ... the three R's,' he wished to render teaching throughout the school system 'more practically and directly subservient to the interests of agriculture and manufactures.'[36] Science, he believed, would serve this utilitarian purpose by teaching future workers to understand the processes and principles involved in the construction and operation of the modern machine technology that was increasingly to be found in Ontario's factories, fields, and mines. On an entirely different plane, Ryerson also argued that science as a subject of study was equal to, and perhaps in some cases better than, the classics in developing the intellectual faculties of the young, particularly when it came to teaching them how to observe and to think.

David Boyle arrived at similar conclusions after studying Spencer, Huxley, and other spokesmen of English science such as John Stuart Mill and John Tyndall. Predictably he emerged from his books and journals a zealot of the cause of science in education. The cause, it must be added, needed its local champions, for Ryerson's legislation took time to be translated into reality. With the supporters of the classics fighting a formidable rearguard action, and with few trained science teachers or laboratory facilities, the campaign for science in the curriculum was destined to be a long one, spanning most of the remainder of the century.[37] Boyle soon learned for himself some of the obstacles that stood in the way. In his first hectic month as principal of the Elora Public School, he attempted to instruct his colleagues in the North Wellington Teachers' Association on how to teach agricultural chemistry. His message apparently went unheeded. 'Very little interest was taken in the subject,' reported the Elora *Observer*, since 'few of the teachers present had taught it in their schools.'[38] Later on, Boyle would face another kind of resistance to his scientific crusade from those religious fundamentalists in Elora worried by the threat to their beliefs posed by evolutionary thought.

How could he help to overcome such inertia and ignorance? It struck him that the answer to this question lay partly within his own limited experience. He would take the object lesson approach to its logical conclusion by creating a school museum. The idea of collecting and preserving biology specimens for class-room use had been made on several occasions in the *Journal of Education*.[39] Boyle also knew that science museums had proven their worth at the university level in Ontario, at some English private schools, and in not a few mechanics' institutes in Britain and the Canadian Maritime provinces.[40] There seemed to be no reason why a collection of natural science specimens would not prove of equal value for teachers in rural elementary schools. Were there not hundreds of valuable and interesting objects lying about within a few minutes' walk of every rural schoolhouse, waiting to be picked up by educators eager to do their part towards unlocking nature's secrets? If he demonstrated the usefulness of a museum in his own school, then surely that would stir interest among his colleagues. Perhaps he could reach beyond the school itself and spark an interest in science among the adult population at large.

Boyle's participation in reconstituting the mechanics' institute, particularly his success in working closely with the news media to drum up community support, proved extremely useful when he launched the museum project in the spring of 1873. 'A Museum is now in the course of formation, in connection with the School,' noted the Elora *News*, 'and contributions of Natural or other curiosities are requested.'[41] The same paper, conveniently edited by Boyle's brother-in-law, Thomas Frankland, urged the residents of North Wellington to rally to the support of the public school museum since its 'collection would soon become highly valuable, and assist in making Elora a point of attraction to many from a distance.'[42] At his own expense, Boyle supplemented the newspaper coverage by circulating handbills soliciting specimens illustrative of the physical and natural sciences and the manufacturing and agricultural processes, as well as archaeological artifacts, old books, manuscripts, pioneer relics, coins, and the like. Letters requesting contributions or exchanges of minerals and fossils flowed out of Boyle's office to descend upon many an unwary government official, scientist, or mining company executive as far away as Newfoundland, Nova Scotia, Montreal, Toronto, Thunder Bay, British Columbia, the United States, Britain, and even South America.

The response of the local community overwhelmed even the optimistic Boyle, who acknowledged all donors in the local press. Equally gratifying were the donations from farther afield such as the large collection of mineral specimens representative of the region north of Lake Superior, sent by a correspondent in the Thunder Bay District. Professor Henry Alleyne Nicholson, the renowned palaeontologist at the University of Toronto, upon receiving a suite of fossils collected by Boyle's students, reciprocated by sending the museum a collection of Devonian corals.[43] By the mid-1870s, the school museum listed other eminent Canadian scientists among its contributors, including Principal J.W. Dawson of McGill University; A.R.C. Selwyn, director of the Dominion Geological Survey; and Alexander Murray, director of the Newfoundland Geological Survey.[44] It was nothing short of amazing that in 1875 the Elora Public School became the first educational institution in Canada to receive a collection of specimens from the Museum of the Geological Survey in Montreal (the precursor of the National Museum of Canada), comprising 277 specimens of Canadian rocks, minerals, and fossils, each named, classified, and catalogued.[45] This donation to the Elora School Museum set an important precedent for the Geological Survey of Canada, which subsequently implemented a distribution program of its duplicate specimens; by the following year it had sent twenty-eight similar gifts to schools and universities throughout the dominion.

Having succeeded with his Canadian sources, Boyle turned his attention to individuals and institutions outside British North America. T.H. Huxley himself, at the Royal School of Mines in London, England, responded to Boyle's communication by sending a small collection of British mineral and fossil specimens. Then, in 1878, the mighty United States National Museum entered into an arrangement with its humble counterpart in Elora and exchanged a shell collection for some Ontario Amerindian stone implements.[46] The Smithsonian Institution also sent Boyle copies of technical pamphlets on collecting and preserving museum specimens, including Charles Rau's *The Archaeological Collection of the United States National Museum, In Charge of the Smithsonian Institution* (1876).[47] By this time, Boyle was taking his curatorial duties very seriously, little realizing that within a decade he would reap the benefits of his expertise in museum methods and philosophy in a professional sense when appointed curator of the Ontario Archaeological Museum at the Canadian Institute in Toronto.

As the Elora School Museum grew apace, Boyle faced the inevitable problem of paying the costs of display cases, and freight and postage charges. Would the tight-fisted trustees agree to assume these expenses? A request for support to Egerton Ryerson and the education office had proved to no avail. 'I asked the "Venerable Chief,"' Boyle wrote sarcastically to Charles Clarke, 'if there was ... likelihood ... of aid being given to school museums, he says he "will give it his best consideration" in other words "you are a fool."'[48] Boyle was too critical of his chief superintendent. This was an age when politicians bore allegiance to the dogma that he who governs least governs best, and when voters had precious little appreciation of the vital place museums could play in the province's educational system. The few museums that did exist – in Toronto at the university, the Canadian Institute, and the normal school, in the several denominational colleges outside the provincial capital, and in Montreal at the Geological Survey (moved to Ottawa in 1880) – had made little impact on the general public. The museum most frequented in Ontario was probably Thomas Barnett's privately owned establishment in Niagara Falls. Although a notorious tourist trap, Barnett's museum housed a respectable collection of natural specimens, historical and archaeological relics, and, according to Toronto historian Henry Scadding, 'some very fine Egyptian mummies.'[49]

Despite the obstacles, Boyle determined to persuade the usually impecunious public and high school boards of trustees to absorb the modest costs associated with the project. The keen interest manifested by the students and their parents, he knew, would help sway the trustees, as would his practice of opening the museum to the public both during and after school hours. A little contrived media pressure, he realized, could also have considerable influence. Subsequently the local press, with Boyle prompting behind the scenes, endorsed the expenditure of public funds on the museum and pointed out how it would provide 'valuable object lessons' and instil among the pupils 'a feeling of proprietorship in the school and its surroundings.'[50] H.A. Nicholson, who, on a field trip to Elora in the summer of 1874 had received considerable assistance in his researches from Boyle and Charles Clarke, willingly threw his prestige behind the museum. In a letter to Boyle, published in the *Observer* in July 1874, he expressed how pleased he was 'to observe the existence of a widespread taste for Natural Science amongst the younger members of the community, and the efforts which you [Boyle] have been making to promote and foster this taste appear to me to be beyond praise.'[51] He concluded with a hope that local funding would soon be forthcoming. Nicholson's wish was realized in December 1874 when, at a special meeting of the public and high school boards, the trustees struck a committee of management for the museum and authorized a modest operating budget of about one hundred dollars.[52]

With annual funding assured, the museum expanded to fill a large room on the top floor of the public school building. By the end of the decade, the primary holdings included a complete set of plants illustrative of the local flora; a variety of local insects, stuffed birds, small animals, and reptiles preserved in alcohol; minerals, rocks, and fossils representative of the region, the province, and the dominion; and a modest collection of archaeological artifacts. In general, the natural science portion of the museum was labelled and displayed in a reasonably sophisticated way. The biological specimens were classified according to family, genus, and species, the geological items by stratum, systems, and formations, and the archaeological artifacts in descriptive typological sequences based largely on function and working methods.

To be sure, the Elora School Museum contained its share of what modern curators would dismiss as a *potpourri* of dust-collecting bric-à-brac. It might well be argued that such exotica as an 'ancient' Japanese almanac donated by a lady in California, a Chinese incense taper, assorted coins, a piece of walrus hide, a backbone and skull of a shark, and 'an old churn cover' into which was driven 'a worn horse-shoe nail' to fend off 'the evil influences of Canadian witchcraft,'[53] did nothing to realize Boyle's goal of making 'our collection a valuable scientific aid to students – not a mere curiosity shop.'[54] From Boyle's perspective, however, as a pedagogue determined to utilize the object lesson approach to guide his students in all subjects from the known to the unknown by the comparative method, these items would all have been viewed as potentially useful in the class-room.

Given the time and place in which it was conceived, the Elora School Museum was a remarkable accomplishment, created by an extraordinary village teacher toiling without guidance to apply Pestalozzian theory and method, and striving to develop an innovative science curriculum. He had not anticipated his own success. 'When I came to reside in Elora permanently,' he wrote in 1878, 'I undertook to organize a small collection of Natural History objects for the benefit of the pupils, solely. Since that time however, the scheme has outgrown itself to such an extent that we now possess what is in many respects the best Museum in Ontario. It contains many thousand specimens illustrative of the geology, mineralogy, ornithology, etc. of the province and Dominion, besides large numbers from other countries.'[55] By 1880, the museum had become a tourist attraction; it was not unusual for a thousand people, mostly visitors to Elora, to view the collections on a civic holiday.[56]

Most importantly, though, the museum served as a vital centre for learning during the 1870s. From all accounts, Boyle's enthusiasm for nature infected his pupils and inspired them to explore and to observe their surroundings. Even the youngest students spent many hours seeking and identifying shell fossils, rocks, and biology specimens for the museum. 'Almost all children in the village upwards of five or six years of age,' Boyle explained with pride, 'can distinguish *Megalomus Canadensis*, quite as readily as they can an Early Rose potato or a Swedish turnip. It is the commonest and most characteristic bivalve in the Guelph formation.'[57] The explosion of student activity extended beyond the sciences to become the stuff of local legend. 'Sitting Bull, in his faraway tent, hob-nobs with an Elora boy,' related Charles Clarke in 1879, referring to one of Boyle's pupils then in the Northwest Territories, 'and thinks it nothing strange that he should be asked to present a pair of his mocassins to the Elora Museum.'[58] In his *History of Elora*, John R. Connon recalled the discovery in 1879 by his school mate, William Bain, of a cache of wampum beads in one of the caves in the gorge. The chance find became a long remembered happening in the village, leaving the other children agape and eager to resume the search for archaeological relics.[59]

The benefits of the field trips, the museum, and Boyle's class-room practices did not go unappreciated by his students. 'Your teaching has helped me through hard places,' wrote one of his pupils attending the Ottawa Normal School many years after leaving Elora. 'Even in teaching, I often, when at a loss to present something clearly, would remember [and] use your methods. Since I came to [the Ottawa Normal School] I have appreciated your teaching more than I did before.' Evidently her masters were 'presenting as new methods' herbariums in the class-room and cabinets for natural science objects. 'To most of the students it was an entirely new idea but I remembered yours.'[60] This letter was written in 1898, seventeen years after Boyle had left the teaching profession!

For David Boyle, his single most gratifying pedagogical achievement associated with the museum came after he had convinced the parents of a deaf mute girl to send their child to school. He made good use of his various collections of specimens to teach the youngster, without the benefit of the spoken word, how to read and to write. He often said afterwards that he learned more about educational theory from that experience than by reading a shelf full of books.[61] His object lesson method had been put to the ultimate test.

III

By the mid 1870s, Boyle had come to think of his museum as a community centre for the 'education of the masses.'[62] He anticipated that the museum would prove useful to the mechanics' institute since both shared common 'practical' educational aims, and, in turn, expected the institute library to serve as a reference centre for the users of the museum, young and old. Still another organization, in this case one specially created to form a symbiotic relationship with the school museum and to generate wider public interest in science, was the Elora Natural History Society. Formed in September 1874 with Charles Clarke, the popular MPP, as president and Boyle as first vice-president and curator, the society attracted a membership of several dozen men and women and senior high school students interested in serious scientific enquiry and rational amusement. The demand for such a group arose gradually out of the success of the museum, the zeal of Boyle and Clarke, and the curiosity generated by Henry Alleyne Nicholson's presence in the village during the summer of 1874. In helping to form a natural history society, Boyle was probably attempting to recreate in Elora the mutually reinforcing scientific and cultural institutions that flourished in towns all over Britain, and in a few Canadian cities such as Toronto, Montreal, Quebec, St John, and Halifax. In Britain, mechanics' institutes (which often housed museums) and natural history societies jointly pursued biology, geology, and archaeology. In Torquay, for example, William Pengelly, a schoolmaster with a passion for geological research and archaeology, first explored the celebrated Kent's Cavern in 1846 under the auspices of the Torquay Natural History Society, and later popularized his discoveries of Pleistocene man by lecturing to the local mechanics' institute.[63] Certainly David Boyle may be seen as the Ontario equivalent of such as William Pengelly in the British Isles.

For two seasons at least, the Elora Natural History Society remained quite active, organizing field trips, providing a forum for serious discussion, and sponsoring an impressive program of monthly lectures prepared by the members themselves. Some of the research papers were good enough for publication, including Boyle's manuscript 'On the Local Geology of Elora,' his first published piece of writing.[64] The field-work undertaken by the members had a salutary influence on the museum since the specimens acquired, after being authenticated and classified, were often donated to the school; this result had the effect of maintaining the scientific emphasis of the museum and offsetting the tendency to highlight the curios and the bric-à-brac. Ironically, the society almost failed because it was too much in earnest. When the members had difficulty finding speakers, the meetings became less frequent, interest waned, and the membership dwindled. Not to be dismayed, Boyle and Clarke breathed new life into the organization in November 1879 by restructuring it as the Elora Natural History, Scientific, and Literary Society. 'While Natural History researches will still maintain due prominence,' explained Clarke, 'scientific discoveries will be canvassed, an attempt will be made to cultivate literary taste, and the social questions of the day will occasionally be written and talked about.' In summing up the achievements of the original group, Clarke believed that it had accomplished much good work. 'The Society,' he concluded, 'has left its traces upon the School Museum, to which it was an excellent feeder. Its labors stimulated the young folk, and I feel sure that there are in Elora today a dozen students of Nature and its workings to every one existent here before the establishment of our Society.' The names of rocks, fossils, flowers, and birds had become 'as familiar as household words ... If the Society were to drop out of existence tomorrow, it would not die without leaving its mark upon Elora and Elorans.'[65] Charles Clarke could take much of the credit for whatever success the society enjoyed. He had been the resident expert on birds and flowers, and a major contributor of ornithological specimens to the school.

The importance of the support and encouragement of a handful of erudite and enlightened social and political leaders like Charles Clarke, and the editors of the several village newspapers – the *Observer*, the *News*, and the *Lightning Express* – can scarcely be over-estimated in Elora's 'intellectual awakening.' These people helped create a climate conducive to the free expression of ideas and liberty of conscience. 'A mind in chains,' thundered

Clarke, 'a mouth fastened with the padlock of rigid conventionalities, a man or woman intellectually shivering with perpetual fear of Mrs. Grundy, is but a sorry sight.'[66] Clarke and others knew that the potential existed in their village to frustrate their efforts on behalf of scientific education. As could be expected in a small, intensely religious rural community that supported the churches of six denominations, there were those fundamentalist Christians who expressed shock over what appeared to be the public school principal's inordinate interest in science, especially Darwinian biology. In his satirical novel describing his school experiences, *The Ups and Downs of No. 7* (1884), published after his retirement from teaching, Boyle dealt savagely with those men of the cloth who thought that the intent of scientists was to undermine religion. The novel portrayed the clergy as an addled, if not ignorant lot. 'I have no doubt,' blurted the Rev. Mr Gubbin, one of Boyle's clerical characters, 'that much of the ... wickedness of the people in our day is directly traceable to the avidity with which they peruse the vile works of such monsters of iniquity as Tom Paine, Tom Huxley, Bob Ingersoll, Henry (I think they call him) Spencer, and that Prince of Darkness, Edward Darwin ... The fact of the matter ... is that we must prevent our young people from reading works that ignore God.'[67] This was almost certainly a reference to the Rev. George Buggin, a Wesleyan Methodist, who used pulpit and press to warn Elorans that 'there are books in the library which are dangerous in their character and demoralizing in their tendency, and which no parents having any regard whatever for the moral character of their children, would knowingly permit them to read.'[68] After Boyle left Elora and began to publish his views on science and evolution, the aptly named Buggin charged that Boyle had been surreptitiously 'poisoning the minds of the people of God' during his residency in the village.[69]

Prior to the publication of Darwin's *Origin of Species* in 1859, most Christians in Elora and elsewhere would have encouraged the study of nature in the belief that the complexity of natural phenomena, the cosmic design, was the most powerful argument for the existence of a supreme intelligence. Darwin, however, massively challenged this comfortable view. His principles of evolution through natural selection, the struggle for existence, and the survival of the fittest raised the frightening possibility that the design in nature was not divinely inspired. Scientists such as T.H. Huxley in England and Ernst Haeckel in Germany concluded that Darwin had undermined teleology, and that the death of teleology was the death of God. While theologians and philosophers pondered the question of chance versus design, of mechanism versus teleology in nature, most Christians tried to grapple with Darwinism at a more elementary level. For them, Darwin had impugned the credibility of Scripture by rendering dubious the description of Creation in the Book of Genesis. Many Christians erupted in anger after the publication of Darwin's *Descent of Man* (1871) in which the author concluded that *homo sapiens* was the descendant of 'a hairy quadruped, of arboreal habits, furnished with a tail and pointed ears,' and that man's mental and moral makeup differed only in degree from that of the apes.[70] Little wonder that many people believed that scientists were determined to destroy religion and that they must be opposed. These opinions were part of the climate in which David Boyle launched his museum of natural science and urged the study of biology in the elementary school curriculum.

Even with the support of the local press, and of the influential Charles Clarke, who held positions of authority in the mechanics' institute and sat on both the museum and high school boards, Boyle did not underestimate the power of the evangelical mind. To assuage the suspicions of the devout, and partly to please his wife who understood the importance of keeping up appearances in a rural community, Boyle prudently swallowed his disdain for organized religions and attended (albeit irregularly) the Free Kirk in the village. On another front, he sought to counter the fundamentalist threat by trying to reconcile science and religion for the fearful villagers. Boyle looked to the writings of New England's 'evolutionary theologians,' specifically Asa Gray's *Darwiniana* (1876), John Fiske's *Darwinism and Other Essays* (1879), and most importantly James McCosh's *The Development Hypothesis – Is It Sufficient?* (1876). These and other reconciliationists refused to accept the conclusions of Huxley and Haeckel that Darwinisn destroyed teleology, and after 1870 they gradually led the main body of religious thought in North America to harmonize science and religion.[71]

Biologists should not be viewed as impious, free-thinking heretics 'whose teaching must be dangerous to the community,' Boyle explained in lectures to both the teachers' association and the natural history society.[72] 'Evolution ... is rapidly becoming the accepted theory of life,' even 'by the thinking portion of the clerical world, which for so long ... denounced this philosophy as an emanation from the Evil One.'[73] The study of the intricacies of nature and living forms, he argued, would still confirm the existence of a Higher Being. 'According to the well-recognized educational principle of proceeding from the known to the unknown, nothing can be more reasonable than to expect that teaching about the creature should prompt to the higher study of what relates to the Creator.'[74] Quoting McCosh at length, Boyle argued that there was no real antagonism between Darwin and Genesis since there was 'a unity in the process of evolution which indicates it to be a system of development originated by God.'[75]

In his attempt to help Elorans and his teaching colleagues work through the disturbing theories of Darwinism, Boyle was extremely cautious, and to a certain extent dishonest. While admitting that the study of the evolution of living forms 'sometimes plays sad havoc with the dogmas,' he did not expound, publicly at least, the full implications of this statement in his mind. Had he done so, he would have nullified his efforts to appease the devout and to have them accept biology in the curriculum. Through his reading, Boyle had retained his belief in God and teleology, but along the way had rejected as myth many of the theological propositions central to Christian faith, including the miracles of Christ, and the Resurrection and the Ascension.[76]

IV

As he hoped they would, Boyle's efforts on behalf of science in the curriculum caught the attention of teachers beyond the confines of Elora. The Guelph *Mercury* and the Fergus *News-Record*, in addition to the Elora papers, kept Wellington County informed of the museum and its acquisitions. Teachers and students from adjacent towns and villages frequently visited the museum, several of them paying Boyle the highest compliment by starting small science museums of their own – nearby Salem and distant St Mary's in Perth County being the first.[77] Following the praise lavished on Boyle and his museum by Henry Alleyne Nicholson in his second volume of the *Report upon the Palaeontology of the Province of Ontario* (1875), Boyle's name came to the attention of educators in Toronto. 'I take this opportunity of saying,' Nicholson wrote in his report, 'that I am indebted for many valuable specimens from the Guelph Formation to the generosity of Mr. David Boyle, … who is an indefatigable and zealous collector, and whose museum in connection with the school over which he presides, is a work of great public utility.'[78] But that was not all. Boyle had discovered a new species of gastropod fossil that an appreciative Nicholson dedicated to him by naming it the *Murchisonia boylei*. Considering the embarrassing circumstances of his appointment to the principalship, what an immense feeling of vindication, mingled with satisfaction and relief, Boyle must have experienced when he received such recognition from an internationally respected scholar and recently retired president of the Ontario Teachers' Association (1873–4). Torontonians again heard of Boyle during the Provincial Exhibition of 1880 when the Elora museum carried off fifty dollars in prizes for exhibits of minerals, fossils, and botanical specimens.[79]

In addition to his museum and scientific accomplishments, Boyle became more widely known and made important contacts as a result of his attendance and active participation on behalf of the teachers of North Wellington at the annual conferences of the Ontario Educational Association. G. Mercer Adam, the editor of a new journal, *The Canada Educational Monthly and School Chronicle*, invited Boyle to contribute an article on 'School Museums' for inclusion in the first volume of the periodical in 1879.[80] In the second volume of the journal, the editor saw fit once again to draw his readers' attention to the progressive efforts Boyle was making to develop a practical science curriculum. 'The Elora Public School,' Mercer Adam noted, 'receives the Weather Probabilities daily from the Toronto Observatory, by special arrangement.'[81]

Locally, throughout Wellington County, Boyle's reputation was enhanced by his frequent addresses on science and science teaching, several of which were later published in the *Canada Educational Monthly*. He was a popular and forthright lecturer who spoke with emotion and authority. These speaking engagements gave him an opportunity to construct his own personal rationale for including biology in the elementary school curriculum. His argument rested on the basic Pestalozzian premise that education must start with a child's own interests and concerns. 'Would it not be the height of folly,' he asked, 'to neglect the inherent tendency [of the child] and to divert the youthful thought into a totally different channel?' Yet that was precisely what most teachers were doing in the class-room by ignoring science, particularly biology. 'Children are natural biologists,' he explained, echoing Herbert Spencer. They eagerly collect 'butterflies and birds' eggs,' they long to own pets, and their minds are full of questions about nature. Instead of a curriculum built around these legitimate interests and inherent enthusiasms of the young – to stimulate their desire to learn – 'the whole drift of education,' he complained, was to force subjects upon the elementary students for which they had no natural inclination.[82]

Drawing upon a wide spectrum of British, European, and North American science promoters, Boyle emphasized that biology was ideally suited to teach the young how to think. 'The day of stupid "cram" and unmeaning "rote" task work has, or ought to have, gone by.'[83] Now, he argued, the prescribed school subjects should be judged by their tendency 'to untrammel the mind, enlarge its horizon, [and] liberalize its view of men and things.' In this regard, biology, more than most other public school subjects, was 'eminently calculated to develop the reasoning as well as the observing faculties of the masses.' Whatever the topic of study in biology, he wrote, whether it was to distinguish species, to observe the process of metamorphosis, or more generally 'to account for the harmony of nature in relation to climatial [sic] adaptability, geographical distribution, [and] local peculiarities, ... all [were] calculated to develop those faculties, the possession of which in their most highly improved condition are as necessary for men of law and divinity, merchants, manufacturers and mechanics' as for the research scientist.[84]

Biological studies, in Boyle's opinion, would also play a major role in the moral education of the young. Of all the moral effects attributable to biology, he waxed most eloquent about 'the beneficently liberalizing influence it exerts upon the student,' especially when it came to encouraging the humane treatment of wildlife. He deplored the slaughter of all forms of game by the vast 'army of pothunters' – 'miserable wretches,' 'short-sighted temporizers,' and 'merciless human brutes,' he called them – who in season and out, shot down game indiscriminately and relentlessly for the sheer sport of it. This type of person, he argued, had all but annihilated the bison and now threatened the moose. Many other species of animals would soon face extinction if the slaughter continued. 'I can conceive of no method so likely to prove effective by way of preventing the extermination of these and many other noble creatures,' Boyle wrote, 'than by a proper system of training in our national schools.'[85]

Quite apart from the moral dimension, there were practical and utilitarian reasons for teaching biology and inculcating an appreciation of all living things among the young. Lacking an understanding of the balance of nature, Boyle wrote, farmers paid a high price annually for their mindless killing of snakes, toads, small game, and birds of prey. Their 'perpetual war of extermination' against the latter, for example, was leading to a huge increase in 'mice of barn and field, moles, squirrels and small vermin,' all to be dreaded by the agriculturalist. 'Every boy and girl,' Boyle concluded, 'should be taught during school ... that an average toad, during its lifetime, is worth more than half a ton of "Patent Insect Powders" – that a well-behaved snake may be valued at very little less as a scavenger – that squirrels form the daintiest tid-bits for the hawks and owls.'[86] It was this kind of useful knowledge that could well save a substantial part of a farmer's crop and spare him much grief. Finally, Boyle pointed out how the discoveries of biologists over the course of the nineteenth century had alleviated suffering and prolonged life by improving health standards, raising the yield of agriculture, and even advancing industry. They had demonstrated beyond doubt the practical value of biological studies, something the schools could ill afford to ignore.

In voicing his practical 'wise-use' conservation ethic, David Boyle joined a growing movement of naturalists and sportsmen across Ontario who were beginning to petition the provincial legislature in the 1870s (petitions that would become a flood in the 1880s), for the protection of their wildlife.[87]

Although he had inherited a love of nature from his parents, Boyle was to some extent stimulated to become an ardent wildlife preservationist by Charles Clarke who himself challenged the prevailing 'pioneer' mentality that encouraged the wanton destruction of the forests and wildlife. Of special concern to Clarke was the need to educate farmers on the value of insectivorous birds, and as MPP for Wellington Centre, he sponsored legislation in 1873 prohibiting the killing of these creatures.[88] Another influence on Boyle's thinking was Egerton Ryerson's *Journal of Education*, which urged educators all through the sixties and seventies to teach their pupils about the complex and inter-related chain of life, and the utilitarian value of many birds and small animals to the agriculturalist. Articles on the need to protect birds found a regular place in the 'Natural Science Section' of the *Journal*; and often, though less frequently, these were supplemented by statements on the economic and sanitary importance of trees and forests.

The concluding thrust in Boyle's argument for biology was to challenge those who believed that the subject matter was 'quite beyond the range of feminine intellect.' He chided the 'poor old conservative souls' who 'endeavoured to limit "women's kingdom" to the kitchen, the nursery and the parlor ... Jane Herschell and Mary Somerville,' he noted, 'have respectively shown the world what the feminine intellect is capable of accomplishing in astronomy and physical geography.' Revealing his Rousseauian-Pestalozzian appreciation for the mother's role in education, Boyle added that 'we want the [future] mothers of our land ... to know vastly more of [biological] studies than is at present the case, and to be able as opportunity may serve to aid the teacher in bringing young people into sympathy with their "poor relations",' or 'misunderstood friends' as he fondly referred to reptiles, insects, birds, and small animals.[89]

Boyle's published and unpublished educational writings in these years evoke almost contradictory impressions. Up close, when dissecting his manuscripts thought by thought, the image emerges of a man who was somewhat unimaginative, an inveterate borrower of ideas, a plodder along the back concessions of science. Ideas did not spring full blown from the brow of David Boyle. He was not possessed of the acute mind or the powerful intellect of a Huxley or a Spencer. He was but one of many Ontario educators grinding the same axe for science, popularizing the ideas of minds greater than his own. To stand back from these manuscripts, however, and view the sum of the parts, gives rise to a more positive assessment of the man. From this vantage point, Boyle's efforts to synthesize the ideas of others amount to something noteworthy in the debate over science in the curriculum. In his lectures and articles, Boyle carefully tied together the two major enthusiasms of his life –

Pestalozzianism and Darwinian biology. Only with the assistance of biology, he concluded, could Ontarians realize the humanistic, liberal, practical, and child-centred ideals that he thought should be at the heart of the educational system.

v

When addressing his colleagues in the teachers' associations and through the *Canada Educational Monthly*, David Boyle did not restrict himself to stirring up interest in a science curriculum. Within the teachers' organizations, Boyle's enthusiasm for science fused with yet another of his causes – the campaign to raise the occupation of public school teacher to the status of a profession in the public's mind. Professionalism went beyond mere curriculum reform and the promotion of progressive teaching methods; it also encompassed the tightening of certification standards, the elimination of the unqualified from the teaching ranks, the establishment of better working conditions, salaries, and pensions, and the fostering of an *esprit de corps*. True to form, Boyle spoke out on all these matters during the 1870s, and carved out a place for himself as a highly regarded spokesman for elementary teachers in the province.

Not surprisingly, the teachers of Wellington County turned to him for leadership; few among them were so erudite and outspoken on educational matters, or so selfless and competent when it came to organizing meetings and leading discussions. In the early seventies, Boyle served as a vice-president of the North Wellington Teachers' Association (1869–72), the president's chair being reserved for the inspector with the improbable name of A. Dingwall Fordyce. Later, after successfully spearheading the effort to reconstitute the North Wellington association into the more broadly based Teachers' Association of the First Division, County of Wellington and Guelph City, Boyle earned a three-year term as president. From these positions of responsibility, he stimulated discussion on every conceivable topic ranging from the place of science in the curriculum to new methods of teaching, the need for better textbooks, particularly in science and Canadian history, and the value of different or optional curricula for rural as opposed to urban schools. If he was not lecturing on topics related to the class-room, Boyle could be found hammering away at one or other of his favourite themes, such as the outrageously inadequate salaries teachers were paid, the problems with the superannuation fund, or the benefits to be gained from abolishing third-class teachers' certificates, an enduring weakness in the public school system.[90]

Towards the end of the decade Boyle widened his horizons in his capacity as the delegate for the Wellington teachers at the annual conventions of the Ontario Educational Association. Here, too, he emerged as a vocal and aggressive spokesman for teachers' rights. The OEA delegates got a fair measure of the principal from Elora after requesting that he prepare a lecture on their superannuation fund. Boyle gave them far more than they bargained for. He researched his paper by circularizing associations, inspectors, and principals across the province in order to present a fully documented and judiciously argued position paper on the problem to the August 1880 convention of the OEA. 'Two things are very plain,' he determined from the responses, and from talks with department of education officials, 'a change is necessary, and ... it is imminent.' To improve the superannuation fund, which was neither self-supporting nor large enough to provide a retirement allowance sufficient to cover the bare necessities of life, Boyle bluntly informed his audience that 'increased contributions will in a very short time be demanded from us. To my mind, such a demand, if we intend to support a fund at all, will be nothing more than right.' But in return for shouldering their full share of the burden, he urged teachers to demand concessions, including more generous provisions for widows and orphans, increased pensions based on a sliding scale for years of service, and the elimination of 'the extreme uncertainty as to how much the [retirement] allowance for a given year would be.'[91]

Boyle's paper was warmly received and served as the basis for the subsequent discussions with the department of education prior to the revision of the superannuation scheme in 1885.[92] So impressed were the delegates with Boyle's diligence that they elected him chairman of the public school section of the Ontario Education Association, a position which entitled him to a seat on the board of directors of the OEA. At the subsequent convention in August 1881 Boyle again made a mark by convincing his colleagues to establish the standing committee on methods of teaching and hygiene, the purpose of which was to encourage experimentation for the improvement of teaching methods, and to lobby for more rigorous ventilation, light, and sanitation standards in the schools.[93] That same year, he also touched on an issue central to the professionalization of any occupation, that is, the necessity of a code of ethics to eliminate the unqualified, and the need to regulate harmful internal competition. Something had to be done, he argued, about 'the host of itinerant incompetents, the nomads of the profession, who seldom remain in a position more than a year,' but who were hired time and again because they had acquired misleading credentials written by ratepayers, ministers, trustees, and even inspectors only too glad to rid themselves of the persons concerned. 'My suggestion,' he stated, 'is that we should use only testimonials in the form of affidavits, properly attested by a magistrate or commissioner. The thoroughly incompetent [teacher] will find it difficult or impossible' to secure letters of recommendation under such a procedure.[94] Little was done to implement Boyle's suggestion, but the cause of professionalism was served by the public airing of such problems.

In his relationship with the teachers' associations, and before that with the mechanics' institute, and the natural history society in Elora, David Boyle indicated that he was not the kind of person who became a member of a professional or voluntary organization for frivolous reasons. Invariably, he joined a group only if he sympathized deeply with its purported objectives. Since his motivation for belonging was reasoned and usually intense, he was incapable of remaining in the background for long, and settled for nothing less than a position of responsibility that required a generous commitment of time and energy. Beyond this motivation, there was something else in his personality that compelled him to undertake an inordinate share of community responsibilities in Elora, to spend every spare moment at his books, to lead crusades for science, and to trumpet the cause of professionalism. In part it was ambition, but it was an ambition governed by insecurity. He was a man possessed by the need to prove himself to those around him, to earn the respect of such as the Elora school trustees or the delegates to the Ontario Educational Association. He was sensitive about the tell-tale signs of his working-class origins, especially the lingering traces of his 'broad Scots' vernacular. He experienced the nagging uncertainties common to the self-made intellectual as to the quality of his knowledge, and the limits of his abilities. 'Want of confidence has always betrayed me,' he confessed to Charles Clarke in 1890, 'and even when owing to the force of circumstances I have been able to accomplish something, I have invariably depreciated my own work. Not that I did not sometimes consider it as superior to that of some other fellow, but that it was so far from what it ought to be according to my ideal. As a mechanic, as a teacher, and in other capacities (or incapacities) I feared to work in the presence of another professional either until familiarity bred its consequent and proverbial contempt, or, until I discovered that the other chap didn't know any more than I did.'[95]

Fortunately, lack of confidence was not a negative factor in Boyle's life. It had the effect of driving him on at a frenetic rate; he worked harder and longer, and as a consequence accomplished more than most of his peers. His was not to be a restful, contented existence. Severe migraine headaches warned on occasion that he was physically and mentally overtaxing himself. The wonder is that he found the time to undertake all that he did. Even the family, social, and recreational side of his life was a full one. Three more children – James, William, and Anne – arrived during the course of the seventies to compete for his time and affection. Few Elorans were more active in the St Andrew's Society or the Mason's Irvine Lodge, no. 203. Outdoor curling in winter replaced the naturalist and archaeological field trips of the warmer months to provide him with whatever physical exercise he required.

Indoors, he found release and pleasure in yet another hobby, writing humorous (although eminently forgettable) poetry, or letters in rhyme to his friends. In the mid-1870s this hobby became a paying proposition when he began to submit humorous letters to the editor of the Elora *Lightning Express*, written in the 'broad Scots' dialect under the pseudonym of 'Sandy McTosher.' These letters proved so popular among the Scottish community of Wellington County that Boyle was encouraged to reach a wider audience by contributing similar pieces, under the *nom de plume* of Andrew McSpurtle, to the *Scottish American Journal*, published out of New York City.[96] For over thirty years the McSpurtle letters appeared intermittently in the journal which reached as many as 15,000 subscribers across North America, mainly Scottish-born immigrants interested in old-country news and the activities of their fellow Scots in the New World. McSpurtle's delightfully funny, earthy, semi-literate, and caustic effusions on social and political topics delighted the subscribers to the *Scottish American Journal*; concerned readers rarely neglected to enquire of McSpurtle's whereabouts when too long a time elapsed between 'epistles.' McSpurtle's account of a meeting with a Sioux Indian in Manitoba is typical of Boyle's unique sense of humour.

Noo, I'm no what ye wad ca' a nairrow-mindit man; in fact, ... I'm ower braid and leeberal in my notions. I can even mak' allooance for puir craiturs being Mahometans, an' Mormons, an' Methodists, an' sic like ...; I can conceive that it lies within the leemits o' possibeelity for an Englishman, ... or a bit jabberin' French body, to be noo an' then the marrow o' a third class Scotchman ..., but when it comes to a skreighin' bluid-thirsty cannibal o' an in-taed Soo Indian gaun aboot ower the prairies, dressed wi' a blanket an' twa o' three feathers – stinkin' like a foumart wi' creesh an' red paint – eatin' deid horses an' dowgs, in total ignorance o' the Shorter Catechism – an' yet, in the face o' a' this paganism, to stan' up an' tell me to my very teeth that his name is McSpurtle! I say its ... the next thing to robbin' a kirk![97]

For Boyle, muzzled to a degree by the nature of his work, particularly in the years ahead as a civil servant, the McSpurtle letters would sometimes serve a cathartic purpose through which he could express his opinions on public issues or social conventions without fear of official reprimand.

Regardless of what doubts or motives inspired his activities, David Boyle enriched the lives of many people during his time in Elora. Prompted and guided by their indefatigable public school principal, Elorans crossed a cultural watershed. Whether in the class-room or the teachers' association, in the museum, mechanics' institute, or natural history society, Boyle stimulated intelligent discussion on pedagogical and controversial scientific themes, sparked 'the spirit of enquiry' among young and old alike, and generally helped lift the veil of ignorance and superstition from the minds of his neighbours. Long after he left Elora, the public library and the museum (as late as 1912 still considered by some to be 'the most important of its kind in Ontario'),[98] attested to his lasting contribution to Elora's social evolution. David Boyle, of course, crossed a watershed of his own during this decade of unremitting activity. For one thing, he had greatly expanded his education, and 'laid down a good broad substratum' of general scientific knowledge.[99] Further, he had established personal and professional contacts among educators and school promoters across the province. In 1881, these two factors – what he knew and whom he knew – became the determinants of his immediate and radically different future.

4

The archaeological outlook
1881–7

I

'Mr David Boyle has been upwards of ten years principal of the Public School here,' reported the Elora *Express* on 6 October 1881. 'Last night the Board [of School Trustees] met and were surprised to receive his resignation.' When he began the school term in September, Boyle could not have known that a few weeks later he would receive a job offer from the Canada Publishing Company in Toronto. The firm had approached Boyle on the advice of G. Mercer Adam, the Scottish-born editor of the *Canada Educational Monthly*, who was in the process of creating an editorial team for the company to produce a new series of readers for the public schools. The department of education, intending to scrap the existing Canadian Series of Readers (issued in 1868 and based on the Irish National Readers), had invited various publishers to submit their own series for possible approval and authorization. Adam recognized that the competition would be fierce, and that a teacher with Boyle's experience and contacts in the profession would be helpful in the publishers' battle that lay ahead.

Boyle could not resist this opportunity. He and other teachers had long complained about the lack of relevant Canadian content in school readers that they considered an inadequately modified version of a series prepared in Britain for British class-rooms. The Canada Publishing Company promised something entirely different in its Royal Canadian Readers. The five-volume series would be 'Canadian in Sentiment – The Product of Canadian Authors, Canadian Compilers, Canadian Artists, and Canadian Educators.'[1] Such a nationalist emphasis promised to elicit considerable sympathy among Ontarians who for over half a century had become steadily more preoccupied with the problem of imported culture and the need to expand their knowledge of themselves through the school system and other cultural agencies.[2] The company intended to illustrate the volumes lavishly and to engage Ontario artists for the task. No expense was to be spared; funding to the amount of $25,000 had been set aside for the project. All in all, it was a major undertaking that fired the ardour of an educational reformer like David Boyle.

Quite apart from believing in the importance of the Royal Canadian Readers project, personal considerations shaped Boyle's decision to drop out of teaching 'for a time at least.'[3] During his late thirties he had begun to assess critically his accomplishments, future goals, and expectations. He had to decide whether to accept his lot in life as a village teacher, or to strike out in new and potentially more rewarding directions. Eventually he faced the fact that his existence in Elora had become too routine and devoid of challenge and intellectual excitement. The tedium of class-room and administrative duties was more difficult to face each year. There was little scope left for personal fulfilment in the museum or the mechanics' institute, once the main outlets for his energies and ambitions. Boyle simply could not resign himself to the thought of stagnating in Elora for the remainder of his life. He had to discover for himself if he possessed the capacity to be something more than a village educator and home-made intellectual. The Canada Publishing Company offered him the opportunity to expand his horizons and to tap his unused potential. Boyle also looked forward to the change of pace and life-style, and the prospect of a 'more health giving and less confining calling'[4] without disassociating himself entirely from the world of knowledge and learning. His responsibilities would include more than editorial duties; he would also be expected to travel across the province, speaking to teachers' associations on the virtues of the new readers. Further G. Mercer Adam promised him regular work as a contributor to the *Canada Educational Monthly*. On top of all these prospects was the anticipation of living in Toronto, with all of its cultural amenities and educational opportunities for himself and his children.

Elorans genuinely regretted the loss of their public school principal in December 1881. A few days prior to his resignation, the students and staff of the school, in an unscheduled assembly, moved Boyle to tears when they presented him 'with a handsome gold watch, purchased at the jewelry store of Mr. Sheppard, and which,' noted the obviously impressed editor of the Elora *Lightning Express*, 'was marked $60.'[5] This was but the first of several tributes. In April 1882 the directors of the mechanics' institute elected Boyle the first life member of their organization in recognition of the fact that it was 'undoubtedly owing largely to his indefatigable efforts that the ... library today occupies the proud position it does.' The following month, at the annual meeting of the First Division, County of Wellington and Guelph City Teachers' Association, he received a 'highly complimentary address, engrossed on vellum,' that extolled his many efforts on behalf of 'educational reform' during his teaching career. Finally, in October, at a public assembly, the school trustees on the museum board made Boyle 'the recipient of a seventy-five dollar silver tea service,' a testimonial to 'his long, arduous, and self-denying efforts in successfully establishing the Elora museum, with its thousands of curious and priceless articles.'[6] The meddlesome editor of the Elora *Lightning Express* seemed oblivious to the right of privacy, and determined not to ignore the price tag on anything. When Boyle sold his house in January 1882 to Alexander Petrie, the new public school principal, the *Express* reported that the transaction was consummated 'for the sum of $700. The property was exceedingly cheap, and Mr. Petrie got a good bargain.'[7]

Scheduled to travel frequently for the Canada Publishing Company, Boyle deferred the move to Toronto for the time being and rented rooms in Elora so that his family might remain among friends and familiar places. Beginning in February 1882 he assumed the task of criss-crossing the province, speaking to teachers' associations and debating with the representatives of the two rival publishing houses that also intended to submit readers for authorization. W.J. Gage and Company were promoting the Canadian Series, adapted for Ontario pupils from a series published in Scotland. The third competitor, James Campbell and Son, had also reached overseas for inspiration and modified the Royal Readers, originally issued by Thomas Nelson and Sons of Edinburgh.[8] The strategy followed by all three houses was to ask teachers meeting in local conventions to pass resolutions in favour of their particular publications. Confusion was endemic as the debate over the three sets of texts raged in teachers' conventions and professional journals for nearly two years.

In most discussions on the issue, Boyle emphasized the nationalist theme, and aimed his most stinging attacks at Gage and Company, his chief competitor. The Gage readers he considered an 'Old Country' series, badly adapted for Canadian children. 'The natural history ... of this continent,' as described in these volumes, Boyle explained, 'will be unrecognizable in Canada ... On page 36 of the Third Book the information is given that "At one time, *indeed not very many hundreds of years ago*, wolves and bears were quite common *in our own country*"; and that "the swiftest dog *we* have is *the greyhound, which is used for pursuing and killing hares.* ..." In Book II., page 10, this further fact in natural history is cited: "Birds have only two legs, but then they have also two wings, *which more than make up*!" ... Of beavers, Book IV., page 17, repeats the erroneous statement that they use their tails as a mason uses his trowel.'[9]

Such devastating criticism could not go unanswered for long. The counterattack came in a most unconscionable way in the pages of Gage and Company's professional magazine for teachers, the Canada School Journal, a rival publication to G. Mercer Adam's Canada Educational Monthly. The editor of the School Journal, Adam Miller, charged that Boyle was 'totally unqualified to represent the public school teachers of this country from a literary point of view.' The evidence cited – his failure to acquire a first-class teachers' certificate in December 1870 because of failing grades in mathematics.[10] Immediately, Boyle's friends rushed to his defence. 'Those who were present at the Wellington Teachers' Convention about a year ago,' wrote 'Vindex,' a correspondent to the Canada Educational Monthly, 'when Mr. Boyle, in a straightforward, manly way, and in the presence of Mr. Gage, gave reasons why teachers should not support the School Journal in preference to the Educational Monthly, will not have far to look for the motive which prompted the attack. If Mr. Boyle had been employed to "get up" a series of mathematical works, some justification might be found for the exposure of his weakness in mathematical subjects. But what have arithmetic and algebra to do with School Readers?' 'Vindex' went on to list ten other subjects in which Boyle had achieved first-class grades in 1870. 'How many teachers can show a better record? ... The malicious attack on Mr. Boyle is a ... standing menace to every teacher in Canada. It says in effect: "Support the Canada School Journal, advocate the introduction of our precious publications, with all their imperfections, into the Public Schools, or we will show up your weak points, and blast your career as a teacher".'[11]

This episode disillusioned and humiliated Boyle. Having his scholastic record dragged across the pages of the professional journals wore off some of the romance of book publishing. What zeal remained for the job would gradually dissipate in the coming months as he wearied of the grind of constant travel and speaking engagements. Fortunately, the work had its enjoyable aspects; there were interviews to conduct with famous personages, including Sir John A. Macdonald himself, the potential subject of a biography by G. Mercer Adam.[12] In September, Boyle began to write the 'School Work' section for the Canada Educational Monthly, in which he proposed examination questions for teachers at different grade levels in all elementary subjects, and provided new ideas (often quoting at length from a wide variety of journals) on teaching theory and method. For David Boyle, at least this facet of his work remained a labour of love.

A scant eighteen months after Boyle entered the book publishing business, the school reader controversy came to a disastrous conclusion for the Canada Publishing Company. The Scottish readers of both James Campbell and Gage and Company were recommended by the central committee of the department of education and authorized conditionally for one year, beginning in June 1883. Notwithstanding the demand among educators for Canadian texts, the Royal Canadian Readers produced in Ontario were rejected. What had happened? Were the Royal Canadian Readers an inferior product? Not if the judgment of teachers across Ontario can be believed, for Boyle received substantial support in the county teachers' associations. G. Mercer Adam was certain he 'smelled a rat.' He alleged that several members of the central committee that recommended texts to the minister were in conflict of interest since they had 'intimate business relations with a firm [W.J. Gage and Company] upon whose Readers they were called to pronounce judgment.'[13] These charges probably reflected more of a 'sour grapes' attitude on Adam's part than they did the truth. Charges of collusion between department of education officials and favoured publishing houses were rife in these years, although investigation failed to substantiate wrongdoing. Besides, Adam's explanation does not account for the fact that the second British series – Thomas Nelson's Royal Readers – also received authorization. In her study of textbook authorization in Ontario from 1846 to 1950, Viola Parvin could only conclude that the Canada Publishing Company's readers were rejected at least in part because 'at the time there was a general lack of confidence in indigenous products.'[14]

With its substantial investment in the Royal Canadian Readers at stake, the Canada Publishing Company despatched Boyle back to the teachers' associations in the autumn of 1883, in a futile bid to stir up a groundswell of protest among the teaching rank and file to force the department of education to reconsider its decision. While he persuaded several more influential associations to endorse his series of readers – South Wellington and East Middlesex to name but two – Boyle soon realized that he was fighting a losing battle.[15] The Royal Canadian Readers were dead and he knew it. So apparently did G. Mercer Adam, who resigned from both the Canada Publishing Company and the editorship of the *Canada Educational Monthly* and emigrated to the United States.

As a postscript to the battle of the school readers, it is interesting to note that neither of Boyle's competitors – James Campbell's Royal Readers nor Gage's Canadian Series – were destined for longevity. Upon becoming minister of education in November 1883, George Ross hastily declared that he desired only one textbook for each subject, and tried to arrange for a composite version of the Scottish series. When the two publishing houses were unable to reach a satisfactory compromise, Ross struck a committee to produce yet another set of readers. This new series, known as the Ontario Readers, received authorization on 26 November 1884, one year and three days after Ross assumed office.[16] Such were the politics of school-book production in the 1880s.

The failure of the Royal Canadian Readers project was actually but one of several reasons why David Boyle chose to leave the Canada Publishing Company in the autumn of 1883. He probably would have resigned before long in any event since he had grown weary of the existence of a harried, itinerant book promoter. He had not foreseen the frustrations of this kind of employment; certainly, it was not the 'health-giving' calling that he had envisioned upon giving up public school teaching. Self-doubt must have haunted Boyle's thoughts as he gradually realized that he had made a bad decision in joining the company. Perhaps he should never have forsaken teaching. Maybe he was deluding himself to think that he could be anything more than a village teacher and an amateur natural scientist. Just how far could he expect the self-improvement ethic to take him?

In time, doubt gave way to latent ambition and a resolve to carve out a place for himself in the book business; he could not yet admit failure and return to the class-room. To an extent, it was an unhappy twist of fate that helped shape David Boyle's destiny at this juncture. The year before, on 27 May 1882, his father, John Boyle, had died in London, Ontario, and bequeathed him a lot and small house. The sale of this property, when combined with the equity from his home in Elora, provided Boyle for the first time in his life with a modest amount of investment capital. With unrestrained enthusiasm, he lunged into business for himself as an independent book merchant; he did so, it must be added, without giving much consideration to the difficult questions of whether or not he possessed sufficient business acumen, or the tempera- ment, to be a success. His store, Ye Olde Booke Shoppe and Natural Science Exchange, was situated at 353 Yonge Street in Toronto, just below Gerrard Street opposite Elm. He moved his family into the living quarters above the shop and opened for business in December 1883. As he organized his new venture, Boyle must have frequently reminisced about his father, and how proud he would have been to learn that his first born had lived up to the artisan ideal of self-culture, and achieved upward mobility into the ranks of the business community. David had confirmed his father's life-long faith in the blacksmith's creed that knowledge and self-help were the keys to inde- pendence, social status, and respectability.

II

Toronto, a city of roughly 100,000 people in 1883, afforded ample opportunities for small businessmen like Boyle. Powerful forces of change were at work in the urban landscape, fostering economic, demographic, and spatial expansion. Industrial development promised to boom under the 'National Policy' of tariff protection. Immigration from Britain would help almost double the city's population by 1891.[17] Toronto was a remarkably British and Protestant city, a city of newcomers; no other Canadian urban centre rivalled it as a destination point of persons from all over the British Isles. Another conspicuous agent of development essential for both the economic and spatial growth of the city was the street railway system, then in the midst of its first period of large-scale expansion.[18] And for the would-be book merchant who dreamed of a provincial market, Toronto, with its railroads radiating in every direction, had no rival as a distribution centre. It was also the centre of education and publishing in Ontario. For Torontonians, the manifest physical growth and the economic and cultural supremacy of their city were a sou.·ce of immense pride. Outsiders did not always share this view, of course. To them, Toronto society seemed in many ways stifling and parochial, a place of intolerant, narrow-minded Protestant bigots and a puritanical middle class only too keen to impose a rigid code of public behaviour on their already 'dull, plodding, bourgeois regime.'[19] As a transplanted Eloran in the provincial metropolis, Boyle came to express elements of both these perceptions of the city.

When he opened Ye Olde Booke Shoppe, David Boyle sought to develop a specialized business around his own interests and expertise. Since he had a keen appreciation of the literary needs of the teaching profession, and a first-hand knowledge of the requirements of the mechanics' institutes, he hoped to acquire their patronage. In addition, he intended to make his shop the haunt of naturalists and the scientifically inclined. With his projected clientele clearly in mind, he stocked his shop with authorized textbooks for public and high schools, considerable non-fiction material, the kind he thought would be desired by the mechanics' institutes, and a fine selection of scientific books and periodicals, much of it material not readily available elsewhere in the city.[20] To complement this inventory, he obtained a large collection of natural history specimens, and established himself as the sole agent for certain brands of 'check and label lists' of Canadian insects, including those prepared by the Natural History Society of Toronto. Not to miss a trick, he also advertised himself as an archaeological specialist, and offered for sale the duplicate specimens of his private collection.[21]

Boyle also pinned his hopes on the business of supplying teachers with class-room materials, a business that had only recently been thrown open to private enterprise by the department of education with the closing in 1881 of the Educational Depository. First established by Egerton Ryerson in 1850, the depository had functioned as a non-profit organization to provide books and school supplies at the cheapest possible price. Under constant attack by private booksellers who considered it unfair competition, the depository was eventually abolished in 1881 when the first minister of education, Adam Crooks, concluded that the general trade could supply the schools 'with more satisfaction, and as cheaply ... with a great savings of provincial funds.'[22] The closing of the depository left a vacuum in the school supply business that was not yet filled when Boyle launched Ye Olde Booke Shoppe.

To reach his intended clients in the city, Boyle had chosen a central location on Yonge Street, just a stone's throw from the normal and model schools and the Ontario School of Art, all of which were then housed in the education department buildings located on what is now the site of Ryerson Polytechnical Institute. The shop also stood within walking distance of the University of Toronto and the religious colleges. As he had hoped, much of his business came from these quarters, mainly in the form of over-the-counter sales to students and faculty, but supplemented on occasion by substantial school supply orders from the education department and the university and normal school libraries.[23] For his potential customers scattered throughout the hinterland of the provincial metropolis, Boyle advertised regularly in the *Canada Educational Monthly*. This expenditure evidently produced results, judging from the shop account book, page after page of which is filled with records of purchases, albeit all quite modest in size, made by dozens of educators from all parts of the province.

On a more substantial scale were Boyle's largest customers, a dozen or so libraries, particularly the mechanics' institutes or free libraries in Elora, Paris, Guelph, Bolton, Cheltenham, Harrison, Uxbridge, Toronto, and Prescott. He could not have been more accommodating to these patrons. If a mechanics' institute enquired about publications on specified topics, Boyle would send a large consignment of books of his choice on approval with no requirement to purchase. The local library simply selected the volumes desired for its shelves and returned the remainder without charge. In Toronto, the parliamentary library emerged as the biggest institutional client of Ye Olde Booke Shoppe. This was a spin-off from Boyle's friendship with William Houston, the parliamentary librarian, with whom he held many things in common, including membership in the Canadian Institute and the Scottish national clubs, and an interest in matters relating to education, literature, and history.

Thanks to Boyle's intense personality and penchant for spirited discussion, Ye Olde Booke Shoppe soon acquired a reputation as a place for stimulating debate on educational topics, scientific subjects, current social issues, archaeology, and history; consequently, it became a gathering point for some of the city's intellectual elite. A.F. Chamberlain, then an undergraduate in modern languages at University College, who went on to become Franz Boas's first doctoral student in anthropology at Clark University, described Boyle's bookstore 'as a sort of forum for the discussion of topics educational and other humanly interesting things,' and recalled 'with pleasure many happy hours spent in such wise.'[24] Daniel Wilson, professor of history and English literature at University College and the renowned author of *Archaeology and Prehistoric Annals of Scotland* (1851) and *Prehistoric Man* (1862), frequented the shop; so too, C.A. Hirschfelder, a member of the Canadian Institute and one of the most active amateur archaeologists in Toronto, James Bain Jr, first chief librarian of the Toronto Public Library, the Rev. Henry Scadding, rector of Holy Trinity Church and the acknowledged historian of the city, and Dr Joseph Workman, the erudite superintendent of the Toronto Asylum. In fact, the list of prominent clients is long, many of them members of the Canadian Institute where Boyle was to find a thoroughly congenial atmosphere in which to expand and to enjoy his scientific and archaeological pursuits.

David Boyle delighted in the life of a book merchant, surrounded by literature of his own choosing, constantly stimulated by his customers, and blessed with more time than he had ever known before to pursue his intellectual interests – and pursue them he did to the full extent of his enormous drive and energy. He was extraordinarily busy, and perhaps too involved in projects and organizations that did not have a direct bearing on his business. Still full of the zeal of an educational reformer, Boyle used his leisure to write and to publish, anonymously and at his own expense, his thinly veiled autobiographical and satirical novel with the awesome title of *The Ups and Downs of No. 7 Rexville, Being a Full, True and Correct Account of what happened in the said School Section during a Period of Twelve Months, more or less, and of some Things that were enacted beyond its Limits, with a few judicious Remarks on Religious Instruction in Public School: The Morality of Fresh Air, Teacher's 'Recommends,' and Bogus Certificates by an Old Maid, (who was 'Plucked')* (ca. 1884). In this work Boyle wielded his pen with the subtlety of a blunt axe to reveal the many defects and injustices he had encountered during his years in teaching. His most bitter words were saved for those clerics and educators – the George Buggins of Elora – who insisted on Bible teaching in the public schools, and who denounced the scientific theories of the day that challenged conventional theological views of natural and human history. *The Ups and Downs of No. 7* stands as a revealing cathartic statement, a psychological break with a past to which Boyle now knew he could not return. In a social and intellectual sense, he recognized that he had achieved what he had hoped to accomplish when he left Elora; the fact that he now rubbed elbows and debated issues with many of the intellectuals who graced the halls of the University of Toronto and the Canadian Institute gave him a heightened sense of his own talents. That these people accepted him as an equal mattered a great deal to him. Ye Olde Booke Shoppe would fail as a business, but it was of enormous importance in Boyle's life in so far as it served as the medium to bring him into contact with the learned and scientific community of Toronto, and with the members of an organization that would determine his future in Ontario archaeology.

Boyle did not confine his literary efforts to his novel. He unleashed Andrew McSpurtle in the pages of the *Scottish American Journal* to vent his anger over various controversies such as the evangelical efforts in Ontario to establish Sabbatarian laws. In Boyle's view, such legislation would only restrict badly needed working-class opportunities for recreational activities and excursions outside the cities. McSpurtle's comments on the subject dripped with sarcasm: 'It's unco pleesant tae see that in Toronto they're takin measures to stop the sellin' o' newspapers on the Lord's Day, an' tae the same en' they made a law i' the Paurliment a week or twa sin pittin' a stop till the rinnin o' steamboats for excursions on the Sawbath. A' thae things are as they should be, an' Toronto can hang up its heid as the maist truly Sawbatarian ceety i' the worl'.'[25] In May 1885 the North-West Rebellion also raised McSpurtle's bile, and brought to the fore some of Boyle's racial prejudices, which, incidentally, he shared with many Torontonians of British stock. He evinced not the slightest sympathy for 'the hauf-breeds an' Indians' or for Louis Riel whom he dismissed as 'a kin' o' mongrel French-Irishman.' 'I houp the lads ... under Gen. Middleton, 'll catch the Riel deevil,' blurted McSpurtle, 'an' ... cairry awa his very scalp.'[26]

In addition to writing for the *Scottish American Journal*, Boyle supplemented his income from the bookstore by continuing to write the 'Classroom Section' for the *Canada Educational Monthly* until 1886, and actively participated in the affairs of the Ontario Educational Association. He could still be counted upon to reiterate his thoughts on current issues such as the superannuation fund,[27] or inadequate teachers' salaries. On 22 October 1886 Boyle was reported to be in Lambton County speaking to the teachers' convention in the Sarnia Model School on the benefits of forming professional organizations. Borrowing one of the catch phrases of the blacksmith, he reminded teachers, particularly those in isolated rural situations, that 'Union is Strength.'[28] In a strongly worded article in the *Canada Educational Monthly*, he argued that educators must take much of the blame for enduring their miserable salaries and poor working conditions. This state of affairs could be mainly attributed 'to the action or inaction of teachers themselves. There has been too much *blind* competition; no common understanding; no organization; no union.'[29]

Boyle proffered an intelligent solution to the salary problem. 'What is suggested is that the Teachers' Association of each county should appoint a committee whose duty it would be to possess itself of all the facts and figures affecting the various school sections, and from these data [on the assessed property values that determine the school-supporting ability of a section] make a fair estimate of what salary each section might reasonably be expected to pay. Intending applicants,' Boyle concluded, 'should correspond with the secretary of this committee before communicating with any board in want of a teacher.' He implored teachers in every county to discuss his proposal. If enough took the suggestion seriously, he hoped that the result might be a *Teachers' Guide Book* for the entire province. Doubtless some did address the problem, but nothing permanent emerged from this premature effort to organize educators for self-protection and professional recognition. In this as in most things educational, David Boyle was ahead of his time.

Following his departure from Elora, Boyle also maintained a close connection with the mechanics' institute movement. Actually, he had been elected in September 1882 to the central committee of the Association of Mechanics' Institutes of Ontario, a position he held for three years. Again he took an activist role on the committee, seeking improvement and demanding the highest standards of library administration. In 1884 he supported President Otto Klotz, who wanted to retain the provincial association's policy of subsidizing speakers on scientific and literary themes and of entitling each local institute to one free lecture annually.[30] On other occasions Boyle spoke out angrily against those local institutes that neglected to use the standard and compulsory classification and cataloguing sheets designed by the department of education. He emerges from these sources as a stern task master, demanding that others meet the same rigorous standards of library 'science' that he had imposed upon the library in Elora. His attitude is revealing, considering that it must have occurred to him that his position on the executive of the Ontario Association of Mechanics' Institutes could possibly work to his pecuniary advantage as a book merchant. Yet it was a measure of Boyle's integrity that he could not strike a servile posture and compromise himself by ignoring irregularities and unacceptable library practices. Instead of being obsequious, he was wont to cry out: 'If Institutes do not send in their reports as required ..., they should not get the Legislative grant.'[31]

Regardless of how much Boyle enjoyed his work and leisure activities as proprietor of Ye Olde Booke Shoppe, there was a basic problem with his enterprise – it never turned a large profit. As his youngest daughter later recollected, he was a 'simpleton about business.'[32] This judgment is borne out by the primitive accounting procedures he used. Only with great difficulty was he able to determine which books had been returned after being sent out on approval. He neglected to collect debts; still to be found in the back of his account book is the unclaimed 'I.O.U. Twenty-five dollars' signed by James Bain Jr in 1884, on the 29th day of an unspecified month – a striking illustration of lax business procedures. Further, by printing an inordinately large run of 2850 copies of *The Ups and Downs of No. 7* at a hefty cost of $356, Boyle squandered much of his cash reserves.[33] Eventually he must have been forced to give the copies away, or to pulp them, judging from the disastrous sales performance of the book as reflected in the accounts. Most unfortunate of all, the strategy of catering to a select clientele of educators and natural scientists rather than to the general public proved to be less than satisfactory from a financial point of view. His renowned clients were rarely extravagant in their buying habits; their modest purchases resulted in a slow turnover in the stock of expensive scientific and other non-fiction literature. Finally, Boyle blithely ignored the details of his business because he was too involved in outside activities, particularly at the Canadian Institute. His children often ran the shop in his absence. In short, he possessed neither the aggressiveness required of the would-be capitalist, nor the inclination to live primarily for the pursuit of profit.

Financial necessity forced Boyle to close his bookstore in 1888. He required the equity tied up in the business to finance his children's education. Susanna, who shared her father's advanced and liberal views on women's 'proper sphere,' was now in medical school, following hard in the footsteps of Dr Augusta Stowe Gullen, who had only recently breached the all-male bastion of the Trinity Medical College to become the first woman trained in medicine in Canada. Susanna Boyle would become a professor at the Women's Medical College upon graduation. David was fiercely proud of his daughter's accomplishments. Meanwhile, his first son, John, required his family's support while studying to be a druggist.

The demise of the bookstore was not an upsetting or bitter experience for Boyle. By 1888 he had created for himself an entirely new and equally congenial career as museum curator and provincially funded archaeologist at the Canadian Institute. That he was able to throw himself body and soul into this work assuaged the disappointment he felt when the doors closed at Ye Olde Booke Shoppe for the last time.

III

When David Boyle joined the Canadian Institute in 1884, it had already played a prominent role in the development of archaeology in Ontario by setting into motion the transition from an era of armchair speculation to what is now identified as the 'classificatory-descriptive period' of American archaeology.[34] The primary emphasis of this period was on the collection, systematic description, and rudimentary classification of the archaeological record by a new generation of professional curators and archaeologists. From the mid-1880s until his death in 1911, Boyle carried to completion the work commenced over thirty years earlier by his precursors at the Canadian Institute.[35]

Incorporated by royal charter in 1851, the Canadian Institute (today the Royal Canadian Institute) had as its goals the 'general advancement of the Physical Sciences, the Arts and Manufactures ...; and more particularly ... the acquisition of those branches of Knowledge ... connected with the Professions of Surveying, Engineering, and Architecture.'[36] With the teaching of science in the provincial universities limited to medicine and 'natural philosophy,' the institute members saw themselves filling a void in the cultural life of the city and province. Their plans included the creation of a science library, a general science museum, and a regular program of meetings to discuss learned papers on various pure and applied science topics, and less frequently on anthropological, archaeological, and literary themes. The best of these papers were published in a new periodical, the *Canadian Journal*,[37] established in 1852.

Such activities were not peculiar to Torontonians. Scientific or learned societies akin to the Canadian Institute were common in other countries, and had already emerged, or would soon be established, in major urban centres across British North America. Since 1824 Quebec City had had its Literary and Historical Society of Quebec, the members of which sometimes wrote and published on scientific themes, particularly geology. The Natural History Society of Montreal, founded in 1827, expanded its usefulness in 1857 when it assumed control of the periodical *Canadian Naturalist and Geologist*. In Halifax, the Nova Scotia Literary and Scientific Society, created in 1850, evolved into the Nova Scotian Institute of Science in 1862, the same year that the Natural History Society of New Brunswick appeared in St John. People in all these places shared a common need for a medium to disseminate information and foster a greater consciousness of their respective regions, and to provide a forum for the discussion of scientific problems and discoveries. Significantly, in almost all the provinces, as in other countries, archaeology was given a decided fillip by the journals, museums, and research launched under the auspices of these scientific groups.[38]

Prior to 1850, however, popular thinking in Canada West on matters archaeological was mainly conjecture and usually shaped by the popular North American myth of the Mound Builders. American antiquarians attributed the mounds that were to be found in their greatest concentration in the Ohio and Mississippi river valleys to a great vanished race. Canadians took naturally to this idea since they were on the fringe of the northern mound zone which stretched from western New York and Ontario into Michigan, Wisconsin, Iowa, Nebraska, and Manitoba (then Red River). In the intellectual climate of the time, few people were prepared to credit the Indians or their ancestors with the intelligence or the degree of civilization required to construct such elaborate earthworks. Instead, chairbound philosophers gave full rein to their imagination and hypothesized an astonishing range of fantastic theories as to the identity of the Mound Builders. Various people argued that the Mound Builders must have been white men, perhaps Danes or one of the ten lost tribes of Israel, or giants or Toltecs or a hybrid race of giant white Jewish Toltec Vikings.[39]

The dominance of speculative thought in archaeological discussions in the Canadas prior to 1850, and indeed throughout North America, can be attributed to several factors. No systematic site exploration or excavation was yet being undertaken.[40] Consequently, without a substantial and reliable store of archaeological evidence available for study and comparison, data upon which to build and to test hypotheses, there was no alternative to guesswork when it came to reconstructing North American man's prehistoric past. Moreover, in Canada West, culturally immature and still undergoing its pioneer phase of settlement prior to 1850, the lack of a periodical literature and museums impeded the development of a scientific archaeology by denying those few interested in the subject a factual basis for generalizing and study.

Just as significant as the want of an adequate foundation of archaeological data was the absence of European models of scientific reasoning, models that would eventually challenge the theological interpretations of natural and human history. A systematic and scientifically based archaeological tradition awaited the general acceptance among the North American learned community of many currents of thought; these included Lyell's geological principles, the knowledge of the Danish Three Age system, the archaeological methods and theories of Thomsen and Worsaae, the recognition of the great antiquity of man following the work of Boucher de Perthes and Pengelly, and, of course, the impact of the Darwinian revolution. Until these intellectual impulses crossed the Atlantic, theological explanations and speculation would dominate writing pertaining to prehistory.[41] It was the transfer of these European ideas and intellectual developments, and the concomitant burgeoning of scientific thought, that became one of the hallmarks of the subsequent classificatory-descriptive period of American archaeology. In Ontario this phase began with the incorporation of the Canadian Institute and the publication of the *Canadian Journal*, and lasted through the First World War.

It might well be argued that the council of the Canadian Institute launched Ontario's classificatory-descriptive period on 12 June 1852 – the date affixed to a widely disseminated circular enjoining interested parties to answer a series of questions on mounds, artifacts, petroglyphs, and aboriginal place names in their localities.[42] The circular was penned by Sandford Fleming,[43] a noted engineer and railway builder, who had been prompted to conduct the archaeological survey by two major considerations. The first was the accelerating frequency of discoveries of ossuaries and village sites by railway navvies and farmers as Canada West underwent its railway era and a period of intensive agricultural settlement. The second and more immediate reason was the publication of E.G. Squier's *Aboriginal Monuments of the State of New York* (1849) for the Smithsonian Institution. Fleming and the council of the newly incorporated Canadian Institute were keen to emulate the research projects of the prestigious Smithsonian.

Regrettably, the responses that were received have not been preserved, although the council did report in December 1852 of 'favourable results' to the questionnaires.[44] It is clear, however, that this first effort to compile a site inventory for Ontario, and to publish the findings for comparative analysis, failed. Upon receiving the circular a half dozen individuals donated small numbers of artifacts, enough to form the 'nucleus of an archaeological collection,'[45] but because the survey was not followed up in ensuing years few donations were subsequently received. Not until David Boyle reissued virtually the identical circular in 1885 did the work of recording the archaeological sites of the province recommence. The specimens donated in the early 1850s suffered a rude fate. They were placed on open shelves, many to be lost over the years. In fact, the entire science museum languished for three decades owing to limited funds, a small membership, and a lack of display space in the institute's home – the converted Haworth house on the corner of Richmond and Clare (now Bertie) streets.

Despite these unsuccessful efforts at site inventory and museum development, the Canadian Institute did serve as the major forum for those interested in archaeology by virtue of the *Canadian Journal* – the first publication in Canada to discuss archaeology on a regular basis – and the efforts of one man,

Daniel Wilson. Yet another Scot, Wilson arrived in Canada in 1853 to assume the chair of history and English literature at University College, Toronto. Almost immediately this industrious scholar and future president of the University of Toronto (1880–92) became a commanding presence on the Canadian Institute council, eventually serving twice as its president (1859–61, 1878–80), and editing the *Canadian Journal* from 1856 to 1859. Wilson's contribution to the development of Ontario's archaeology lay primarily in his introduction of a scientific approach, and the international perspectives he brought to the fledgling discipline.

Wilson came to Canada West as one of Britain's leading prehistorians; in fact, it was Wilson who coined the word 'prehistory.' In his monumental compilation of Scottish antiquities, *Archaeology and Prehistoric Annals of Scotland* (1851), he was the first scholar to apply the Danish Three Age concept to British archaeology.[46] Once in Canada West, he soon took up as his hobby anthropology in its widest sense, encompassing the fields of ethnology, prehistory, physical anthropology, and linguistics, and published within ten years a broad synthesis of the cultural history of the New World entitled *Prehistoric Man; Researches into the Origin of Civilisation in the Old and the New World* (1862).

Daniel Wilson was perhaps the first Canadian-based writer to articulate a purely scientific rationale for archaeological endeavour. '[The] object of the intelligent collector,' he wrote in the *Canadian Journal*, 'is not the mere gratification of an aimless curiosity, or the accumulation of rarities of difficult acquisition, but the preservation of objects calculated to furnish valuable scientific or historical truths.'[47] Although Wilson accomplished little field-work of his own, he urged others to apply a scientific approach during excavations. In the *Canadian Journal* he outlined for his readers the basic principles essential to good excavation, especially the importance of preserving everything unearthed on site and the necessity of a complete description of all sites, including the position of each artifact, no matter how trivial.[48] Wilson also carried over the scientific method into the analysis of artifacts when he subjected prehistoric copper implements to chemical tests in a laboratory and belied the theory of a long forgotten Indian technology for smelting copper. His own most important scholarly research, work that spanned both archaeology and physical anthropology, were his osteological studies. In a seminal article in the *Canadian Journal*, 'Brain Weight and Size in Relation to Relative Capacity of Races,' he argued that cranial capacity was not a dependable means for determining the relative intelligence or ability of various races or individuals.[49]

As editor of the *Canadian Journal*, Wilson opened its pages to those influences giving rise to a scientific archaeology on both sides of the Atlantic. The journal regularly featured the writings of eminent European prehistorians, particularly articles supporting the geological proofs of the antiquity of man, including Charles Lyell's celebrated defence of Boucher de Perthes's work in the Somme River valley and of the British cave finds. Analytical reviews, sometimes hostile, of major books by Darwin, Huxley, Lyell, and Ernst Haeckel on evolutionary theory as it pertained to man were also regular fare.[50] Under Wilson's direction, the *Canadian Journal* also became the first periodical to record archaeological discoveries and field-work in Ontario.

Notwithstanding the importance of Wilson's contributions to the development of a scientific approach to archaeology,[51] his influence did have limits. The fact remains that as late as 1884 there existed no major museum collection representative of Ontario prehistory. No publication was yet devoted exclusively to the description, classification, and interpretation of the archaeological record. And with the exception of such notables as C.A. Hirschfelder and Professor Charles Joseph Taché, a physiologist at Laval University, few competent amateurs toiled in the field. David Boyle's words rang true when he remarked in 1886 that 'hitherto, nothing has been done here [in Ontario] beyond a little mercenary, pettifogging collecting, without system, and without any aim outside of how much the "specimens" would fetch in $ and ¢.'[52]

Still, there were positive signs of change in the air. Public interest in matters archaeological, a prerequisite for government support, was on the rise by the late 1870s. Wilson and the Canadian Institute could take some of the credit for this development in the Toronto region. More generally, dozens of popular books and periodicals – the kind of literature that we have seen was shaping David Boyle's outlook in Elora in these years – stimulated a wider interest in prehistory, particularly in the Mound Builder controversy. The brilliantly written and imaginative books of the New England historian Francis Parkman, whose eight-volume series *France and England in North America* appeared between 1851 and 1892, also supported the archaeological impulse in Ontario by quickening the public's enthusiasm for the history of New France. Newspapers were taking a keen interest in everything related to the subject of Indian prehistory. The regional and the Toronto press eagerly printed the details of any new find; even so minor a discovery as the cache of wampum in the Elora Gorge by one of David Boyle's students in November 1879 rated a paragraph in the Toronto *Globe*.[53] Scarcely a month slipped by in Toronto in the late seventies when either the *Globe* or the *Mail* did not inform its readers of recent archaeological developments abroad, whether in North and South America, Britain, Europe, Russia, or the Near and Middle East.

Closer to home, during 1878 and 1879, events in Manitoba stoked up interest in the Mound Builder issue as reports of excavations into the earthworks along the banks of the Red River came to the public's attention.[54] Ontarians followed these activities with great curiosity and with a *soupçon* of jealousy. Stung into action by the example of the Manitoba Historical and Scientific Society, Daniel Wilson, during his second term as president of the Canadian Institute (1878–80), urged his colleagues to organize similar field expeditions with a view to forming 'a museum of the primitive history of Canada,'[55] and to approaching the government for funds. Given the questions being asked in the press as to the relationship of Ontario's prehistoric past to the remarkable discoveries being made elsewhere,[56] and given the example of archaeological progress in other jurisdictions, it was only a matter of time before other voices would be heard demanding that the Ontario government assume its cultural responsibilities and fund archaeological investigations and museum activity.

This, then, was the state of archaeology and the intellectual climate of opinion on matters pertaining to prehistory in Ontario when David Boyle opened his bookshop in December 1883. It was a climate suited to an activist like Boyle, a person disinclined to sit by idly and merely talk of museums and government subsidization. Significantly, even before leaving Elora, he had taken a noteworthy initiative on behalf of archaeology in the province. Towards the end of December 1879, he pushed a resolution through the Elora Natural History, Scientific and Literary Society urging the provincial government to subsidize 'a Provincial Museum for the preservation of Indian relics and Canadian Antiquities' since 'there now existed no institution of the kind in the Dominion.' The time seemed opportune because 'a large Parliament House was soon to be erected [in Toronto at Queen's Park] and at a small additional expense this accommodation could be provided.'[57] Boyle's major argument for such a publicly funded museum was extremely important, since he was one of the first to express what can only be described as Ontario's version of 'the birth of a conscience' about the expropriation of antiquities.[58] Boyle denounced the fact that 'many precious relics of a bygone system of civilization were being removed from the country simply for want of a place to accommodate them ..., and even Professor Wilson had ... [sent] a large number of these relics to the Museum at Edinburgh.'[59] One is reminded here of the arguments posited by Auguste Mariette in Egypt, at the time the director of the Egyptian National Service of Antiquities, who put an end to the uncontrolled exportation of Egyptian archaeological treasures. It was Mariette's obsession to see that these priceless relics found a permanent home in modern Egypt in the National Museum of Egyptian Antiquities, an institution of his own creation.[60]

Not surprisingly, soon after arriving in Toronto, David Boyle determined to see that a publicly supported museum of Ontario archaeology became a reality. This object gradually became his new all-consuming passion. Over the next quarter century, he would build upon the foundation laid by Wilson and the *Canadian Journal*, and develop fully the classificatory-descriptive period of Ontario archaeology with its cautious scientific approach and incipient professionalism. Where Wilson had failed to undertake or to stimulate field-work, to build up a museum collection illustrative of Ontario's prehistoric past (an essential step for the development of scientific archaeology), and to establish a journal devoted exclusively to archaeology, David Boyle would succeed. Ontario archaeology, in short, was on the threshold of new possibilities.

IV

Early in 1884, Boyle joined the Canadian Institute, eager to pursue his scientific interests in what he considered a major and prestigious learned society. His timing could not have been more fortunate since the institute's prospects were just then beginning to brighten after an extended period of financial difficulties and slumping membership. The sale of a parcel of land in 1882 had reduced the heavy mortgage debt incurred with the construction of a new building on the Richmond Street site in 1877. That transaction, combined with an expanding membership (236 in 1884, up from 139 the year before),[61] and the addition of younger, more progressive-thinking men at the helm, bode well for the future. Foremost among these young leaders stood the thirty-nine-year-old corresponding secretary (1882–6), and soon to be president (1886–8), William Henry Vander Smissen, a lecturer in German and a librarian at University College.

David Boyle, too, quickly discovered that there was ample room for improvement. He was shocked at what passed for a museum at the institute. How appalling, he thought, that one of Canada's premier scientific organizations, located in the cultural heart of Ontario, had been unable to match the efforts of the Elora Public School in museum activity. Vander Smissen felt the same, and condemned the fact that while 'many valuable and interesting specimens have been presented to [the] museum, both biological and archaeological, ... a great portion has disappeared,' a consequence of several changes in location and want of funds to build proper display cases.[62] Yet, as Boyle pondered over the remnants of the badly managed collections, excitement tempered his initial indignation. On the positive side he saw that a great opportunity beckoned for someone with his special experience and interests. He knew at once that he would respond to the challenge posed by this failed museum by seeking the appointment to the curator's position. Some weeks later he laid claim to this volunteer post by donating his personal archaeological collection, consisting of some nine hundred specimens, to the institute. After this generous and calculated attention-getting gesture, the curatorship was his for the asking, and the members elected him to the position in May 1884.

A variety of motives and personal considerations had prompted Boyle to seek control of the museum and to pursue his amateur interest in archaeology. For one thing, the curatorship would project him into the centre of activities at the institute; he could not abide the thought of remaining an anonymous and ineffective member of an organization for any length of time. But more than this interest, the opportunity he saw in the museum seemed especially attractive since he was in the process of redefining his intellectual goals. After years of serious reading into the literature of natural science, he had laid down 'a good broad substratum' of general scientific knowledge. It was now the time, as he put it, to 'select some department as his speciality ... What is demanded by the age,' he explained, 'is not mere repetition of what we hear or what we read, but an expression of what we have seen, and of what we know, an elucidation of some hitherto dark spot in study, or, in other words, a genuine contribution to the fund of knowledge.'[63] Ontario archaeology, he concluded after joining the institute, would be his speciality. In this neglected and largely untilled field, he might make his contribution to knowledge as curator of a revived Canadian Institute Museum.

What had led him to choose archaeology as the primary focus of his intellectual endeavour? Why not one of his other scientific interests? Actually, had the circumstances of his life been slightly different – another city and scientific organization, for instance – he might well have channelled his prodigious energies in a totally different direction, towards some aspect of biology, geology, or palaeontology. He did not join the Canadian Institute intending to become an archaeologist. Only after he saw the old museum collection languishing from want of attention, and decided to assume control, did his future as an Ontario archaeologist begin to take shape. Boyle keenly appreciated the archaeological traditions of the institute, particularly the pioneering efforts of Daniel Wilson to lay the foundation for serious archaeological research in the province, and understood it to be his responsibility as curator to build upon that foundation. Interestingly, there is no indication that Wilson himself personally encouraged Boyle to take up the torch that he had carried for decades. In the early 1880s, Wilson had little time for the institute, burdened as he was as president of University College after 1880. Years later, when Boyle reflected upon those people who had directly assisted him in this stage of his career, he named W.H. Vander Smissen as his chief supporter, and gave Wilson not so much as a mention.

Whatever his doubts as to his ability to further Wilson's archaeological work, and there must have been some, the challenge of following in the footsteps of this enormously respected scholar was irresistible. 'Aim high,' Boyle used to tell his students in Elora, 'you are then more likely to hit something of value than otherwise. Whatever you do, let it be done your best. Although the "Ladder of Fame" is pretty well crowded from the middle downwards, there is plenty of room at the top.'[64] At the Canadian Institute Museum he intended to follow his own advice and seize the opportunity to work his way to the top of the archaeological ladder in Ontario, not an unrealistic goal for a hard-working, intelligent individual, especially considering the paucity of competition. Thus, a combination of factors, including an amateur's enthusiasm for museums and archaeology, the Wilson legacy at the Canadian Institute, and sheer ambition, moved Boyle into a serious pursuit of archaeological knowledge. At this time, however, he gave no thought to becoming a full-time professional archaeological museum curator. As in Elora, he expected to fulfil his curatorial responsibilities in his leisure hours away from the bookstore. Only several years later, when his business proved to be a disappointment, and when he had successfully lobbied the provincial government for operational funds, did he consider trying to make a living out of his avocation. Boyle became Ontario's first professional archaeologist more by luck, both good and bad, than by design.

In February 1885 W.H. Vander Smissen began his campaign to reorganize the Canadian Institute and reinvigorate its program. Aware of the example of the Royal Society of Canada, established in Ottawa in 1882, which had divided its operations into special sections devoted to the various branches of science, and French and English literature, Vander Smissen struck a committee to consider whether the Canadian Institute should do the same. Boyle, James Loudon, a professor of physics and mathematics at University College, and a future president of the University of Toronto (1892–1906), and seven others joined Vander Smissen on the committee which subsequently endorsed the latter's proposals on reorganization.[65] The policy paid dividends later that year when the Natural History Society of Toronto agreed to become the biological section of the Canadian Institute. Four more sections were established during 1886–7 (architectural, geological and mining, philological, and photographic). The reorganization had an immediate and beneficial impact on the museum. The new biological section, its members anxious to create a decent repository for their natural history specimens, agreed to guarantee the interest on a one thousand dollar loan for two years when the council resolved to renovate the third floor of the building as a museum of

natural history and archaeology. Tenders were called in 1886 and construction began later that same year.

Meanwhile, David Boyle tried to make the most of a situation so obviously
conducive to change and expansion. With Vander Smissen's blessing, he
contrived a strategy in the spring of 1885 for the development of archaeology
in Ontario, a strategy that closely paralleled the tactics he had used
successfully in creating the Elora School Museum. First, he planned to issue
circulars soliciting information for an inventory of archaeological sites and
resources, and requesting 'persons in possession of relics to forward them to
the institute for the purpose of ... [forming] an archaeological exhibit worthy
of the Province of Ontario.'[66] On the basis of his experience in Elora, Boyle
hoped that by the end of the year the museum would receive an influx of
accessions. Public interest in the project would then be aroused, and he would
be able to speak authoritatively about the extent of the untapped archaeological resources across the province. At that point he would be prepared to
appear, cap in hand, before the provincial government and ask for funding to
proceed in 'a systematic and scientific manner in the formation of an
archaeological museum.' In April 1885 Boyle prepared his circular by dusting
off Sandford Fleming's original questionnaire drafted thirty-three years
earlier and editing it for brevity. He asked of the readers:

1. Is there any mound, tumulus, or intrenchment in your neighbourhood?
2. Are there any elevations which, from their regularity or for any other reason
   suggest an artificial origin?
3. What are the dimensions and area of these from actual measurement? If possible,
   give a plan with sections.
4. What are the physical features of the situation and vicinity?
5. Are there any evidences of the place having been surrounded with posts or
   pickets?
6. Are there still, or were there before 'clearing,' trees of large size within the area of
   the work? If so, state kind and size, also number of annual growth-rings on largest
   stump.
7. Are stone or bone weapons of any kind, or fragments of pottery ploughed up in
   the neighbourhood?
8. Have any copper implements of native manufacture been discovered? What?
9. Have any iron or copper articles been found indicating intercourse with
   Europeans? What?
10. Are there any local names of Indian origin in your township or neighbourhood? If
    so, kindly make a list of them, indicating their correct pronunciation, stating their
    meaning, and the local or traditionary circumstances from which they originate.

11. Names of township and county, and numbers of lot and concession in which any mound, ossuary, intrenchment, old village site, or battle-ground exists.
12. Name of any local collector of Indian relics, or of any persons who are interested in Canadian Archaeology.[67]

Boyle and Vander Smissen personally absorbed much of the cost of printing and mailing the one thousand circulars to 'representative men of all classes,' including newspaper editors, public school inspectors and rural teachers, doctors, clergymen, and municipal councillors across southern Ontario.[68] The strategy worked very well. By October, the Toronto *Mail* reported that 'the appeal made by the Institute ... is meeting with a hearty response from all over the country.' Local newspapers had assisted greatly by publishing the circulars and enjoining their readers to support the cause – the *Globe* and the *Mail* in Toronto were especially supportive in this respect.[69] Letters poured in to Boyle, 'some expressive of sympathy with the project, some giving information regarding specimens, some promising assistance, and others extending hearty invitations to explore in promising localities.' These letters came in sufficient numbers to surprise Boyle himself who was thrilled by the 'rapid expansion of our knowledge as to the number of places ... worthy of examination and survey.'[70] The York Pioneer and Historical Society placed its collection of some one thousand specimens in the custody of the institute (a mixed blessing considering the members had neglected to catalogue the provenience data for each item), while a dozen other individuals came forth with smaller donations.[71]

Among the early donors were George E. Laidlaw and Andrew F. Hunter, both of whom would figure prominently in the future of Ontario archaeology as it made the transition from a pastime of antiquarians to the status of a professional discipline. Laidlaw, the son of a Victoria County farmer on Balsam Lake, fell victim as a boy to the 'romance' of relic hunting upon discovering the wealth of prehistoric artifacts around 'The Fort,' his family homestead. Likewise, A.F. Hunter, born of pioneer stock in Innisfill Township, Simcoe County, discovered archaeology as a youngster whilst exploring the rural landscape of what used to be Huronia. In 1885, the twenty-two-year-old Hunter, an undergraduate in honours mathematics and physics at the University of Toronto, found his interest in history and archaeology stimulated enormously both by Daniel Wilson in the class-room and by David Boyle at the Canadian Institute. 'I was at the opening meeting [of the season] of the Canadian Institute,' he wrote to his parents in November 1885. 'They have a very nice collection [of archaeological artifacts] for a beginning. If you hear of any relics of such nature, beg them for me for the museum. I have got acquainted with Mr. Boyle, the curator.'[72] The following summer Hunter was to be found exploring the ruins of Ste Marie II on Christian Island for specimens to send to Boyle; it was the beginning of the field-work that would earn Hunter a lasting place in the archaeological record.

The circulars also generated the first field-work Boyle undertook for the Canadian Institute. During the summer of 1885, he examined several sites in Beverley Township, Wentworth County, including the James Dwyer farm ossuary I (an historic Neutral burial pit) and a historic Neutral village on the James Rae farm. Accompanying Boyle were James Bain and an artist friend, Arthur Cox, FRSA. Boyle returned to the Dwyer farm in October, this time with the Reverend T.T. Johnstone of Ancaster, and 'engaged the services of four stout men to handle spades and shovels.' Several other curious neighbours joined the excavation during the day and helped exhume 'a large number of valuable relics, including an almost perfect clay cup, four perfect clay pipes, a small, neatly-carved human head in stone, about one thousand pieces of white wampum, and many other specimens.'[73] The Toronto *Globe*, which reported the excavation, echoed Boyle's sentiments in concluding that the 'prospects are excellent for the formation of a first-class collection of aboriginal relics,' and invited the public to judge for themselves by viewing the artifacts on display in the window of Ye Olde Booke Shoppe.[74]

Ironically, just as it became clear that Boyle's plans were succeeding, the possibility of archaeological research being assumed by a federal government agency became the subject of a spirited discussion in the Toronto press. From September through November 1885, the *Mail*, followed by the *Week*, came out strongly in favour of the dominion government establishing a bureau of archaeology and ethnology, with a small professional staff, and an annual budget of about $25,000.[75] 'It is high time,' argued the *Mail*, 'if we in Canada intend to contribute our quota to the sum of human knowledge concerning this race, that we should undertake the work of exploration and research according to scientific methods ... Public money cannot be put to better use than in getting at the truth about man.'[76] The question called for immediate action: 'We are so desperately bent upon the affairs of the present, that we have no time to devote to the numberless monuments bequeathed to us by the people who preceded us on this continent. They are fast being obliterated, the mounds in Manitoba being converted into roothouses and cattle byres by the intensely practical settler; and in a few years, when wealth may bring with it a taste for learning, we shall look in vain for the precious [monuments and relics].'[77] What apparently triggered the barrage of editorials in the *Mail* was the editor's fascination with the idea of the vanished race of Mound Builders, an interest stimulated by excavations being undertaken at the time by George Bryce and Charles Bell of the Manitoba Historical and Scientific Society.

Soon after, Charles Bell wrote from Winnipeg and confused the issue by suggesting that instead of a federal bureau, a Dominion Archaeological Society be formed, funded by its members, to work in association with the Royal Society and the museum of the Geological Survey in Ottawa.[78] In a subsequent letter to the *Mail*, George Laidlaw agreed with Bell, but suggested instead that such a national society deserved public as well as private support.[79] That none of the participants in this debate gave the Canadian Institute the slightest mention brought a prompt response from a concerned David Boyle in his paper, 'The Archaeological Outlook,' delivered to the institute on 21 November 1885.[80] The speech represents a benchmark in his career and in the evolution of an Ontario archaeological tradition. Here Boyle confidently laid down the broad outlines of his future work as a provincial archaeologist.

'We shall hail with delight any efforts made towards the prosecution of archaeological research, from a really national standpoint,' he claimed. But regardless of any federal scheme, 'Ontario owes it to herself as the richest, most populous, and most advanced Province, to work her own territory to the best advantage ..., and to form an archaeological museum in the City of Toronto – the Queen City – the City of Schools ... the principal literary and scientific city in the Province, if not in the whole confederation.' What angered Boyle most about the recent discussion in the *Mail* was the assumption that Ottawa would become the central depository for the fruits of most archaeological and ethnological research. That prospect alone, he argued, negated the other 'immense and peculiarly advantageous opportunities' that might otherwise accrue from a federal bureau of ethnology or a Dominion Archaeological Society. After several visits to Ottawa for the Canada Publishing Company, Boyle had come to hold the place in contempt as pretentious and culturally barren, a miserable excuse for a nation's capital.

The Canadian Institute in Toronto, Boyle went on, funded by the provincial government, should assume responsibility for archaeology in Ontario. 'If we take the whole Dominion as a field,' he explained to his attentive audience, 'the magnitude of the undertaking is too great either for our Society or for any similar organization to entertain for a single moment, and when it is clearly understood how much is involved in the prosecution of the task, it may be doubted whether even our own Province is not more than we can hope to work to the best advantage.' Few understood just exactly what methodical and scientific archaeology entailed. It included far more than the 'actual digging up' and collecting of artifacts. 'To do these things,' he explained, 'is little more than stepping upon the verge of the study.' Collecting was but the beginning of the task. 'Archaeology can only be said to possess any genuine public interest in so far as it is a handmaid to its elder sister, history, and it is the purpose of the Institute so to prosecute its researches in this line that its records and specimens may be mutually instructive.'

To achieve this goal, he added, 'it is required in the first place that we make as full and complete a record as possible of every spot in the Province that gives or has given any indication of having been in any way identified with the life-history of our aborigines.' As the systematic inventory is carried out, each site 'should be collated [with] every passage in the narratives of our early travellers for the purpose of identifying ... those localities that are most intimately associated with the historical exploration of the country.' Then, too, every site 'should be accurately measured, sketched, thoroughly explored and fully described.' This approach would necessarily entail a study of the Mound Builder question. Exploration parties should be despatched to the Rainy River area of north-west Ontario to examine the mounds which Boyle believed formed 'the very outposts of the territory occupied by the Mound Builders.' Perhaps the answers to the Mound Builder controversy lay here, in Ontario! 'Who were the people that erected these immense earth heaps, and did they move from the north southwards or *vice versa?*'

In the interest of science, Boyle continued, the findings of all site surveys and excavations must be published following the example of 'our American cousins in their issue of beautifully illustrated documents ... Besides all this, the preservation and proper display of the illustrative objects will prove of no small importance. These must be arranged in suitable cases and be properly classified for the purpose of comparing one with the other.' Ideally, this method should result in a first-rate museum that would 'attract students from distant lands and enable the scientific investigator of the future to thank heaven for the somewhat tardy foresight that has provided for him ... a feast of fat things.' Boyle estimated that the complete programme of site inventory, excavation, interpretation, classification, exhibition, and publication, would require the expenditure of a minimum of '$5,000 to $6,000 annually for four or five years, and twice either of these sums might be employed to good advantage.' What Boyle and his contemporaries considered princely sums, and the time frame they set for the completion of their work, must leave the modern researcher breathless, if not incredulous.

Regardless of the narrow provincial scope Boyle placed on the Canadian Institute's archaeological program, he still considered his scheme 'national work,' a patriotic duty; the proposed museum in Toronto would still comprise 'a really national collection.'[81] His attitudes were quite typically Ontarian, indeed even more narrowly Torontonian. By stamping his provincial perspective with a national seal of approval, Boyle had fallen into a powerful current of provincial thought that began after Confederation with the nationalist effusions of Canada First, and that extends down to the present.

In retrospect, there is something amusing about Boyle's somewhat self-serving effort to keep the spotlight on the Canadian Institute and a Toronto museum. The possibility of Ottawa establishing a bureau of ethnology at this time was quite remote. Apart from those who briefly discussed the idea in the *Mail* and the *Week*, the demand for such an agency simply did not yet exist. True, an incipient Canadian school of anthropology was quietly emerging, led by such men as Daniel Wilson, Horatio Hale, and Principal John William Dawson of McGill, but these people were still part-time hobbyists, unable to carry out a national programme.[82] Not until 1910 were the circumstances ripe, and the professional ethnologists available for such a bureau, when Dr Edward Sapir was appointed director of the anthropological division of the Geological Survey centred at the new Victoria Museum in Ottawa.

Nor was Charles Bell's notion of a self-supporting Dominion Archaeological Society likely to succeed. His idea was ill-conceived, tossed out on the spur of the moment, in defiance of the fact that if the leading provincial scientific and historical societies could not muster sufficient funds among their membership to carry on archaeological field and museum work, the prospect of a national organization doing so were dim indeed. Bell himself did not follow up his idea with any determination. In fact, by February 1886 he was to be found in Ontario speaking to the Canadian Institute and petitioning Oliver Mowat to subsidize an institute expedition to the Rainy River mound zone.[83] Still, the discussion and the emotions raised in Toronto during the fall of 1885 had been most valuable; they had spurred Boyle on to clarify his objectives. Early in 1886 he was ready to lead a delegation to petition the premier for funding.

The Canadian Institute's 'Memorial to the Hon. Oliver Mowat'[84] was for the most part a restatement of the scheme and rationale set out in 'The Archaeological Outlook.' In this submission Boyle added to his argument by attempting to shame the government into action by showing that Ontario lagged behind other jurisdictions in archaeological matters. 'For a great many years,' he explained to Mowat, 'this line of study has been pursued in almost every one of the European countries, and to a considerable extent ... in the

United States and Mexico ... Your memorialists wish to place the student of Ontario on an equal footing with the student of other lands.' Time was of the essence, stressed Boyle. 'Already, it is to be deplored, that in the progress of settlement, many opportunities to investigate, to authenticate, and to compare have been lost beyond recall; thousands of existing traces are disappearing annually.' He concluded his memorial with a request for 'a legislative grant of not less than [five] thousand dollars to be expended during the current year under the auspices of the Canadian Institute which society will engage to act subject to the control of the Legislature, and as its custodian of all that may go to form a Provincial Archaeological Museum.'

If either Premier Mowat, once a president of the Canadian Institute himself (1864–6), or Minister of Education George Ross, whose department would fund the program, had any sympathy for the objectives outlined in the memorial, they stifled it upon hearing the demand for an initial grant of five thousand dollars. They would not consider endorsing such a large expenditure, particularly with an election in the offing that year. Boyle had seriously misjudged what he could realistically expect from a government committed to prudent management, a *laissez-faire* philosophy, and the liberal creed of 'he who governs least, governs best.' Five thousand dollars was a sobering figure to a government that operated the province with total annual revenues amounting to a modest three million dollars and a civil service of fewer than seven hundred people.[85] The amount requested by the institute looms large when it is noted that the legislative aid to the province's seventy-four mechanics' institutes in 1879 amounted to a mere $22,885.26.[86]

There may have been another factor behind the government's reluctance to fund archaeology – David Boyle himself. Apparently he was held suspect by George Ross, one of the most powerful figures in the Liberal party. Boyle's political philosophy and voting behaviour was not at issue; in years past he had staunchly supported 'Sandy' Mackenzie and the federal Liberals against Macdonald and the 'National Policy' of tariff protection, and had backed Charles Clarke, Wellington County's champion of Mowat Liberalism. What bothered the minister of education were Boyle's views on Darwinian evolution. Ross believed that he must be an agnostic or worse, and considered such a person an unworthy recipient of a Christian government's largess. Ironically, it was the Roman Catholic dean of St Catharines, William R. Harris, who discovered that Ross held such an opinion of Boyle and tried to rectify the situation. Harris wrote to Charles Clarke in October 1885: 'I have been very favorably impressed with Mr. Boyle's ability and would like very much to see him in some position where his talents would have room for expansion. In conversation with the Honorable Mr. Ross, I was given to understand that he was of the opinion that Boyle was an agnostic ... Would it not be well for you to set the Minister right on this matter ... as I believe you to be a friend of Mr. Boyle's.'[87] That Clarke had not yet reached the minister on this matter before the Canadian Institute delegation made its presentation is a distinct possibility.

Archaeologically, 1886 proved to be a lost year in Ontario, following the provincial government's rejection of the institute's first petition for financial assistance. Without the grant, the council of the Canadian Institute was unwilling to subsidize any field-work during the summer; Boyle would have worked without remuneration during his holidays but he had to have his expenses defrayed. Only in the museum could one find any signs of progress. Under Vander Smissen's leadership, the council loosened the purse strings and voted one hundred dollars for display cases to house the artifacts acquired the season before. Boyle spent much of his leisure time away from his bookstore studying and arranging the collection. He bemoaned the fact that he still lacked sufficient case room for the 'fine geological specimens' from years past, but was encouraged enough to report that 'before the close of another year it may be reasonably hoped that the whole collection [natural science, geological, and archaeological] ... will be put in proper shape for study.'[88] Somehow, through these months, he maintained his faith in the possibility of achieving his goals. 'It is my intention,' he wrote boldly in November to Frederic W. Putnam at the Peabody Museum in Harvard University, 'to visit and examine every old trail, portage, encampment, ossuary, etc. known to exist in this province, and to put the result in book form.'[89]

Shortly after the provincial election of December 1886, with the Mowat Liberals settled snugly back into their accustomed place of power, the council of the Canadian Institute deemed the time appropriate to approach the government again for an archaeological grant. The delegation went before George Ross in February 1887 with a much keener sense of what was politically possible. Instead of the five thousand dollars requested the year before, Boyle asked for a mere fifteen hundred dollars.[90] For this money, he argued, the government could expect to receive a great deal in return. 'Every specimen found [will] become the property of the province – the rarest, best, or otherwise most valuable to be preserved in some central place, open to the public; the less rare or valuable to be distributed among local schools, or other collections in various parts of the province.' After undertaking the program outlined earlier, the institute would be quite prepared to turn the collection over to the University of Toronto or the education department if the minister so wished. 'It ought to be distinctly understood,' stressed Boyle, 'that the province has no money to expend for the support of a mere curiosity shop. Every specimen should have a distinctively scientific value, having attached to it a label giving all the necessary particulars.' In reply to Ross's questioning, Boyle insisted that archaeological research 'must be done through the government,' whether by a civil servant, or a Canadian Institute curator with quasi-official status by virtue of the provincial funding he received. Boyle was diplomatic enough to suggest that the minister might wish to develop the program entirely under his own department and with personnel of his own choice. Stretching the truth a little, Boyle claimed that 'the Institute has no particular desire to do the work, so long as it is done. We have only undertaken it in view of the fact that we were losing much of the best material, by its deportation to the Museums of Europe and the United States.' Naïvely, he now estimated that the program might be accomplished in three years; 'after that the work would be but light and occasional, and could be performed by the person in charge of the collection at the University or elsewhere.'

George Ross responded warmly to this more modest request for funds, and the less confident, more deferential tone of Boyle's brief. Soon after, in the spring of 1887, he informed the Canadian Institute that his department would provide a one thousand dollar grant for the coming year and would publish an archaeological report of the year's activities. Whatever doubts he may have once entertained about David Boyle's religious persuasions seemed to have dissipated; Ross was now prepared to accept the fact that as the official curator of the Canadian Institute, and as the quasi-official provincial archaeologist (the title was not formalized), Boyle would receive a portion of the grant as a salary and for travelling expenses.

In one significant area, however, the minister chose not to take action. The delegation in February had requested that he introduce legislation to protect archaeological sites, modelled on the British Ancient Monuments Act (1812). The institute hoped that under such legislation all identified sites would 'be declared public property and be made inviolate to all bric-a-brackers and pot-hunters until examined by some competent person appointed for that purpose.'[91] Quite likely, the government believed that such legislation, while useful in theory would be difficult to enforce. Boyle himself had admitted as much in 'The Archaeological Outlook.' Unfortunately, it so happened that Ontario would not move to protect its archaeological resources through legislation for another sixty-six years, until the passage of the Archaeological Sites Protection Act of 1953.

Bolstered by the injection of government funds and the opening of the partially completed museum on the third floor of the Canadian Institute in

May 1887, the future of archaeology in Ontario looked promising. Within a year David Boyle would divest himself of Ye Olde Booke Shoppe to become Canada's first full-time professional archaeologist. The transition from teacher to archaeologist had not been easy. For seven years he had struggled to find a suitable occupational alternative to teaching and now, whether he realized it or not, his search was over. Significantly, each phase of his career during these years was consistent with the essential theme of his adult life – his commitment to the acquisition and imparting of knowledge. Despite the abrupt changes in occupation, these years of transition can scarcely be seen as a break with Boyle's past. He may have developed new interests, but he never lost sight of older ones. In 1887 he was no less the Pestalozzian educator than he had been in Elora. Now his class-room was the archaeological museum; his students, anyone who entered its doors; his method, still the object lesson, but now through the archaeological record. He still pursued science with a passion, and he was more than ever an advocate of self-culture.

5
The archaeological reality 1887–94

Conflicting emotions swept over David Boyle in the spring of 1887 as he pondered the task that faced him. The thought of creating a museum for representative collections of Indian antiquities from all regions of the province was exhilarating, but the immensity of the program Boyle had defined in 'The Archaeological Outlook' gave him spells of anxiety, particularly since he intended to accomplish his goals in his leisure hours away from Ye Olde Booke Shoppe. At best, he could foresee spending four weeks in the field during the spring and summer months to collect as many artifacts as possible for classification and exhibition in the fall and winter. One thing was certain; to realize his objectives he would have to encourage local amateur archaeologists to join in his work by donating their private collections, locating sites, describing and surveying their finds, and in some cases, by excavating on his behalf.

Starting in late April, Boyle fled his bookstore for intervals of one to four days to investigate promising leads in various parts of southern Ontario. On 30 April he examined middens in York Township at the late prehistoric Jackes (today Eglinton) site, before heading east on 11 May to open several mounds on Tidd's and Hay Islands in the St Lawrence River near Gananoque. From Boyle's description, these mounds, all traces of which have disappeared, are thought to be characteristic of Ohio Hopewell burial mound influence on the Point Peninsula culture. A week later Boyle travelled west to Beverley Township, Wentworth County, to authenticate the site of a palisaded historic Neutral village on the William Gilbert farm (today the Mount or McDonald site). June 9 and 10 found Boyle near Port Colborne in Humberstone Township salvaging what he could from the Bearss site, a prehistoric Neutral ossuary recently discovered near the Erie shoreline. Towards the middle of the month he made a one-day inspection of an 'early trading post' and burial pits on the Baby Estate at the southern end of the Humber River trail, south of Lambton Mills. Shortly after, on 29 June, he left for Nottawasaga Township where he spent four days with James Bain. Here they resumed their work of the previous year looking for and examining Petun villages and ossuaries including the Lougheed site and the Beecroft ossuary. After that trip, Boyle's field-work for the year was virtually complete, save for a day's visit in July to the Tuscarora Reserve in Brant County to study the wampum belts held in trust by the aged Mohawk chief and 'fire-keeper,' *Ska-na-wa-tih* (John Buck), and two short trips in October, one to Beverley Township and the other to the Seabrook farm in Komoka, Middlesex County.[1]

It could not be expected that in rushing around the Ontario countryside in short bursts of activity, Boyle's excavations in his first year would be models of good field technique. The average length of time he spent at each location was often less than a day. Compared to the procedures of latter-day archaeologists, his modus operandi in the field might appear crude and un-scientific, his excavations being little more than an antiquarian's raid for the purpose of collecting museum specimens. For instance, he trenched several mounds in a single day on Tidd's Island in order to verify that they had been produced artificially, and to recover the primary interment and associated burial goods.

While acknowledging that Boyle's excavation technique left a great deal to be desired, to judge him by modern criteria would be a gross anachronism. Apart from a precious few individuals like Britain's General Pitt-Rivers, whose total and systematic excavation and recording of sites was outstanding, Boyle's excavations were standard for the late-nineteenth century. In fact, his efforts in the field from 1887 on were a marked advance over the work of any of his Ontario predecessors. The procedures he used were scientific in intent. His method was that of an ardent empiricist who believed that archaeology, like all the sciences, must be characterized by 'calm, close, careful and prolonged investigation, and ... carried on in such a manner as to avoid every possible element of error.'[2] It was not his way to march into the field to substantiate preconceived theories; rather, he was willing to observe before reaching conclusions. No matter how brief his site visit, he recorded and later published in his annual *Archaeological Reports* the main natural and archaeological features of each location and the surrounding landscape, and made rough measurements of the same. He scoured the vicinity for surface artifacts, and noted the provenience of each item. After trenching a mound, earthwork, or ossuary, he wrote an accurate description of his findings at each stage of the dig, including the relative position of everything found. His descriptions were not as complete as one would find in modern reports, but they remain invaluable references to this day. David Boyle, it should be emphasized, was the first person in the history of Ontario archaeology to record and to publish a systematic record of his excavation procedures and findings.

Furthermore, the descriptive analyses of his excavations contained in the *Archaeological Reports* were devoid of the speculative thinking of the past; instead, Boyle's analysis was informed and based on a wide knowledge of geology and natural science. Take, for example, this assessment of one mound on Tidd's Island: 'A trench was dug from the margin to the centre of the elevation, but with the exception of a few flint-flakes and some charcoal near the surface, everything went to show that the mound was one of natural formation, the strata of fine and coarse sand reposing on each other undisturbedly.'[3] Similarly, his authentication of the palisaded historic Neutral village site on the Gilbert farm in Beverley Township was a solid example of scientific analysis: 'After having had a portion of the marked ground ploughed from side to side, and the loose earth carefully removed with spades, we found unmistakable evidences of the old palisades. Only a few decayed fragments of wood were found, but sufficient to prove that the posts were pine; and the discoloration of the earth caused by the subsidence of the vegetable mould into the old cavities in the lighter colored sub-soil, indicated that the stakes had been from four to six inches in diameter, and about the same distance apart. The enclosed space was almost circular, being 180 yards in diameter from east to west, and 140 yards from north to south.'[4] Nothing so detailed pertaining to an archaeological excavation in Ontario had appeared in print before.

No one became more conscious than Boyle himself of his own limitations in the field; no one regretted more than he the lack of time and operational funds that prevented him from placing more emphasis on site excavation. As early as his third report he would decry his inability to undertake 'moderately accurate surveys of all aboriginal locations, with drawings of fortified works, and exact data relating to materials, patterns, depths, soils, ash-heaps, position of bodies, with particulars relating to skulls, modes of burial, presence or absence of European influences, and many other details requiring experience, time and labor to record satisfactorily.'[5] Soon after he complained again that 'the character of our operations is unsatisfactory – it lacks thoroughness. Many localities demand weeks and months of examination, but the limited resources of the Institute render this impossible. The progress of time serves but to prove the futility of our attempts to grapple with the task of Ontario's archaeology otherwise than in the most superficial manner.'[6] Given the circumstances under which he toiled, David Boyle accomplished what was possible, and resigned himself to the fact that others would have to undertake the careful surveys and systematic excavations of the sites he had only been able to examine on a preliminary basis.

Despite the restrictions that adversely conditioned his work, Boyle still managed to add some eight hundred specimens to the museum during 1887, partly the result of his own activities in the field, but mainly by purchase and donation. He possessed a remarkable talent for convincing individuals to donate or sell their private collections to the Canadian Institute Museum.[7] By all accounts he was a man who genuinely enjoyed meeting people from all walks of life. His ebullience, his sparkling sense of humour, his skill as a raconteur, and his varied background enabled him to relate to farmers, artisans, businessmen, and professionals alike. When promoting his cause, he was as much at ease chatting with weathered farmers and labourers in a tavern as he was taking afternoon tea in an upper-middle-class matron's sitting room. Wherever he travelled he charmed those he met, and usually left them only too glad to donate specimens or to collect on his behalf. In return he would acknowledge all such favours by mentioning even the most minor contribution in his reports. The *coup* of his first season's work on the road occurred in October 1887 when, during his stay in Middlesex County, he made a side trip to Strathroy. Here he persuaded amateur collector Joseph W. Stewart to sell his excellent and documented 'cabinet of nearly six hundred specimens, nearly all of which are among the best of their kind procurable.'[8] Meanwhile, other donations had arrived through the mails in response to the second distribution of the site inventory questionnaire earlier that year.[9] Again, as was the case with the initial mailing in April 1885, the circular proved effective in eliciting information, donations, and generating a wider interest in matters archaeological.

The task of classifying and cataloguing his growing collection and developing typologies proved worrisome for Boyle. He would have preferred to study at first hand the classification schemes of some of the major American archaeological repositories, such as the Smithsonian Institution in Washington, DC, or Harvard's Peabody Museum in Cambridge, Massachusetts,[10] instead of relying upon his reading of the archaeological literature, and common sense. The practice of British curators, who by this time emulated the Danes in dividing prehistory into chronological periods based on the Three Age system, and classified artifacts according to these eras of time, proved of little use. 'European aboriginal relics,' Boyle explained, 'are classified as palaeolithic or neolithic, according to their degree of finish, the latter being of more recent origin and of superior workmanship. In this country, however, no such distinction can be made, for we find the rude and the more elaborate forms in various degrees of finish, in such circumstances as to indicate that all were made and used by the same people contemporaneously.'[11] Having little appreciation of the chronology, time depth, and culture sequences of Ontario prehistory – a problem shared by all American archaeologists during this period – Boyle adopted a classification scheme that was essentially descriptive taxonomy.

He began by sorting the specimens into four broad categories according to functional criteria:

1st. Those of which we know the mode of production and their uses, e.g. arrow heads.
2nd. Those of which we know the mode of production, but are uncertain as to the use, e.g., so-called breast-plates, and banner stones.
3rd. Those of which we know the use, but not the mode of production, e.g., certain kinds of finely drilled beads;
4th. Those of which we know absolutely nothing.[12]

Within each of these categories the artifacts were classified into types according to their modes or diagnostic attributes. Boyle then analysed, exhibited, and wrote about each class or type of artifact separately from the others. It did not occur to him to consider the specimens within a cultural framework; he classified all his material in undifferentiated sequences that encompassed enormous geographical areas. For instance, he grouped all 'rough flints' from across the province in one display case, and subsequently added American, British, and French specimens for comparative purposes.[13] All North American archaeologists did the same for the simple reason that the concept of culture complexes or units had not yet been clearly developed. Later, as Boyle's work progressed and his data base grew, an awareness of geographical and cultural variations in archaeological assemblages would begin to creep into his classification. For the time being, the important thing was that he was heading in a positive direction towards the systematic and objective examination of his specimens.[14]

If the class of artifact permitted, as with clay or stone pipes, Boyle evoked the evolutionary principle and arranged his material in typological sequences 'from the rudest to the most elegant.'[15] That an evolutionary bias should influence his interpretation of the collections was typical of the period, and to be expected, given his Darwinian perspectives. He was at one with most late-Victorian archaeologists who conceived of prehistory largely as a record of progress and evolution[16] and who, influenced by such anthropologists as E.B. Tylor, L.H. Morgan, and Daniel Wilson, read into the material remains of the past a chronicle of human progress from savagery through barbarism to civilization. Boyle's archaeological assumptions were also shaped by his intimate knowledge of geology and palaeontology. These scientific interests had not been neglected after leaving Elora; on the contrary, he maintained his reading in these fields, and at the Canadian Institute became curator of the geological and mining section, formed in April 1887. Thus Boyle, the palaeontologist *cum* archaeologist, was prone to analyse and exhibit an archaeological artifact type in much the same way as he did a palaeontological fossil specie, that is, by tracing progressive evolutionary development in each instance.

Perhaps the most noteworthy dimension of Boyle's early analysis, classification, and exhibition of the artifacts was the emphasis he placed on ascertaining the function and the method of producing each of the specimens in his possession. Case B in the Canadian Institute Museum contained dozens of 'Broken and Unfinished Articles Showing Methods of Working,' while a major portion of each *Archaeological Report* was reserved for the description and analysis of new accessions with the focus on their function and how they were made. In this dimension of his work Boyle proved to be quite effective, since he brought to each problem the experience and the common sense of the skilled blacksmith possessing an extensive knowledge of tools and working methods.

Typical of the application of the artisan's knowledge was the following analysis in his first *Report* pertaining to the production of beads:

We have in our cases several pieces of hard, close-grained stone partially cut into strips preparatory to being squared, or rounded, and bored. We learn from this and other specimens that the rough block of stone was first polished on two sides, so as to present even surfaces for marking off and for being ultimately sawn through by means of flint-flakes. Probably this sawing process was aided by water. When a moderately deep cut had been made on both sides, the strip was broken off, cut into lengths, and bored; but how the boring was done, when the holes required were so small, it is not quite so easy to understand. Beads, broken lengthwise, enable us to see that the process was carried on from each end; but here certainty ceases.

Another specimen found on the Lougheed farm in the Collingwood area, a historic Petun site, proved 'that the Indians understood a method of cutting stones somewhat similar to the plan known as "plug and feather," which we employ in our quarries to-day; a series of holes has been bored in line close to each other, the necessary or unnecessary piece of material has been broken off, and then friction has been resorted to for the purpose of removing the projecting portions between the holes.'[17]

A cautious empirical approach, devoid of dogmatism, characterizes this and all of Boyle's analysis and interpretation of the artifacts. His expertise was not coupled with an inflated ego. He never became a 'theory-maniac' as he called those archaeologists who drew conclusions on the basis of little or no evidence. 'There are not a few writers,' he noted on the subject of banner stones, 'who express themselves glibly as to the application of almost every specimen that comes under their observation, but the truth is that regarding a large number of types we are totally ignorant of the purposes they served in aboriginal economy.' If Boyle was uncertain, he declined to make a conclusion and humbly admitted his ignorance. Yet he also showed at the outset that he possessed the courage of his convictions, and took a stand on controversial matters in American archaeology. The question of whether or not prehistoric Amerindians applied heat to copper to work it, or to harden it, greatly intrigued the 'smithy' in Boyle. 'It is pretty well known,' he wrote, 'that the aborigines mined, in a rude way, the native copper which is found so abundantly on the north shore of Lake Superior, and that they succeeded in hammering portions of it into ... weapons, cutting tools, or personal ornaments. It is extremely doubtful that they employed heat in any way for the purpose, although many writers are inclined to adopt this view. That they may have employed grooves, or what blacksmiths call "swages," in wood or stone into which the metal was pounded to give it the required form is not unlikely.' He pointed to a specimen of an adze in his collection, 'the outer or convex side' of which showed no signs of hammering, giving support to his 'swage theory.' He was forthright enough, however, to admit that the flaw in his hypothesis was the absence of 'swage-stones' in the known archaeological record.[18] Most archaeologists today would probably agree with the essentials of Boyle's argument that early Amerindian artisans worked their copper simply as a stone with special non-chipping qualities, and manufactured their artifacts out of nearly pure copper, either cold or slightly heated (a possibility he did not discuss), and hammered them into shape with the assistance of appropriately grooved stone or wood – the precursors of the formal blacksmith's swage.

In his first *Archaeological Report* Boyle did not clearly articulate his motives for emphasizing function and working methods but did so in subsequent publications. His primary reason was to study technological evolution, to trace man's progression from the most primitive tools and technology to the 'miraculous' engines and tools of the late nineteenth century. With this end in view, he urged the preservation of 'not only perfect and highly finished specimens of all kinds, but the very rudest in form as well, and especially those on which the workmanship appears to be incomplete. The former may serve to exemplify the lower types from which the ideally perfect weapon or tool has evolved.'[19] The second reason for making 'a close and patient study of function and working methods' was 'to understand the modes of thought, manners of life, and conditions of early society ... To learn the uses of [artifacts],' he explained, 'is to arrive at a knowledge, not only of how the ancient people lived, but of how they thought which is of even greater importance, for if we can ascertain this we are on the highway to an understanding of much that it would be extremely interesting to know relative to aboriginal mental development, and consequently valuable as a contribution to the history of our race in its progress from the rudest to the highest and most refined manifestations of humanity.'[20]

All these ideas are suggestive of Boyle's perception of himself as an archaeologist. Despite a background in biology and geology, as an archaeologist he did not see himself as a natural scientist like many European prehistorians with similar training and interests. Certainly he exploited many of the methods and techniques of the natural scientist, but in common with Daniel Wilson before him, and indeed with most American archaeologists, he considered himself primarily an anthropologist (archaeology he believed to be a 'department' of anthropology), and secondarily a historian interested in reading the story of man's society, economy, and ideas into the material remains of the past. Later in his career he would take considerable interest in comparative ethnology to supplement the archaeological record, on the assumption that modern tribes of Indians preserved stages in human development that could throw light on prehistoric social and spiritual life.

Such were the basic concepts and attitudes shaping David Boyle's thoughts and actions as he busily classified his artifacts and arranged them in display cases during the fall and winter of 1887–8. He recognized that he had embarked on a never-ending curatorial process that would demand a major portion of his time each year. A good museum, he wrote, must constantly change and grow; 'the arrangement and classification' must never 'be regarded as satisfactory or final. Museums, like libraries of humble origin, require frequent changes and rearrangements corresponding to the increase and variety of the collections.'[21] To some extent, Boyle was making a virtue out of a necessity in propounding this important principle of museology, for by the end of the next year, the size of his collection had doubled again, requiring considerable alterations in the displays. Inevitably, because he worked in isolation, he made mistakes. 'I intend ... to paint a number on each specimen, and to catalogue them all,' he promised in 1888.[22] The cataloguing method he devised involved beginning a new series of numbers for each class of specimen; unfortunately, in a very short time the collection grew so rapidly that this procedure became very confusing and had to be abandoned in 1890 in favour of a straight serial system for artifacts of every type.

Although he lacked any formal training as a curator, David Boyle was second to no other museum administrator in Canada. He was remarkably modern in his thoughts as to the purpose of a museum. The ideal museum, he argued, must not be totally research oriented; above all else it should be a teaching institution, a place of learning for the general public. He deplored those museums in which 'a number is all that serves to identify the pieces, and constant reference to a catalogue is thus involved on the part of him who wants to get information.' Such practices only acted as a barrier to those studying the collections. 'This ... is not my idea of how either to popularize a collection, or to facilitate the work of the student. Everything possible should be done to enable young and old, learned and unlearned, to examine with pleasure and profit, at the least possible expense of time and trouble. This object can be obtained only by means of copious and legibly written, or printed labels.' Thus a conscientious labelling practice, combined with the annotated catalogue made available in 1889, became the basis of the interpretive program at the Canadian Institute Museum.[23]

II

Perhaps the area in which David Boyle made most progress in his first years as an archaeologist and curator at the Canadian Institute was public relations. As he had done earlier on a more limited scale for the Elora School Museum, he proved himself a master in promoting Ontario archaeology. Rarely did he miss an opportunity to feed information to the press, particularly as he passed through the various regions of the province. In Toronto the *Mail* emerged as a strong supporter of his work. 'Mr. Boyle is to be congratulated on the result of his exploration,' the *Mail* editorialized after the Tidd's Island excavations. 'It is a great pity this sort of thing had not been done for national purposes many years ago, but much may be accomplished yet. Let farmers, teachers, commercial travellers and persons of leisure render assistance in every possible way by communicating any knowledge they possess on this subject to the Canadian Institute.'[24] Reporters from all the Toronto newspapers, intrigued by word of a major accession, would at one time or another eventually grace the doors of the museum; to a man they would be overwhelmed by Boyle, some perhaps more than others after imbibing a glass or two of Scotch whiskey filed away in a convenient cupboard. They would later wax eloquent about the reception they had received, and about 'Mr. Boyle's untiring energy and activity,' or 'the genial and entertaining curator ... who is ever ready to instruct the uninitiated in the history and uses of the numerous Indian relics on exhibition.'[25]

The Canadian National Exhibition in Toronto also afforded opportunities for promoting archaeology. Two hundred dollars of the first archaeological grant went to the project to erect a memorial on the site of the old French trading post, Fort Rouillé, on the exhibition grounds. Toronto historian and past president of the Canadian Institute, the Rev. Henry Scadding, had been pushing this cause for several years, and by 1887 had convinced most levels of government and the city's mercantile community to contribute to his campaign to mark this 'cradle spot' of the city's trade and commerce.[26] On the occasion of the annual exhibition on the fair grounds in August, Boyle exploited the opportunity for informing the public of his work by preparing what became a highly acclaimed archaeological display; he received that year's gold medal of excellence from the exhibition board for his trouble.[27]

Of all the public relations projects initiated in the first year, none was more effective than the *Archaeological Report*, a journal destined to appear annually and to become the first periodical published in Canada devoted primarily to archaeology. Some two thousand copies of the report were published by the department of education, an indication that George Ross was well pleased with Boyle's efforts. The reports were distributed to members of the legislative assembly and the Canadian Institute, all donors to the museum, newspapers, and eventually to curators and archaeologists elsewhere in North America, and to anyone else interested enough to request a copy. Boyle wrote his reports, initially at least, as basic primers in prehistory for those unfamiliar with the American and British literature on the subject. He reasoned that if people could be made to identify and to understand the function of the artifacts they found, and how these specimens were produced, their interest in the subject would deepen. Farmers and youngsters might be encouraged to preserve the 'scientifically valuable objects' that they too often 'lightly esteemed, or neglected and lost.'[28]

Judging from the swelling list of donors, young and old, as the years passed, and the popularity of his heavily illustrated and readable journal, the early educational objective was achieved to a considerable extent. 'It is gratifying to be able to state,' Boyle noted in the third *Report*, 'that the interest in archaeological matters has increased very considerably throughout the province, since the inception of our scheme to place ourselves as nearly as possible abreast of other countries in this respect ... Old collectors have been encouraged to go on, and many new ones have entered the field.'[29] He went on to mention another beneficial result arising from the reports – 'the very general determination arrived at by almost all who pick up specimens, not to let them go out of the country.' In every publication he took special pains to express his outrage over the fact that 'immense quantities of material' have been exported to 'the most celebrated museums in Europe and America.'[30] In so doing, he was single-handedly stimulating 'the birth of a conscience' in Ontario about the indiscriminate exportation of the province's archaeological resources to foreign repositories.

After the gratifying reception given his first *Archaeological Report*, Boyle worked to refine and expand the educational dimension in subsequent issues. Recognizing the need among amateur collectors for reference sources to facilitate comparative study and artifact analysis, he persuaded A.F. Chamberlain, then a fellow in modern languages at University College, Toronto, and an avid ethnologist and part-time archaeologist, to fill this gap. Chamberlain's annotated 'Contributions Towards a Bibliography of the Archaeology of the Dominion of Canada and Newfoundland,' appeared in three instalments from 1887 to 1891. Nearly a decade later Andrew F. Hunter continued and embellished this valuable reference source by compiling an even more comprehensive and specialized 'Bibliography of the Archaeology of Ontario.'[31] Boyle also included in his reports such helpful articles as lists of tribal names and their synonyms,[32] and extracts transcribed from rare documentary sources that he believed woud 'throw light on portions of history and archaeology' for his readers. These included: '"A Short Account of the Maquas Indians in New Netherland; Their Country, Stature, Dress, Customs and Magistrates, Written in the Year 1644." By John Megapolensis, Jun., Minister There,'[33] and the 'Short Historical and Journal Notes by David Pietersz, de Vries, 1665.'[34] On other occasions he drew upon less esoteric sources to help his readers understand Amerindian social and economic conditions. In the third *Archaeological Report*, for example, he received permission from Francis Parkman to quote extensively from *The Jesuits in North America* on the history of the Petun.

Boyle also intended his *Archaeological Reports* to demolish the popular stereotype of the North American Indian as a war-like savage, in short, the image perpetuated in the 'penny dreadfuls' and other 'books of professedly higher aim' that dwelt on the recent history of Indian troubles in the western United States. Many authors portrayed the American Indian as having 'a diabolical grin on his countenance, a war-club in his blood-stained hand,' and 'his dishevelled locks matted with the gore of his innocent victims.'[35] Boyle liked to remind his readers that 'the every-day life of the old American savage was superior to that of peasants in some civilised communities today ... In the region of the aesthetic,' he argued, 'the Indian, even of this northern latitude, occupied an immensely higher plane than the class just mentioned. He understood the effect of colour, and employed it to some purpose, both in personal decoration and on articles of manufacture; his sense of the elegant in form is well illustrated in the graceful outline given to many of his coarse clay vessels, his pipes of stone and clay, and in the great variety of beautifully fashioned objects.' Boyle cited L.H. Morgan's work on the Iroquois to explain that the prehistoric Amerindian was also a deeply religious person who 'may be fairly placed among the first of the animists. To him, everything visible and tangible was the abode of a spirit.'[36]

III

David Boyle's solid progress at the museum and his enormously successful public relations initiatives during 1887, culminating in the distribution of the first *Archaeological Report*, paid dividends early in 1888. George Ross, basking in the credit that had fallen on his department, renewed the archaeological grant for the coming fiscal year (1888–9). But more importantly, perhaps, Ross spoke in support of Boyle when his name was proposed as an assistant to the commissioner in charge of the Ontario mineral exhibit planned for the Centennial Exposition of the Ohio Valley and Central States in Cincinnati, scheduled to take place from 4 July to 27 October 1888.

Premier Oliver Mowat appointed the Hon. Timothy Warren Anglin, a long-time Liberal politician from New Brunswick, and then editor of the Toronto *Tribune*, as commissioner to oversee the Ontario exhibit. David Boyle and Charles Canniff James, a professor of chemistry at the Ontario Agricultural College in Guelph and a future deputy-minister of agriculture (1891–1912), were chosen to assist him. When offered this post, which required him to take up residence for five months in the United States, Boyle finally decided to sell his bookstore. Now that he had been given the opportunity to feed at the patronage trough of Mowat Liberalism, he anticipated being able to make a living as a professional archaeologist and all-purpose curator for the government. With the equity from the bookstore, the Boyles purchased a modest house at 316 Berkeley Street, about three-quarters of a mile east of the Canadian Institute on Richmond Street.

By May 1888, after visiting or communicating with all the principal mine operators in the province, tons of ore specimens began to arrive in Toronto for exhibit in Cincinnati. Boyle and C.C. James selected and catalogued some two thousand specimens weighing approximately ten tons for shipment by train to Ohio in June. 'In the placing of [these] articles in the space allotted to Ontario at the Exhibition,' reported Commissioner Anglin, 'the taste and skill of Mr. Boyle and Prof. James merit a hearty recognition.'[37] The two assistants, as it turned out, got along famously; they shared a great deal in common including a love of science, literature, and history. Later in their careers they would work together again, this time in the cause of heritage preservation as leaders of the Ontario Historical Society after 1898 – Boyle as secretary (1898–1907), and James as president (1902–4). Once the exhibit had been designed and arranged, Boyle settled into a regular routine of greeting the public, assisting businessmen interested in purchasing Ontario minerals, and enthusing potential investors intrigued by recent developments in New Ontario, particularly by the impressive copper-nickel discoveries in 1883 on the CPR main line at a place called Sudbury.

Life in Cincinnati provided Boyle with many diversions in his leisure time. 'This is a most musical community,' he wrote to Charles Clarke, 'banjos, guitars, pianos, violins ... abound ... Serenading parties are quite often heard even near the "wee sma' 'oors." '38 Boyle frequented the city's art gallery and public library, and attended many concerts. 'Liberati's band is here from New York,' he wrote, 'he is divine, you bet. All the bands here are very good.' He also enjoyed long walks to view the grand houses and manicured gardens in the exclusive neighbourhoods of Clifton, Avondale, and Walnut Hill. The downtown core he found less to his liking. 'I don't feel at all well,' he confided to Clarke. 'I am afraid I've caught malaria in this infernal odiferous hole.' In one of the McSpurtle 'epistles' for the *Scottish American Journal*, he described Cincinnati 'as dirty a toon as I ever saw, excep' Greenock, an' I dinna ken but it's even waus than it.'39 In the market-place, hucksters who retailed 'all sorts of edibles,' grated the ear 'with cries that remind one of Liverpool' or 'the utterances produced by average brakesmen on the G.T.R.'40 Surprisingly, Boyle, who was not a supporter of strict Sabattarian laws, was shocked by the wide-open social and commercial activity on a typical Cincinnati Sunday. His belief in the working class's right to steamboat and picnic excursions on a Sunday in Toronto was one thing, but unregulated business, theatres, and saloons on the Sabbath offended even his sensibilities. 'This city is worse than "Soadum an' Gemorry," ' concluded the feisty Andrew McSpurtle.

If there was one regrettable aspect to Boyle's sojourn in the United States, it was the loss of an entire season of archaeological field-work in Ontario. 'But, I am pleased to be able to inform you,' he wrote in his second *Archaeological Report* (1887–8), 'that the work of collecting ... has not ... been a total blank, as ... I was enabled to gather a considerable number of specimens [in Ohio], many of which differ considerably from the types found in this country.'41 Upon arriving in Cincinnati, he lost no time in making contact with local archaeologists in the city and in nearby Lawrenceburg, Indiana, including the very capable Warren K. Moorehead, an emerging figure in American archaeology. Boyle expected to learn much in this centre of the ancient Mound Builders – now known as the home of the Adena and Hopewell cultures. Two of his contacts – identified as Drs Craig and S.H. Collins of Lawrenceburg – secured for Boyle 'the rare permission to open a number of mounds' and to appropriate the contents for the Canadian Institute Museum. In addition, he purchased specimens from nearly a dozen states and procured plaster casts of several engraved stone tablets characteristic of the Adena people. 'For more than a quarter century,' Boyle wrote in an impish mood, 'have our American scientific neighbours acted towards Ontario in a most friendly manner, visiting us frequently, carrying off to Washington and elsewhere every specimen worthy of preservation in their cabinets, and it seemed to me only fair even at this late date, to evince a spirit of good fellowship by way of reciprocity. It is therefore gratifying to state that acting upon this principle we have been able to add about five hundred objects of interest to the Provincial Archaeological Museum.'[42]

Despite his long absence from Toronto, the Ontario collections continued to grow apace thanks to individuals like James Dickson, a public lands surveyor based in Fenelon Falls, and Dr Rowland B. Orr of Maple, both of whom sent in specimens. After returning to Toronto in November 1888, Boyle purchased the large and well-documented 1400-piece collection belonging to William Matheson who resided in Lucan, the small village north of London of 'Black Donelly' notoriety. The Matheson collection was valuable in so far as it was 'exhaustively illustrative of a limited area' of five townships in Middlesex County. To cap off the accessions for the year, Boyle was pleased to receive samples of British and French lithics sent by a friend of J.H. Pierce, president of the biological section of the Canadian Institute.[43]

The Cincinnati sojourn proved to be a period of no little importance in Boyle's professional and personal development. He returned to Canada after this association with his American colleagues with a better appreciation of his own archaeological expertise. His American counterparts, to his surprise, were no better trained or intellectually equipped than himself to study and to discuss prehistory. This new-found confidence manifested itself in the second *Archaeological Report*, in which Boyle demolished the hypothesis of an official of the Smithsonian Institution that polished 'birdstones,' stylized effigies of nesting or sitting birds, were designed for a game of chance. The birdstones, according to this authority, were said to be shaken in a vessel that was then turned upside down on a flat surface; 'the count was reckoned for or against the player, in accordance with the number found standing or fallen when the vessel was removed.' This hypothesis was nonsense, argued Boyle: '1st, because the bases of some are rounded off so much, or are so narrow, that it requires careful adjustment to make them stand at all. 2nd, many are

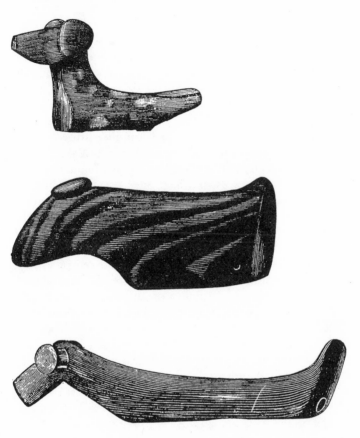

Birdstones (*Archaeological Report 1887–8*)

top-heavy and therefore easily overbalanced ... In the third place, what is perhaps the strongest reason why these objects were not so employed, consists in the fact that they seldom show any signs of abrasion.' As for famed anthropologist Henry Schoolcraft's argument that birdstones served as 'knife-handles,' Boyle argued that since 'no blades have ever been found showing any arrangement for attachment to articles of this sort, it must be concluded that this was not their purpose.' Birdstones and similar objects, he suggested, were probably 'worn partly as articles of personal adornment and partly as amulets or luck-stones.'[44]

IV

With the arrival of spring 1889, David Boyle grew impatient to get back into the field after a hiatus of over eighteen months. For various reasons his field-work would be interrupted frequently in the years to come – entire seasons would be lost – but he was about to enjoy a stretch of three summers documenting sites, conducting brief excavations, and collecting specimens for the museum. Late in May he travelled west to Clearville, situated in the south-east corner of Orford Township in Kent County near Lake Erie, to investigate a large prehistoric village site reported by Thomas Boon, one of his contacts in Bothwell. Boyle found 'two village sites occupying different levels' on a small plain surrounded by steep bluffs of from ten to thirty-five feet in height. These natural defensive features were supplemented by man-made earthwork embankments. At the western embankment of the upper-level site, he discovered an immense kitchen midden, the ashes of which gave up a rich variety of shells, bones, skulls, broken pipes, and pottery.[45] Impressed by his initial findings, Boyle acquired permission from the owners to make a more thorough examination and returned on 16 July with Thomas Boon and several labourers. For three days they dug into the ash beds, drove trenches into the embankments which they discovered had been palisaded, and used a sounding rod to locate 'soft-places.' Using this technique, Boyle discovered an ossuary containing the remains of eight persons. On the basis of his total findings, he concluded that the Clearville site 'must have been occupied at widely separated periods by at least two, and perhaps three different tribes.'

The site description in the *Archaeological Report for 1888–9* proved to be one of Boyle's best, although even for the times it was diagrammatically weak, lacking cross-section drawings. He recognized stratigraphy and distinguished between pottery styles; this data enabled him to determine a rough occupation sequence for the site.

The broken pottery found near the base of the middle embankment were large and coarse and without ornament, and the flint-flakes were different in color and appearance from those nearer the surface. The houses of these people would occupy the enclosed spaces, and in accordance with this we find beds of ashes at depths varying from two to four feet, and alternating with thin layers of sand all over the area in question. A bed of ashes four feet from the surface was found below the eight skulls and other bones already mentioned. The deepest of these were probably left by those who threw up the earthwork, and this view is confirmed from the correspondence in appearance between the potsherds and flint flakes found at the greatest depths here,

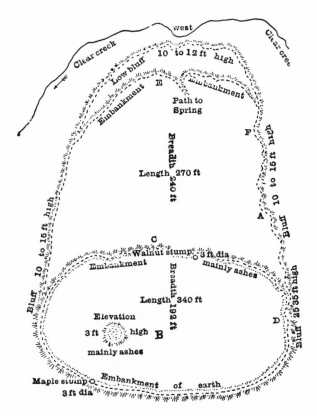

Clearville site (*Archaeological Report 1888–9*)

with those found deep in the embankment. By the time the second people took possession it is likely that every trace of former occupation had disappeared, and the new arrivals [settled] ... close to the middle bank on the higher, or easterly side, finding the western slope convenient as a dumping-ground for refuse.

The grave in which the eight skulls were found, he believed to be 'comparatively recent, and the work of a third people. Aside from the freshness of the remains,' he argued, 'it is not reasonable to believe that those who fortified the place would bury within the enclosure. In addition to this the existence of ashes below the bones goes to show a more ancient possession of the spot by others.'[46]

What Boyle primarily excavated at Clearville was a multi-component ancestral prehistoric Neutral village site of the Late Woodland period that dated back to circa 1500 AD, a site inhabited off and on by its various occupants for a period of about one hundred years.[47] In 1889, of course, no one could have known all these facts. Lacking the archaeological basis and interpretive techniques to discuss scientifically questions of culture and absolute chronology, Boyle simply ignored problems of dating the site or identifying the peoples who inhabited the area. Not for over half a century, until 1939, when Wilfrid Jury of the University of Western Ontario re-excavated Clearville did anyone begin to grapple with these matters.[48] Today students are assisted by new interpretive techniques, refinements in stratigraphic methods, concepts of culture units, of local sequences, of seriation, of traditions and horizons, and, after 1950, the carbon-14 method of chronometric dating, none of which had yet been developed when Boyle was active in the field.

Still, Boyle's excavation of the Clearville site, and his interpretation of the archaeological data, rank among the best work of its kind in Canada in the late nineteenth century. His conclusions of a triple occupancy have been borne out by subsequent research. The pity is that Boyle, the solitary professional in the province, lacking both adequate operational funds and support staff, was never able to refine his excavation technique beyond the level of competence demonstrated on this occasion. Because of the burden of his multifarious tasks, rarely was he able to devote as much time to other sites as he did to Clearville.

During June, between his visits to Clearville, Boyle spent more than a week in Nottawasaga Township in Simcoe County. Here he continued the exemplary work begun four years earlier of conducting a systematic field survey to discover 'the position of every known locality' in the township associated with the historic Tobacco Nation or Petun and their prehistoric forbears. His survey had been a lengthy and deliberate process involving a study of the historical record, such as the *Jesuit Relations*, questioning known collectors, inquiring of farmers and exploring the land afoot, tramping the hills, valleys, and streams, his eyes alert to the tell-tale flint chips, potsherds, and other clues of Amerindian activity. The results were very satisfactory, for he located and recorded the lot and concession number of ten village sites, twenty-one ossuaries, an earthwork, and three potteries. 'A reference to the map-diagram,' Boyle explained in his *Report*, 'will show that all the locations marked extend in a direction from north-west to south-east, that is to say, corresponding with the range of hills that stretch through the township of Nottawasaga.'[49]

As far as Boyle was concerned, his archaeological work on the Tobacco Nation was now complete. He had provided the site locations to enable 'any

Archaeological map of Nottawasaga Township (*Archaeological Report 1888–9*)

future explorer with "reasonable means," to economize time in making a more detailed survey, or in excavating for relics.' More importantly, he wrote, 'it is gratifying to be able to state that our cases now contain a moderately good representation of all that is procurable to illustrate the social condition of ... [the Petun].' To round out his field-work and museum collection, Boyle penned a historical narrative of the Tobacco Nation, based both on his own research and his study of the published sources. It was a noteworthy synthesis for the time, emphasizing such themes as burial practices, the construction of villages, agricultural production, diet, and trade.[50] He dared even to correct the formidable Francis Parkman who had argued that the Petun, like the Huron, temporarily scaffolded their dead prior to the periodic ossuary burials associated with the great ceremony of the 'feast of the dead.' From his field research, Boyle had 'found numerous evidences that among the Tobacco Nation, inhumation, was the prevalent, if not the sole mode of preliminary disposal.'

One of Boyle's purposes in conducting the Nottawasaga field survey was to provide a model for others to emulate. 'The whole of this neighbourhood should be examined carefully, [and] as soon as possible,' he wrote. As luck would have it, one of his protégés was already in the process of doing precisely that – the young Andrew F. Hunter, now graduated from the University of Toronto, and who that same year had purchased the Barrie *Examiner*. Encouraged and inspired as an undergraduate by both Boyle and Daniel Wilson to pursue archaeology, he had determined to make the prehistory and history of Simcoe County his own. For several years he had been keeping a detailed catalogue of village and ossuary sites for the counties of Simcoe, York, and Ontario. By 1889 he was well enough along in his work that Boyle asked him to prepare a paper for the *Archaeological Report* to accompany his own study of the Petun. The result was a strikingly innovative manuscript in which Hunter took a geographical approach to archaeological interpretation by plotting the distribution of French relics in what he identified as 'Huron' sites in the three counties.[51]

By that time Hunter had compiled a record of some four hundred sites, most of which he had personally investigated:

Villages: Simcoe (218); York (33); Ontario (14)
Ossuaries: Simcoe (122); York (5); Ontario (6)

He broke down the data statistically, township by township, twenty-three in total, to show the percentage of sites containing French relics. 'It will be observed,' he wrote, 'how rapidly the percentage of villages where French relics have been found falls off after leaving the first few townships in the remote north beside Georgian Bay. This was the district occupied by the Hurons in the time of the Jesuit missionaries of the seventeenth century.' South of a line drawn from east to west through Kempenfeldt Bay on Lake Simcoe, less than 20 per cent of all known village sites yielded French relics; those that lacked such artifacts Hunter dated prior to 1615, the date of Champlain's journey to Huronia. 'In York and Ontario Counties there is but one case in each, so far as the writer has ascertained, of European relics having been found at Huron village sites.' Based on the archaeological and historical records, Hunter argued that prior to 1615, the Hurons, fleeing the League of the Iroquois, had entered Simcoe County from the south, from around the Toronto area and the north shore of Lake Ontario. Recently archaeologists have posited a far more complicated story of conflict, migration, and the fusion of peoples than Hunter ever imagined; nevertheless, his was a solid and imaginative first response, based primarily on archaeological research, to the question 'Whence came the Huron of Champlain's time?' and anticipated the northward movement theory developed by J. Norman Emerson in 1954 and still recognized by archaeologists today.[52]

The appearance of Hunter's paper in the *Archaeological Report for 1888–9* was an event of some significance, for it marked the beginning of one of Boyle's valuable contributions to Ontario archaeology. From this point on the pages of the reports were opened to the research papers and field notes of the several talented amateur archaeologists who toiled in the province. Knowing that Boyle wanted to publish the results of their work, that he would gladly edit and constructively comment on their written submissions, and that he would guide their reading in the published literature, encouraged them to pursue their archaeological investigations. It is doubtful that people like Hunter, George Laidlaw, and others would have gone on to make the important contributions they did, had it not been for Boyle and the support he gave through his journal.

After Clearville and the Nottawasaga expedition, Boyle undertook two more minor 'digs' before the end of the 1889 season. In mid-August, he and James Bain examined a seventeenth-century historic Neutral ossuary in Humberstone Township near Port Colborne (today the Tennessee Avenue site), on the property of an American-owned summer resort called 'The Solid Comfort Club.'[53] Before they arrived, a deputation of municipal officials and doctors from 'a neighbouring city in the United States' had already descended upon 'Solid Comfort' in an unsuccessful bid to secure the find which included rare specimens of whole pottery. Unfortunately, Boyle was no more successful than the American deputation since the wealthy patrons of the club took the relics home with them later that year. Finally, on 5 September he joined Dr Rowland B. Orr and several others to examine the Maple Village site and to open the Keffer ossuary in York and Vaughan townships, respectively, north of Toronto.

All in all, 1889 was a good year in the field for David Boyle. The Clearville excavation and the Nottawasaga survey made up for any disappointments. And there was the added excitement of attending the meeting in Toronto in late August of the American Association for the Advancement of Science. This occasion enabled Boyle to strike lasting relationships with many of North America's most eminent archaeologists. He listened enthralled to Major John W. Powell's address on the 'Evolution of Music' and to Garrick Mallery's 'Israelite and Indian,' in which the author examined the myth that the Amerindian was descended from the ten lost tribes of Israel. To be accepted at the meeting as an equal by the greats and near greats in the profession and to guide them through his museum was an experience that Boyle, the ex-blacksmith and self-taught archaeologist, could never forget. Charles C. Abbott, after touring the museum, wrote in the guest book: 'Its value for scientific purpose is very great, and already there is gathered here the material for comparative study.'[54] W.M. Beauchamp of Baldwinsville, New York, a prominent archaeologist connected with both the Smithsonian Institution and the New York State Museum at Albany, added: 'I have been both greatly pleased [and] profited by examining the valuable collection of Indian artifacts in the Canadian Institute, among which are some that would be beyond price to any antiquarian, [and] will prove of the highest use in solving some questions of early history.'

The Peabody Museum's Frederic Ward Putnam also recorded his impressions: 'I have found very much of importance to me in my study of the skulls of American peoples. The collection of skulls for Ontario show clear resemblances with those found in the old burial places of Massachusetts.' Encouraged by Putnam, Boyle went on to include in his *Archaeological Report for 1891* a full study of his crania collection, including engravings and measurements.[55] The study, conducted in accordance with recognized international rules and procedures, was made by two recent graduates of Trinity Medical College – Letitia K. Meade, a practising physician in Hamilton, and David's daughter, Susanna P. Boyle, MD, CM, by then a demonstrator of anatomy in the Toronto Women's Medical College.

The establishment of lines of communication with American archaeologists was another of the important developments of David Boyle's early work. It meant that his findings would be incorporated into the mainstream of north-eastern American archaeology. Through ongoing personal contact, and through the exchange of journals and specimens with individuals and museums in the United States, he saw to it that his efforts became widely known, and that his *Archaeological Reports* were cited for comparative purposes in publications below the border.[56] As a consequence, Boyle avoided the fate of his counterparts in Nova Scotia and New Brunswick who, without the benefit of personally knowing the Americans, were virtually ignored in archaeological circles to the south. Their significant findings on shell heaps, for instance, were not even mentioned by archaeologists working along parallel lines down the eastern seaboard of the United States.[57]

Following the meeting of the American Association for the Advancement of Science in Toronto, Boyle spent the remainder of 1889 diligently classifying and exhibiting his growing collection, and preparing a fifty-five-page catalogue for the museum as part of his *Archaeological Report for*

1888–9. Then, suddenly, late in the year, he was struck down by excruciatingly painful migraine headaches that had him bed-ridden on and off for months. As late as 1 July 1890, he wrote to Charles Clarke that he was 'speaking in the presence of death. The sort of head affliction I have can't last long without getting better or worse, and it does not get much better often.'[58] Anxiety about his financial state of affairs did little to help his condition. Since the Cincinnati Exposition no more political plums had come his way; incredibly, his major source of income was the paltry salary of three hundred dollars allocated from the archaeological grant to the Canadian Institute. In December 1889, faced with the possibility of Boyle's resignation, the institute executive belatedly acknowledged their curator's desperate financial plight and voted him an increment of one hundred dollars. In addition, they approached the federal government for additional funds to subsidize archaeological research, but with no success.[59] After being rejected by Ottawa, Boyle confided to A.F. Hunter in March: 'I have such a weight on my mind the whole time regarding the question of household supplies that I often think of pulling up stakes and striking off somewhere else. Of course it is hard to think about relinquishing work that is only fairly begun but I have struggled so long, working in the public interest and foolishly neglecting to a large extent my own that I am now almost in despair.'[60]

By any standard, a salary of four hundred dollars was an outrageously inappropriate level of remuneration for the work Boyle was accomplishing for the province. His counterparts at the Smithsonian Institution, for instance, received from $1500 to $3600 annually depending on the nature of their positions; even a lowly messenger at the Smithsonian earned $480.[61] Most anyone else with Boyle's talents would have been driven out of Ontario archaeology and the Canadian Institute Museum into another more lucrative line of work. But not the unconventional, stubborn Boyle, especially now that he had finally found a career that fulfilled his abiding commitment to learning and self-culture, and allowed him to maintain his links with education generally, to contribute to scientific knowledge, and to write. He would complain often about his salary and threaten to resign if it was not augmented. Even more distasteful, he had to become something of a political manipulator. Take, for example, the following letter to G. Brown Goode, the executive secretary to the United States National Museum:

I cannot tell you how grateful I am to you for the use of the phrase 'I find it very valuable,' [with reference to the latest *Archaeological Report* sent to him by Boyle], as it will go far towards keeping alive the more than half extinguished interest (and always languid interest) manifested by the 'powers that be' towards our archaeological work.

I am afraid you can scarcely realise the difficulties under which we labor ... I am well-nigh disheartened, and would gladly welcome any change. If the authorities knew such to be my intention, or if they thought such a probability imminent, perhaps they would wake up. Is there the remotest chance for any employment about the u.s. National Museum? Were you simply to ask the Hon. G.W. Ross, Minister of Education, relative to the tenure of my engagement, he might see things in a new light. Pardon, my dear sir, the liberty I take in making this suggestion, but when I tell you how ardently I love this work, and that all I do has to be performed by fits and starts, ... at a remuneration varying from $200 to $400 per annum, as the funds may stand, you will see my plight.[62]

It is not known whether Goode went along with Boyle; but the letter indicates that in the final analysis David Boyle could not bring himself to give up an occupation that suited him so perfectly.

With the arrival of the digging season in May 1890, Boyle had recuperated sufficiently, albeit temporarily, from his headaches, to begin one of the most active seasons of field-work in his career. He travelled first to south-west Ontario, to Elgin County, where he examined the impressive double-walled Southwold earthworks, the remnants of a strongly defended late prehistoric Neutral village, circa 1450–1500 AD. A chilling, relentless spring rain made digging impossible and restricted his activities to measuring and jotting down a description of the site.[63] Still, the trip turned out to be profitable in terms of acquisitions for the museum since Boyle's companion to the earthworks, Dr Charles B. Tweedale of St Thomas, donated his extensive case of Elgin County artifacts assembled over many years by his father.

A few weeks later Boyle spent several days on the Six Nations Indian Reserve near Hagersville in Tuscarora Township. Accompanied by Dr P.E. Jones, a superintendent on the reserve, he examined a late prehistoric Neutral village on the Baptiste farm and a nearby encampment where 'a line of ash-beds' some twelve hundred feet in length could be traced.[64] Later, he teamed up with a local collector, Cyrenius Bearss, who farmed near Port Colborne, and travelled to Point Abino on Lake Erie in Bertie Township, Welland County 'To many people in this country,' Boyle wrote, 'it is a source of wonder where the Indians procured their "flint," but to the dwellers along the eastern end of Lake Erie this matter is plain. Immense quantities of chert are found in the limestone forming the outcrops near the shore ... For miles along the sandy beach heaps of flakes may be seen ... [Here] the Indian fletcher carried on his trade both for "home and foreign consumption," as relics of this kind are found in all parts of the country corresponding in appearance with the Lake Erie material.'[65] Near these sources of flint, Bearss directed Boyle to the site of a historic Neutral encampment where they found evidence of

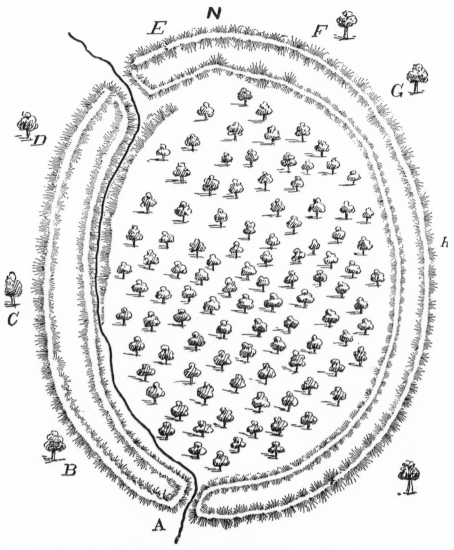

The Southwold earthworks (*Archaeological Report 1890–1*)

several longhouses, one of which, judging from the ash-beds, may have been some 360 feet in length.[66]

In mid-June Boyle headed north to Victoria County to spend several days with George Laidlaw at his ranch, 'The Fort,' located on Balsam Lake on the Trent system of inland waters. Laidlaw had discovered three prehistoric/

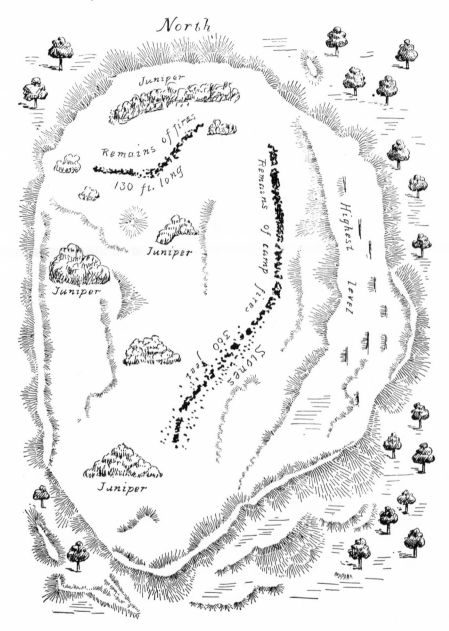

Point Abino village site (*Archaeological Report 1890–1*)

early-protohistoric village locations, the most promising of which (today the Coulter site) lay on his property. Here Boyle unearthed considerable potsherds and several bone needles, and located two rows of single graves, about twenty in total, the skeletal contents of which had badly decomposed. Because of 'the situation, depth, order and regularity' of these graves, he thought that the people responsible for them were not Huron who normally buried their dead in communal graves on high ground. The advanced stage of bone decomposition suggested 'that the bodies were placed here long anterior to the beginning of the seventeenth century, a period we can fix with certainty in connection with some Huron ossuaries in which the bones may still be found in a comparatively sound condition.' From his analysis of Balsam Lake ceramic styles, he noted 'a curious blending of the Huron with something that appears to be of a different origin,' and hypothesized that the people who made the pottery might possibly have been an early 'branch of the Huron themselves.'[67] Eventually the absence of ossuaries in the area led Boyle to the conclusion that the Balsam Lake people were Algonkians, possibly the Cheveux Relevés. To explain the apparent Iroquoian influences on the Balsam Lake ceramic styles, he invoked the concept of diffusion. 'We know quite well that the Hurons were in frequent alliance with neighboring Algonkin peoples,' he explained; consequently, 'there must have been a considerable amount of intercourse between those of different stocks.'[68]

George Laidlaw, a trifle less cautious than his mentor, went a step further in his interpretation of the data, and it was to Boyle's credit that he was willing to permit him to state his case. Laidlaw believed that the ceramic fragments of Balsam Lake might be linked to the pottery styles of the St Lawrence Iroquois, or 'Hochelagans' as he called them. His hypothesis was not un-informed speculation; rather, it was based on a careful comparative analysis of the existing published literature. 'It is evident,' he concluded, 'from the different modes of burial and from other minor details, that this country was inhabited by a people which were absorbed or exterminated by the Hurons, or else they sought shelter with the Hurons from the savage forays of the Iroquois. This people may or may not have been the Hochelagans of Cartier; the evidences rather show that they were.'[69]

The Balsam Lake findings opened a pandora's box of questions as to the migration and fusion of peoples in late prehistoric/early-protohistoric south-east Ontario. 'It is not definitely known how the Hurons got to their country,' Laidlaw explained. 'If they came from the east they probably occupied this region for a period in their westwardly drift; or they may have come into their own country from the west, conquered this people [around Balsam Lake], and assimilated the survivors at a period previous to their being known to the whites.' Another possibility was that the area 'may have been the westerly limit of the Hochelagans, who, according to [J.W.] Dawson, [principal of McGill University (1855–93), and author of *Fossil Men and Their Modern Representatives* (1880)], inhabited the Island of Montreal and the country to the north and west of the St. Lawrence. From this tribe the Hurons may have sprung and survived.'[70] Before these questions could be answered definitively, however, Laidlaw recognized that the area between Balsam Lake and the Ottawa River, and south to Lake Ontario, 'will stand a great deal of investigation.' Ninety years after Laidlaw penned these words, the 'investigation' is still far from complete, and the debate still goes on over the identity and origins of the prehistoric peoples who lived in Victoria County and their relationship both to the Huron and the St Lawrence Iroquoians. Significantly, Laidlaw's 'Hochelaga hypothesis' is now seen by some archaeologists as a benchmark in the development of our understanding of Ontario Iroquoian prehistory; yet, it was not until after the Second World War that university-trained scholars began to pursue the implications of his statements and to suggest answers to the questions he raised.[71]

George Laidlaw emerged as one of David Boyle's most reliable and gifted co-workers. In addition to his diligent surveys and excavations, artifact analysis and interpretation, this popular rancher and reeve of Bexley Township in Victoria County publicized his archaeological work through the weekly newspapers and elicited donations on the Canadian Institute Museum's behalf from dozens of people in his community.[72] On the occasion of Boyle's visit to 'the Fort' in June 1890, Laidlaw in turn, gave most of his private collection to the museum. With the Laidlaw collection in his possession, Boyle returned to Toronto flushed with his good fortune. This was the third major donation of the season, for in addition to the Laidlaw and Tweedale collections, W.G. Long of Lansing, York County, had placed in Boyle's care six hundred specimens gathered from four townships.[73] By this time Boyle had come to recognize that artifact types were unique to different tribes and regions across Ontario. He now understood that 'a critical examination of minor variations in form, finish or material, is often sufficient to enable a conclusion to be arrived at relative to the local or tribal origin of a given specimen.' This result was particularly true of pottery, he wrote. 'Within certain limits one may distinguish even by means of a small fragment what is characteristic of certain areas.'[74] Already these perceptions had begun to influence Boyle's classification of the archaeological record along geographical lines as he set aside a special case to display the Clearville specimens.

Early in June 1890 Boyle travelled to the historic and scenic town of Niagara-on-the-Lake to attend a special summer session of the Canadian

Institute. That the institute was meeting there in the first place can be credited to Boyle and A.F. Chamberlain. Recognizing that the institute could more effectively promote its objectives and boost its membership if it became known to more people, they had urged that occasional meetings be held outside the provincial capital.[75] At Niagara-on-the-Lake Boyle presented his paper 'Archaeological Remains, A Factor in the Study of History,' which provided his new audience with an overview of his work and a reminder that 'the Niagara peninsula is but scantily represented' in the cabinets of the museum. Following the Niagara meeting, he set off for Midland and the ruins of Ste Marie, the Jesuit missionary centre established in 1639 to minister to the Huron confederacy. From Midland he pushed north and cursorily investigated several sites near Parry Sound.

In describing this trip in the *Archaeological Report*, Boyle raised a theme that would become increasingly central to his public relations efforts – the preservation of historic and prehistoric sites. It distressed him to see Ste Marie, a place that formed 'a closely connecting link through the French, between ourselves and the Hurons,' desecrated by relic hunters. 'Can anything be done to preserve it from further speedy decay? We have no castles, or keeps, or feudal mansions to connect us with the past of our country. We have no legendary lore to excite our wonder or to test our credulity ... The wish to maintain all that is left of a once famous structure is not childish, nor foolish, nor retrograde.' For Boyle, who had been raised on tales of Scottish heroism and awestruck by the grand ruins that dotted the landscape of Scotland, patriotism based on knowledge of the past was an essential ingredient of any national sentiment. 'Throughout Europe, historic ruins are regarded by the people with feelings of veneration as well as pride. Parents and grandparents,' he reflected with his own childhood in mind, 'delight to tell their oft told tales in connection with the days of yore, pointing to the cairn, or the cromlech, or the mouldering walls in the neighbourhood, to attest the truth of the uncanny, but veracious (or otherwise) stories, and in this way the young folk have their interest awakened or incited in the history of their own country, and are all the better for it.'[76]

Boyle was not advocating an expensive reconstruction of Ste Marie, but rather the simple preservation and maintenance of the ruins. 'Might not the enterprising Midlanders make a move in this direction?' he asked. 'The accomplishment of such a work would be a credit to them. Four hundred dollars, perhaps less, would prove ample to buy the land, fence it, restore the outline of the fort, and erect a tablet setting forth in brief the history of the spot.' By raising the issue in the *Archaeological Report* he hoped to prick the conscience of local citizens and politicians for neglecting the place. He realized that local initiative was essential if such sites were to be preserved, especially after the provincial government had declined to introduce heritage conservation legislation along the lines of the British Ancient Monuments Act as suggested by the Canadian Institute several years earlier.

Considering the importance he attached to the site, Boyle went several steps further in an effort to stimulate local interest. He approached A.F. Hunter about the possibility of arranging for a special session of the Canadian Institute in Simcoe County, and for the creation of a historical society as the preliminary steps in a campaign to save Ste Marie.[77] Henry Scadding, then in the midst of organizing a province-wide network of pioneer and historical associations, seconded Boyle's suggestions. Consequently, for a year Hunter discussed the idea of a historical association in the Barrie *Examiner* before establishing the Simcoe County Pioneer and Historical Society in November 1891. Just prior to its formation, the Canadian Institute had met in summer session at Penetanguishene and Christian Island where the delegates resolved to pressure the various levels of government to preserve the remains of both Ste Marie I and II.[78] Regrettably nothing came of all these efforts. The historical group in Barrie attracted only a handful of active members, and they chose to expend their energies and limited funds researching their pioneer ancestors and publishing the results. For his part, Boyle unsuccessfully memorialized the various township and municipal authorities in the region, and even mooted the idea of the Canadian Institute purchasing the site of Ste Marie through public subscription. His proposals fell on deaf ears.[79] Had the place been connected with loyalist or pioneer heroics, or the War of 1812, his chances of success would have improved. Alas, late-nineteenth-century Ontarians in this era of imperialist ardour, 'Equal Rights,' and Protestant Orange bigotry showed little interest in the remains of an old French Jesuit missionary outpost. Ste Marie would have to await a more sympathetic generation before knowing happier days.

If Ste Marie topped Boyle's list of sites worthy of preservation, the Southwold earthworks ran a close second. 'When we consider how few really well preserved land-marks of the original people remain in Ontario it is deplorable to think that in a few years this earthwork with all its distinctive characters [sic] will be levelled in the course of cultivation ... One cannot help wondering why municipal corporations ..., scientific bodies, or wealthy individuals do not make some effort to preserve all that is possible of such extremely interesting works.'[80] Boyle cited the example of Frederic Ward Putnam, curator of the Peabody Museum, who in 1886 had persuaded a group of Boston women to organize a fund drive on the museum's behalf to purchase and to care for the great Serpent Mound in Adams County, Ohio.

Why could not local people do the same in Elgin County? Boyle asked. 'The Southwold earthworks, though less extensive, are quite as interesting in relation to the anthropology of Ontario as is the Serpent Mound to that of Ohio ... The works cover an area little exceeding three acres, the purchase of which with the right of access, need not cost a very large sum.'

Though no group rushed to act upon Boyle's suggestion to purchase the earthworks, local effort did play a significant part in the protection of the site over several decades. In April 1891 there appeared the Elgin Historical and Scientific Institute in St Thomas, under the presidency of James H. Coyne, the county registrar. In part, at least, thanks to Boyle's prompting, the new society had as one of its primary objectives 'the investigation of Indian forts and mounds, and their preservation as far as practicable.'[81] Almost immediately, W.E. Campbell, an engineer and one of the members of the institute, prepared a survey plan of the earthworks and presented a copy to Boyle. Meanwhile, James H. Coyne wrote a splendidly researched paper entitled 'The Southwold Earthwork and the Country of the Neutrals' which appeared in the *Archaeological Report for 1892–3*. For some forty years, until the property was acquired by the dominion government and incorporated into the national parks system, the Elgin Historical and Scientific Institute acted as a self-appointed guardian of the site.[82]

After the journey to Midland and Parry Sound in the summer of 1890, Boyle had no thought of undertaking another major archaeological expedition that year until he received word in early September from Alexander Robertson, a correspondent in Madoc, of a possible undisturbed ossuary in the northern extremity of Addington County. If there were indeed an ossuary in this remote area, Boyle knew it would be a unique and important find. Quickly, he contacted A.F. Chamberlain and set out by Grand Trunk Railway to Belleville, then north by rail (picking up Alexander Robertson *en route*) to the hamlet of L'Amable, just south of Bancroft in Hastings County. With 'tent, food, cooking utensils and spades' stowed in a two-horse rig, they set off on a grueling four-day, sixty-mile return trip to Weslemkoon Lake in north Addington. The going in the Shield country was brutal. 'Up and down hills frightfully steep, over rocks acres in extent, across corduroy bridges and "swampaducts,"' skirting innumerable lakes – and all, it turned out, for nothing! They found a site on a plateau near the lake, 'marked by broken bones, but in such fragmentary condition that it was impossible to say whether they were those of human beings or of other animals.' This, it appears, had long passed for an ossuary in local folklore.[83]

Frustrated, yet determined not to return to Toronto empty-handed, they made their way back to Bancroft to meet Dr T.A. Beeman, who guided them to Baptiste Lake where a small band of Algonkian Indians resided. Here Boyle observed a birch-bark canoe being constructed in the traditional fashion and recorded the various steps in this soon-to-be-lost art for the *Archaeological Report*. Later, while A.F. Chamberlain talked at length on matters of philology and tribal legend with the chief of the band, François Antoine (*Ag-wah-setch*),[84] Boyle paddled to the western end of the lake and superficially examined a prehistoric Algonkian campsite on Grassy Point. Two miles distant on the south shore, he scampered 120 feet straight up a cliff face to investigate a cave that figured in local Algonkian mythology, but found nothing of significance. Although something of a lost cause archaeologically, this trip had proved one thing: at forty-nine years of age, his migraine headaches notwithstanding, David Boyle remained in sound, if not vigorous health, and was not so close to the deathbed as he had imagined earlier that year.

After the very full 1890 season, it is not surprising to find Boyle retracing his steps the following spring to complete work left undone the summer before. In May 1891 he revisited the Southwold earthworks to complete the preliminary excavation hampered by the weather during his first visit. While in Elgin County, he also inspected, on the Pound farm in Malahide Township, a prehistoric earthwork village site now dated to about 1400 AD, its earthworks almost ploughed level; and on the Dalby farm, two mounds, each twenty-five feet in diameter, which he concluded were kitchen-middens.[85] Subsequent intensive cultivation obliterated all traces of these earthworks, and had Boyle failed to document their location, they would have been lost to the archaeological record.

Apart from the journey to Elgin County, Boyle devoted the remainder of his field-work in the 1891 season to the relatively neglected eastern portion of the province. Upon receipt of a letter from Arthur Brown, a public school inspector in Dundas County, he hastened to Morrisburg in Williamsburg Township. A few miles outside town he discovered the remains of what he considered to be 'the most easterly circular embankment in Ontario' – the remains of a mid-fifteenth-century prehistoric St Lawrence Iroquois village known today as the Beckstead site. One elderly local resident recalled seeing the place in 1816 when the earthworks stood three feet high and enclosed an area of about five acres. 'All that remains,' wrote Boyle, 'is a few feet of the bank ..., so inconspicuous ... that none but persons who know of its former connection would regard it as other than a hummock ... Having cut a section through it, however, the evidence was conclusive that the earth had been thrown up artificially, besides which, we found fragments of pottery at various depths as low as three feet.'[86]

That summer Boyle also had cause to revisit Baptiste Lake near Bancroft in Hastings County when informed by Dr T.A. Beeman of the discovery there of a large Indian burial ground. 'I am sorry that before I succeeded in reaching it,' he reported, 'a number of amateurs had so destroyed the surface marks and disturbed the graves that my examination was not nearly so satisfactory as I could have wished.' Still, the site justified his trip north since he found about forty graves, 'all single and arranged in rows ..., some being encircled on the surface with stones placed close to each other, and some having no such arrangement.' From the burial practices and grave goods, many of which were European made, Boyle concluded that the site was historic Ojibwa. 'Taken altogether,' he explained after studying and arranging the artifacts later in the fall, 'the case containing the material from the shore of Baptiste Lake is one of the most complete and, therefore, most interesting and instructive in the museum. The bone tools are dissimilar to anything else we have ..., and I have not seen anything like them figured or described elsewhere.'[87]

Later that summer Boyle once again returned to eastern Ontario, this time to Addington County where he teamed up with Dr M.I. Beeman of Centreville, and Dr T.W. Beeman of Perth to examine several sites in the Varty Lake area. The Beemans of Bancroft, Centreville, and Perth, all medical men, were the Canadian Institute's staunchest allies in the region. They stimulated an interest in archaeology among dozens of people and, like George Laidlaw in Victoria County, convinced many of their acquaintances to give up their specimens to Boyle. The Beemans also subsidized archaeology by playing host to Boyle when he visited them, thereby cutting down on his expenses, and by introducing him to local luminaries such as John W. Bell, ex-MP for Addington, and Peter McLaren, a senator and wealthy lumberman, who extended many courtesies and assistance.

T.W. Beeman of Perth emerged as the most serious amateur archaeologist of the three, and spent his summers surveying and examining sites along the Tay River and the shores of Rideau Lake in Lanark and Leeds. His efforts were facilitated by Mrs Peter McLaren who often placed her steam yacht, the 'Géraldine,' at his disposal. The first record of his valuable field-work appeared in the *Archaeological Report for 1891*. He wrote:

From all appearances the Rideau seems to have been the principal Indian resort as here are found in greatest quantities, evidences of an occupation that must have been extended over a great length of time ... [There] is a marked difference in the weathering of different specimens. The pottery also shows two different periods of time, and possibly two distinct peoples. As a rule the older pottery was far superior in make and ornamentation to the newer ... About the lake, every bit of sandy beech [sic] on the banks along the mouth of a stream emptying in the lake, was sure to yield large numbers of specimens. Following up the streams, every small lake showed one or more old village sites.[88]

The area, in fact, was giving up ground slate points and gouges that subsequent archaeologists would date back to the Archaic period (ca. 5000–1000 BC), and other artifacts characteristic of Middle and Late Woodland cultures.

With the season's field activities complete after the trip to Addington in the summer of 1891, Boyle returned to Toronto to face a busy autumn of administrative and curatorial duties. The correspondence generated by his public relations efforts had increased considerably and now 'occupied an unusually large portion of time … Many of the letters received are from farmers and young people; from the former, generally, with regard to features observed on the farm, and from the latter, asking for information about specimens they have found, and where they may procure books that will lend them assistance in … the study of archaeology.' The schoolteacher in Boyle demanded that he write to each youngster a lengthy handwritten note of encouragement and guidance. 'In a large number of cases correspondents ask for copies of our reports, but these, I am sorry to say, we cannot always send as the issue [2000 annually] is too small to supply the increasing demand. During no other period since the commencement of this work have so many requests and invitations been received to go here and there for the purpose of examining this or that locality. Only want of time and means has prevented this being done in many cases.'[89]

Beyond his archaeology-related activities, Boyle sought to supplement his meagre income over the winter of 1891–2 by writing a book on elementary educational theory and practice entitled *Hints and Expedients: A Pocket Book for Young Teachers*.[90] John W. Bengough, the brilliant political cartoonist and editor of *Grip*, cleverly illustrated the volume with pen and ink drawings. In this work, completed in February 1892, Boyle made use of his entire stock of practical and proven teaching techniques and threaded them together with what amounted to the fullest and clearest expression of his version of the Pestalozzian method. Remembering his own struggle to find his way in the one-room schoolhouse of Upper Pilkington, he wrote the volume primarily for the young, inexperienced rural teachers of the province. The book did not become a best seller or provide its author with substantial royalties; nevertheless, it was a labour of love that he would have repeated without a qualm.

As Boyle penned his *Archaeological Report for 1891*, he reflected upon a development about which he was justly proud. It gave him great pleasure to watch the blossoming talents of Hunter, Laidlaw, and Beeman, all of whom he considered his protégés. They were a new breed of amateur archaeologist, people of 'true scientific instinct' and not mere 'curiosity hunters' – serious students who conscientiously devoted 'attention to the literature of archaeology generally, as well as to its scientific bearings from the points of view afforded by their own localities.'[91] So seriously did these individuals take their archaeological avocation that they genuinely felt guilty if they happened to fall behind in their reading. 'It is something even to incite or foster a praiseworthy sentiment of this kind,' Boyle had earlier explained to the minister of education, 'and the Canadian Institute has the satisfaction of knowing that it has done much in that direction.'[92] In the history of Ontario archaeology, Hunter, Beeman, and Laidlaw were transitional figures between the antiquarianism of an earlier generation and the professionalism of the next.

Had modesty not stood in the way, Boyle might well have continued chronicling his achievements since joining the institute seven years earlier. He had taken up where his precursors had either failed or left off. Boyle had lobbied for and acquired operational funds; he had established the first journal in Canada devoted exclusively to archaeology, a scientific journal free of the speculative nonsense of the past. In the field, he had done extensive work himself, including excavations and site surveys, and had managed to stimulate others to do likewise. A small but professionally administered museum of Ontario archaeology had become a reality. Boyle and his new breed of amateurs, supported by a host of antiquarian collectors, were busily assembling the foundation of data upon which scientific archaeology and sound interpretation could be built. Already he had established a good reputation among the North American archaeological community. He had been one of the first people in the province, and was certainly the most vocal, to advocate the preservation of archaeological sites; similarly, he had denounced the unregulated export of the province's prehistoric heritage by foreign collectors and had nurtured a public conscience about such activities. And on top of all this, he had generated a wider interest, if not understanding, among the educated public about Ontario's archaeology. It was a remarkable record of achievement for just one man working on a shoestring budget and within such a short period of time.

v

As Boyle put the finishing touches to his *Report for 1891*, and to *Hints and Expedients for Young Teachers*, he finally received the news for which he had been waiting since the Cincinnati Exposition in 1888 – the Ontario government again required his services, this time to prepare a geological exhibit for permanent display at the Imperial Institute in London, England. This appointment was most welcome since it relieved him, temporarily at least, of his financial worries. He had been complaining for years to his friends that the Mowat administration had unfairly overlooked him in favour of less qualified 'Grits' when it came to the dispensation of jobs related to geology. 'Let me tell you a "good one",' he had written to Charles Clarke in July 1890. 'About three weeks before the elections a great big somewhat aged gentleman called on me saying that he had been appointed by the Government to go and visit all the mines in the province for the purpose of collecting information as to capacity, resources, etc., etc., and that he had been told that I would post him as to localities, routes, and owners and personally aid him in his quest. He also said that although he was appointed, the fact was not to be made known until after the election.' After perusing a few pages of one of Boyle's reference sources on minerals, the visitor came to the subject of nickel and exclaimed: ' "Nickel, that's a mineral too is it not?" His name is Slaght, ... a Baptist Minister from Simcoe County ... This was a job that would have suited me,' Boyle remarked, 'especially as I have been all over the ground two or three times. Cuss 'em.'[93]

The provincial government's decision to establish a mining exhibit in London, England, represented one element of an emerging strategy to promote economic growth in northern Ontario. It was a policy shaped by the Royal Commission on Mining appointed in 1888, which, after travelling the length and breadth of the province, had waxed poetic about Ontario's untapped mineral resources and the potential for the growth of new towns, trade and commerce, investment, jobs, and the opening of hitherto untouched tracts of the Laurentian Shield.[94] The commission recommended in 1890 that the government revise its mining legislation and take a variety of initiatives to educate domestic and foreign capital and to assist the private sector to develop the province's mineral wealth. On the basis of this advice, the Mowat administration appointed Archibald Blue in 1891 to organize a Bureau of Mines (1892), established a School of Mines in Kingston (1893), and provided technical training to miners and prospectors in northern Ontario communities. With the object in view of attracting British investors and buyers to New Ontario, the government decided to display its minerals at the Imperial Institute in London. Doubtless, it was people like Archibald Blue and William Hamilton Merritt, both close friends of Boyle in the Canadian Institute and both members of the mining commission, who reminded those who controlled the patronage strings of the splendid job Boyle had done in Cincinnati, and thereby helped to gain him the appointment.

Another arduous task demanding Boyle's attention that summer was the removal of a large portion of the specimens from the Canadian Institute on Richmond Street for exhibition in the Toronto Public Library at the corner of Church and Adelaide streets. As early as 1889, Boyle had complained that the third-storey location at the institute was unsatisfactory owing to 'the impossibility of having it thrown open to the public at reasonable hours. There are probably thousands of people in this city,' he had complained, 'who are totally unaware that there is even a small collection of such objects; ... few throughout the province know of its existence, and tourist visitors never hear it mentioned.'[95] At the time, these considerations were not sufficient to prompt any changes. Not until 1891, by which date the archaeological collection (composed of about 15,000 specimens) had outgrown its accommodation, did the institute executive address the museum problem. Then, through the treasurer, James Bain, also the chief librarian for Toronto, a tentative agreement was made to place the entire archaeological section under the auspices of the public library board. However, adverse reaction at city council soon put an end to this plan. According to Boyle, one prominent alderman 'declared ... that he would not give twenty-five cents for all the old bones [the museum] contained!'[96] After this rebuff by the city fathers, the institute and the public library board worked out an alternative scheme whereby a portion of the specimens would be displayed in the central library. Boyle was delighted that the public would now be able to view the collection 'all day, and not only during afternoons as formerly.' Despite the improvement, it did not escape him that even this situation could only be viewed as a temporary solution. 'Extension can proceed but little further under the ... arrangement,' he explained, 'and increased accommodation must, before long, be found here or elsewhere.'[97]

Initially Boyle had hoped to complete his various curatorial and geological tasks in time to undertake some archaeological field-work during the late summer months of 1892. But no sooner had he solicited and prepared the mineral specimens for shipment to the Imperial Institute, and designed a 'colossal map' of Ontario depicting the various mining regions (it caused a minor sensation when displayed in London), than his services were required for at least another year in the cause of mining promotion. In anticipation of the World's Columbian Exposition scheduled to open in Chicago, Illinois, on 1 May 1893, the government appointed him superintendent of the mineral exhibit planned for this much-heralded event. Since the organizers of this world's fair had also provided for an Anthropology Building, and planned for a major international conference on anthropology in August 1893, the minister of education agreed to appoint Boyle superintendent of an archaeological exhibit as well, the displays of which were to be prepared from the collections in the Canadian Institute Museum.

As far as the mining exhibit was concerned, Boyle felt that he had the job well in hand. Based on his earlier experiences, he anticipated no trouble soliciting specimens from the mining companies for what he intended to be a spectacular exhibit of all the commercially valuable mineral material known to exist in Ontario. Already the nucleus of a collection lay at his disposal in the form of duplicate pieces assembled earlier that year for the Imperial Institute, as well as the material from the Cincinnati Exposition still on display at the Queen Victoria Niagara Falls Park. Despite these initial advantages, Boyle's complacency was soon shattered by the mine operators, who virtually ignored the five hundred circulars mailed out requesting the loan of specimens. Evidently these businessmen had grown weary of repeated demands from bureaucrats in Toronto and sceptical of the benefits to be derived from geological exhibits. 'This apparent reluctance to act, on the part of so large a number,' Boyle explained, 'rendered it imperative to spend much of the available time in travelling over the province for the purpose of coming into personal contact with the owners of mines and mining properties.'[98] In a mild state of panic, he set off to cover the ground from the Ottawa Valley to Fort William along the CPR main line, then later moved down through the counties of Peterborough, Hastings, Addington, Frontenac, Lanark, and Renfrew before swinging back to a few locations in the south-western part of the province. To his great relief, upon his return to Toronto, the prospectors and mine and quarry owners to whom he had spoken inundated him with thirty-five thousand specimens varying from less than an ounce to twelve thousand pounds each, with an aggregate weight of fifty tons! Of these, Boyle selected fifteen hundred pieces for the exhibit. An inordinate amount of preparation went into the design of the displays. The smaller specimens had to be arranged in glass table cases, the larger ones shaped into polished cubes of various sizes according to regulations laid down by the exposition authorities. Knowing what to expect in Chicago, Boyle planned on going beyond the normal display method of providing simple labels indicating the mine and location of each specimen. He prepared a sixty-four-page catalogue for distribution that afforded 'an ample fund of information relative to sources and extent of supply, varieties, analyses, and exhibitors with their post office addresses. With this object in view,' he explained, 'each specimen was designated by a number painted upon it for ease of reference in the catalogue.'

The introduction to this publication quoted freely from the optimistic report of the mining commission of 1890. For the more casual visitors to the exhibit, Boyle worked on another huge wall map, twelve by eighteen feet, illustrating the geological features, mines, railways, and principal urban centres, and providing a plethora of information on the social and economic condition of Ontario. 'All the printed matter,' he noted, 'was legible at a distance of thirty feet.'[99]

The Ontario mineral exhibit in the Palace of Mines at the World's Columbian Exposition, which opened on 1 May 1893, was truly something to behold. At the centre of a court, occupying 150 square feet, stood a spectacular nickel display 'containing at its base samples of the ore, weighing some thousands of pounds each; surmounting this were cones of matte, and crowning all was a magnificent specimen of the pure metal, weighing 4,600 pounds.' Around this impressive trophy provided by the Canadian Copper Company of Sudbury, Boyle arranged a collection of multi-coloured polished marble pillars, and three circular terraced pyramidal stands, seven feet high and lined with plush, two of which were set aside for a grand petroleum-products display. Prominently located on one of the petroleum pyramids stood a bust of that most slippery of politicians, Sir John A. Macdonald, modelled out of paraffin wax by the Toronto sculptor Hamilton McCarthy. Stand upon stand of polished cubes of stone, massive sheets of mica, myriad fertilizer products, 'heaps of gold ore' stacked close to the main entrance, large samples of iron ore, and some 150 square feet of glass table cases containing smaller and valuable mineral pieces, boggled the imagination of the public. All of this Boyle decked out with dozens of flags, carefully designed maps, framed photographs, decorated wooden archways, carved shields bearing the provincial coat-of-arms, several 'excellent heads of the common deer,' and an 'enormous and handsomely mounted moose head,' under which was hung rather unceremoniously the mandatory portrait of Her Majesty, Queen Victoria. The commissioner in charge of all the Ontario displays at the exposition, Nicholas Awrey, MPP, was ecstatic over Boyle's creation. 'The results show,' he reported, 'that no more efficient and pains-taking man could have been found to do the work.'[100] That the judges awarded thirty-four prizes to various aspects of this one exhibit was further testimonial to the quality of Boyle's efforts.

At the very least, the mineral exhibit in Chicago served to awaken people outside the province to the potential of Ontario's mineral resources. Some one million visitors trooped through the mineral court. 'The immediate results were all that could be reasonably wished for or expected,' wrote Boyle. 'From a purely educational standpoint the effect was good. Here, for the first time, did a large number of people learn something about our province, its extent, capabilities and resources. The variety and abundance of our minerals proved to many little short of a revelation.' In addition to the many tourists, 'thousands of explorers, miners, manufacturers and capitalists found here special objects of consideration, and it is safe to say that the collection ... attracted more than the average amount of intelligent attention.'[101] Commissioner Awrey added: 'No foreign government represented at the Exposition failed to send experts ..., the result of which will be, I have no doubt, the investment of large sums of foreign capital in developing the northern section of our country.' Awrey was also delighted that during the exposition 'the scientific journals of New York and Pittsburgh devoted a great amount of space' to the subject of Ontario's nickel and iron ore fields. Finally, the exhibit also generated dozens of inquiries and a large correspondence between Chicago and the mine owners of Ontario.[102]

David Boyle thoroughly enjoyed his work at Chicago. Many years later, one of his friends, R.M. Haseltine, chief inspector of mines for Ohio, upon receiving a photograph of a pipe-smoking Boyle with feet on desk at the museum in Toronto, remembered some of the good times they had enjoyed together. 'The easy posture reminds me forcibly as you appeared in the office of the Ontario Mining Exhibition at the World's Columbian Exposition,' remarked Haseltine, 'and recalled the many pleasant hours I spent in that historic room consuming tobacco and exchanging ideas. I am not unmindful of the exhilarating influences that I imbibed from the little brown jug in the cubbord [sic].'[103]

As the exposition drew to a close on 31 October 1893, Boyle found himself swamped with requests for exchanges of specimens. 'The result is,' he reported in January 1894, 'that the province is now in possession of valuable mineral material from many parts of the world at a comparatively trifling cost.' Upon the return of the exhibit to Toronto, he was assigned the task of distributing much of the collection between the School of Practical Science at the University of Toronto, the new School of Mines in Kingston, the Toronto Technical School, and the Imperial Institute in London, England. 'No better disposition could possibly be made of such material, but,' he added, never one to miss an opportunity to speak out for museum development in Toronto, 'it is extremely desirable that in the capital of the Province there should be a [museum] collection of all our minerals *for the use of the people*, as well as for examination by prospectors and capitalists.'[104]

In his capacity as superintendent of the Ontario archaeological exhibit at the World's Columbian Exposition, David Boyle received further accolades for his performance from Commissioner Awrey. 'In archaeology Ontario was once more to the front as the only province having an exhibit.' Mr Boyle, Awrey noted, 'secured honors, only second to the Smithsonian Institute [sic]' – a reference to the prize diploma and medal of excellence awarded to the Ontario display. 'Our exhibit was not large,' Boyle reflected, 'but it was choice.'[105] Commercially, there was nothing to be gained from the archaeological exhibit, 'but it was thought advisable,' he explained in a burst of Ontario First chauvinism,

that our province should place itself on record as a country which, possessing the best educational system in the world, was able to stand, side by side, in such a purely scientific kind of exhibit with the most advanced nations of either hemisphere ... Students from many quarters visited the Exposition mainly to examine the contents of the anthropological building, and it would have been derogatory to Ontario should she have no place there. This was one reason, but another was the hope that many Canadians, seeing there for the first time so many beautiful specimens picked up 'at home,' might be inspired or incited to aid us in the formation of a truly worthy national collection in Toronto.[106]

In preparing the exhibit, Boyle had selected a sample of about six hundred of the best and most characteristic specimens in the Canadian Institute Museum. Since he knew that his time in Chicago would be largely occupied in the Palace of Mines, half a mile distant from the Anthropology Building, he enlisted the services of his second son, James, who had just completed his sophomore year of medical school, to arrange and label the collection. All the specimens were placed under glass in twelve handsome cherry-wood table cases, each two by six feet, set out in two double rows of six each. The space allocated to Ontario was small, but ideally located at the main entrance of the Anthropology Building. Boyle saw to it that his display struck the visitor's eye immediately upon entering the building by covering it with a multi-coloured cloth canopy supported by a tastefully designed framework of wood and iron painted in contrasting colours of deep brown and bronze. A gold-lettered glass sign declaring 'Archaeology of Ontario,' long festoons of red, white, and blue bunting, wreaths of maple leaves, several British flags, and, lacking another moose head, 'two fine portraits of Queen Victoria' provided the finishing touches to the exhibit. For distribution to the more serious students of archaeology, the minister of education authorized the publication of three thousand extra copies of the *Archaeological Report for 1892–3* which contained a catalogue of the exhibit. 'This was the only publication issued in connection with any exhibit of the kind in the Anthropological building,' Boyle proudly noted.[107]

If David Boyle had any regrets about his sojourn in Chicago, it was that his responsibilities at the Palace of Mines prevented him from attending to the visitors passing through the archaeological exhibit, and meeting those who took more than a fleeting interest in prehistory. Furthermore, he fretted over his failure to arrange as many exchanges with foreign museums as he had anticipated. He found himself frustrated at every turn by the promoters of the newly organized Field Museum of Natural History in Chicago, an institution that enjoyed the active support of the influential and persuasive Frederic Ward Putnam, the person in charge of the Anthropology Building. Despite these problems, Boyle still managed to acquire, by the exchange of mineral specimens, several hundred archaeological pieces from Illinois, Ohio, Wisconsin, Tennessee, New Mexico, and France. 'We were especially fortunate,' he noted later, 'in being able to procure by purchase for a comparatively small sum, what is, without doubt, the best collection of ancient Mexican [Aztec] relics in British America.'[108]

Perhaps the high point of the World's Columbian Exposition for Boyle was the Congress of Anthropology held in August 1893. The names of the speakers and delegates to the conference reads like a 'who's who' of American archaeology and anthropology in this period and included: Franz Boas, D.G. Brinton, F.H. Cushing, W.H. Holmes, O.T. Mason, J.W. Powell, F.W. Putnam, and Harlan I. Smith.[109] David Boyle made the most of this opportunity to renew old acquaintances and to strike new friendships. One in particular was of no little significance. 'I consider it a piece of rare good fortune to have met you in Chicago and to have assurance of your interest and sympathy in my archaeologic work,' wrote William Henry Holmes of the Smithsonian's Bureau of Ethnology. 'I have just gone carefully through your various archaeologic publications in the Canadian Institute reports and am delighted with them. They are full of valuable information, and in all cases, though writing in scraps as made necessary by the annual report system, you have gone right to the root of things.'[110] Holmes, one of the outstanding figures in American archaeology, went on to request permission to cite Boyle's pottery studies and to use the illustrations of Ontario ceramic styles contained in the *Archaeological Reports* for his forthcoming manuscript on 'Aboriginal Pottery of the Eastern United States,'[111] published by the Smithsonian Institution. In this seminal work, Holmes synthesized the existing literature and systematically examined hundreds of ceramic collections for differences in style and design, materials, and methods of manufacture, and delineated for the first time the several pottery regions of the eastern United States.

In the year following the World's Columbian Exposition, the Canadian

Institute benefited in other ways as a consequence of the connections Boyle had made in Chicago. Former Principal G.S. Ramsay of the University of New Mexico in Albuquerque, who had succumbed to Boyle's charm, made a gift of some thirty specimens of Pueblo pottery, while Dr S.H. Collins of Lawrenceburg, Indiana, whose relationship with Boyle dated back to the Cincinnati Exposition, donated his private collection of about 350 specimens, mainly flints from Ohio, Indiana, and Kentucky. Furthermore, there were exchanges of artifacts with major museums like the United States National Museum in Washington, DC, Northwestern University in Chicago, and the Field Museum of Natural History. A dozen amateur and professional archaeologists also made good their promises to exchange material; these included Clarence B. Moore of Philadelphia, best known for his activities in the south-eastern United States, particularly Florida, where he located and excavated important sites while working out of his private houseboat.

On the whole, then, in spite of the fact that Boyle had devoted nearly two years of his time to his geological and mining duties, the Canadian Institute Museum had not fared badly. Actually, archaeological work in Ontario had also gone on uninterrupted thanks to the small band of ardent amateurs like Beeman, Coyne, and Laidlaw, who continued to collect for the museum and to write up the field notes of their surveys and excavations for the *Archaeological Report*. Once back in Ontario, Boyle spent the first months of 1894 completing his reports on the Chicago mining and archaeological exhibits for Commissioner Awrey, and writing and editing the *Archaeological Report for 1893–4*. Returning the geological specimens on loan to their owners, and disposing of the remainder to various repositories kept him employed until late spring.

In April 1894 Boyle was deeply grieved by the death of one of his closest friends, Joseph Workman, for twenty-one years the superintendent of the Toronto Asylum for the Insane (1854–75). The two men had first met through Charles Clarke in Elora and had come to admire each other's talents and personalities. 'Modesty,' Boyle wrote of Workman, 'was one of his most characteristic qualities – he made no pretensions to encyclopaedic knowledge – never hesitated to confess his ignorance ... A most remarkable feature was his disposition to accept and adopt new, if apparently well-founded, scientific and theological theories ... In the light of modern discovery he had no respect for moss-grown theories.'[112] Workman would have probably written precisely the same of Boyle. Over the years they had enjoyed many hours together in vigorous discussion ranging from science to literature.[113] When Susanna Boyle toiled through Trinity Medical College, Workman followed her progress with great interest, provided encouragement when it was needed, and gave her access to his own extensive library. In tribute to his friend, Boyle published a short biographical sketch entitled *Notes on the Life of Dr. Joseph Workman* (1894), read initially as a memorial address before the Canadian Institute.

With the arrival of May, David Boyle readied himself for an active archaeological season in the field pursuing the most promising leads that had reached his office during the previous two years. To his dismay, however, his plans came to naught when the minister of education refused to authorize the expenditure of the archaeological grant for that year. Boyle's letters asking for clarification went unheeded. Spring slipped into summer as he puttered around the museum now so overcrowded he could not find adequate space for his new acquisitions. Dr T.W. Beeman of Perth, who dropped in during June, became incensed to learn that many of the Lanark County artifacts were still unopened and stored in the basement of the Canadian Institute. Moved by Boyle's despair over his career and deepening financial plight, he and others wrote angry letters to George Ross protesting the withdrawal of the grant and the inadequate museum accommodation.[114] Under these baleful circumstances, it was to be expected that by July 1894 an embittered David Boyle began to think that his work as a provincial archaeologist had come to a conclusion.

6

Archaeology, history, and ethnology, 1894–8

I

Minister of Education George Ross had good reason to withhold the archaeological grant for 1894 from the Canadian Institute – the previous year's funds had been misappropriated! In Boyle's absence at the World's Columbian Exposition, the institute's executive had spent a portion of the grant for 1893 to bind pamphlets and journals in the library. Ross may have also been reluctant to subsidize an organization beginning to show the effects of lack-lustre leadership, financial problems, and declining membership. The sad truth was that a general malaise had already set in that would see all the various sections, with the exception of the biological section, fade out of existence by the end of the dacade.[1]

David Boyle was also becoming disillusioned with the institute and the lack of vision manifested by its leaders. As early as 1890, in a paper entitled 'The Canadian Institute of the Future,'[2] he had chastised the members for ignoring the problems troubling their organization. He pointed to such things as their dwindling numbers, the overcrowded conditions in the reading room, library, and museum, the inconvenient location of the Richmond Street building, and the practice of meeting on Saturday nights. His solutions were many: 'Summer and winter meetings elsewhere than in Toronto; special meetings in the rooms during the regular session, with invitation to the public; ... increased annual payments and an entrance fee; removal to larger and more conveniently situated premises, and a change in the night of meeting; failing increase of revenue and ability to secure better accommodation, to hand the library and museum over to the City Public Library, or the books alone to it, and the museum to the University.'

Not unexpectedly, the reaction to this unsolicited and controversial paper by the curator had been mixed.[3] While the members pursued some of Boyle's minor recommendations, such as the peripatetic summer meetings and the museum arrangements with the Toronto Public Library, they ignored the major proposals. The results were unfortunate, for until the institute moved north to a new building on College Street in 1905 and enjoyed a resurgence of activity just prior to the First World War, it was doomed to struggle along in a condition increasingly more dead than alive. By 1894 Boyle was thoroughly disgruntled with the institute executive for this inertia and for jeopardizing the archaeological program by misusing the government grant and incurring the wrath of the minister.

Actually George Ross probably never intended to end his department's support of archaeological endeavour. What he wanted, apart from admonishing the institute by withholding the grant, was more control over the expenditure of monies. This intent became apparent late in the summer of 1894 when Ross informed the institute that he would renew the archaeological grant, but under certain conditions. In future, he or his deputy minister would authorize major expenditures, including the curator's salary of four hundred dollars, and Boyle would henceforth report directly to the minister of education instead of to the council of the institute. 'I have entered into a new arrangement as to the Museum,' Boyle explained to A.F. Hunter some time later, 'one quite independent of the Canadian Institute (so-called). The new conditions are better than the old ones, but still far from being satisfactory – i.e., there is not a living in the business.'4

It appears also that Ross was already planning to sever his department's relationship with the Canadian Institute Museum by housing the provincially owned archaeological, science, and art collections in an expanded Ontario Provincial Museum at the normal school. For the time being, because of the lack of accommodation for the archaeological artifacts at either the institute or the Toronto Central Library, Ross discouraged Boyle from undertaking any field-work and collecting that year. Instead, Ross set him to work writing a popular synthesis of Ontario archaeology for use by the 'many teachers and others ... who are particularly desirous to know something about the Indians of our own country.'5 The outcome was Notes on Primitive Man in Ontario, completed in three months by November 1894 and printed as the Archaeological Report for 1895.

Although the bulk of Primitive Man was merely a rehash of old reports, some aspects of the volume are noteworthy insofar as they throw light on Boyle's thinking on several fundamental issues in debate among North American archaeologists. Most of his ideas were derivative, but they indicate that he was conversant with the published literature and capable of discussing it with critical understanding. One issue Boyle felt compelled to discuss was: Whence came the Indians of North America? To begin, he dismissed the possibility of an independent origin for the Amerindians; he was no poly-genesist – nor were any other Canadian anthropologists for that matter[6] – and subscribed to the idea of the unity of mankind derived from a common origin. Most scholars, he explained, believed that the Amerindians came from Asia, by way of the Bering Strait, although they disagreed on the source of the migration, some suggesting China, Japan, or Malaysia. Still others, he continued, argued in favour of a migration from Northern Europe across an ancient land bridge by way of Iceland and Greenland.[7]

Evidently Boyle's interest in this debate had been fuelled by Otis Tufton Mason, a curator with the United States National Museum, who had written 'Migration and Food-Quest: A Study in the Peopling of America' for the July 1894 issue of the *American Anthropologist*. Mason's thesis that inhabitants of the Indo-Malayan archipelago discovered North America as a consequence of a deliberate search for food made little sense to Boyle. If men came to America via the Pacific, he countered, they came by accident, courtesy of ocean currents that flowed towards the mainland.[8] Boyle leaned towards the views of such as Daniel Wilson, Cyrus Thomas of the Smithsonian, and Canadian anthropologist Horatio Hale, all of whom accepted the idea of multiple origins for the North American Indians. 'It is highly probable,' Boyle wrote, 'that a more thorough and comprehensive study of all data will ... lead to the conclusion that the continent was peopled from two sources, one part coming to the Atlantic coast, the other to the Pacific side.'[9]

After reviewing the debate over the origins of the North American Indians, Boyle attempted to relate these theories to the question of the antiquity of man in Ontario. Several years earlier, in the *Archaeological Report for 1892-3*, he had speculated that the Amerindians had been in the province a relatively long time. He based this hypothesis on the discoveries of rudely worked 'palaeolithic-like' flints by Charles C. Abbott in the Trenton gravels of New Jersey, and other alleged 'Early Man' finds in the United States.[10] While admitting that 'no authenticated discovery of co-glacial relics in Ontario' had yet been found, he believed that the proof would soon be forthcoming. However, by the time he penned *Primitive Man in Ontario*, his faith in these ideas had been shaken by William Henry Holmes, then of the Field Museum in Chicago. Holmes, explained Boyle in *Primitive Man in Ontario*, 'has recently made an exhaustive study of the Trenton gravel-beds, whence Dr. Abbott procured his specimens, and has expressed his utter disbelief in the palaeolithic character of the finds.'[11] Wisely, Boyle left the issue of 'Early Man' in Ontario in doubt, and offered no conclusions of his own. In first endorsing Abbott's theories and in accepting the credibility of the 'Early Man' finds of other American archaeologists he had stepped too hastily into a matter which, before being resolved, awaited more refined excavation techniques and rigorous scientific standards of proof. Archaeologists would remain uncertain about the antiquity of man in America until geologists had fathomed the mysteries of Quaternary geology, and established the dates of the Pleistocene period. Not until 1926, when chipped stone projectile points were found in association with extinct bison remains near Folsom, New Mexico, did the fog of confusion about the antiquity of man in this hemisphere begin to lift. [12]

Without evidence that the aborigines had inhabited Ontario for any appreciable length of time, Boyle was unable to come to grips with the chronological dimension of the province's archaeology. For the most part, Ontario prehistory remained for him an undelineated time plane of historically known tribes and their ancestors, particularly the Iroquoian-speaking peoples who inhabited southern Ontario. At the time, Boyle knew little of the prehistory of the Algonkian peoples in Ontario and virtually ignored that subject in *Primitive Man*. His main interest was the origins and migrations of the Iroquoian tribes. In addition to his own field research, Boyle's thinking on this question had been shaped by Horatio Hale, author of the widely acclaimed *Iroquois Book of Rites* (1883). Hale argued that the entire Iroquoian-speaking family shared a common origin near the mouth of the St Lawrence River centuries before European contact. As their numbers increased, dissensions arose among the various branches of the family, with the result that different bands broke off from the main group and migrated west and south. Eventually these groups settled around the Great Lakes in the territories they were known to occupy when contacted by the Europeans. 'It is probable that the Neuters or Attiwandarons were among the first to leave the main body,' Boyle suggested. 'Regarding their movement there is not even a tradition, but their situation beyond the most westerly of the Iroquois, and the fact that they had no share in the Iroquois-Huron feuds, point to an earlier and wholly independent migration.' According to Hale's analysis of Wyandot legends, the Huron, after leaving the St Lawrence Valley, migrated west along the southern shore of Lake Ontario to Niagara, but were then forced by their Iroquois enemies in New York State to relocate first in the Toronto area, before moving north to Georgian Bay. From Boyle's standpoint, this analysis would have seemed quite plausible since it reinforced A.F. Hunter's south-to-north migration theory posited in the *Archaeological Report for 1888–9*. Also, according to Hale, another branch of the St Lawrence Iroquoians arrived later in what is now Simcoe County via the Ottawa River after 'the overthrow of the Hochelagan dominion.' [13]

Boyle's overview assumed a relatively shallow time depth for the Iroquoian phase of Ontario prehistory – he spoke in vague terms of centuries. He also assumed the culture of the Iroquoian tribes to be similar and static. This view explains his statement in the *Archaeological Report for 1886–7* that 'in all the chief characteristics of aboriginal life ... there would appear to have been scarcely any difference among the tribes that inhabited this portion of Canada.'[14] Still, as he wrote *Primitive Man in Ontario*, he recognized that the prehistory of the province did not begin with the migration of the St Lawrence Iroquoians; the existence of 'a more archaic type of specimen' indicated that Ontario had been occupied for an undetermined period prior to the Iroquois. Boyle warned his readers to avoid the temptation of viewing these earlier inhabitants as the lost race of Mound Builders.[15] Just a few years earlier Cyrus Thomas's monumental work on the Mound Builders for the Smithsonian Institution, published in the *Twelfth Annual Report of the Bureau of Ethnology* (1894), established once and for all that the builders of the mounds were none other than the ancestors of the American Indians. 'There was for a long time a disposition to impose upon us a fictitiously specialized race known as the Mound Builders,' wrote Boyle in *Primitive Man in Ontario*. 'The truth is that Indians, while possessing many points of agreement in character, presented as much tribal divergence as one may find among any savage people anywhere else, and the Mound Builders were only Indians with a predilection for the construction of earth-heaps.'[16] To explain the disappearance of the earlier inhabitants of Ontario, he invoked the idea of the invasion of the various branches of what are now referred to as the St Lawrence Iroquoians, which led to the 'speedy and overwhelming extirpations of tribe by tribe as have fallen within historic scope.'[17]

This, then, in broad outline, represented David Boyle's interpretation of Ontario prehistory. From the perspective of modern knowledge, it seems an incredibly limited and flawed analysis, based too much on suspect ethnological evidence such as Hale's study of oral traditions. Archaeologists now are quite certain that the Iroquoian peoples inhabiting Ontario in historic times did not migrate into the area as Boyle thought. Iroquoian culture seems to have evolved within southern Ontario after about 500 AD as the indigenous Woodland peoples gradually became dependent on agriculture.[18] Furthermore, Boyle's synthesis lacked both a chronological dimension, and an appreciation of the presence and complexity of earlier prehistoric cultural groups and the many changes and developments they underwent over time. The historic Algonkian tribes, moreover, were mentioned only to be dismissed without the slightest hint as to their origins or antiquity.

The failure to grapple with chronology and culture sequence was typical of all North American archaeologists in the 1890s, and for good reason. Boyle and his contemporaries lacked the archaeological basis available to modern students to discuss questions of time and culture scientifically. For instance, the failure of the 'Early Man' claims to withstand critical scrutiny deprived prehistorians of the proof of the existence of a long-term sequence of cultures in North America. Also, because the concept of micro-change in culture had yet to be developed by the anthropological-archaeological fraternity in America, the data so far unearthed in Ontario did not suggest to Boyle any significant culture shifts other than those he had identified. Blithely unaware of the importance of small-scale change in culture over time, he understood culture change in gross terms, as a series of dramatic shifts from savagery to barbarism to civilisation, or from palaeolithic to neolithic.

Perhaps the most important factor inhibiting late-nineteenth-century archaeologists from coming to grips with chronology and culture sequence was the slow acceptance of the stratigraphic method. Without stratigraphy, archaeologists could not develop the concept of micro-change in culture through time, for example, by applying to potsherds stylistic and associational seriation on a similar principle. In addition, the failure of the 'Early Man' finds, the trend in anthropological circles led by Franz Boas and his students to reject cultural evolutionism,[19] and the fact that many archaeological sites, particularly in eastern North America, were not conducive to stratigraphical excavation, were further reasons why the method did not become basic to American archaeology until after 1914. Prior to this date, stratigraphical digging was undertaken only in the crudest manner, for instance, as Boyle applied it at Clearville.

II

Nearly four years had slipped away since the summer of 1891 when David Boyle last ventured into the field in the cause of Ontario archaeology. During that period correspondents had informed him of scores of sites. Finally, with the arrival of the 'digging' season in May 1895 he was permitted by the minister of education to investigate the most promising leads, particularly several earthworks that had been reported near Waterloo and Berlin (now Kitchener) and London. 'The first earthwork visited this year,' Boyle reported on what was probably the remains of a late prehistoric Neutral village, 'is in a field near the Berlin and Waterloo general hospital ... Although cultivation has to a large extent levelled the banks surrounding this village site, enough remains to show that they formed a large semi-circle enclosing about four acres.'[20] Still lacking adequate operational funds to excavate and to survey, Boyle's site research continued as in the past to be short and unsatisfactory. 'While it is desirable that [such sites] should be accurately surveyed,' he explained, 'the cost of such work has stood in the way, and I have therefore confined myself to making measurements with the tape-line, taking angles in a rough way by means of a pocket compass, and preparing drawings which give some idea of the outline and proportions of the embankments.'[21] He concluded his description of the Berlin-Waterloo earthwork with a familiar plea for its conservation 'for park purposes' by the local community. As time advances, he argued, this 'pre-historic landmark ... will be regarded with increasing interest. When it is too late, the unavailing query will be in the mouths of many, why was this not done?' How prophetic Boyle's statement proved to be, for his message went unheeded and the site subsequently disappeared without a trace. He was decades ahead of his time in his call for site preservation.

A second late prehistoric Neutral village site Boyle visited that spring – known today as the Lawson site and dating to circa 1500 AD – suffered a more agreeable fate. Located north of the city of London on what was then the Shaw-Wood farm overlooking the Medway River, this important location is now the home of the University of Western Ontario's impressive Museum of Indian Archaeology. One might have doubted this happy outcome in 1895 when Boyle arrived on the scene to make a preliminary investigation. 'The spot has long been known to relic-hunters,' he complained, 'and large quantities of what should have been valuable material, have been dug from it. Unfortunately, in most cases ..., the only object was to secure specimens without reference to any other consideration, and despite the objections of the proprietor, almost every foot of available surface has been turned over, until the original appearance of the place may only be guessed at.'[22] When Boyle returned for a second visit 'to make a somewhat thorough examination of all the ground,' he was horrified to discover that 'a few nights previously the most promising-looking spots had been attacked by a party of relic-hunters, and the ground was left in such a condition that anything one might find would possess little value.'

Angry, but not to be denied, he verified former measurements, collected surface specimens, drove trenches into the earthworks in an unsuccessful search for 'traces of stake-holes,' and examined the 'numerous hollows from three to four feet in width and averaging about a foot in depth' which he decided might have been used for storing grain. 'This place is worthy of more minute examination,' Boyle observed, 'and a survey of it should be made in such a way as to embody every detail within the area.'[23] Following this work on the Shaw-Wood property, he briefly visited the nearby township of North Dorchester in Middlesex County to examine what appeared to be another prehistoric Neutral village site, the embankments of which were still partly visible on the Jackson and Sharpe farms on concession 5.[24] Rough diagrams of both the 'Shaw-Wood' and the 'Jackson-Sharpe' sites appeared in the *Archaeological Report for 1894–5*.

On the basis of the information he had gathered over the years, Boyle considered it timely to inform his readers of his conclusions on Ontario earthworks and to cast them into a comparative framework with the more famous Ohio earth structures. 'The people who constructed earthworks in this Province,' he explained, 'never attempted anything of such huge dimensions as are found in many of the States, notably in Ohio, where there are continuous embankments enclosing hundreds of acres. Nor are our embankments comparable to theirs so far as mass is concerned, for, while, as at Fort Ancient, earth-walls rise to heights of from five to fifteen feet, it is seldom that those in this country ever exceed even the former figure ... Neither did the early inhabitants of our Province exhibit any desire to distinguish themselves, or to commemorate events, by the erection of mounds.' This last statement was surprising considering his discoveries of burial mounds in 1887 on Tidd's and Hay Islands in the St Lawrence River, and his knowledge of T.C. Wallbridge's report of dozens of mounds along the Bay of Quinte shoreline in the *Canadian Journal* for 1860. Boyle would be forced to revise his assessment the following year when he made several startling site discoveries in the Rice Lake area south of Peterborough.

The reason for the existence of all the earthworks in Ontario, he maintained in 1895, was defence. 'Situated anywhere, but especially on a plain, low banks of earth, not exceeding perhaps more than six or seven feet in height, could scarcely in themselves have afforded adequate protection by way of defence, and it is almost certain that they were constructed as the footholds or foundations of stakes or palisades, as described by Champlain, Cartier and others.' Boyle's digging technique had not yet been refined enough to be able to authenticate the existence of palisades at most earthwork sites. 'In the construction of these enclosures,' he concluded, 'advantage was taken of any natural declivity that might add to the outward height of the works, if to the extent of no more than two or three feet.' The proximity of a stream for drinking and fishing purposes, he noted, and the presence of fruit and nut-bearing trees and bushes influenced the selection of any encampment. In this analysis of Ontario earthworks, David Boyle was following the long-standing policy of North American archaeologists who considered it their first priority, as Joseph Henry stated in his *Annual Report of the Smithsonian Institution for 1874*, 'to collect all possible information as to the location and character of ancient earthworks.'[25]

With his earthwork priority out of the way, Boyle turned now to the necessity of visiting his mainstay volunteers in the field, particularly A.F. Hunter, George Laidlaw, and T.W. Beeman. Andrew Hunter, it turned out, was unavailable; having just sold the Barrie *Examiner*, he was preparing for a trip to Britain. George Laidlaw and T.W. Beeman, however, were eager to entertain Boyle and go over their new discoveries with him. Hence, during the first week in July he spent a leisurely few days in Victoria County looking over several of Laidlaw's recent finds, the most interesting of which were the dozens of shallow pits, in rows, near a village site in Bexley Township close to Victoria Road Station. 'We opened several of them to a depth of ten feet, or until the undisturbed soil was reached, but in no case was there anything to indicate a purpose in making such pits. The absence of charcoal and ashes gave no color to the supposition that they had been fireplaces, and the probability is that they were used as *caches* for corn.'[26]

Before travelling east to Perth to meet Beeman, Boyle investigated several ossuaries reported by correspondents. The historic Huron Bowman ossuary in Flos Township, Simcoe County, proved of interest in that it contained four brass Jesuit finger rings as well as other European and native relics.[27] Also of significance was the ossuary located on the Syer farm in Manvers Township, south of Lindsay in Victoria County.[28] 'The most important feature connected with this ossuary,' he noted, 'is the fact of its position so far east, and to be able to record this alone is of some value.' He cleaned out the pit completely, describing the excavation in some detail. From the nearly six hundred bundle burials Boyle retrieved 'fifty-seven very good crania' for the museum, but the pit proved barren of other archaeological data. 'Not a flake of flint, nor a fragment of pottery was seen during the two days engaged in the work of opening.' He also discovered a village site a few hundred yards away in a nearby field. As news of his dig spread through the township, Boyle learned of another ossuary on the Fallis farm which he examined briefly in inclement weather. These finds raised many questions in his mind. 'The presence of a bone-pit, or communal grave, has hitherto been regarded as sufficient proof that the district was within the territory occupied by the Hurons, but the fact that examples of ossuary sepulture are found so far away as Manvers, the nearest point of which is twenty-four miles south-east of Lake Simcoe gives rise to one or two queries. Was this within the limit of the Huron country? ... Or was this method of burial adopted by a neighbouring people? Or had this been a place of sojourn by the Hurons on their way towards the other side of Lake Simcoe?'

More complicated still was the identity of the prehistoric people who inhabited the shores of Rideau Lake in Leeds and Lanark counties. Some time during late July or August, Boyle and T.W. Beeman were the guests of Mrs Peter McLaren of Perth who put her yacht, the 'Géraldine,' at their disposal for two days to explore the archaeology of the lake, the water level of which happened to be unusually low that year. At Plum Point in North Elmsley Township and at the immediately adjacent Squaw Point in South Elmsley, Boyle examined two sites of what had evidently been 'populous and long established' prehistoric villages.[29] Almost every yard of shoreline at Plum Point, the larger of the two village sites, yielded evidence of occupation. 'The soil itself consists largely of ashes to the depth of a foot, and even more in some places.' Boyle also noted the relative scarcity of potsherds compared to village sites to the west.

Two features characterized the specimens recovered from Rideau Lake. 'One of these is the disproportionately large number of poorly finished celts or hatchets ... That ... the lack of symmetry and polish on the celts in question was not due to a deficiency of taste or skill on the part of the workman,' Boyle explained, 'is borne out by the unusually large number of well-made "gouges" produced by the same people.' Beeman, in fact, had already donated some fifty of the latter to the museum. 'Nowhere else in the province have so many tools of this kind been found in proportion to the number of other relics ... Taken altogether,' he concluded, 'the collection of gouges from this section is remarkable,' and perhaps unique 'so far as the whole continent is concerned.' Boyle recognized that the Amerindians who had fashioned these implements pre-dated the Iroquoian tribes, and concluded that they were 'a pre-Iroquoian Algonkin people.'[30] Actually, these artifacts were characteristic of the Laurentian Archaic culture and dated back to between 2000 and 3000 BC.

Perhaps the single most interesting aspect of Boyle's field-work during the 1895 season was the discovery and recording of the magnificent rock painting site on the huge granite escarpment north of the narrows of Lake Mazinaw, a site that is now part of Bon Echo Provincial Park. When told of these pictographs by Beeman, he was sceptical. 'Warned by many disappointing experiences, my belief in the existence of real rock paintings was very weak. I was prepared to see streaks and stains, the result of oxidization, but no work of human agency, although I had heard of such at this place many times during the last twenty years. It did not, however, take long to convince even the most cautious ... that the markings here were the work of ... savage man.' What had prompted Boyle after so many years to follow up the reports of the Lake Mazinaw pictographs and visit the site only accessible by canoe? Most certainly it was the recent publication of Garrick Mallery's massive eight-hundred-page manuscript, 'Picture-Writing of the American Indians,' in the *Tenth Annual Report of the Bureau of American Ethnology* (1893). This volume, which contained the results of Mallery's researches since 1876, was the first systematic attempt in North America to record and to classify Indian rock paintings; it inspired Boyle to emulate Mallery's work and to record graphically this fascinating and almost totally neglected dimension of Ontario archaeology.[31]

Boyle was spellbound by what he saw at Bon Echo; there were over a hundred painted symbols scattered along a mile of the cliff face. Even today, no other pictograph site in Ontario rivals this one in terms of the quantity of rock paintings to be found.[32] Boyle could perhaps be excused for exaggerating the significance of his find in claiming that the Bon Echo pictographs were 'among the best illustrations the world affords' of 'pictographic art' which, everywhere have 'led to the achievement of what we call Literature.'[33]

Regrettably, his attempts to photograph the paintings failed 'owing chiefly to the lack of sufficient contrast between the natural and artificial colors, even when these were distinct enough to the eye.' Anticipating this problem at the time, and taking advantage of the 'mirror-like' water and splendid weather, he and Beeman stood precariously in their canoe and rapidly pencil sketched many of the paintings. Their technique, shaped by the speed of their work, left a great deal to be desired in the quality of the sketches published in the *Archaeological Report*. Boyle sensed that his tracings of the often 'indistinct and unknown characters' were error ridden. 'One's imagination, or even his desire to see some special shape, may lead him, more or less unconsciously, to give a line a twist or a turn that another might reverse, or perhaps not observe at all.' Weather conditions, the time of day, the position of the observer each had an effect on his work so that 'even the same observer on two or more occasions might produce so-called copies wholly dissimilar from each other, and all unlike the work of another copyist.'[34] Time has shown that the Boyle-Beeman sketches do contain inaccuracies – given their lack of artistic training this result is not surprising. Nevertheless, the record they left is still considered invaluable.[35]

Boyle correctly attributed the paintings to an Algonkian people, perhaps Ojibwa since they 'exhibited a fondness for recording important events on stone, bark and skin,' and had 'attained to a higher excellence in pictography than was reached by some others of the same great division.'[36] Apart from describing the paintings and speculating what individual symbols represented, or stating that groups of symbols seemed 'to tell complete stories,' Boyle was unable to interpret the meaning of the paintings. Most of these art forms, in fact, remain unfathomable. 'If they were intended as messages,' Kenneth Kidd has suggested, 'some were probably addressed to the attention of other Indians; some to the inhabitants of the spirit world. Any which were not, strictly speaking, messages may have been memorials of one sort or another, illustrations of myths, or markers of spots of some ritual or other significance.'[37]

Owing to the extent of his responsibilities, Boyle was unable to carry on systematically his pioneer work of recording Indian rock art. During the remainder of his career, he managed to record only three more rock art sites. In June 1906 he sent his temporary assistant, W.H.C. Phillips, to examine two sites north of Lake Temagami on Diamond and Lady Evelyn lakes.[38] The following year Boyle himself ventured north to Nipigon Bay and sketched pictographs 'found at the base of a precipitous rock, some four or five hundred feet high, on the north side of the bay, about five miles east of Nipigon station on the Canadian Pacific Railway.'[39] Apart from these efforts, he could only encourage his readers to record any rock art sites that came to their attention; but none apparently did. During these years William McInnes, who had no association with Boyle, sketched some eighteen rock art sites in northern Ontario while employed by the Geological Survey of Canada. Beyond this effort, little more was done for another sixty years until the mid-1950s, when Kenneth Kidd of the Royal Ontario Museum initiated the first systematic field recording program of Indian rock paintings of the great Lakes, a program conducted by the late London artist and teacher Selwyn Dewdney.

The 1895 season in the field had been an extraordinarily active and productive one for David Boyle; some 3500 specimens had been added to the museum since the last report. Success in collecting, however, only intensified the serious problem of overcrowding at the museum. 'Cases are so close together,' grumbled Boyle, 'that two persons cannot pass each other in the spaces.'[40] He also fretted over the 'constant danger of destruction by fire, in the third storey of a very combustible building, and in a room lined with varnished wood.'[41] Working conditions at the museum had become so bad that he could barely fulfil his curatorial responsibilities. Lacking the space to incorporate the new specimens, he perforce postponed the cataloguing, and the reclassification and rearrangement of the collection. By the autumn of 1895, the situation had become intolerable. Most of the members and the executive of the Canadian Institute, more interested as they were in scientific subjects other than archaeology, turned a deaf ear to his complaints. The institute continued its slide into an abyss of lethargy and stagnation. There was no movement afoot to expand the museum or to move to another building. The membership continued to decline. The historical section, to which Boyle had belonged since its inception in February 1890, failed to meet after 1893, and the geological and mining section showed signs of following suit. A frustrated David Boyle determined to register a protest about this state of affairs and resigned from the Canadian Institute in November 1895.

His resignation was more a symbolic gesture than anything else. He continued to receive his salary through the institute since it still administered the archaeological grant for the department of education. And although Boyle had forfeited the curatorship by resigning, he continued in an unofficial capacity to oversee the archaeological collection. 'I have attended to correspondence, and interviews with visitors (sometimes by appointment) and have generally looked after the business,' he explained in June 1896.[42] Even had he stayed on as curator, it is not likely that he would have accomplished much more than he did in the way of rearranging the museum, for by February 1896 it was known that George Ross intended to expand the provincial museum at the normal school and place the archaeological collection at the institute under its auspices. Whether he had been curator or not, the rearrangement would have waited until the move to the new quarters.

Boyle was too wise to assume that the appointment as curator of the new archaeological section at the normal school museum would fall to him automatically. Prior experience with the ways of the Liberal patronage system had taught him not to take such things for granted. Thus, to lay claim to the post, he marshalled his influential associates to lobby on his behalf. Toronto journalist Alexander Fraser, a leading figure in the Gaelic Society of Canada and the Sons of Scotland, and a Liberal who had the ear of George Ross, was one of those who rallied to Boyle's side after receiving a plea for assistance. 'I have missed numerous opportunities to improve my condition,' wrote Boyle, 'and now I find myself compelled to live on a pittance of $600 a year in the City of Toronto – the salary of some school caretaker and of third rate clerks in good business houses.' As for Ross's intention 'to put another storey on the main building of the Ed. Dept. for Museum purposes,' Boyle stated 'with all due modesty' that he had earned the curator's position; 'and yet, the probability is that unless some one should intrust himself in my behalf, it will go to a better church man or a better politician than I am, and yet I prefer my mental freedom to the highest gift of ecclesiastical and political shysters.'[43]

On various occasions during 1896, friends like Fraser, T.W. Beeman, Senator Peter McLaren of Perth, and O.A. Howland, MPP for South Toronto and an avid history buff, all spoke to Ross and Premier Mowat in Boyle's favour; this support afforded him some comfort as he waited anxiously for news from the minister of education. It became apparent, though, that George Ross intended to wait until the expansion of the provincial museum neared completion towards the end of the year before announcing his choice for the curatorship of the archaeological section. David Boyle, who had earned the right to a modicum of financial and professional security, would have to suffer months of emotional turmoil before learning whether or not the politicians would allow him to continue his chosen work.

III

During the first six months of 1896 Boyle did not sit idly worrying about developments at the normal school. He continued to carry on correspondence with various archaeologists such as Stewart Culin, director of the department of archaeology and palaeontology at the University of Pennsylvania.[44] Culin relied heavily upon Boyle for data pertaining to the games of the early Canadian tribes as he prepared his manuscript of 'Games of the North American Indians,' which eventually appeared in the *Twenty-fourth Annual Report of the Bureau of American Ethnology* (1907). More importantly, throughout this period, Boyle laid aside archaeology for the most part and pursued another project; he had accepted the commission offered by the municipality of Scarborough, then a largely rural community on the eastern outskirts of Toronto, to write the centennial history of the township. The work had to be completed rapidly before the civic celebrations planned for June 1896. For a curator in limbo, the timing of this task could not have been more fortuitous.

With so little time to research and to write the Scarborough volume, Boyle relied upon local volunteer committees associated with the centennial celebrations in the township to assist him in gathering information. He also engaged the services of two accomplished women writers to prepare six of the twenty-one chapters in the book: Sarah A. Curzon, an activist for women's suffrage since the 1870s, author of *Laura Secord: The Heroine of 1812* (1879), and a founder and first president of the Women's Canadian Historical Society of Toronto (established 1895); and Mary Fitzgibbon, a granddaughter of Susanna Moodie of *Roughing it in the Bush* fame. Even with this support, Boyle had to work at a feverish pace to finish the volume on schedule, but finish it he did. Today the volume stands as a classic example of late-nineteenth-century local history, exhibiting both the best and the worst traditions of the *genre*.

The *History of Scarboro* may well be likened to a historical version of Boyle's *Archaeological Reports*, with their emphasis on reconstructing prehistoric Amerindian living conditions and socio-economic patterns, their classificatory-descriptive thrust and scientific intent. For instance, Boyle neglected traditional political themes – a significant departure in itself – and tried instead to describe for his readers the various aspects of pioneer society and economy. 'The time is past,' he wrote, 'when history was supposed to be merely a record of political events, of campaigns in the field of war, and of great discoveries. Important as these are, they do not by any means constitute the sum total of history; and hence we find considerable attention now being given to sociological features in the growth of nations; and as nations are but aggregations of communities, it would seem that intelligent citizenship implies a knowledge of facts pertaining to the development of institutions and industries in young settlements of modern, as well as of ancient date.'[45] Instead of one continuous narrative he opted for a thematic approach. Like an archaeologist classifying his data, Boyle systematically broke down his information into twenty-one short chapters on topics such as topography, archaeology, pioneers, farm life, domestic life, roads, trades, churches, schools, libraries, and so forth.

The approach taken in the *History of Scarboro* indicates that Boyle viewed history as he did archaeology, as an empirical discipline and a legitimate science. This was a relatively new conception of history, as it was of archaeology; in fact, both disciplines had been developing along parallel lines through the nineteenth century. The exponents of 'scientific' history were still refining the critical methods by which to handle the documentary sources and to establish properly 'scientific' standards. Boyle, of course, had no training of this kind and little appreciation of such critical procedures, nor for that matter did many other people at the time in Canada. Even in the university system a historical profession was only just emerging in 1896, and the writing of history had not yet been solidly established on a critical foundation of exhaustive and scrupulously accurate research methods.[46] All the same, through his wide reading of British and European history and his archaeological experience, Boyle grasped the essential approach of 'scientific' history and avoided philosophic speculation, overt bias and judgment, and lengthy commentary and analysis. He stuck to the strict presentation of his documentary information. 'No attempt has been made,' he explained, 'to produce anything but a bare statement of facts, beyond supplying introductions to the chapters, and such connective passages to the information as seemed necessary to put the material in tolerably readable form.'

In the spirit of the German historical tradition, Boyle aspired in his history to show only what really happened.[47] He transcribed document after interminable document, establishing cause and effect when required. Generalizations and conclusions he often considered unnecessary since the facts were thought to speak for themselves. Like all the exponents of the 'scientific' approach, he failed to understand that fact, theory, and interpretation were integrally related parts of any historical narrative.[48] Boyle's history was fundamentally shaped by his assumptions of progress and evolution. The book, as factual and objective as it may have seemed to him, contained a powerful underlying organizing theme and bias; it was meant to illustrate a century of gradual progress up to a glorious present. Notwithstanding these considerations of method, Boyle's *History of Scarboro* and the many similar works of local history comprise a noteworthy stage in Canadian historiography. Because the best of them were for the most part factually accurate and eschewed the bias and polemics of earlier studies, they added to that movement which marked the initial development of a critical historical scholarship in Canada prior to the First World War. These local studies, moreover, preserved an enormous amount of information which otherwise might have been lost. Again one is struck by the parallel with Boyle's work in archaeology, for one of his major contributions in that discipline was to assemble the data base upon which later generations of university-trained researchers could construct a more scientific archaeology.

In June 1896 Boyle had one more historical commitment to fulfil before turning his thoughts back to archaeology. He had promised to deliver a paper on the 'Philosophy of Folk Lore'[49] to the Hamilton meeting of the Pioneer and Historical Association of the Province of Ontario on 3 June. Collecting folklore had been one of his leisure pastimes for most of his adult life – a consequence of a happy childhood spent listening to members of his family relate the old-time tales of rural Ayrshire and the 'sons of Vulcan.' There were three varieties of folklore, he informed his audience. 'The mythical is purely fabulous; the traditional usually has at least a thin substratum of fact; and the proverbial may be referred to as condensed experience pithily expressed.' Predictably, he concluded his paper by urging people to preserve examples of this aspect of their culture. 'The folk-lore of Canada,' he explained, 'especially of Ontario, and the other western provinces, is mainly a heritage from the Mother Countries; still we are not wholly without material of the traditionary kind, quite distinct from our rich aboriginal field, and it should be the duty of some one or more persons to set about collecting these waifs and strays.' Acting upon his own advice, he did just that himself the following year and for a brief period wrote a Canadian folklore column for the Toronto *Globe* which generated considerable response from the readers.[50]

Boyle's participation at the Ninth Annual Meeting of the Pioneer and Historical Association was the beginning of a long relationship with this organization. In 1898, the provincial association would be restructured as the Ontario Historical Society with Boyle, himself, as the first secretary (1898–1907). The association had been founded in 1888 by Henry Scadding to serve as a clearing-house and lobby for the burgeoning number of local historical groups that were appearing in communities across southern Ontario.[51] No single explanation accounts for the emergence of these historical societies, some dozen of which existed by 1896. Interest in the study of history at the local level was a general North American trend, and the example of American state and local historical associations galvanized Ontarians to follow suit. The realization took hold in Ontario, as it had in the United States, that historical documents, artifacts, sites, and buildings were being neglected or destroyed at an alarming rate.[52]

Through the short-lived historical section of the Canadian Institute, David Boyle had already responded to this realization and emerged as a prominent figure in the heritage movement. Beyond his campaign to save archaeological sites, he had been involved in the successful effort in the early 1890s to pressure the department of militia and defence in Ottawa to keep the historical buildings at Fort George in better repair.[53] In 1890, he had also pushed a resolution through the historical section and led a delegation to discuss with Premier Mowat the possibility of the government underwriting the cost of publishing the correspondence of Governor Simcoe and military documents of early Upper Canada recently acquired by the Dominion Archives.[54] Boyle and others in the section such as Henry Scadding, William Canniff, and Ernest Cruikshank also urged Mowat to appoint an archivist to gather 'valuable historical documents in the possession of private families' and 'to procure the interesting relics of pioneer life for a provincial museum.' Mowat ignored these suggestions for reasons of economy but the ideas remained topical among the local history groups and were eventually pursued with considerable success by the Ontario Historical Society after the turn of the century.

Variations of the program carried out by the historical section of the Canadian Institute were undertaken by each of the local historical societies in the province with the result that they established themselves as the chief vehicles for popularizing the past in these years. They published a great deal of local history, preserved documents, erected the first monuments and plaques, organized gala historic fêtes and pilgrimages to historic sites such as the battlefields of 1812, and established the first of dozens of pioneer historical museums that remain a permanent part of Ontario culture. By the late 1890s, governments and the public became aware for the first time of the value of preserving their historical resources.[55]

All this activity did not come about simply because of the American example, or a mere desire to preserve heritage. Underlying the sudden appearance of historical societies after the mid-1880s was a complex of ideological currents, of nationalist aspirations and pride, doubts, and apprehensions. Economic depression, the apparent failure of the 'National Policy' of tariff protection, the federal Liberal party's flirtation with Commercial Union and Unrestricted Reciprocity, and the suspected machinations of the annexationist forces, ignited an explosive debate in Ontario over the future of the dominion. Arguments over annexation, independence, and the British connection became one of the great national pastimes in the late eighties and early nineties. Meanwhile, racial and religious divisions wracked the Canadian body politic as the Riel execution, the Jesuits Estates controversy, and the Manitoba school question also became bitter issues. Such a climate provided fertile ground for the historical society movement. The founders of these groups, including David Boyle, were a zealous lot who clung to the belief that history could shape a common national outlook, powerful enough to heal the rents in the Canadian social fabric and to combat the deeply feared continentalist threat by propagating the message of imperial federation.

In all their activities, most of the historical societies sought to present a view of Canadian and Ontario history (many Ontarians equated the two) that supported the notion that imperial federation was the logical end towards which Canada had been evolving since 1783. The loyalist interpretation of Canadian history became the vehicle by which many of these societies disseminated their imperialist message.[56] In brief, the tradition portrayed the loyalists as the very cream of society in the American thirteen colonies, who suffered by choice unspeakable depredations and atrocities, the loss of country and all material possessions, for the sake of high principle and religious and moral values. In particular, they adhered to the institutions and philosophy of the British constitution, and to imperial unity. During the War of 1812, according to this tradition, the Canadian militia, allegedly composed mainly of loyalists and their kin, and inspired by Isaac Brock, successfully defended, preserved, and perpetuated the principles of the British constitution and of imperial federation upon which Canada was said to be founded. Suddenly, the loyalist landing places, the decrepit military posts and the weed-choked battlefields of 1812–14 took on a new significance when presented as sacred ground, symbolic of the traditions and achievements of the country's loyalist founders.

Ancillary to this primary nationalist impulse for creating local historical societies were a number of other powerful motives. Civic boosters, especially those in the towns of the Niagara peninsula close to the battlefields of the War of 1812, used history to acquire for their communities a share of the national glory. A skirmish such as that which took place at Stoney Creek in 1812 was heralded as a 'victory that has very few equals.'[57] Feminists like Sarah Curzon and Mary Fitzgibbon of the Women's Canadian Historical Society saw in history a tool by which to promote their demands for equal rights by illustrating what a vital role women had played in the development of the nation. Personal and familial pride of accomplishment was yet another factor motivating members of the early historical societies. Some of the elderly members were pioneers themselves; others were descendants of loyalists and pioneers who sought the social status that came from being related to those who founded the province.[58]

David Boyle, in common with most who belonged to the heritage movement, subscribed to the imperialist variety of Canadian nationalism. Canada's future as a nation, he believed, lay within the matrix of the Empire, and he generally sympathized with most of the schemes – whether commercial, political, cultural, or military in nature – that promised to bring about closer imperial ties. To immunize young Ontarians from the 'infection' of continentalism, he looked to the loyalist version of history to instruct schoolchildren about the meaning of their British-Canadian identity. Boyle seemed to believe that patriotic indoctrination could be achieved even by the ostensibly unbiased 'scientific' historian simply by serving the youngsters large dollops of the facts and avoiding the 'braggart or vain-glorious spirit.' The facts would speak clearly and 'objectively' of 'one of the most brilliant and instructive histories any country could desire,' especially since the imperial heritage was an essential part of the Canadian tradition. 'The history of our Empire,' he wrote, 'is the most glorious history pertaining to any empire or republic that has ever existed. We as Britons have done more than our share in the advancement, in the civilization, in the humanizing of our race.'[59]

Some twenty years before, Boyle had already strongly identified with efforts to indoctrinate the young with patriotic attitudes based on an understanding of Canadian history. As a student and a teacher in Wellington County in the 1860s and 1870s, he had been struck by the lack of patriotic enthusiasm among the schoolchildren of his adopted country and tried in his own small way to rectify that situation in his class-rooms. At the Niagara meeting of the Canadian Institute in July 1890 he had supported the motion, inspired by a speech by the arch-imperialist spokesman William Kirby, author of *The UE: A Tale of Upper Canada* (1859), that 'Canadian history be given a more important place in the school programmes and University curriculums in the different provinces,' and that school texts be prepared 'having a more pronounced spirit of patriotism evident in them.'[60] By the time the Pioneer and Historical Association of Ontario took up the same cry in the 1890s, Boyle felt right at home among its members. Following him at the podium at the Hamilton meeting in June 1896 was an old friend, Joseph H. Smith, a public school inspector in the city, who spoke eloquently on 'The Teaching of Patriotism in the Public Schools.'[61] For these imperialist historians and educators, continentalism was tantamount to treason. They condemned those who spoke in favour of closer ties with the United States, particularly Goldwin Smith, the one-time professor of history at Oxford. Even the conferring on Smith of an LL D by the University of Toronto in 1896 raised Boyle's ire. In one of the McSpurtle 'epistles' Boyle commended those graduates of the University of Toronto who declared that henceforth 'they'd hae naething to dae wi'' an institution that gies ony honor till a man who haivers anent the desirabeelity o' makin' the United States pairt an' paircel o' the Domeenion o' Canada.'[62]

In Boyle's mind, the teaching of 'patriotic' history had another function in addition to combating the spectre of annexation, and that was to help assimilate youngsters of different racial and religious backgrounds to an Anglo-Saxon norm. Linguistic and cultural uniformity, he believed, were essential for a strong united Canada. The question of assimilating immigrants would become a critical issue for Boyle and others in the historical society movement during the prosperity of the Laurier years after 1896, when waves of non-Anglo-Saxon 'foreigners' spilled across the Atlantic. In the early 1890s, however, his chief concern was the problem of Anglicizing French-speaking Canadians outside of Quebec. Like so many Ontarians of British descent in this era, Boyle was convinced of the Anglo-Saxon's superiority and unrivalled 'capacity for advancement' and certain that Anglo-Saxon civilization was 'the highest form that has ever been developed.'[63] In the estimation of Boyle and most Ontarians, Canada was, and must remain, a British-Canadian nation.

Following the growth of ultramontane nationalism in Quebec after Confederation, the Northwest Rebellion, the election of the *Parti National* in Quebec, and the influx of francophones into the eastern counties of the province, Ontarians like Boyle had grown apprehensive about French-Canadian intentions. Their anger knew no bounds with the passage of the Jesuits Estates Act in 1888, legislation that challenged their nationalist ideal for cultural homogeneity outside Quebec since it symbolized to them more than anything else an aggressive French-Canadian determination not only to survive but to expand.[64] Boyle joined actively those who called for the disallowance of the act. 'The great majority of the people of Ontario,' he wrote to D'Alton McCarthy, one of the leaders of the unsuccessful disallowance battle, 'are prepared to support any man who will vigorously take hold of, and endeavour to have the principles of Equal Rights to all, carried out.'[65] The Equal Rights movement, which initially sprang up in Ontario to secure disallowance, soon developed into a widespread agitation against the use of French in the schools of eastern Ontario and against the extension of Catholic separate-school rights throughout the province.

Subsequently Anglo-Saxon nativism emerged as a movement in Manitoba where the provincial government passed legislation in 1890 denying public support to denominational schools in which many thought French-Canadian culture was propagated. Boyle applauded the Manitoba Schools Act partly as an attempt to curtail institutions that nourished French language and culture, and partly because he believed that any step towards establishing a non-denominational and secular school system was a positive reform. It was not that he was anti-Catholic; rather, he viewed all organized religions with suspicion and believed that religion was a dimension of life better left to the home and the church. In one of the McSpurtle letters, Boyle, speaking from his own bitter experiences, lashed out against the consequences of maintaining confessional schools in Manitoba or elsewhere: 'I carena whether it be Praisbyterian, Episcopaulian, Methody, Catholic, Morman, or Mahometan – the result'll just be sae mony combinations an' cliques firm i' the belief that because they hae been made to unnerstaun that this or that faith is the true faith sae faur as their eternal salvation is concerned, nae man is caupable o' being a mechanic, a lawyer, a doctor, a policeman, a magistrate, a sheriff, an alderman, an auctioneer, or even a member o' the Legislature, withoot he blieves in accordance wi' the tenets o' the particular creed that for the time being ... is i' the ascendant.'[66]

If his views on imperialism and Anglo-Saxon racial superiority were two pillars of Boyle's national concept, an intense Scottish cultural nationalism was another. His fondness for, and pride in, old-country ways and traditions waxed as he grew older, not an unusual development in Scottish immigrants who more than the English, Irish, and even the Welsh, were retentive of their cultural heritage.[67] Since arriving in Canada, much of Boyle's social life had revolved around the Scottish community. He regularly attended the banquets, concerts, and games of the several Scottish immigrant clubs such as the Burns, St Andrew's, Caledonian, and Gaelic societies. He curled with his Scottish cronies until his early fifties when age began to slow him down. Each year, the Boyles celebrated Burns and St Andrew's nights and stoked up their sentiment for the homeland through music, song, and story. On these occasions, they and their friends wore sprigs of heather, piped in the haggis, recited 'Tam O' Shanter' and other Burnsian favourites, imbibed the traditional Scotch whiskey, and indulged in old-country dancing. On New Year's eve they celebrated 'Hogmanay' – the chief social event of their year – and went 'first footin' the following day. Pictures of Scottish glens purpled with heather and models of Clydeside ships adorned the walls of the Boyle home.

The cultural nationalism of the Scottish community went beyond the social dimension, however. 'It beehooves us,' commented an unusually serious Andrew McSpurtle, 'to cultivate upo' ... oor families a love for Scottish history, Scottish enterprise, an' Scottish leeterature ... Not only should we bring up oor bairns in "the nurture an' admonition," etc., but we should sit doun wi' them whiles an' crack aboot the "Land o' brown heath an' shaggy wood." We ocht tae make them un'erstan' that altho' by a mere accident they hae been brocht intil the worl' on the wrang side o' the Atlantic, they are notwithstandin' not only Canadians or Americans but Scottish Canadians an' Scottish Americans.'[68] David Boyle, it seems, had worked out his own cultural identity in the New World, an identity that was neither wholly Scottish nor wholly Canadian.

Interestingly, his Scottish cultural nationalism did not spill over into the political sphere in the form of agitation for political self-determination for the homeland. His imperialism and his Scottish nationalism were not incompatible, although he was quite sensitive about Scotland's legal equality within both the United Kingdom and the Empire. Woe to any public figure who mistakenly substituted the word 'English' for 'British' in his public statements. 'It has been noticed by many Scotsmen of late,' wrote an angry Boyle to an unsuspecting Prime Minister Laurier, 'that in your public addresses you almost constantly refer to the *English* people, the *English* parliament, the *English* government, and so on. The culmination of this unintentional offence was reached, when in your address before the Caledonian Society of Montreal ... you spoke of Scotsmen as being loyal to *England's* queen ... On this account we claim as we always have done, *Our Rights*, and one of these is that our share as partners in the Empire shall be recognized in accordance with fact, in the use of the terms Great Britain, Briton, and British.'[69]

IV

It was late August 1896 before David Boyle received the first positive indications that he would be retained as the archaeologist-curator following the transfer of the Canadian Institute collection to the Toronto Normal School. The first sign came when the minister of education authorized the expenditure of the archaeological grant for 1896 and informed Boyle that he might conduct field-work that September. Ross also gave Boyle cause for hope by instructing him to prepare plans for the construction of display cases for the new museum extension. Subsequently, Boyle submitted specifications based on information received from F.W. Putnam of the Peabody Museum at Harvard University.[70] 'The new premises will be ready in a month or so,' Boyle wrote to A.F. Hunter in September, 'and [the minister] intends to get new cases! I hope he will make some arrangements also that will yield me a decent livelihood, but this he mentioned not.'[71] Despite some lingering uncertainty, Boyle had good reason to be optimistic. In high spirits, he ventured forth into the field during the first week of September for what was about to become the most thrilling four weeks of his archaeological experience.

To humour his friend H.T. Strickland of Peterborough who was convinced of the existence of burial mounds on his property on Rice Lake, a sceptical Boyle headed east to Peterborough County. The site in question was in Otonabee Township on the crest of a hill at Mizang's Point near the mouth of the Indian River on the north shore of Rice Lake. As he plodded around the property which he noted had often been raided by relic hunters, Boyle observed one oval and four elliptical mounds and what appeared to be a zig-zag embankment nearly two hundred feet in length.[72] He ruled out a geological origin for the elongated embankment since it lay in an east-west direction across the line of glacial deposition and, given the location of the structure, also discounted the possibility of the mound being a defensive earthwork.

To commence the excavation, Boyle chose the oval mound at the eastern extremity of the long earth structure. He drove a trench five feet wide across the mound and made another cut from the western end to meet the first trench, 'the two thus forming a large "T".'[73] His initial scepticism about the artificiality of the mounds soon dissipated upon finding in the first opening two skeletons in a sitting position, and a skull and long bones at a depth of two feet which he concluded were comparatively recent burials.[74] At levels below three feet in the second trench he found another skeleton lying on its right side, evidently placed there prior to the construction of the mound, as well as a human skull, an animal mandible, canine teeth, mussel shells, and charcoal. Near the centre of the mound he also unearthed 'burnt human bones, but not associated with ashes or charcoal,' several pottery fragments, and at the base level, 'a circle of stones rudely put together about three feet in diameter' without a trace of charcoal or ashes.

While his hired labourers trenched and sieved the oval mound, Boyle carefully studied the long zig-zag embankment. For a wider perspective, he backed away from the structure to a ridge some fifty feet distant to the west. Suddenly it struck him – that end of the embankment was tapered. He scurried to the other extremity of the structure – it rose abruptly to a height of four feet! His mind raced and his thoughts turned to the Great Serpent Mound of Adams County, Ohio. Could this be an Ontario equivalent? Caution prevented him from making such a hasty conclusion. Back and forth he

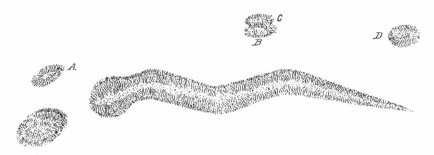

Ground plan of the Serpent Mounds site (*Archaeological Report 1896–7*)

walked, over and around the structure, observing it from every direction. Whatever his vantage point, he kept visualizing the head of a serpent at the eastern end of the mound, a tapering tail to the west, and three well-marked convolutions. A rapid measurement of the structure confirmed that each of the zig-zag sections was roughly forty feet long. That clinched it in his mind; the builders had meant the structure to be serpentine. And what's more, the position of the oval mound, accurately in line with the head and neck portion of the long structure, suggested 'the ancient combination of serpent and egg,' just as in Adams County, Ohio. Before taking spade in hand, he was almost convinced that a burial effigy mound lay before him, the only example of its kind in Ontario.

As soon as the workmen had finished with the oval or 'egg' mound, they opened the serpentine structure in two places – the first about seventy feet from the 'tail' in a place left relatively undisturbed by pothunters, the second at the eastern extremity near the 'head.' There was no question as to its artificiality, for they discovered a 'much-decayed' human bone in the first cut, and 'comparatively recent burials' less than eighteen inches from the surface near the 'head' of the serpent. Later Boyle opened the four elliptical mounds lying along the south or lakeward side of the serpent and in every case found human remains.

He could not resist immediately informing George Ross of his discoveries. 'The identification of this as a serpent mound,' Boyle wrote on 6 September, 'may be regarded as the most important contribution that has been made to the archaeology and ethnology of Ontario ... I am duly impressed with the significance of my identification, and in announcing it, am well aware that the statement will raise doubts and denials on the part of many, so that I have been extremely cautious in arriving at a conclusion which was forced upon me by the logic of the situation, and came to me quite contrary to every expectation.'[75] Almost at once, Boyle began to pressure the minister to

The Serpent Mounds site in 1896 (*Archaeological Report 1896–7*)

preserve the site as a provincial park. 'When the value of this ancient earth-structure is estimated ethnologically, I feel warranted in making the suggestion that the small area on which the mounds stand should be secured as the property of the province, and preserved intact for the study and admiration of all who are interested in problems affecting the human race, and its development in America.'[76] The area contiguous to the mound site was ideal for recreation purposes; 'as a summer resort the situation is unsurpassed by any on the lake.'[77]

Even George Ross got caught up in Boyle's excitement. He authorized a survey and encouraged Boyle to sound out the owners on the cost of purchasing the property. Astonishingly, when the owners offered the four-acre site for $450, Boyle advised the minister to turn the offer down. 'As the whole farm (68 acres) is held at $1,100, the price asked is too high by half'[78] – a puzzling conclusion considering his thoughts on the significance of the place. Perhaps Boyle sensed that the government would not look kindly upon any request for large expenditures or costly, long-term management commitments. If so he was right, for the province had no intention of providing more parks for the people after creating Algonquin Park in 1893 and Rondeau Park in 1894. Besides, there was virtually no local political pressure in the Peterborough area for such a facility, in spite of yeoman efforts to generate interest in the idea the following year by the Ethnological Survey Committee of the British Association for the Advancement of Science and the Peterborough Historical Society.[79] It was fortunate indeed that the mounds were protected by the owners. Eventually the property was purchased by the Hiawatha band of Mississauga Indians in 1933, and leased to the Ontario Department of Lands and Forests in 1956, as a provincial park – sixty years after Boyle had first proposed the idea.

As soon as the local press announced the discovery at Mizang's Point, people throughout the county began to provide information about other possible mounds and village sites in the area. This information prompted Boyle to undertake an immediate field survey of the Rice Lake–Trent River shoreline and islands. The results of that reconnaissance, conducted during the rest of September, were impressive. On the Miller farm, situated at the mouth of the Otonabee River, he located three burial mounds, one of which had been converted into a root cellar. He excavated the other two and uncovered four individual burials and miscellaneous artifactual material. One specimen, a large engraved marine-shell turtle effigy,[80] the back of which was 'rudely ornamented with concentric circles, scrolls, and shallow depressions or borings' greatly excited Boyle. 'So far as I know,' he reported to Ross, 'this is the only specimen of its kind that has yet been unearthed, and its value in

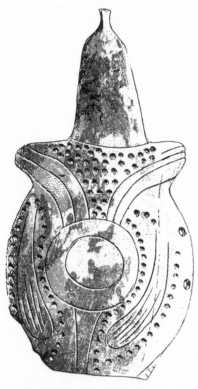

Shell gorget, Miller mounds (*Archaeological Report 1896–7*)

estimating the culture of our Canadian Mound Builders cannot well be over-estimated.'[81]

After excavating the Miller mound group, Boyle made his way along the north shore to Cameron's Point at the eastern extremity of Rice Lake near the head of the Trent River. Here he located three more burial mounds and a shell midden. Nearby, on the east side of Birdsall's Bay he also discovered a late prehistoric Huron site that produced potsherds, pipes, 'arrowheads' and 'an unusual type of mealing-stone.'[82] At this juncture, Boyle received word of an ossuary (today the late prehistoric Neutral Main ossuary) just discovered in Beverly Township. He decided to leave the Cameron's Point excavation in the capable hands of W.G. Long of Toronto, who had considerable archaeological experience in both Manitoba and the Dakotas. Long trenched each of the structures so as to cross-section them at right angles. Altogether he found twenty burials, a number of them intrusive, and evidence of stone arrangements associated with the primary interments.[83] Having completed this task, Long, acting under instructions from Boyle, moved on to East Sugar Island about a mile to the east of the Serpent Mounds site. Here Boyle met up with him on 15 September and together they opened two small mounds and noted the existence of at least two others. The most interesting was the 'Princess Mound' which contained seven intrusive burials, and near the centre, a skeleton 'half-seated,' with the legs 'drawn up behind' and the hands 'on the breast.' Around the neck, they found an eight-strand necklace of copper beads and shell disks. Near the right arm was 'a very perfect stone tablet' or biconcave gorget of translucent 'Mexican onyx,' and a little beyond an enormous copper adze weighing some three and a half pounds.[84]

Following these exciting discoveries, Boyle spent a few days in Toronto before returning to Rice Lake on 22 September to survey the Trent River below the lake. His luck continued, for he located three more burial structures on the Preston farm about four miles downstream in Asphodel Township. One of these earth-heaps seemed to be a combination of mound and ossuary since it contained a mass grave of seventeen individuals covered with a layer of hard clay, above which he found the disarticulated remains of human cremation in the form of a charred human leg and rib-bones in a bed of ashes.[85] For another week he continued his reconnaissance for mounds along the Trent River below Rice Lake with no further success and, before heading home to Toronto, made a cursory examination of the area between Peterborough and Lakefield, which was equally barren of results.

After his work in Peterborough County during September 1896, Boyle was forced to revise his conclusions of the previous year that Ontario earthworks were all defensive embankments built to support palisades. The Rice Lake structures were certainly burial mounds and the 'Serpent and Egg' mounds at Mizang's Point seemed to fall into a burial-effigy classification. Since he could find no evidence of large permanent village sites near any of the mound groups, Boyle suspected that the sites were 'merely ceremonial in character,' centres which people from the interior visited intermittently. As for the identity of the builders, he could only conclude that they were a people who preceded the Huron-Iroquois occupation, perhaps a much earlier Algonkian tribe. 'It is not recorded that the Huron-Iroquois were mound builders,' he explained, 'and we must therefore regard the earthworks in question as the product of a people who preceded them. Indians they were, undoubtedly, but Indians of different tastes and habits from the Huron-Iroquois, as well as from any members of Algonkin stock met by the white man in this part of America.'[86]

Boyle's work in the Rice Lake–Trent River area was of no little

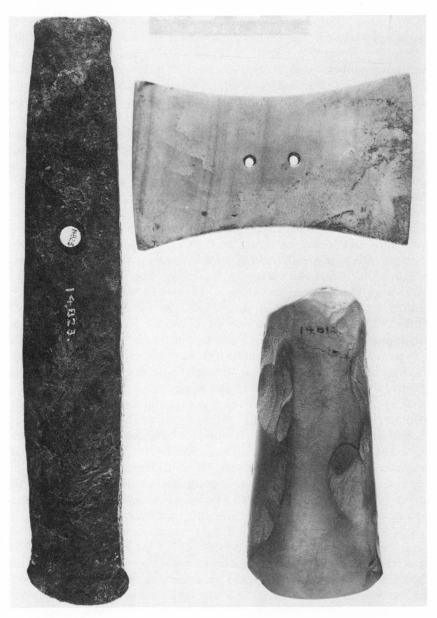

Adze (14812), onyx gorget, and copper celt (14823), Princess Mound, 1896 (ROM Toronto)

consequence. With one exception[87] he had located and excavated all the Middle Woodland burial-mound groups in the area that archaeologists since the Second World War have dated between AD 100 and 300. His work is all the more significant since many of the mounds no longer exist; the only data available for the structures at the Miller site, on East Sugar Island, and the Preston site are contained in the *Archaeological Report for 1896–7*. While the earliest mounds, such as mound C at Cameron's Point, have yielded grave goods of the Ohio Hopewellian type, it is now generally believed that these burial structures were the product of a weak Ohio Hopewellian influence on a Middle Point Peninsula people indigenous to the Trent water system. These cultural influences probably arrived in the province by way of New York State where there flourished a local Point Peninsula people more heavily influenced by Hopewellian ideas.[88] Whether the elongated mound at Mizang's Point was intentionally built up over time in the shape of a serpent (in which case it may be related to the Great Serpent Mound of Adams County, Ohio, seemingly Adena), or not, remains a point of contention.[89]

After the Rice Lake survey in September, the remainder of Boyle's field-work for 1896 was anti-climatic. He spent a week in October in the Balsam Lake area with George Laidlaw, and twice travelled to Innisfil Township near Barrie to examine what Andrew Hunter insisted was an enormous serpent effigy some 1230 feet in length.[90] Eight years earlier, Hunter had recorded the serpentine feature of this embankment but thought nothing of it until the discovery at Mizang's Point. Boyle, after excavating the Innisfil structure and finding no artifactual material, concluded correctly that the irregularly shaped embankment was a natural geological feature. Alas, Hunter, his judgment warped by 'serpent mania' and 'sun worship' theories, fumed with anger that his mentor would deny him a share of the limelight, and proceeded to write up his personal views for the *Archaeological Report*. The manuscript, dogmatic and speculative, reflected Hunter at his worst. He built up the specious argument that a complex of four villages surrounded the alleged serpent effigy, all of which contained ceremonial centres, 'the entire group apparently making what is known ... as a Cosmic System, having the effigy at its centre.'[91] Boyle responded that he did not 'take much if any stock in so-called "Serpent Worship" and still less in what you call "cosmic".' All the same, he respected Hunter's wish to voice his opinion. 'The views are yours, you have a right to them, and it is as fair that you should express them, as that I should express mine ... At any rate ... your paper will set people a-thinking.'[92] Andrew Hunter never forgave Boyle for casting doubt on his conclusions and their personal relationship deteriorated from this point on.

Towards the end of November 1896 George Ross at last named David

Boyle the curator of the new archaeological section located on the third floor of the Ontario Provincial Museum in the Toronto Normal School. The question of the curator's stipend, however, remained unsettled until the following May when the appointment was confirmed by an order-in-council granting him an annual salary of one thousand dollars to be charged against the government's 'Unforeseen and Unprovided' fund.[93] While still far below the pay scale of his counterparts in the United States, the amount at least provided the Boyles with a welcome measure of financial security for the first time since leaving Elora.

Much to his dismay, Boyle soon discovered that the change of venue from the Canadian Institute to the education department simply substituted one set of frustrations and disappointments for another. He expected to finish cataloguing, reclassifying, and displaying the archaeological collection by the spring. Yet by May 1897 the new cases and shelving had still to be installed in the room allocated to archaeology. The cause of the problem was George Ross himself, a fussbudget who insisted on supervising everything from room allocations to the purchase of cases and shelving. His interest was commendable; but it also had the effect of hindering progress and shackling the curators of the various sections of the museum. The upshot of Ross's interference was that Boyle had not yet put his collection entirely into order by the official opening of the provincial museum on 17 June 1897. Boyle's lack of authority to make even minor decisions caused him no end of trouble with Andrew Hunter who took it as a personal insult that Boyle would not pay for photographs he had taken on his own initiative of the Innisfil serpentine ridge. 'I had not any authority to pay for the photos you took in Innisfil,' Boyle tried to explain, 'I feel as keenly as you do ... the injustice of non-recompense for work performed in the public interest, but I am helpless in the matter. Here I am no more than a little boy, without an ounce of authority or discretionary power ... I simply cling to one prerogative, viz., that I shall arrange material as I please.'[94]

To his credit, Boyle exercised that prerogative in a splendid fashion. For years he had been waiting for the chance to reorganize the collection that now comprised some twenty thousand specimens. In a report to the Geological Survey of Canada, he described the contents of the museum under the following categories:[95]

(1) Stone pipes 150
(2) Clay pipes 200
(3) Copper tools and weapons 60
(4) 'Bird' amulets 40

The Toronto Normal School, home of the Ontario Provincial Museum
(*Archaeological Report 1913*)

Main Archaeological Room, Ontario Provincial Museum
(*Archaeological Report 1911*)

(5) 'Huronian' slate objects 30
(6) Stone tubes 25
(7) 'Butterfly' stones. 30
(8) Clay vessels: Ontario 13
                 Pueblo 60
                 u.s. Mounds 70
                 Cliff dwellers 1
(9) Crania: Indians 200
            German 6
            Mummey 6
(10) Aztec specimens 700
(11) Plain and grooved celts . . . . (several × 100s)
(12) Iron tomahawks 50
(13) Gouges. 150
(14) Pottery . . . . .innumerable
(15) Shell objects. 200
(16) Wampum beads. xxx
(17) Flints 1000x
(18) Chipped tools 1000x
(19) b.c. Ethnology collection (small)
(20) Brit. Guiana collection (small)
(21) New Hebrides collection (small)

While rearranging this material, Boyle made a major innovation and introduced a new dual system of classification. In addition to the purely descriptive taxonomy of the past with its functional emphasis and cross-cultural and evolutionary biases, his new scheme also took geography and culture into consideration. There had been hints of this approach earlier when Boyle had displayed both the Clearville and the Baptiste Lake artifacts in separate cases, but now he began to arrange George Laidlaw's impressive Balsam Lake collection of more than one thousand pieces so that all the specimens were placed in groups, each of which represented one of the village sites (thirty-one by 1900) examined by Laidlaw.[96] 'I have always thought that material from [different regions] should be kept together and not scattered,' Laidlaw wrote to Hunter. 'Then one can compare localities at a glance, which is what men like we want.'[97]

Regrettably, Boyle restricted his use of this method to the artifactual data from the Balsam Lake area. He did so partly because his concern was not to study local sequences and cultural variation, but rather to illustrate the social life of the prehistoric Amerindians in general. 'Thus arranged,' he explained with reference to the Laidlaw collection, 'one can see at a glance what may be

Pagan village burial ground, Christian Island (*Archaeological Report 1897–8*)

called an object picture representing in some measure the every day life of those who occupied the Balsam Lake district, and as this life did not differ very much from that of other aborigines in this province, the grouping will thus answer a general purpose.'[98] Furthermore, Boyle was discouraged by those he considered his superiors from arranging his collections by localities. For example, G. Brown Goode, the assistant secretary in charge of the United States National Museum, suggested instead that 'if the number of specimens under any one subject will allow, ... it would be well to separate them from the general series so as to show its evolution, i.e. in the Museum the jacknife is taken and each stage of its development, as far as possible is shown.'[99] This, of course, is what Boyle had been doing all along. One can only surmise what conceptual and interpretive advances would have occurred had he followed his own instincts and pursued his new classification method more rigorously with a view to comparative analysis of regional variations in the data, and local cultural development.

Despite the onerous tasks associated with the opening of the expanded provincial museum, Boyle endeavoured that summer to balance his curatorial responsibilities with occasional field-work. His most ambitious trip took him to Christian Island in Georgian Bay where he investigated the remains of a 'pagan' Indian village and burial ground, and excavated the historic Huron *Ahoendoé* ossuary. He dated this burial pit to the spring of 1650, and explained it as a consequence of the dreadful winter of famine suffered by the Huron Indians in 1649 after they were driven from Ste Marie 1 by the Iroquois.[100] Subsequent to this expedition, Boyle escaped the confines of the museum to investigate a late prehistoric Neutral site at the confluence of the Grand River and Whiteman's Creek in Brantford Township. He also excavated the Pound farm site in Malahide Township, Elgin County, which he had first visited in 1891. 'This place is worthy of further and much closer examination,' Boyle reported, 'the whole field apparently having been a place of human resort in pre-historic days.'[101] Not for another forty years, until Dr Philleo Nash of the University of Toronto excavated this location during the summers of 1938 and 1939, did the Pound site receive the close examination demanded by Boyle.

v

The discovery of the Rice Lake mound groups in September 1896 and the opening of the expanded Ontario Provincial Museum in June 1897 were both nicely timed to give Boyle some well deserved recognition in the international scientific community, particularly among the members of the British Association for the Advancement of Science who met in Toronto in August 1897. Archaeology took a prominent place at the convention. The president that year, Sir John Evans, the noted British prehistorian, addressed the delegates on the reasons for considering archaeology a science.[102] The BAAS members were also afforded the opportunity to visit the Serpent Mounds which, since Boyle's discovery, had become a stopping-off point for the Rice Lake excursion boats. Boyle also gave conducted tours of his museum and managed to persuade Sir John Evans to donate a small collection of British palaeolithic celts. That Boyle impressed the BAAS executive became apparent when he was appointed to the standing committee to organize an ethnological survey of Canada chaired by Dr George Mercer Dawson of the Geological Survey of Canada.

This committee immediately launched two initiatives in Ontario in the hope that it might capitalize on the interest generated by the BAAS convention. Urged on by Boyle, it lobbied both the provincial and municipal authorities to set aside the Serpent Mounds as a provincial park, but to no avail. Their second initiative was more successful. On Chairman Dawson's instructions, Boyle and James Mavor, a political economist at the University of Toronto, descended upon George Ross in November 1897 to request the establishment of an annual ethnological grant. The minister denied them the grant, but he did agree later to allow Boyle to pursue as his major task for the coming year an ethnological study of the 'pagan' Iroquois on the Six Nations Reserve near Brantford.

The appointment to the BAAS Ethnological Survey Committee afforded

Boyle the excuse he needed to branch into comparative ethnology – a dimension of anthropological activity that he had thus far been forced to neglect because of the pressures of his work. Even before the appointment, he had reached the conclusion that since his museum was now sufficiently representative of Ontario prehistory, 'the time has arrived when it is desirable to pay more attention to the ethnology of our own and other continents than we have done.'[103] In this, as in most other matters, he was following in the footsteps of his American colleagues who, led by Major John Wesley Powell, chief of the Smithsonian Institution's bureau of ethnology, had forged intimate links between archaeology and anthropology. Restricted by the nature of their data to the technological aspect of man's development, but desirous of understanding man's social, mental, and moral evolution, archaeologists everywhere routinely used the so-called comparative method to supplement their research with ethnological data. They did so in the belief that contemporary Amerindian primitives would furnish valid information about prehistoric cultures. John Fiske, whom Boyle cited in the preface to the *Archaeological Report for 1891*, explained the method this way: 'The more advanced societies have gone through various stages now represented here and there by less advanced societies; ... there is a general path of social development, along which, owing to special circumstances, some peoples have advanced a great way, some a less way, some but a very little way, and ... by studying existing savages and barbarians we get a valuable clue to the interpretation of pre-historic times.'[104]

Another aspect of the comparative method that intrigued Boyle was the concept of 'survivals.' From his reading of E.B. Tylor's *Primitive Culture* (1871), he understood survivals as any idea or phenomenon which, having originated under certain causal conditions in the prehistoric past, continued to exist in modern times regardless of the fact that the original conditions no longer applied. The great evolutionary anthropologists of the nineteenth century like Tylor and L.H. Morgan, whose publications greatly influenced Boyle's thinking, regarded survivals as traces of prehistory and helpful building blocks in the task of reconstructing the evolution of present-day institutions.[105] As early as 1886, in one of the first papers he presented to the Canadian Institute, entitled 'The Persistence of Savagery in Civilization,' Boyle had already applied the concept in a general if not very profound way to argue that many modern manners and customs betrayed their lineage to prehistoric man.[106] He identified as survivals such latter-day customs as hunting for pleasure, the prevalence of crime, and a child's 'savage impulse' to inflict pain on birds and small animals. The tobacco habit, games of chance, superstitions and folklore, modern man's penchant for 'half-cooked or nearly raw meat' and 'rotting or rotten cheese,' were but a few of the 'inherited proclivities' bearing 'strong resemblances to savage ways.' Many of man's 'highest moral, social, political, artistic and scientific achievements,' added Boyle, echoing Tylor, should be viewed as having 'their beginnings far away back in the stream of time.'

If the comparative method and the concept of survivals were fundamental to his theoretical baggage as he ventured into the ethnology of the Grand River Reserve, so, too, were his notions of racial determinism. Unlike either Daniel Wilson who was unique in not being a racialist in his views, or the coming generation of Boasian-influenced anthropologists who held to the ideal of moral and ethical relativism in the study of the other cultures, Boyle's thinking was tainted by many of the same racial assumptions that permeated the books of Tylor, Morgan, Spencer, and the other evolutionists to whom he was intellectually indebted.[107] Like them, he believed that race and culture were interdependent, and that cultural traits were carried in the 'blood,' and not merely determined by climatic, dietary, and governmental factors. Some 'races of men do not possess, or do not exhibit the same capacity for advancement,' wrote Boyle. 'Some are today as they were a thousand years ago – in little more than intellectual infancy – some in boyhood, and not a few in stunted manhood.'[108] The American aborigines were not a very progressive people, he argued, because beyond a certain point they lacked inventiveness and 'adaptiveness'; they did not invent the wheel, for example. 'The American Indian with all his sagacity stuck hard and fast at the wheel, and there is reason to believe that every race, with the exception of our own has a "sticking place".'[109] In Boyle's estimation, the contemporary American Indian still exhibited many of the personality traits of a child; both were deemed to be credulous, illogical, inveterate liars, cruel, superstitious, irresponsible, and lacking the desire for economic gain.[110]

Although Boyle did not consider the American Indians the equal of the Anglo-Saxons, his racial beliefs did not prevent him from respecting Amerind virtues (bravery, self-denial, filial affection, and gratitude), or from admiring their accomplishments as mechanics and artists. He even hypothesized that some Indians would have reached the stage of civilization had they been left undisturbed by European culture.[111] Nor did his assumptions of Anglo-Saxon superiority prevent him from striking a warm and close relationship with the people on the Six Nations' Reserve. He lived with them while on the reserve, and welcomed them into his own home in Toronto, even when they arrived unannounced. His friends along the Grand River appreciated his attempts to reconstruct Iroquoian prehistory and his efforts to preserve their cultural heritage; indeed, the Mohawks had already expressed their gratitude by adopting him into their tribe in 1892, and naming him *Ra'-ri-wah-ka-noh'-nis*, a word meaning 'an ambassador' or 'one who is sent to do business between the two peoples.'[112]

As an adopted Mohawk, Boyle enjoyed 'unqualified Indian courtesy' during his several sojourns on the reserve to study the traditional pagan religious ceremonies. He began by spending ten days in late January and early February 1898 observing the Mid-Winter Festival with its ceremony of the Burning of the White Dog. On 8 May he returned for the Cayuga After-Seeding or Spring Sun Dance, and again at the beginning of harvest time for the festival of the Green Corn Dance. The purpose of his ethnological research was to prepare for the first time a study of the beliefs and customs of the roughly one thousand Iroquois who still held to their old religious beliefs. As with his archaeological field-work, time and money prevented him from following the preferred 'modern methods of [anthropological] investigation' which required 'years of close study' and 'intimate social intercourse' with the people under scrutiny. 'One worker,' Boyle also admitted, 'during one season, cannot hope to cover all the ground.'[113]

These problems aside, he was fortunate to be able to depend upon a reliable interpreter, J.O. Brant-Sero, a Mohawk with a knowledge of all the Iroquois dialects. Considered to be 'one of the brightest and most intelligent Iroquois ever born on the Reserve,' Brant-Sero went on the following year to pursue a career in North America and Europe as a lecturer on the Six Nations Indians. To supplement his field studies, Boyle also brought to Toronto the headman of the ceremonies in the Seneca Longhouse, *Ka-nis-han-don*, who provided the words and speeches and the music for songs at the major festivals. On these occasions, *Ka-nis-han-don's* utterances were recorded and interpreted by Alexander T. Cringan, musical superintendent of Toronto Public Schools, who also prepared musical scores for the various songs.[114]

The *Archaeological Report for 1898* was largely made up of Boyle's 150-page manuscript on conservatism among the Iroquois on the Six Nations' Reserve; it remains to this day, the author's biases notwithstanding, a solid and reliable piece of ethnological research. As in all his work – archaeological and historical – the strength of the study lay in Boyle's determination 'to give facts only.'[115] His accurate and detailed descriptions of the dances, games, customs, myths, and beliefs associated with the 'pagan' festivals, as well as his translations of songs and speeches, are timeless documentary sources of information. All the data, he explained, 'have been verified out of the mouths of two or three witnesses at least, and sometimes of many more.' To place his findings within a wider historical framework, he also provided an excellent synthesis of the existing literature on Iroquois mythology and its development over time and drew upon the leading authorities to explain the reasons for such ceremonies as the Burning of the White Dog.

Since the major thrust of the study was to determine the extent to which ancient Iroquois rites had been changed by Christian influences, Boyle saw fit to examine the important religious movement at the beginning of the nineteenth century initiated by the prophet Beautiful Lake* (*Ska-ne-o-dy-o*), said to be the half-brother of Cornplanter, the Seneca sachem.[116] After experiencing what he interpreted as a supernatural visitation, Beautiful Lake exhorted the Iroquois, and all Indians for that matter, to renounce white ways and to maintain the ancient religious traditions. Boyle explained how Beautiful Lake's mission had much in common with those of the prophets of other nativist Indian movements in the same period.[117] Ironically, as Boyle noted, Beautiful Lake's creed – with its monotheistic notion of a Great Spirit, and the promise of an eternal happiness in a heaven reserved solely for those Indians who followed the dictates of his religious teachings, moral code, and message of temperance – was not unaffected by Christian influences.[118] Nevertheless, the prophet's reform gospel, conservative in intent and deeply rooted in the old ways, won a substantial and lasting following among the Six Nations. Boyle discovered through his own research that a century of Christian missionary work and European cultural pressures had yet to eradicate those ancient rites and the impact of Beautiful Lake.

'The wonder ... is,' Boyle eventually concluded, 'not that Iroquois paganism has been to some extent modified by Christian influences, but that it has been modified so little.'[119] He believed that the music, the songs, the dances, the speeches, and the ceremonies he had witnessed were almost pristine examples of the prehistoric forms.[120] But, he added, they were often mere survivals since the origin and meaning had long been forgotten. 'Their maintenance is purely conservative. Even the significance of the words of the song is lost, and in many of the ceremonial rote-speeches in connection with the feasts, words and phrases are employed respecting which even the oldest medicine man has no knowledge ... The same is true with regard to such customs as the "scattering of ashes," the spraying of heads with sweetened water, the anointing of heads with sunflower oil, and several other rites.'[121] Boyle marvelled at the resilience and stability of Iroquois tradition, but these traits only went to confirm his preconceived belief that 'American Indians are not a progressive people. They assimilate European notions very slowly, and, at best, somewhat imperfectly. Tradition and usage are more powerful than appeals to action along new lines, even when the advantages of the latter

* Now generally called Handsome Lake

course are made plain. It is only when tradition has been deprived of its power by the segregation of individuals from national or tribal associations that tradition itself ceases to govern.'[122]

To give Boyle his due, the *Archaeological Report for 1898* remained for the most part free of his racial biases. It was primarily in the closing pages, when he digressed from the primary theme of religous rites and launched into a quite unnecessary section on 'Disease,' that his views on race became manifest. For his information he relied upon a statement provided by Dr L. Secord of Brantford, a medical officer on the reserve.[123] Secord painted an appalling picture of a community where the death rate was thirty per thousand, three times the provincial average. Many of these deaths were said to be preventable, the product of 'ignorance, superstition, filth and indifference.' Fully 30 per cent of infant deaths under one year of age he attributed to congenital syphilis. Upon receiving this assessment, Boyle was unable to resist ending his report with a 'political' statement quite out of keeping with the rest of his manuscript. He recommended the appointment of a new type of Indian agent by the dominion authorities, one who had the confidence of the Six Nations' Council and who would be required to spend most of his time on the reserve acting as 'guide, philosopher and friend' to his charges. 'It would be the duty of such a one,' he explained, 'to advise and to suggest, with power when necessary, to enforce measures for domestic comfort and public health.'[124] Clerics and schoolmasters were of little use since they were without influence among the pagans.

Boyle, in fact, expected the new agent to accelerate the process of assimilation on the reserve, regardless of the wishes of the Indians. If judiciously approached, he argued, the Iroquois could be made to improve their living and sanitary conditions. 'We sent "instructors" to our red brethren in the North-West,' he noted, 'why not to those on our own doors?' The fact that many Indians on the reserve could not speak English had to be surmounted, for without knowledge of English, they were 'by necessity as well as by inclination isolated from elevating influences; with good reason they are suspicious of "white" interference, but, notwithstanding these and other difficulties, it is time to save them from themselves ... In a word, the Indians actually invite disease, and seem to pay gladly for deaths. The first step towards radical improvement would be to teach every Indian to speak and read English.' With that remark he concluded his study of the 'pagan' Iroquois.[125]

In stating his opinions so bluntly, Boyle invited criticism from those long associated with the missionary efforts on the reserve. Perhaps because his reports were not popular reading among the general public, or because the controversial section was buried deep in the manuscript, the attack when it came was belated and token. 'We ... note that not a picture is shown in this report of any of the fine brick residences and churches ..., nor of any of the accomplished ... professional men who belong to the Six Nations,' wrote one Anglican critic to the minister of education some two years after the *Report* was published. 'Very little else but Pagans and Pagan Rites, which is calculated to create a very false impression of the advancement and civilization of the Six Nations.'[126] The assertion that the Indians actually invited disease was condemned as 'outrageous and libellous falsehood.' Boyle refused to retract a word. 'There is not an unkind, or an untruthful word in anything I have written. If any irritation exists ..., it has been fomented by busybodies who have been disappointed.'[127]

Had he intended to undertake a long-term and systematic ethnological survey of the Grand River Reserve in the years ahead, Boyle might have faced some opposition to his work as a consequence of some of the undiplomatic things he had written. As it turned out, however, his ethnological field study was a one-time effort. With the exception of a brief return visit in 1899 to record the Cayuga Sun Dance, he simply did not have the time to devote to anthropological pursuits because of his mounting curatorial, historical, and purely archaeological responsibilities. In fact, during 1898, the weeks spent on the Six Nations' Reserve deprived Boyle of any opportunities to undertake archaeological field-work that year. He devoted the remainder of his time to the museum. New acquisitions had to be processed, particularly since the number of donations was increasing following the publicity associated with the opening of the Ontario Provincial Museum. Dealing with the correspondence was almost a full-time job in itself. In the *Archaeological Report for 1898* he claimed to have received 982 letters and sent out 1085 communications, all handwritten and without secretarial assistance.[128]

VI

By the end of 1898, David Boyle recognized that he had attained the goals that he had set for himself fifteen years earlier upon joining the Canadian Institute and becoming a serious student of Ontario prehistory. He had built up the best archaeological museum in Canada. He had contributed to scientific knowledge, and he had reached the top rungs of the archaeological ladder in North America. To be sure, the realities of Boyle's professional life failed to meet his earlier, naïve expectations. After years of financial sacrifice and deferred gratification, he was still grossly underpaid and overworked. Little wonder that he asked himself on occasion whether the struggle had been worth the bother, and toyed with the idea of emigrating to the United States. Happily for Ontario archaeology such notions usually dissipated each year when the tributes to his work poured in following the distribution of the *Archaeological Report*. It was a source of immense satisfaction that scholars like Stewart Culin of the University of Pennsylvania considered his publications 'full of the most useful information of the most permanent value';[129] or that the renowned Frank H. Cushing of the Smithsonian's Bureau of Ethnology would write the following testimonial about Boyle's study of the 'pagan' Iroquois; 'Were it in my power by either word, or contribution, I could not say too much or give too much or do too much, in aid of such work as you are endeavoring.'[130]

Closer to home, Boyle's efforts to preserve Ontario's heritage had earned him enormous respect among the ranks of the historical society movement. In recognition of his contributions, he was elected first permanent secretary of the recently created Ontario Historical Society in June 1898. That Boyle received this honour can also be attributed to the influence of his old friend in archaeology, James H. Coyne of St Thomas, the registrar of Elgin County. Upon being elected to the presidency of the Pioneer and Historical Association of the Province of Ontario the year before, Coyne had begun to expand its usefulness. In March 1898 he had asked Boyle to assist him by serving as secretary pro tem of the association. Together, they struck a special committee that set about to restructure the old Pioneer and Historical Association along the lines of the highly successful state-supported historical societies in Wisconsin, Michigan, and Ohio. The radically revised constitution submitted by the committee and ratified in May 1898 broadened the basis of the provincial historical association by providing that in addition to the affiliated local historical groups, any individual might become a member of the Ontario Historical Society. The society would continue to promote the interests of the affiliated local history groups, but now it also aspired to a much more ambitious program. The constitution boldly declared:

The Society shall also engage in the collection, preservation, exhibition and publication of materials for the study of history, especially the history of Ontario and of Canada; to this end studying the archaeology of the Province, acquiring documents and manuscripts, obtaining narratives and records of the pioneers, conducting a library of historical reference, maintaining a gallery of historical portraiture and an ethnological and historical museum, publishing and otherwise diffusing information relative to the history of the Province and of the Dominion, and in general encouraging and developing within this Province the study of history.[131]

This was a grandiose statement of intent. Evidently the OHS anticipated filling the massive void occasioned by the absence of other provincial historical agencies.

For obvious reasons, Boyle leaped at the chance to be connected with this program. Apart from believing in the cause, he saw career opportunities for himself should the OHS realize its objectives of establishing a museum, archives, and library complex. He knew that he would be the obvious choice to administer any such project. And on the basis of official reaction, it seemed that Coyne's scenario for the society might be obtainable. As a key Liberal party organizer in Elgin County, Coyne had long known George Ross, who sat for adjacent West Middlesex; and this close political connection apparently paid dividends when the OHS leader went begging to the minister of education for provincial funding. The upshot of their discussions during late 1897 and early 1898 was that in March Ross agreed to support the society's objectives by providing an annual grant of $500 and by publishing without cost the society's *Papers and Records.*

George Ross's decision to subsidize the Ontario Historical Society was probably prompted by several considerations, both ideological and political. He already enjoyed a reputation as a nationalist and imperialist sworn to transform the schools into more effective agencies for fashioning patriotic attitudes and sentiments among the younger generation. He made the study of Canadian history compulsory in the elementary grades, and ordered history texts to be standardized and rewritten by Canadians. Patriotic exercises were encouraged in the schools on national and imperial holidays, and Ross himself prepared a teachers' aid for such occasions entitled *Patriotic Recitations and Arbor Day Exercises* (1893). In supporting the Ontario Historical Society, Ross obviously recognized that an effective historical association would bolster the patriotic work of the department of education by arousing pride in country and empire through the study of the past. 'An historical society should be educational,' he explained, 'and while scholarly and exact in its methods, it should reach the masses in its results – it should appeal to our domestic affections as well as to our national pride and our patriotic aspirations.'[132] No doubt the minister of education was also aware that his promotion of a popularly based provincial historical society, led by a prominent Liberal associate from south-western Ontario, could not hurt his chances to succeed the ailing Premier Arthur S. Hardy, whose retirement was rumoured, particularly after his near defeat in the general election of March 1898.

Whatever Ross's motives, David Boyle benefited from the minister's interest in the Ontario Historical Society. In June 1898 at the annual meeting of the society held on the Six Nations' Reserve at Ohsweken, the members elected him their permanent secretary at a salary of one hundred dollars per annum. Their choice was virtually predetermined by Ross himself who agreed beforehand to Coyne's suggestion that if Boyle were secretary he might include as part of his daily work at the museum the routine office business of the Ontario Historical Society. 'The Minister of Education is heartily with us,' wrote Coyne to Andrew Hunter. 'It seems to me, that by using the Educational Department Buildings as our headquarters with our Corresponding Secretary in charge there, & our Library, Museum, etc., established in the buildings, we can indirectly get the equivalent of a large annual grant.'[133] These were heady times for both Boyle and the Ontario Historical Society; their future together would be an interesting and productive one.

7

Primarily a museum man 1899–1905

I

With the completion of his study of the 'pagan' Iroquois in 1898, and his appointment that year as secretary of the Ontario Historical Society, David Boyle reached the apex of his career. In the few years of activity that remained to him, his contributions to Ontario archaeology and ethnology would be acknowledged and applauded by his peers on both sides of the Atlantic. Ironically, this recognition came just at the time that his active period of field research was drawing to a conclusion. With the burden of co-ordinating the Ontario Historical Society programs added to his already overwhelming curatorial tasks, he found himself more than ever confined to his office. Rare were the opportunities to escape the provincial museum and get out into the field. Only when word of an extraordinarily promising archaeological find reached his desk – usually one associated with a mound, earthwork, or ossuary – did he succumb to the temptation of the dig.

Such were the circumstances of a brief trip to Pelee Island in the summer of 1899 when he excavated several earth structures, two of which were certainly burial mounds, all Middle Woodland manifestations about which archaeologists still know very little.[1] Two years later, in August 1901, Boyle examined another mound group situated on three bluffs on the east side of Jordan Harbour in Lincoln County. These so-called Yellow Point Mounds may have been marginal components of the New York Point Peninsula people.[2] To the end of his career, Boyle remained perplexed as to the age of such mounds and the people who erected them. 'It is absolutely impossible, and, from the nature of the case must always remain impossible,' he concluded in 1901, 'to arrive at anything like assurance [sic] with regard to the date when any pre-historic earthwork was constructed.' He speculated that the builders of these structures must have had some contact with the Mississippi Valley Mound Builders, but he remained uncertain as to the nature of that connection.

What seems most likely is that they [Ontario mounds] were the work of some straggling bands from the main body [of those Amerinds who settled in the Mississippi Valley] during its southward movement (if it was a southward one), or of some bands which for one reason or another found their way back here shortly after this latitude had been passed, and before the making of huge mounds had become a matter of so much importance, as it afterwards did. Failing this, we can account for our mounds only on the supposition that the Algonkins, or their predecessors, whoever they may have been, went so far towards imitating their fellows to the south.'[3]

The discovery of the Parker earthwork two miles east of the St Clair River near Corunna, Lambton County, in 1901 prompted another of Boyle's rare field trips during these years. In customary fashion, he recorded the features of the site and helped Alfred Willson, a civil engineer and manager of the Canada Company, survey the embankment. Surprisingly, they failed to notice four circular burial mounds situated just outside the structure. This association of burial mounds and village, the several openings in the earthen walls, as well as the ceramic styles and other features, made this site unique. Archaeologists now think that the principal occupants of the Parker earthwork, identified as the 'Wolf Phase,' came out of Michigan in Late Woodland times.[4] Boyle sensed the earthwork to be significant, and pleaded for its conservation. 'As in the case of the Southwold earthwork, and in that of the Otonabee Serpent Mound,' he wrote, 'it is very desirable that steps should be taken to preserve this interesting example of early Indian occupation ... Some of us may live to see the time when provision will be made in law to prevent the destruction or removal of such ancient landmarks, as in some other countries.'[5] Fate was not to be as kind to the Parker earthwork as it was to the others; the site was partially razed in 1976 by the Dow Chemical Company.

It took the discovery of a late prehistoric Huron ossuary on the Stubbs farm near Bradford in Simcoe County to lure Boyle into the field during the summer of 1902. Upon arriving at the site he discovered that the local inhabitants had looted the burial pit. 'A ghoulish craze seemed to have taken possession of many people,' reported Boyle. On the principal streets of Bradford, skulls served as ornaments on many window-sills, 'while in not a few sitting-rooms they occupied prominent places on centre-tables.' Nobody could be persuaded to donate their 'gruesome specimens' to the provincial museum. 'At least one man,' explained an incredulous Boyle, 'contemplated having the top of his skull sawn off to form an ink-bottle stand! Of course he meant his Indian skull, but this was a mistake!'[6]

Although David Boyle firmly believed it was still his professional duty to maintain a semblance of a balance between his field-work and curatorial responsibilities, no longer did he feel the urgency of years past, when he had anxiously travelled back and forth across the province mindful that his annual operational funds might suddenly be terminated at the whim of a politician. Now, with the archaeological collection well established and his position relatively secure, he could leave most of the work of collecting artifacts, conducting regional field surveys and site inventories, and filing field reports to a growing number of competent amateur archaeologists. These included old stalwarts such as Laidlaw and Hunter, and newcomers such as F.W. Waugh in Brant County, R.T. Anderson in Elgin, L.D. Brown in Oxford, William Brodie in York, Frederick Birch in Grey, J. Hugh Hammond in Simcoe, and W.J. Wintemberg in Oxford and Waterloo.[7] The value of these people was recognized officially after the turn of the century by Richard Harcourt, the minister of education (1900–5), who consented to pay a portion of the expenses of the regular contributors to the *Archaeological Reports*. George Laidlaw continued to send Boyle his excellent field notes which detailed his systematic reconnaissance of Indian sites in North Victoria. By 1903 he had described, diagrammatically recorded, and excavated a total of thirty-nine sites in the Balsam Lake area.

By far the outstanding field man working for the provincial museum in these years was Andrew Hunter. Ontario archaeologists will be forever indebted to him for painstakingly examining and recording every Indian site that came to his attention. By foot, horse and buggy, and bicycle, he had scoured the fields, ridges, valleys, and old raised beaches of Simcoe County, systematically interviewing farmers, until he had compiled some 637 site references in his notebooks. The bulk of these extraordinarily rich sources of information was written up for the *Archaeological Reports* from 1899 to 1903. Hunter carefully described the sites and classified them (whether village, ossuary, or trail), pinpointed the lot and concession number, located them on maps, and analysed clusters of sites in relation to the topographical features of each township. He even managed to work out a rough chronology for many of the sites, by recording and plotting the presence or absence of French relics, and by relating groups of sites to the old raised beaches. Thanks to Hunter, the archaeological record of Huronia is the most complete of any region in the province.

Andrew Hunter's outstanding contributions aside, he also proved to be the most troublesome of Boyle's associates. A solitary and idiosyncratic individual, he was incapable of taking criticism from his colleagues. To those who dared contradict him he revealed a side of his personality that was aggressive, rude, and vindictive; in short, he could be, as David Boyle found out to his surprise, a curmudgeon of the worst sort. The relationship between the two friends began to sour in 1896 when Boyle refused to accept Hunter's theory that the so-called Innisfil serpent mound was man-made. The following year, Hunter also took it as a personal affront that the donations he had made to the provincial museum did not receive the preferred treatment accorded to the Laidlaw–Balsam Lake artifacts, which were then being arranged by village site in separate cases. That Hunter would react so petulantly may have been a function of the anxieties and frustrations of underemployment and a stagnating career. After selling the Barrie *Examiner* in 1895, Hunter had been at loose ends, desperately wanting an occupation in the archaeological or historical field. In fact, he coveted either one or both of Boyle's positions as archaeological curator at the provincial museum and secretary of the Ontario Historical Society. The longer he went without permanent employment, the more his jealousy of Boyle ripened. He convinced himself that he was the better scientist of the two – after all, had he not an MA in Physics from the University of Toronto to prove it? – and by far the more productive archaeologist.

Regrettably, Hunter sought his place in the archaeological community by devious means. To begin with he made every effort to besmirch Boyle's reputation among his colleagues and government officials. 'He [Boyle] complains of being overworked,' Hunter wrote to George Laidlaw in December 1898. 'If he would always work to advantage he would have lots of spare time, but he is as fussy as a wet hen and does not accomplish as much real work in a day as some men do in an hour.'[8] To officials in the department of education, Hunter deplored both the 'quantity and quality' of Boyle's work as compared to his own.[9] Combined with his behind-the-scenes attack on a man who still considered him to be a friend, Hunter schemed to carve out a career for himself in archaeology by paralleling Boyle's activities. He exploited his Liberal political connections and convinced George Ross to dip into the patronage funds in order to reimburse him for his submissions to the *Archaeological Reports*. By 1902, when Boyle's other volunteers acquired the same concession, Hunter received eight dollars per thousand words, nearly twice the going rate. Hunter also endeavoured to establish a rival archaeological journal based on his own research in Simcoe and adjacent counties. Anticipating that such a journal would show up Boyle's *Archaeological Reports* as an inferior product, and perhaps eventually supersede them, he convinced local Liberals that there were sound political reasons to promote his idea. For instance, the journal would please the Catholic vote by popularizing the history of the early missions.[10]

When Boyle got wind of this proposal, he hastened to convince the minister to resist the pressure for a separate publication. One *Archaeological Report*, he argued, served all purposes, scientific and political; there was no need for a rival journal. Beware of Hunter, he warned. 'He is an extremely persistent and pertinacious gentleman – always bound to carry his point, and he will harp on all his requirements as long as there is any hope.'[11] How prophetic! The following year, 1902, Hunter not only demanded five hundred copies under separate cover of his report on village sites in Oro Township, but an increase in his stipend as well.[12] Again Boyle moved to thwart his would-be-rival. 'His work is undoubtedly quite good,' he explained to Harcourt, 'but no better than that of Col. Laidlaw, and of Messrs. Waugh, Wintemberg, and Anderson, some of whom have contributed yearly without a cent of remuneration ... I would also like to point out that if it be decided to print for him 500 or any number of extra copies of his matter, there would not seem to be any reason why our other friends should not make a similar claim.'[13] The minister accepted the logic of Boyle's arguments and denied Hunter both his requests.

As time passed, Hunter began to lose all sense of balance and moderation, particularly after there appeared in the *Archaeological Reports* two articles that challenged his conclusions as to the location of the Huron villages of St Ignace II (where Jean de Brébeuf and Gabriel Lalement were said to have been martyred) and *Cahiagué*. In the *Report for 1902* A.E. Jones, SJ, of St Mary's College, Montreal, rejected Hunter's site identification for St Ignace II on the Hogg River, and located it instead on the 7th concession of Tay Township near Waubaushene. For years afterwards Hunter railed that Jones's theory was 'utterly without proof or probability.' He wrote to General John S. Clark of Auburn, New York: 'I think it was Boyle who sent Jones up here on his flying visit ... to "puncture" my work, but I think the "puncturing" has not been in my work. At any rate, the rubbish that Jones has divested himself of has been freely printed by Boyle at the people's expense. It looks learned, but it is a bag of wind.'[14] Hunter's disposition soured further after J. Hugh Hammond, an Orillia solicitor, published his '*Cahiagué*' in the *Archaeological Report* for 1904 and disputed Hunter's conclusion as to the location of yet another important Huron village.

To suggest as Hunter did that Boyle printed the Jones and Hammond manuscripts simply to undermine his reputation is absurd. Jones was a highly regarded scholar who based his conclusions on a thorough knowledge of the historical records, as well as imaginative field reconnaissance.[15] Similarly, J. Hugh Hammond's arguments for locating *Cahiagué* in South Orillia Township also seemed plausible, at least as plausible as Hunter's hypothesis that the village site was to be found in Oro Township; both their studies were based on a careful sifting of the available documentary and archaeological evidence. Had Hunter been singled out for attack in the *Reports*, he may have

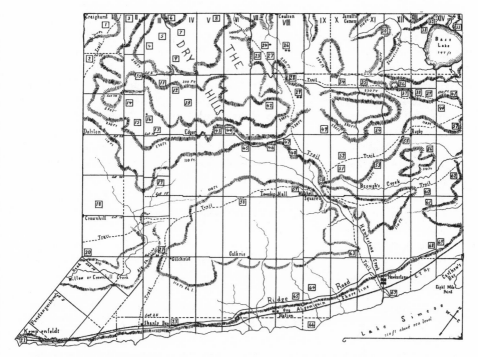

Archaeological map of Oro Township, Simcoe County, drawn by A.F. Hunter
(*Archaeological Report 1902*)

had reason for complaint; however, such was not the case. Even A.E. Jones
was not above criticism. His arguments as to the site location of *Ekaren-
niondi*, the standing rock from which the Petun village of St Mathias took its
name, was persuasively challenged by Frederick Birch in the *Archaeological
Report for 1903*.[16] The amusing thing about these early disputes over village
locations is that few of the participants, forced by necessity to rely on
inadequate evidence, have been borne out by subsequent study. In fact, the
controversy over both *Cahiagué* and St Ignace II goes on to this day.[17]

All the same, following the appearance of the Jones article in 1902 Hunter's
ire knew no bounds, and his letters to the department of education became
imperious in the extreme. 'As the chief part of the reading matter on this Oro
map cannot be seen without a microscope,' he declared to Harcourt with
reference to the galley proof of a map for the *Archaeological Report for 1902*,
'I refuse emphatically to permit such a caricature to appear in print with my
report.'[18] The minister's reply was devastating: 'The tone of your letter is
inexcusably harsh, and if another such letter reaches me I will return your

manuscript, and you may do with it exactly as you wish ... It is desirable that there should be uniformity in the design of our report, and I am determined to treat all contributors alike.'[19] Undaunted and unrepentant, Hunter resurfaced the following year and again denounced Boyle for denying him an enlarged map for his report on North and South Orillia townships. On this occasion he directed his invective to the deputy minister, who, as it turned out, was no more sympathetic to Hunter's position than Minister of Education Harcourt.[20]

This unseemly course of events finally ended in 1904 when Hunter received permanent employment with the Geological Survey of Canada. Ontario archaeology suffered as a consequence, for he subsequently dropped out of the archaeological limelight. For this outcome he had only himself to blame; he was the victim of his own personality. Hunter possessed the talents and the energy to build a career in archaeology, perhaps even to fill Boyle's shoes after his debilitating stroke in 1908. But it was not to be. Instead, William John Wintemberg replaced Hunter as the stellar performer on Boyle's team and went on to become Canada's outstanding archaeologist between the two world wars.

From the moment they first met in 1897, David Boyle instantly liked and admired Wintemberg who had just turned twenty-one years of age. In this intense, studious, and largely self-educated young man, the son of a blacksmith of Alsatian ancestry, Boyle must have been struck by the many parallels with his own experience. During his upbringing in Waterloo County, Wintemberg had developed an insatiable appetite for science in general. He owned an impressive private library, and had assembled a modest archaeological collection of some five hundred artifacts. 'I do not merely gather these specimens for the sake of getting a larger number together, but for the purposes of study,' he wrote in one of his first letters to Boyle. 'I have been greatly helped by the information given in your annual reports.'[21] During these years Wintemberg conducted systematic archaeological surveys of Waterloo and Oxford counties. In Blenheim Township, Oxford County, he actually visited every single farm during his investigations. By 1900 he was adept at distinguishing between Neutral and pre-Neutral sites.[22]

Wintemberg's emergence as a professional archaeologist prior to World War One was an arduous and frustrating experience. He wrote to Boyle in February 1898: 'As I am – owing to continued delicate health – out of employment at my trade (printing) and desiring to obtain employment where I could be outside most of the time, and being, also, anxious to engage in scientific work, could you tell me, or do you know any person engaged in archaeological, geological or biological field work with whom I could get

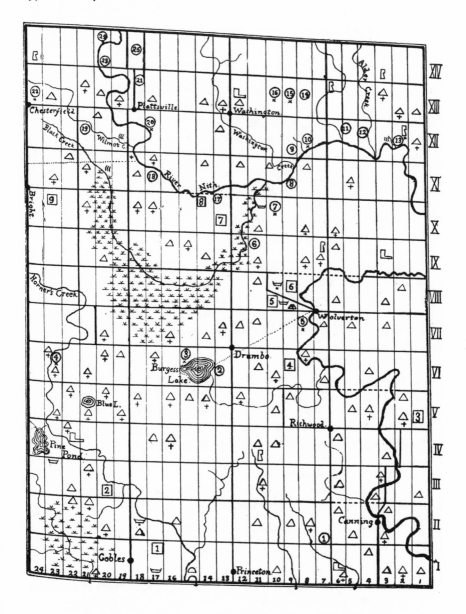

Archaeological map of Blenheim Township, Oxford County, drawn by W.J. Wintemberg (*Archaeological Report 1902*)

employment as an assistant? Salary no object so long as I could make a living.'[23] Boyle was unable to do much for him apart from providing an occasional few weeks' work at the museum. He tried in vain to find Wintemberg suitable employment with one of his many contacts. Had the choice been his, Boyle would have hired him in an instant. In 1903 he described his young protégé as the 'one man whom I would care to trust' in a curatorial capacity at the provincial museum.[24]

Wintemberg moved to Toronto about 1902, and for nine years worked at various trades such as printing and stencil-making. Although financial constraints curtailed his diligent field-work, as an alternative he frequented the provincial museum where he prepared exhaustively researched studies of various types of artifacts. These included his lavishly illustrated 'Bone and Horn Harpoon Heads of the Ontario Indians,'[25] and 'The Use of Shells by the Ontario Indians.'[26] Boyle granted his protégé full intellectual freedom in publishing these articles, even when he disagreed with his conclusions. In 'Are the Perforated Bone Needles Prehistoric,' Wintemberg postulated that this artifact type was confined to the Iroquoian family and claimed a European origin for eyed, bone needles. Although Boyle did not agree with the latter argument, he printed the manuscript on the grounds that 'Mr. Wintemberg is a close and intelligent observer, and his remarks are worthy of consideration.'[27]

Wintemberg followed Boyle and most other North American archaeologists in focusing on the functional interpretation of the material, and in projecting ethnographical insights back into prehistory. By present-day standards, his initial efforts at functional analysis and interpretation appear to be quaint but relatively sound. In undertaking such studies he was breaking new ground in Ontario archaeology by attempting to reconstruct the life ways of past peoples. His work also demonstrated that for the first time sufficient artifactual data was available in a museum setting for a scholar to prepare scientific studies on specimen types distributed across the southern portion of the province. For that development David Boyle could take most of the credit.

11

Although the weight of Boyle's curatorial and historical society responsibilities after 1898 curtailed his activities in the field and forced him to rely on his team of quasi-professional co-workers, he was able to devote more of his time in the museum to artifact analysis. As a consequence, some of his best reports on function and aboriginal working methods appeared in these years. For

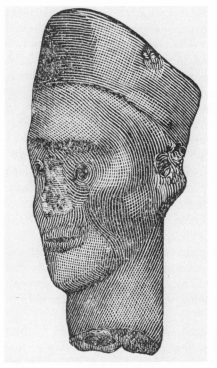 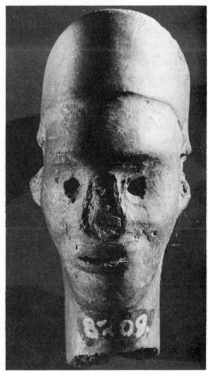

Effigy pipe, Clearville site, 1889. The line drawing appeared in the *Archaeological Report 1888–9*; the photograph was taken from the original in the Royal Ontario Museum (ROM, Toronto)

instance, using as his evidence the magnificient pipe collection at the provincial museum, he took issue with Joseph D. McGuire who, in his 'Pipes and Smoking Customs of the American Aborigines, based on material in the United States National Museum,' had concluded that all but the simplest straight tubular pipes smacked of European influences. From his own experience Boyle knew this theory to be wrong, and convincingly marshalled the evidence to prove his point. 'To admit that our Indians were indebted to Europeans for every notion respecting the shapes and decorative devices in pipe-making is to deny that the aborigines possessed any imagination, or much mechanical ability,' he argued.[28] Such a notion flew in the face of an immense body of archaeological evidence.

McGuire also drew a spirited response from Boyle for suggesting that sheet-copper found in the Ohio mounds, and socketed copper implements unearthed elsewhere, were not prehistoric. The Ontario evidence, argued Boyle, clearly indicated that 'long before The Discovery' the aborigines had developed the use of the copper socket and tying hole.[29] It seemed to him that too many archaeologists such as McGuire exaggerated the extent of European influences on Amerindian cultures, and wrongly assumed that prehistoric man in America lacked even a modicum of inventiveness. Boyle went on to accuse William M. Beauchamp of this same transgression for suggesting that 'no New York or Canadian Indian ever made a bone comb until he had European hints' and possessed steel tools.[30] This contention, Boyle retorted, did not stand up to critical analysis. Interestingly, on this point Boyle received the full support of the internationally celebrated Egyptologist, William Flinders Petrie of University College, London, England. 'On reading your ... report of 1903,' he wrote to Boyle, 'I can at once answer your debate as to the possibility of the bone combs ... having been made without steel tools. They are very closely like the prehistoric Egyptian combs, made when copper was scarce and little worked, and no other working metal known; it is certain that flint must have been the tool material. I add some outlines for you to compare, only don't set off some wiseacres proving that the Amerinds came from Egypt, 6000 B.C.!'[31]

The debates with McGuire and Beauchamp were carried on in the best scholarly tradition, free of the acrimony that characterized Boyle's discussions with Andrew Hunter. In order that his colleagues might respond to his arguments[32] in the same issue, Boyle sent them advance copies of his own criticisms. For a self-educated man, he had a finely developed sense of what constituted scholarly intellectual debate. His approach was obviously appreciated. 'I think legitimate criticism is of interest to all students,' commented McGuire upon receiving his advance copy, 'and adds to knowledge when intelligently expressed.'[33] McGuire later penned a glowing review of the *Archaeological Report for 1903* for the *American Anthropologist*,[34] in spite of the sharp criticism of his own work it contained. 'The Report as a whole,' he confided privately to Boyle, 'I frankly believe to be your best one.'[35] Similarly, neither did William Beauchamp take offence at Boyle's critical analysis of his work. He held Boyle's opinion in high esteem. 'Don't forget reports for me,' he had written several years earlier. 'Can't do without them.'[36]

In fact, by the turn of the century the *Archaeological Reports for Ontario*, replete with regional field reports and Boyle's own notes on artifact types and working methods, had become widely appreciated and sought after by archaeologists across North America and Europe. Cyrus Thomas of the

Smithsonian 'highly appreciated' receiving them, and always examined them 'with care, interest and profit.'[37] The *Reports* were used and cited by Frederick Ward Hodge in his *Handbook of American Indians North of Mexico* (1907), published by the Smithsonian Institution. Renowned British scholars such as Flinders Petrie, Sir John Evans, and W. Boyd Dawkins perused them regularly. So too, did the popular French prehistorian, the Marquis de Nadaillac, who praised Boyle's work in the prestigious *L'Anthropologie*. Not only were Boyle's *Archaeological Reports* being reviewed regularly and sympathetically in the best journals, but the leading professional organizations in the English-speaking world began to acknowledge his contributions in a variety of ways. The British Association for the Advancement of Science, for instance, made a special request of the Ontario Minister of Education that Boyle be permitted to address the BAAS annual meeting in Bradford, England, in September 1900, a request to which the minister acceded. That same year, the Anthropological Institute of Great Britain and Ireland asked Boyle to serve as their 'Corresponding Member' in Canada, a position of no little prestige that required him to keep the institute informed of current matters of an anthropological nature in the dominion.[38]

Two years later, a special committee made up of delegates representing the Anthropological Society of Washington, the American Ethnological Society, and the anthropological section of the American Association for the Advancement of Science further acknowledged Boyle's pre-eminent role in Canadian archaeology and ethnology by inviting him to support their effort to unite American anthropologists in one powerful organization. He accepted without hesitation, and thus became a founding member of the American Anthropological Association established in June 1902 during the Pittsburgh meeting of the AAAS. Shortly after, he was appointed to the editorial board of the *American Anthropologist*, the official organ of the American Anthropological Association. President W.J. McGee explained that Boyle's membership on the committee was required to 'give the journal something of an international character.' As the sole Canadian, he was expected to 'direct appropriate contributions toward the journal' from among his associates across the dominion.[39] In serving on this board from 1903 until his death in 1911, Boyle was in impressive company; his name appeared along with such luminaries as the redoubtable Franz Boas of Columbia University, F.W. Putnam of Harvard, F.W. Hodge of the Smithsonian, W.H. Holmes of the United States National Museum, A.F. Chamberlain of Clarke University, and A.L. Kroeber of the University of California.

That David Boyle was now internationally recognized as Canada's foremost archaeologist and ethnologist did not escape the attention of some

influential figures in the Toronto academic community. This fact first became apparent in the spring of 1900 when Professor George M. Wrong of
the University of Toronto History Department attempted to entice Boyle
and his archaeological collection into the university structure. 'In regard to
the Ethnological Museum,' Wrong enquired, 'is it possible to negotiate a plan
for amalgamating the two museums [referring to the archaeological section of
the provincial museum and the university collection] on the basis of their
being housed under your charge at the University? You know what excellent
accommodation we have there.'40 Although the two men met to discuss this
scheme, nothing came of it. Most likely the government gave short shrift to
Wrong's suggestion that the archaeological section of the provincial museum
be moved out of the normal school, when just three years earlier the building
had been renovated at considerable expense to accommodate Boyle's
collections.

It was most unfortunate that Ontario archaeology did not fall under the
aegis of the University of Toronto at this time. Had the transfer been made,
the trend towards professionalism would have been given an enormous boost.
Experience in the United States, where archaeology, ethnology, and higher
education had already been linked, suggested that the teaching of these
subjects at the university level would have soon followed. Professor Wrong's
idea was an excellent one; the pity is that he did not make this suggestion a few
years earlier when Boyle had desperately sought to escape the confines of the
Canadian Institute. As a result, Canadian universities were destined to lag far
behind their American counterparts in pursuing ethnological and archaeological studies. It was not until 1926 that Thomas F. McIlwraith established the
country's first anthropology department at the University of Toronto; and
not until 1938 that McIlwraith hired Dr Philleo Nash, the first professional
archaeologist to teach prehistoric archaeology at a Canadian university. With
the appointment of Dr J. Norman Emerson in 1946 at the University of
Toronto, the first serious program to train Canadian archaeologists in Canada
finally was launched.41

III

If Boyle was upset that the University of Toronto scheme failed to
materialize, his disappointment was soon forgotten. A scant three weeks
following his discussions with Professor Wrong in mid-June 1900, the
minister of education declared that he was prepared to send Boyle to Britain
that summer to present a paper to the BAAS annual meeting in Bradford. It
came as a pleasant surprise that a government that steadfastly refused to

augment Boyle's salary of one thousand dollars had consented to grant him four hundred dollars to travel abroad, presumably to promote the province's stature in science and education.

A month later, in early August, David and Martha Boyle were en route to New York City and the start of a grueling two-month itinerary that took them to Liverpool, Paris, London, Edinburgh, and Glasgow, with a pilgrimage down the Clyde to Greenock and on to the Ayrshire countryside of David's youth. As tourists, the excursion met their every expectation. They particularly enjoyed the sights of Paris – the Eiffel Tower, the Louvre, the palaces of Versailles and Luxembourg, and the World's Fair – and the traditional tourist haunts, theatres, and concerts of London. In a professional sense, the trip was no less fulfilling. At the BAAS annual meeting on 5 September 1900 Boyle's paper 'On the Paganism of the Civilized Iroquois of Ontario' was warmly received and later published in the *Journal of the Anthropological Institute* (1900). While in France and Britain, Boyle also made a study of several of the outstanding archaeological collections, including those at the Louvre and the British Museum. He discovered that his modest archaeological museum in Toronto compared favourably with the best that Europe had to offer. 'So far as labels, arrangement and classification are concerned,' he reported to the minister of education, 'little was seen that could suggest any improvement on our own methods.'[42] Ethnologically, he confessed, the provincial museum was woefully deficient.

Boyle's admiration for the ethnological collections in the major European museums strengthened his resolve to place considerably more emphasis on the anthropological side of his work. Upon returning to Toronto, a stream of letters soliciting donations flowed out of his office to various museums and to religious missions all over the world. Within two years, missionaries in such far-flung outposts as the New Hebrides, Angola, Bella Bella, BC, and Herschel Island near the mouth of the Mackenzie River, obliged him by sending crates full of samples of native dress, ornaments, weapons, and utensils. Meanwhile, George Laidlaw, who served (1901–2) in the Canadian contingent during the Boer War, and Frederick Hamilton, a correspondent for the Toronto *Globe*, sent material from South Africa. Exchanges with other museums also proved beneficial. In 1901, for example, George A. Dorsey of the Field Columbian Museum in Chicago sent Boyle some two hundred specimens peculiar to Paraguayan tribes in return for duplicate Ontario archaeological artifacts.[43] Soon after, exchanges were arranged with the Imperial Museum in Tokyo and the Australian Museum in Sydney, New South Wales. By 1903 Boyle had gathered sufficient material to warrant the opening of a separate ethnological room in the provincial museum.

Finally, the European excursion proved beneficial in another, quite unexpected way. In Edinburgh, Boyle stumbled upon the gallery of the sculptor, D.W. Stevenson, ARSA, and was enormously impressed by a display model for a statue of Scotland's bard, Robert Burns. Upon his return to Toronto, Boyle convinced the local Burns Monument Committee, of which he was a member, to procure a copy of Stevenson's statuary which, thanks to Boyle's preliminary negotiations, was acquired 'at a very moderate cost.'[44] The monument, one of many erected in cities across North America in these years by Scots imbued with the cult of Burns, was donated to the City of Toronto and unveiled in Allan Gardens on 21 July 1902.

Boyle's two-month trip abroad provided a needed respite from the pressures of work. During his travels the realization struck him that at fifty-eight years of age, a recognized expert in his profession, the time had arrived to curb his ambitions and his hitherto frenetic expenditures of energy. The first thing he determined to do upon returning to Toronto was to resign as secretary of the Ontario Historical Society. 'The present condition of affairs,' he wrote to the minister of education in November 1900 to explain his reasons for resigning, 'is such that at many times I am compelled to give more attention to the Society's work than to the Museum, while the truth is that the Museum itself requires even more attention than I am able to give it even when I have nothing else to do.'[45]

During his two-year tenure as secretary, Boyle had conscientiously, and without complaint, handled the enormous amount of office routine, committee work, and annual meeting arrangements with characteristic zeal. Next to President James Coyne, he was perhaps the person most responsible for establishing the OHS on a firm footing in its formative years. His membership campaign netted the society some two hundred members. He forged a close relationship between it and the historical section of the Ontario Educational Association by arranging joint meetings each year and by convincing many educators to join the historical society, including such worthies as James L. Hughes of Toronto, Joseph H. Smith of Hamilton, John Dearness of London, and Adam Shortt of Queen's University, Kingston. Boyle's responsibilities also included preparing a substantial annual report, and helping to edit the *Ontario Historical Society Papers and Records*. On top of all these efforts, he actively participated on the committees to establish patriotic monuments to Laura Secord at Lundy's Lane (unveiled 22 June 1901) and to John Graves Simcoe at Queen's Park (unveiled 27 May 1903).

Furthermore, by personal communication and circular letter, Boyle had assiduously solicited books, documents, and historical artifacts to establish the nucleus of a provincial historical library, museum, and archives along the lines of the Wisconsin Historical Society, as envisioned by James Coyne when he reorganized the OHS in 1898. Towards this end, Boyle had worked closely during the first half of 1899 with the Women's Canadian Historical Society of Toronto in organizing the 'Great Canadian Historical Exhibition' at Victoria College in late June. He personally obtained monies for the event and gave freely of his time and advice in the setting up of the displays. The exhibition comprised thousands of items gathered from across Canada, so many in fact, that it took a catalogue of 150 pages to list them all. To complement the exhibits, the OHS organizers laid on a full schedule of lectures and concerts. People flocked into Victoria College during the two-week run in such numbers that they forced an extension of the exhibition for an additional three days. According to *Saturday Night*, the event proved to be 'one of the successes of a very bright season.'[46]

If the weight of the workload at the Ontario Historical Society was one factor in Boyle's decision to resign as secretary in November 1900, another was the realization that the society would not achieve, at least in the forseeable future, its grandiose plans to establish a publicly supported provincial library, archives, and museum building on the Wisconsin model. As early as June 1900, James Coyne bemoaned the fact that 'the Society is hampered in its operations for want of funds.'[47] Coyne, his impeccable Liberal credentials notwithstanding, had been naïve to think that the department of education would be any more generous in supporting the OHS than it had been in funding Boyle and archaeology. Eventually the government would make provision for a provincial archives and a museum of history in Toronto, although in ways quite unexpected by the Ontario Historical Society. In 1903, for instance, the Ross administration responded to heavy OHS pressure and appointed a provincial archivist, but as part of the civil service.[48] This development meant that Coyne's vision of a public archives under OHS auspices would not be realized. And by another cruel twist of fate, the OHS hope for a provincial historical museum foundered in the wake of a more powerful claim by Toronto's intellectual and social elite for a first-class museum dedicated to the full sweep of man's world development. Such an institution, the Royal Ontario Museum, eventually opened its doors in 1914.

Much to Boyle's astonishment, resigning as OHS secretary proved to be more difficult than he ever imagined. He was nonplussed to learn that the executive council refused to accept his resignation; he was simply too important a connection with the education department to be lost without a struggle. Besides, Boyle represented 'cheap labour' at an annual salary of $100, especially since he conducted OHS business during office hours at the museum. Only Andrew Hunter, also a member of the executive council, advised that Boyle be permitted to step down – a not unexpected suggestion since he coveted the position for himself. Hunter argued, without basis in fact, that Boyle was the cause of the society's financial plight. 'Intimations I have had,' Hunter wrote confidentially to James Coyne, 'lead me to understand that he [Boyle] has been extremely averse to contributing even the smallest part of his earnings to the Government campaigns.' This stance, he continued, probably shaped 'the attitude of the Government toward him and every matter with which he is connected. The delegation that urged the Government to give the society a larger grant last winter could not have been more influential than it was, and yet what was the result?'[49] To their credit, nobody else on the executive took such arguments seriously.

Under the threat of losing their secretary, the OHS leaders tried to convince the minister of education to provide Boyle with an assistant curator to free a portion of his time for historical society matters. The only concession they obtained from Harcourt was a new typewriter for Boyle and the promise of some stenographic assistance. Still, these trifles, combined with the moral suasion of his friends on the executive council, proved sufficient to convince a reluctant Boyle to remain on as secretary. Not surprisingly, though, a mere six months later, in June 1901, a harried Boyle, in the midst of setting up an Ontario archaeological exhibit at the Pan-American Exposition in Buffalo, New York, threw up his hands in exasperation at his inability to conduct OHS business as efficiently as he wished, and resigned a second time. On cue, the executive council repeated its lobby to retain Boyle's services, and this time convinced the minister of education to provide him with some part-time curatorial assistance at the museum. Again Boyle relented and withdrew his resignation. One of the first to benefit from this development seems to have been W.J. Wintemberg, hired for five weeks to help Boyle arrange and supervise the impressive archaeological display at the Pan-American Exposition. Their exhibit, as it happened, was awarded the silver medal in its class.

The OHS decision to retain Boyle's services was probably a mistake. Even with additional help at the museum, it was only with great difficulty that he was able to do an adequate job of carrying on the society's business. His enthusiasm flagged badly under the monotonous and oppressive routine. On occasion he was embarrassed by his own inefficiency; for instance, the *Annual Report of the OHS for 1902* which he prepared was 'such a mess of error and misses' that he forbade its wide distribution.[50] During this period, moreover, the membership drives that he had conducted so successfully during his first two years as secretary ground to a halt. Fortunately, the society did not depend entirely upon Boyle's effectiveness; rather, the strength of the OHS prior to the First World War lay in the availability of a rich pool of talented and dedicated activists. These included James Coyne, Charles Canniff James, the deputy minister of agriculture, George Pattullo, the registrar of Oxford County, Collingwood journalist David Williams, Clementina Fessenden, the reputed originator of the Empire Day concept, and Frederic Barlow Cumberland, vice-president of the Niagara Navigation Company. These people were deeply committed to the society, motivated as they were by an insurgent British-Canadian nationalism sharpened by growing nativist fears over the effects of the massive flow of immigration into Canada during the Laurier boom. The opportunity to be associated with these activists, and the fact that he shared their concerns, probably accounts for Boyle's decision to continue on as OHS secretary until 1907 despite his misgivings.

By 1900, economic expansion and a growing national pride and consciousness had dispelled most of the earlier annexationist fears of the 1880s and 1890s. The buoyant optimism and pride inspired by Ontario's material prosperity explains part of the OHS leaders' urge to create symbols of their heritage and otherwise to preserve their past. At the same time, however, Boyle and others were keenly aware of the fragility of the developing Canadian character in a period noted for its rampant materialism and massive immigration. They believed that material prosperity could not alone provide a satisfactory foundation upon which to build a nation state. The 'greatness of a nation' depended as much upon the 'character of the people' as 'the magnitude of the population or the wealth of possessions,' preached Barlow Cumberland. Patriotism rooted in an understanding of the OHS's version of Canada's past could help to mould a people's character; it 'arises to wrest the people out of their selfishness, and fuses them mightily into a pervading fervid fellowship – a process of amalgamating power arising from a spirit of self-sacrifice, rather than of self-seeking.'[51] Such ideas, presented in the spirit of reform, had great appeal to Boyle and others who called into question the quality of life in an increasingly urban and industrial Ontario. They offered an aroused patriotism as the essential purgative for the spiritual ills of a society seemingly dominated by unbridled materialism.

Another and more powerful consideration impelled Boyle and his colleagues to develop patriotic sentiments in this era of prosperity. They feared the possibility that the influx of immigrants, particularly those from central and southern Europe, would endanger their British-Canadian character. Like most English-speaking Ontarians, the OHS leaders believed that Canada was and should remain an Anglo-Saxon country embodying 'the highest principles of Christianity and civilization.' Their collective thought hinged on concepts of social Darwinism, Anglo-Saxon superiority, the 'white man's burden,' and the myth of the superiority of the northern races. Moved by these concerns and beliefs, they continued to champion the cause of imperial unity and stepped up their patriotic activities. These included the promotion of Empire Day and flag exercises, the building of inspirational monuments, the introduction of symbolic decorations into the schools, the preservation of historical sites, especially those connected with the loyalists and the War of 1812, the creation of pioneer and historical museums, the collection of documents, and the publication of patriotic history.

For Boyle, one of the few pleasures associated with the position of OHS secretary involved supporting contemporary imperialist demands for imperial penny postage and legislation to encourage the entry into the country of British rather than American newspapers and magazines. The following quote from one of the McSpurtle 'epistles' captures the intensity of Boyle's feelings on these questions: '[Joseph] Chamberlain's the man we've to thank for ocean penny postage. Hoo des this look to the everlastin' smaert Yankee? Here we Britishers are awa ahead o' the "greatest people in the whole world!" ... Rule Britannia! Britannia rules the waves! Hip, hip, hip, hooray! hooray! an' a teeger. Hooray!'[52]

It was something of a paradox that while, on the one hand, Boyle and his friends boasted of their superior Anglo-Saxon qualities, their thoughts, on the other, were riddled with doubts as to the future integrity of the British-Canadian character under the impact of European immigration during the Laurier era. 'What are we to do with our foreigners?' asked James Coyne, giving voice to a question that worried concerned educators, clergymen, journalists, and politicians across Canada.[53] Moderate elements within the Ontario Historical Society eschewed restricting immigration, and instead believed in the capacity of the schools, churches, and national and historical societies to assimilate all immigrants so that unwanted alterations in the national character would not occur. A patriotic history to them was a vitally important tool in the process of absorbing 'foreign elements.'

David Boyle took a more pessimistic and extreme position in this debate than did the majority of spokesmen for the OHS. He demanded an exclusionist immigration policy against those peoples he considered inferior and non-assimilable. Citing his credentials as an expert in ethnology, he wrote to Frank Oliver, the minister of the interior (1905–11), that 'it appeared to be extremely foolish on the part of any government to introduce as settlers representatives of peoples whose history had shown them to be incapable of high civilization, or of any kind of civilization at all worthy of the name.' Central and southern Europeans like the 'Poles and Sicilians' he believed to be 'utterly incompetent,' 'without an immense amount of training,' and un-worthy of 'being called civilized people.' Echoing nativist propaganda heard frequently in the United States, he associated these immigrants with urban crime and vice. 'The cost consequent on the introduction of such peoples into any country, will in all probability far outweigh the returns.'[54] 'Hindoos and Sikhs' were also unwelcome. In their case, he explained to Henri Bourassa, the French-Canadian *nationaliste* leader, himself an exponent of tighter im-migration laws, 'it was not so much a matter of civilization as perhaps of physical incapacity to assimilate themselves to climactic conditions.'[55]

In uttering such views, David Boyle was expressing the standard clichés and prejudices of his times, and the racial theories of late-nineteenth-century anthropology. His response, and that of OHS spokesmen in general to the immigrant issue, was consistent with a wider North American pattern of attitudes. During the 1880s and 1890s, when earlier waves of newcomers from continental shores had reached the United States, a similar nativist reaction against non-Anglo-Saxon people had swept that country. So-called American patriots, arguing that to be great a nation needed an homogeneous people, called for a reawakened sense of nationality and set into motion a campaign for flag exercises, pledges, symbols of a patriotic history, and the like.[56] Insofar as it was presented as a partial remedy for the immigrant crisis, the Ontario Historical Society program prior to World War One was simply a northern extension of the nativistic outburst that had occurred earlier in the United States.

IV

If David Boyle proved at times to be a mediocre secretary of the Ontario Historical Society following his two unsuccessful attempts to resign in 1900 and 1901, there was good reason for his substandard performance. His re-sponsibilities at the provincial museum increased enormously after October 1901, when the minister of education requested that he accept the new position of superintendent of the entire museum. The institution had become a major administrative headache for the department of education as the various individuals and groups in charge of specific collections quarrelled over space and funding.[57] Worse still, since no one person had general oversight in the museum prior to Boyle's appointment, and since the several curators possessed different levels of competence, the overall quality of the institution had deteriorated to the point that it was becoming an embarrassment to the government.[58] After reviewing the personnel at his disposal, the minister chose Boyle as the individual most likely to bring order out of the confusion.

The new superintendent wasted not a moment in preparing lengthy, hard-hitting memoranda on the state of the provincial museum. 'A finished or stand-still museum is a dead museum,' he explained in November, and several departments had long ago reached the state of being moribund. 'Except in the matter of a few busts of local celebrities, nothing has been added ... in the way of statuary for a quarter of a century or more, and the same may be said respecting copies of the old Masters.' In some departments specimens were left in a state if disrepair. Most of the museum, with the exception of archaeology, was badly labelled. There was no catalogue to assist visitors. The museum lacked adequate security and caretaking staff. All in all, it had become quite shabby looking. 'Our rooms frequently become so dirty that ladies have to move about with uplifted skirts; the glass in the wall cases becomes obscured as a result of finger marking, and the table cases go for days without even a suspicion of a duster.'

The unsatisfactory condition of the institution, Boyle continued, was largely owing to inadequate funding. He noted that the Pennsylvania State Museum received an annual grant of close to fifty thousand dollars. 'I believe that in many other States the appropriation runs from $5,000 to $15,000. Even the lower figure would be to us like a Godsend, if only for a year.' In comparison, the operating funds for the provincial museum in 1901 came to about $2600 and that included Boyle's salary! He concluded that under such circumstances the museum had 'for many years' utterly 'failed to serve its legitimate purpose' of ministering to the diverse educational needs both of serious students and the general public.[59]

The minister of education read with disbelief Boyle's assessment of the provincial museum. He knew the place had its problems, but surely this was a gross exaggeration of the truth by the new, overly enthusiastic super-intendent. Harcourt reacted by asking several knowledgeable individuals, including Charles Canniff James, Dr William Brodie, a prominent naturalist, John Ross Robertson of the Toronto *Telegram*, and Byron Edmund Walker, general manager of the Canadian Bank of Commerce, to make their own separate judgments. To a man, they confirmed everything Boyle had written.[60] Walker's analysis was the most detailed and devastating of the lot. That Ontario was in great need of first-rate, publicly supported museums, Walker had no doubt, but the provincial museum was in such a miserable condition that he advised that most of it be scrapped or distributed to the smaller university collections. 'My advice is,' he wrote, 'advance and develop as far as possible the one good thing you have, the Archaeological and Ethnological Department, and get rid of the rest. In this Department you can do something which will bring credit to all concerned.'[61]

Although his assessment may have been correct in most respects, Walker's drastic solution was not realistic. Politically, it was not possible for the department of education to dismantle the museum after spending considerable sums on its expansion. More significantly, despite its seedy appearance, it was popular among culturally starved Ontarians, some fifty thousand of whom trooped through its halls annually.[62] 'There is no institution in Canada which is better known to the population generally than this one,' claimed Boyle. 'It is from our collections that many thousands have learned (and continue to learn) all they know of Art, Ancient and Modern; of the fauna of our own and other countries; of Ontario's floral forms, and of material illustrative of aboriginal life ... What "we saw" in the "Normal School Museum" forms ... a frequent subject of conversation at rural gatherings and in domestic circles.'[63] Since it played so important a part in the cultural life of the province, the museum could not easily be terminated. To have delivered the *coup de grace* in 1902 would have been premature since there was no alternative at the time, and there would be no alternative until the Royal Ontario Museum opened for business a decade later. At least the review of the museum by Walker and the others served a useful purpose. Their reports moved the minister to grant Boyle a permanent stenographer, and the authority to effect a list of minor improvements to the displays and to begin implementing policies for upgrading the weaker departments. During the ensuing months, Boyle plunged into the task of relabelling the museum with the energy of a man half his age.

The position of superintendent of the provincial museum meant so much to David Boyle that when offered the post in October 1901 he accepted it for a mere one hundred dollar increase in salary. This response is particularly revealing when just the year before he had grown so frustrated in his inability to augment his income that he began to look for alternative employment. At the time he had written a frank letter of complaint to the minister: 'There is certainly no other person in America doing anything like the same quantity or quality of work ... who is so poorly paid ... [A] salary of $1000 is not only too little to support the small amount of dignity that ought to attach itself to [my] position, but is too small to maintain a decent livelihood, and involves cheeseparing economy.'[64] Despite this situation, Boyle still accepted the superintendency at virtually his old salary. Even more significant was the fact that in May 1902 he turned down the position of director of anthropology at the Pennsylvania State Museum at three times the pay! 'You were always a damn fool along the money line anyhow but I think this is madness,' wrote one of those who had recommended Boyle for the post over such a capable candidate as Gerard Fowke. 'Canada is too slow a country and you will never get $2000 there if you live to be as old as Methusslah [sic].'[65]

Before many months had passed Boyle would entertain second thoughts about rejecting the Pennsylvania offer; at the time, though, he had good reason for remaining in Toronto. For one thing, at sixty years of age he could not abide the thought of walking away from his accomplishments at the provincial museum for the sake of monetary compensation alone. No matter how much he complained about his salary scale, the fact remains that he loved his work and took enormous pride in his archaeological collection. Moreover, what he lost in financial terms, he gained ten-fold in self-esteem. The thought that he, David Boyle, had been given control of the Ontario Provincial Museum left him dumbfounded. In his mind, he now held the most prestigious curatorial position in Canada. Since his first association with the Ontario educational system in Wellington County, he had looked upon the provincial museum with awe and deep respect. He took it for granted that most everyone else who had taught, or who had been a student in Ontario over the past half-century, did the same. No matter how paltry the salary, he now had charge of a recognized cultural centre of national reputation. One could not easily give up such a position.

Still, Boyle's initial self-satisfaction and enthusiasm would wane over time, beginning with his attendance at the New York meeting of the International Congress of Americanists in October 1902. The congress, a scholarly association established in 1875 to study the archaeology and anthropology of the Americas, convened every two years alternately on each side of the Atlantic. Boyle joined the organization in 1902 to take advantage of the opportunity afforded those who attended the meeting that year to tour most of the major museums in the eastern United States. The delegates first convened in New York City (20–25 October) at the American Museum of Natural History for a program of learned papers and instruction in museum practices. The following week they set off on a marathon railway excursion that took them to the United States National Museum and the Smithsonian Institution in Washington, DC, the University of Pennsylvania Museum in Philadelphia, the Carnegie Institute in Pittsburgh, the Eden Park Museum in Cincinnati, and the Field Columbian Museum in Chicago.[66]

Although a new member of the congress, one of 219 delegates representing nineteen countries, Boyle received special attention and courtesies from the organizers. By chance, he was but one of two Canadians in attendance (the other being Edmond Roy, FRSC), and also the only official corresponding member of the Anthropological Institute of Great Britain and Ireland. The New York meeting of the congress attracted the élite of the North American anthropological fraternity. 'Many valuable papers were read,' reported

Boyle, 'but the main profit arose from personal contact with those pursuing similar courses of study in both Hemispheres.' He delighted in the opportunity to spend endless hours in conversation, both wet and dry, with many old friends and new acquaintances.

Apart from the benefits of conversation with his fellow archaeologists and ethnologists, Boyle absorbed many lessons from his tours of the various museums. On the positive side, he reported to the minister of education: 'I can freely say that our own museum, comparatively small as it is, did not in many respects suffer by comparison and this with due modesty I may state is especially true in relation to our Archaeological arrangement. In Biological matters we are generally far behind, but no collection contains better prepared specimens than those in our Ornathological [sic] room.' On the negative side, the trip confirmed what Boyle already knew – that the provincial museum was inadequately funded by many thousands of dollars annually. 'In every instance, it appeared that the funds available for carrying on museum work exceeded what is thought sufficient in this Province by from $9000 to $100,000 either in the shape of public grants or of private beneficence.' All the museums he visited were provided with 'laboratory or workshop accommodation.' Such facilities, argued Boyle, were 'a prime necessity in every live museum and without it the display of material in the cases must suffer to a very great extent.' At the time, his combined office and workshop space was an incredibly cramped six- by eight-foot room. 'Assistants and attendants were numerous in the best institutions, each Department having one or more ... I saw no institution so badly "manned" as ours is.' Caretaking staff were kept constantly at work. 'Cleanliness I found to be regarded as a *sine qua non* everywhere, and in this respect our museum suffered most by comparison ... When foreign visitors come here, ... one cannot but feel ashamed.'[67]

On the basis of these findings, Boyle recommended in confidence to the minister what he considered absolutely essential if the provincial museum was not to 'fall short of present-day requirements.' At the very least, he required an appropriation of five thousand dollars annually. With this funding he planned to launch a modest purchasing program, hire assistants for each floor 'to keep the cases clean, answer questions civilly, and be above the suspicion of tips,' and to seek out an experienced assistant superintendent capable of mounting and maintaining displays, preparing labels, repairing specimens, and attending to visitors. 'This would still leave your Superintendent plenty to do and afford him opportunity to do it as well as modern museum methods demand.'[68] The minister seemed genuinely sympathetic to these suggestions.

'I have read your private report ... with great interest and pleasure,' he replied to Boyle. 'When we come to prepare next year's estimates I will go over the whole matter with you.'[69]

Alas, the minister's words were not to come true. Boyle's expectations were shattered a few months later when he learned that the museum appropriation for 1903 amounted to a mere $1950.[70] Furious, he began to lash out in every way he could, by rallying his friends in the Liberal party to protest on his behalf, by threatening to resign, and notwithstanding the possibility of dismissal, by taking his grievances to the readers of the *Archaeological Report*.[71] 'Of late,' he wrote in the *Report for 1904*, 'the French word *musée* has been introduced as a name for any collection of monstrosities, alive or dead, exhibited in some place where, too often, the ... attractions consist of not very high vaudeville performances, and it is not unusual to hear the Provincial Museum referred to by the ... name.'[72]

This was not meant to be carping, vindictive, and negative criticism, for Boyle supplemented his attack with a vision and a philosophy for the museum. 'If a public museum has no educational value it cannot be said that there is any reason for its existence. It is the duty, therefore, of those who are concerned in the maintenance and management of such an institution ... to lead in the adoption of new methods, rather than to lag, or to [imitate] tardily those of ... more progressive institutions.' Furthermore, every 'reasonable accommodation' should be made for the serious researcher. If done properly, he added, the museum will fulfil its responsibility as a 'national museum' and become a mecca for all students of science. In addition to the research function, Boyle urged that special facilities be provided for youngsters. 'In some progressive cities there are children's museums, that is to say, small typical collections of local flora and fauna, besides instructive material of some other kinds, the character of which necessarily accommodates itself to the situation and circumstances of the town and its locality.'[73] If nothing else, classes of schoolchildren from the city schools should be encouraged to visit the museum on weekdays during class time instead of on Saturdays which was then a standard practice.

For the general public, he added, the museum should provide more than 'a place in which many pleasant hours may be spent merely in sightseeing.' That would not suffice to achieve his educational objectives: 'Every museum ... worthy of the name,' he explained, 'should institute courses of lectures, or of familiar talks, for the benefit of those who care to attend.' Moreover, the curator must strive to create a pleasant learning environment. 'Every possible means should be employed to make visitors feel at ease,' he wrote, harkening back to his Pestalozzian notions of education regarding the close relationship between a pleasant environment and learning, 'particularly ... when people from the country parts are concerned. They are naturally somewhat more constrained in the surroundings than are those who live in towns, and have frequent access to public places. Such visitors should be assured ... that the institution is public property, that strangers are cordially welcomed, and that there need be no hesitancy in asking for information.'[74]

David Boyle ended his attempt to shame the government into action with one final 'exhaustive report' to the minister of education in October 1904. He reiterated the now familiar theme that the 'condition and management' of the provincial museum had become 'quite antiquated' and until proper funding was made available he would be 'totally destitute ... to apply any remedy.'[75] It was all to no avail. The political manoeuvring and public criticism failed to elicit the hoped for response from a government that, on many other counts, was not responding to the needs of urban Ontario. Indeed, three months later this general reticence to formulate policies and implement reforms with a wide appeal to the voters of urban Ontario played a substantial role in the defeat of George Ross's administration in the election of January 1905.[76] Thirty-three years of Liberal rule in Ontario had come to an end; no one was more pleased with the development than the superintendent of the provincial museum.

With the coming to power of James Pliny Whitney's more urban-oriented 'progressive' Conservative regime, Boyle knew that he would be dealing with an administration more sympathetic to cultural institutions. It just so happened that Premier Whitney himself had been a habitué of the museum; indeed, he had spent so much time there that the reporter responsible for the 'Intimate Interviews' section of Saturday Night remarked facetiously on 9 July 1904 that he 'felt almost sure Mr. David Boyle had secured him [Whitney] for a summer engagement.' Doubtless the future premier of Ontario had heard the superintendent's long recitation of grievances on more than one occasion. That Boyle had launched his assault on the museum policy of the Liberal administration on the eve of its demise was purely fortuitous; all the same, it served nicely to ingratiate him with his new political bosses.

The Whitney government moved swiftly in coming to grips with the problems of the provincial museum. Dr R.A. Pyne, the minister of education, accepted in principle Boyle's objectives and philosophy for the institution, and at once provided funds for additional curatorial, custodial, and clerical staff.[77] Much to Boyle's delight, the government also increased his salary by nearly 40 per cent to $1500 per annum, still paltry by American standards, but substantial enough to afford him a measure of dignity and self-respect he had for too long been denied. This increment meant all the more since it came in spite of a Conservative retrenchment policy initiated to deal with the deficit left by the previous administration. At last, in his sixty-third year, David Boyle was able to put his financial and professional anxieties behind him. He had only a short span of good health and activity remaining to him, but at least the next few years were destined to rank among the happiest and most gratifying of his life.

8

Ambition fulfilled, 1905–11

I

During his final years as superintendent of the Ontario Provincial Museum, David Boyle narrowed the gap between his ideal of a modern museum and the reality at the normal school. He was happiest in times like these when circumstances permitted him to work methodically towards a preconceived goal. The remedy for all problems at the provincial museum was, of course, financial, and it was his good fortune that the government proved willing, indeed eager, to administer the cure. In the budgets for 1906, 1907, and again 1908, the department of education allocated to the museum sums of money that were lavish by previous standards. By 1908 the funding for the institution approached eleven thousand dollars annually, nearly twice the amount granted in the final year of Liberal rule; meanwhile, Boyle's own salary jumped to a respectable $1800.[1]

Charles Canniff James, the deputy minister of agriculture, had once remarked in 1902 that the Ontario Provincial Museum was the most inadequately staffed institution of its kind in North America, the only place to his knowledge 'where the exhibits are left to the honesty and good conduct of visitors.'[2] By comparison, after three years of Conservative administration, the place hummed with activity. The department of education provided Boyle with the funds to hire Dr William F. Brodie, one of Ontario's foremost naturalists, as a full-time curator, and W.H.C. Phillips as a temporary assistant for the archaeological section. Provision was also made for full-time clerical, cleaning, and security personnel. Administratively, the museum took on a character that was more vital and thoroughly professional. Display standards and techniques had been upgraded; regular changes were being made to the exhibits throughout the museum. Gone were the dusty, insect-infested natural science relics that dated back to the Ryerson era. Most importantly for Boyle, the educational potential of the institution was

The first archaeological map of Ontario, prepared by David Boyle in 1906 (*Archaeological Report 1906*)

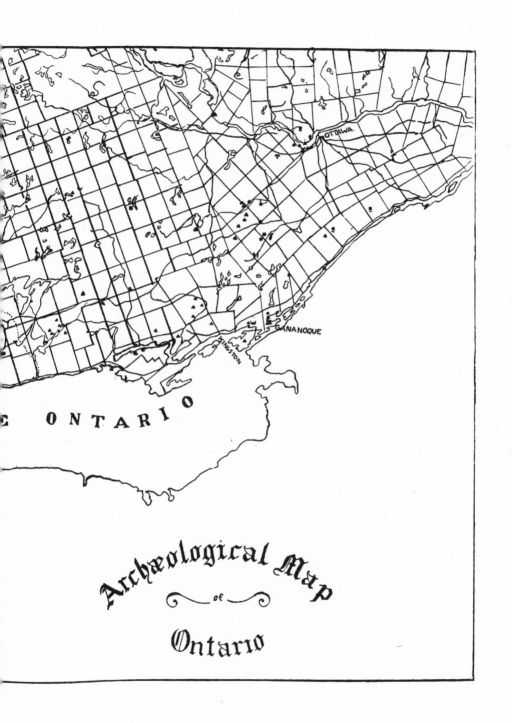

enhanced with the publication of a new catalogue, the addition of more informative labels, and the availability of a courteous, knowledgeable staff. Most certainly these years stand out as the halcyon period of the old Ontario Provincial Museum. With proper funding, the superintendent accomplished almost everything he considered necessary to bring it up to 'present-day standards.' Boyle even had the opportunity to undertake projects long contemplated such as the preparation of an archaeological map of Ontario, which appeared in the *Archaeological Report for 1906*.

The harmony Boyle knew in his professional life in these years spilled over into his family affairs. During the summer of 1905, after receiving his first salary increase, David and Martha Boyle purchased a small new brick bungalow at 78 Walker Avenue in a fashionable middle-class neighbourhood just west of Yonge Street, a few blocks south of St Clair. By this time their five children had all left the family fold. Susanna, the eldest, now married, lived in Minneapolis; she was a slight disappointment to her father in that she had put family before career and practised medicine only on a part-time basis. John owned a drugstore in Vancouver, Jim had a medical practice in Edmonton, and William, in Montreal, worked in the dry goods business. Anne, the youngest, then in Winnipeg, was the frustrated member of the Boyle progeny. She had desperately wanted to attend university in the late 1890s but the family's financial straits had made this goal impossible. Cast as she was in the same mould as her indomitable father, Anne Boyle determined to make her own way in the world. In Winnipeg she demonstrated how close she was to David in temperament by helping to form the Women's Civic League and by becoming an ardent exponent of women's suffrage. After 1912 she successfully pursued a career in journalism.

With the changed circumstances at the museum after 1905, Boyle found himself with the free time and the motivation to indulge in outside interests and rational amusements. This situation represented a dramatic change in mood from the previous few years when he had complained of being 'a common drudge, without a moment's leisure to pursue with pleasure, or with profit, any literary or scientific bent ... My duties are so continuous and so laborious that I have neither the opportunity nor inclination to assist myself in this way.'³ But conditioned as he was by the deeply ingrained artisan's self-improvement ethic of his youth, Boyle, even in his old age, still could not abide leisure without purpose. Only begrudgingly did he accompany his wife on an extended cross-Canada vacation to Vancouver, with a side trip to visit relatives in Arizona, during the summer of 1906. Since the western sojourn had no relation to his work, it had seemed superfluous. 'I find it very difficult to make up my mind to go away at all,' he had written prior to the trip, 'for the reason that there is so much work to do here.'[4]

Perhaps the most interesting project Boyle took up in his spare hours was the writing of a book of original children's nursery rhymes. The birth of his first grandchild, Adelle, William's daughter, prompted him to complete a task which he had begun about 1903. As in all his work, there was a purpose in writing the book beyond a grandfather's sentimentalism and a fondness for small children. These nursery rhymes and jingles had their inspiration in the same motivation that underlay his historical and archaeological endeavours – patriotism. His rhymes were suffused with Canadian content aimed solely at Canadian children. 'While "Ride a cock-horse," "Old Mother Hubbard," and the like, have by right of occupation, made good their claim to stay,' he explained, 'there would seem to be a reason why some rhymes with a flavor of Canada should find a place in our homes, if only for patriotic purposes, in a small way.'[5]

To prepare the coloured drawings for the book, Boyle chose Charles W. Jefferys, a young artist of much promise who then made his living illustrating stories for newspapers and magazines. Jefferys would eventually become the unrivalled master of the pictorial side of Canadian history, and a president of the Ontario Historical Society (1942–4). He had been one of the early members of the Toronto Art Students' League and at the time helped produce the renowned Art League Calendar (1893–1904) in which Canadian themes were zealously explored and the verses of some of the country's leading poets illustrated. Together he and Boyle produced a lavishly and magnificently illustrated volume of verse which appeared in 1908 under the title of *Uncle Jim's Canadian Nursery Rhymes for Family and Kindergarten Use.*

Full of delightful jingles and rhymes of nonsense and humour for the very young, the book was a pioneering effort in the *genre* of Canadian children's literature. It virtually stood alone with its emphasis on traditional Canadian pastimes (sleighing and lacrosse), geography, and place names.

Tommy Temper had a fall
He bumped his brow and gave a bawl;
As soon's his head had struck the floor,
Niagara never gave such a roar.

The standard symbols of Canadian patriotism – beaver and maple leaves – not to mention references to other distinctive Canadian flora and fauna, were sprinkled liberally throughout the volume.

A foolish little Beaver
Once tried to fell a tree
Across St. Lawrence River,
Two miles, or maybe three.

It gnawed a great big maple
Ten nights, or maybe more
Which fell, but wasn't able
To touch the other shore.

Had this young Beaver gone to school
As little boys and girls do
It would not have been such a fool
As to have acted so.

There were also verses dedicated to a variety of social and political themes, ranging from the governor-general to the folklore of the Canadian Indians ('Omemee' and 'The Pretty Wabigoon'), the Canadian National Exhibition in Toronto, and the Canadian Pacific Railway.

Tell me, Tommy Tattlewell, come tell me now I beg
How far I take the C.P.R. from here to Winnipeg?
'I see,' said Tommy Tattlewell, 'the answer's very clear.
You'd have to travel twice as far as half way there to here.
But if you take this for a joke, or only idle talk,
Don't go to Winnipeg at all, or if you do go – walk.'

Boyle was acutely aware that simply because he had succeeded 'in making one line end with "rig" and another with "pig",' he was scarcely able to proclaim himself 'a Second Shakespeare.' Even in the twilight of his life, he remained uncertain of himself when venturing into unfamiliar fields of endeavour, so much so that he insisted the book be published anonymously. How appalled he was when the *Canadian Magazine* reviewed the volume and gave away his identity. 'If you only knew how taring, rearing, ripping, ranting mad I was when I saw that you had mentioned my name in connection with the work,' he wrote to the editor, 'you would avoid me as you value your life, if we were to face one and other in a ten acre field.'[6]

II

As he ended his career, David Boyle relished the role many people encouraged him to play as the grand old man of Ontario archaeology and ethnology.

Much stouter now, he looked every bit the part with his shock of white hair and flowing beard. While the spring may have disappeared from his gait, he had lost none of his remarkable sense of humour or capacity for winning friends. He had not sought nor even consciously fostered his image as patriarch of the Canadian anthropological fraternity; it had come naturally, the consequence of three decades of accomplishment and his own charming personality. In any case, Boyle found himself in increasing demand as a speaker, not only at the usual functions of civic and educational groups in Toronto, but also at institutions of higher learning across the province. The Ontario Agricultural College at Guelph invited him to address a gathering of nature study teachers in June 1905, while Queen's University convinced him to deliver a series of six lectures on ethnology in late October 1906.[7]

Meanwhile, Boyle was also courted by the International Congress of Americanists. At the Stuttgart meeting (1904), the executive directors appointed him to a committee, along with Dr Robert Bell of the Geological Survey, Monseigneur LaFlamme of Quebec City, and Franz Boas of Columbia University, to organize the next meeting of the congress planned for Montreal in September 1906. On Boas's suggestion,[8] Boyle decided to make a special contribution to this event by producing his *Archaeological Report for 1905* as a handbook of Canadian ethnology to be distributed free at Montreal. Beginning in June 1905, Boyle, with Boas's assistance, hurriedly commissioned specialists to prepare manuscripts on the various aspects of the 'Ethnology of Canada and Newfoundland.'

'In the following papers,' Boyle wrote in his preface to the anthology, 'we have brief, general accounts of Canadian aboriginal people – something never before attempted in anything like a methodical and scientific way by writers who have made special studies of our Indians.'[9] Boas himself prepared numerous sections on 'Physical Types of Indians of Canada,' 'The Indian Languages of Canada,' 'The Eskimo,' 'The Salish Tribes of the Interior of British Columbia,' and 'The Tribes of the North Pacific Coast.' Cyrus Thomas submitted an introductory 'Historical Account,' while A.F. Chamberlain wrote on 'The Beothuks of Newfoundland' and 'The Kootenay Indians,' Clark Wissler on 'The Blackfoot Indians,' the Reverend A.G. Morrice on 'The Canadian Denes,' Charles Hill-Tout on 'The Salish Tribes of the Coast and Lower Fraser Delta,' and William Jones on 'The Central Algonkin.' All in all, it was an impressive collection of essays written by some of the leading ethnologists in North America.

For his part, Boyle prepared a section on 'The Iroquois' in which he posited a revisionist interpretation of the origins of the Iroquoian-speaking tribes, an interpretation that rejected the views he had expressed earlier in *Primitive*

Man in Ontario (1895). In that work, Boyle had accepted the theory popularized by Horatio Hale that 'the Iroquois came south-west from the north shore of the lower St. Lawrence.' Now he argued that Hale's theory, based largely on oral traditions, was suspect. Had the Iroquois originated in the St Lawrence Valley, Boyle asked, would not their legends and folklore have contained some references to the Eskimo, and to the fauna of the sea? Based on his further study of Micmac and Wyandot oral traditions, he hypothesized instead a southern origin for the Iroquois, perhaps in Kentucky and southern Ohio.[10] At some undetermined time in prehistory, he explained, 'one great dispersal, or various minor dispersals of these people' may have taken place. Since the philologists recognized the Huron language to be the oldest Iroquoian tongue, the Huron ostensibly left the main body first and migrated to what is now Simcoe County. They were subsequently followed into prehistoric Ontario by migrations of Wyandots, Petuns, Tionnontates, Attiwandarons, and Eries, all apparently offspring from the same main stock.

Finally, according to this theory, those of the main stock who remained in Ohio migrated north-west 'dropping by the way, bands subsequently known as the Cherokees, Tuscaroras, Andastes,' then moved east 'until they reached Acadia, now New Brunswick and Nova Scotia, finding their way eventually to the north shore of the St. Lawrence river, or gulf ... whence they ... spread westwards to Stadaconé (Quebec) andHochelaga (Montreal).' The archaeological record, in Boyle's mind, bolstered this hypothesis. Did not the existence of mounds and earthworks along the shorelines of Lakes Ontario and Erie give credence to the notion that the Iroquois migrated from the Ohio region, for it was there that the Mound Builder culture first flourished. 'Had the Iroquois come to this part of the country from the northeast directly, or indirectly,' he observed, 'they would scarcely have brought with them this custom.' That this rather fabulous hypothesis raised more questions than it answered Boyle did not deny, and he was the first to recognize the extremely speculative nature of his paper. 'Although much has been *written* regarding the origin of the Iroquois as a people,' he admitted, 'we [still] *know* absolutely nothing.'[11] Boyle's contribution to the 'Ethnology of Canada and Newfoundland' demonstrated that to the end of his career he remained the iconoclast, ever willing to question conventional wisdom.

The appearance of the 'Ethnology of Canada and Newfoundland' in the *Archaeological Report for 1905* did not represent a startling departure from the traditional contents of the journal. Since his study of the 'pagan' Iroquois in 1898, Boyle had been supplementing regional archaeological studies with ethnological papers of various kinds. In the *Reports* for 1899 and 1902, for instance, music specialist Alexander Cringan had continued his analysis of

Iroquois folk-songs. In fact, he and Boyle brought to Toronto several native singers who recorded their music on 'graphophone cylinders' with the result that some one hundred authentic melodies were thereby preserved. Increasingly, Boyle's interest in comparative ethnology prompted him to include in the *Reports* more articles pertaining to the cultures of the Canadian Indians beyond the borders of Ontario. Some of these manuscripts were of no little value, such as William E. Connolly's study of the Wyandots (1899), the Reverend R.W. Large's 'Mortuary Customs in British Columbia' (1904), and 'The Killing of *Moostoos* the *Wehtigoo*' (1903) – the latter being the transcript of the trials in Fort Saskatchewan and Edmonton of certain Cree trappers charged in 1899 with the murder of one of their companions whom they believed to be possessed of an evil spirit or '*Wehtigoo*.'[12] Occasionally the *Reports* even included papers of ethnological topics beyond Canada, such as Frederick Hamilton's 'Rough Notes on Native Tribes of South Africa' (1900), and the Reverend Dr W.R. Harris's 'The Caribs of Guiana and the West Indies' (1903).

That Boyle chose to include these exotic ethnological manuscripts in the *Archaeological Reports* was a pity. One of the strengths of the journal had been its specific and systematic emphasis on the archaeological and cultural heritage of the Ontario Indians. Once the reports branched out ethnologically beyond the provincial borders, and especially into Latin American and African themes, they lost some of their impact and special character. Perhaps Boyle included these works for want of Ontario-related research material. His own field-work had been severely curtailed; A.F. Hunter's connection with the museum was strained; and George Laidlaw was in South Africa. Officially, at least, Boyle rationalized his decision to readjust the focus of the *Reports* to encompass a wide range of ethnological themes on the grounds that the papers often served as informative companion pieces for recent collections acquired by the museum. Besides, Boyle's priorities had gradually shifted since 1898. One of his primary objectives as superintendent was to develop the Ethnological Room, to make it 'illustrative of Canadian aboriginal life, ... not by any means of extravagant pretensions, but one worthy of our Province and its position in the Dominion.'[13] In addition, he was of the opinion that 'the contents of our cases are now such as to require at least fairly good and typically representative material for comparative purposes from other lands.'[14]

The change of emphasis in the *Archaeological Reports* found favour among the members of the British Association for the Advancement of Science and the International Congress of Americanists who had long urged Boyle and other Canadian scholars to take a greater interest in ethnology, particularly that of the western Canadian tribes. Boyle's stature at home and abroad was further enhanced by the publication of the 'Ethnology of Canada and Newfoundland.' It helped earn him both a term as a vice-president (1906–8) of the Congress of Americanists, and election in November 1907 as an honorary member of the Anthropological Society of Italy.[15] A few months later in February 1908 yet another honour came Boyle's way when he was awarded the prestigious Cornplanter Medal for Iroquois Research. Boyle was the third recipient[16] of the medal, named after the famous Seneca sachem, and awarded every two years by the Cayuga County Historical Society in New York State. Apparently so many honours and awards in quick succession had left Boyle a trifle jaded. 'Will it be much of a swell affair? I mean in the gathering,' he wrote to William Beauchamp prior to attending the festivities associated with the presentation of the Cornplanter Medal. 'Kindly let me know, because if it is likely to be that character I would rather stay at home.' Not at all, replied Beauchamp. 'The presentation will be a simple affair ... The society's rooms will not *put on style*. Fashionable people don't take to historical work.'[17] With that assurance, Boyle dutifully attended the ceremony on 18 February 1908.

III

There was but one discordant note in these otherwise harmonious years for David Boyle – his severe headaches returned to slow him down. It was cruel irony that now, with the support staff at the museum to enable him to engage in a few weeks' archaeological field-work each summer, ill-health and the effects of age sapped his desire for travel and physical activity. He managed to undertake one major expedition in 1907, a relatively easy trip by CPR to Nipigon Station on the north shore of Lake Superior. Here, with the assistance of his companion, Clarkson W. James, secretary of the department of education, he recorded the rock paintings on a cliff face along the Nipigon Bay shoreline.[18] That Boyle, once in north-western Ontario, did not muster the enthusiasm to push on to excavate several of the legendary mounds in the Rainy River area – a project in which he had long been interested – indicates his declining state of health.

Following the accidental discovery by a building contractor of an Indian burial ground on the Niagara escarpment near the village of St David's in April 1908, Boyle set out on what proved to be his last field trip. What he found was a major historic Neutral cemetery some five or six acres in extent. The site, he concluded, comprised 'the most extensive Indian burial ground so far known in this Province.' Regrettably, the thrill of this discovery was dampened by the fact that when he arrived on the scene, he found the place occupied by several dozen 'men and boys – some even from the United States – who were making havoc of the graves. These people,' he reported bitterly, 'were merely curiosity hunters, and as a matter of course were quite successful in finding and carrying away a considerable number of excellent specimens, [and] ... in putting the ground in such a condition that no one could make any intelligent examination of it.'[19]

A few weeks later, towards the end of May 1908, Boyle suffered a debilitating stroke. For a fortnight he lay unconscious, near death. His daughter, Susanna, rushed home from Minneapolis, and Jim from Edmonton, to be at his side during what they thought were his last hours. 'I have no recollection of their visit,' he would write later.[20] To the surprise and delight of his physician, he regained consciousness in early June and began a grim three-month period of rehabilitation. He fought his illness with characteristically methodical determination. 'My attention has been wholly occupied with trying to get better,' he wrote in September.[21] By October he had recovered sufficiently to spend a few hours a day at the museum; this first stroke had merely left him weak and his memory slightly confused.

Alas, just when the ordeal seemed to be over, Boyle was struck down by a second paralytic stroke in April 1909 which left him permanently incapacitated. 'I am afraid David will not be of much use any more,' wrote a saddened George Laidlaw to Andrew Hunter. '2 strokes in less than a year will probably be followed closely by another.'[22] Boyle's plight evoked enormous sympathy among those who knew him. Out of respect, the Canadian Folk-Lore Society, an organization which Boyle had just helped to establish in 1908, elected him an honorary president. The University of Toronto also moved quickly to acknowledge his accomplishments as an archaeologist and ethnologist by conferring upon him the honorary degree of Doctor of Laws. Since Boyle was unable to attend the regular ceremonies at the university, the administration decided to hold a special convocation on 10 June 1909 at his home on Walker Avenue. What thoughts must have crossed the ex-blacksmith's mind as a row of carriages brought to his door a crowd of dignitaries and faculty dressed in their academic gowns and brightly coloured hoods. As he lay on his sick-bed, a black robe over his nightshirt, J. Ramsay Wright, the vice-president of the University of Toronto, placed varsity's crimson hood over Boyle's shoulders.[23] Those who attended this unique event found themselves swept with mixed emotions, their delight tempered by the sure knowledge that the man who lay before them had not long to live.

Boyle lay paralysed for another nineteen months. He died on the afternoon of 14 February 1911.

IV

'I am expressing to you Sir Daniel Wilson's *Prehistoric Man.* A work like that seems out of date now and not up to much. There is nothing definite in it, and too much generalities. I think old Sir Daniel was a sort of 'off-hand' archaeologist. A good many of his statements to my mind are not borne out by latter-day investigation' (George Laidlaw to Andrew Hunter 1 April 1911).[24]

George Laidlaw was quite correct; significant progress had indeed been made in the development of American and Ontario archaeology during the half-century since the appearance of Wilson's *Prehistoric Man* in 1862. During that period David Boyle stands unrivalled as the most prominent and influential figure in the development of the Ontario archaeological tradition; he dominated its so-called classificatory-descriptive period. This was a period of incipient professionalism across North America, when a more scientific archaeology displaced the armchair speculation of the past, and when the emphasis of those interested in prehistory turned to the collection, systematic description, and rudimentary classification of the archaeological data.

It was David Boyle who conceptualized and single-handedly launched in 1885 the program that eventually laid the groundwork for the development of Ontario archaeology as a systematic and scientific discipline. At the Canadian Institute, and later at the Ontario Provincial Museum, he assembled an outstanding collection of Indian artifacts representative of the southern portion of the province. It was Boyle who introduced the invaluable *Archaeological Reports* for the Ontario Department of Education in 1887 – the first periodical in Canada devoted primarily to the study of the archaeological record. Together, the museum collections and the contents of the *Reports* provided a foundation of data and insight upon which scientific archaeology would be based.

During his career as the sole professional archaeologist in the province, Boyle assumed responsibility for a staggering variety of tasks. He lobbied successfully for operational funds. He became Ontario archaeology's public relations man who aroused the provincial consciousness on matters archaeological, and educated government and public alike on the value of encouraging the study of the province's prehistoric and historic past. Over and over again, he reminded Ontarians of the importance of museums for the proper housing of antiquities, and articulated a museum philosophy that still has a remarkably modern ring. For Boyle, a museum served a dual purpose, as an educational institution for the general public, and as a research centre for scholars and students of all ages. He likened a museum to an organism which, to live, perforce must constantly change and grow.

Boyle also undertook a vastly greater amount of field-work in the province than had ever been conducted before. He compiled invaluable site inventories, carried out systematic field explorations, and conducted excavations. More important, he encouraged such worthies as Andrew Hunter, George Laidlaw, T.W. Beeman, and William J. Wintemberg to do the same. All their work was carefully described in the *Archaeological Reports* – a practice that in itself was of no little importance. By modern criteria, their field technique was crude, but compared to the efforts of their predecessors, it was a noteworthy improvement. Witness, for example, Boyle's excavation of the Clearville site. Finally, to Boyle must go the credit for discovering and/or initially investigating many of the province's major archaeological sites including the Rice Lake–Trent River mounds, the Southwold and Parker earthworks, the Pelee Island and Yellow Point mounds, the Clearville and Lawson sites, and the Bon Echo pictographs.

From the outset of his career, Boyle also marched in the van of those seeking legislation to protect archaeological and historical resources. While he failed to move the provincial government to take action, he often generated sufficient interest locally to ensure that a protective eye was kept on some of the province's key sites. Furthermore, he gave rise to the 'birth of a conscience' in Ontario about the wholesale and indiscriminate exportation of antiquities to foreign museums and private collections. In voicing such concerns, he proved to be decades ahead of his times.

With Boyle, too, came the first modest steps towards the professionalization of Ontario archaeology. The signs of this development are to be seen in the government-sponsored museum, and in the scientific attitudes and empirical approach that conditioned the work of Boyle and his cohorts. The trend to professionalism was also cultivated through his regular interaction with his counterparts at major expositions, and through his active participation in such organizations as the British and American Associations for the Advancement of Science, the International Congress of Americanists, and the American Anthropological Association. Only in one major respect did Ontario lag in comparison with trends towards professionalism to the south; here, archaeology made little impact on university curricula through 'an academic alliance with anthropology.'[25] This state of affairs was largely the consequence of the elementary state of Canadian anthropology prior to the establishment in 1910 of the anthropology division of the Geological Survey of Canada.

Notwithstanding the weak university connection, David Boyle did begin the process of raising archaeology in Ontario to the level of a respectable scholarly discipline. Perhaps the provincial universities were little affected, but academics and professionals in the United States and Britain certainly took notice of his accomplishments. They did so because from the beginning of his tenure at the Canadian Institute he was determined to work and to write within a wider North American framework, not surprising since his main source of archaeological stimulation came from the ideas and methods of his peers in the United States. As a consequence of this approach, and of the carefully developed lines of communication with his American colleagues, Boyle ensured that his work was incorporated into the mainstream of northeastern American archaeology.

As a corollary to his close relationship with American archaeologists, Boyle shared their failures and weaknesses. The chronological dimension of Ontario prehistory eluded him; so, too, did the complexity of the province's aboriginal cultural evolution. Lacking an understanding of the concept of microchange in culture, he failed to exploit stratigraphy to grapple with both chronology and culture sequence. In classifying his data Boyle adopted a descriptive taxonomy characterized by cross-cultural, evolutionary biases with an emphasis on functional interpretation. There were only slight hints of future developments in his occasional classification by geographical locale (as in the case of the Clearville and Balsam Lake collections), and by culture (as in the case of the Baptiste Lake Algonkin specimens). It did not occur to him to pursue rigorously these promising innovations in taxonomy with a view to the comparative analysis of the regional variation in the data, and of local cultural development. Yet given the interpretive vacuum in which he worked, the fact that he handled his specimens in a systematic, objective, if only descriptive way was a major step in the right direction.

Whatever the shortcomings of Boyle's approach, they scarcely detract from his pivotal and unique importance in Ontario, and indeed Canadian, archaeology prior to the First World War. He bridged the gap between the antiquarians of the first half of the nineteenth century and the professional archaeologists of the twentieth. Beginning himself as an uninformed antiquarian collector in Wellington County during the 1860s, by dint of sheer effort, dedication, and intelligence he helped shape the Ontario archaeological tradition as he struggled to carve out a career for himself at the Canadian Institute. Because he blended both the enthusiasm and disinterested devotion of the amateur with the methodological rigour of the professional, Boyle was the ideal person for the times. His own experience taught him to appreciate the importance of the amateur collectors in the enormous data-gathering process that lay before him. Thus, from the outset of his tenure at the Canadian Institute, he assiduously cultivated an outstanding team of regional volunteers. He instructed them by personal contact and through the *Reports*, edited and published their field notes, while gradually encouraging in their work a noteworthy degree of professionalism. Having learned by trial and error himself, Boyle remained open-minded, and largely free of the orthodoxies and rigid methodological convictions that often limit the vision of university-trained scholars. Never did he reveal himself to be contemptuous of his amateur co-workers' opinions; on the contrary, he invariably tolerated, and regularly published, views that differed from his own.

When David Boyle died in 1911 he was succeeded at the Ontario Provincial Museum by Dr Rowland B. Orr, a long-time amateur collector and friend of the museum, then a physician in suburban Parkdale. Orr was a political appointee, his Conservative leanings being of more consequence to those who selected him than the fact that he had little curatorial experience. With his appointment the trend towards professionalization in Ontario was given a rude setback. For the next twenty-two years, Orr held the position of curator of the archaeological section at the provincial museum. He proved to be adequate, but failed to introduce many innovations either in the museum or in the field. Not surprisingly, then, after 1911 the centre of gravity in Canadian archaeology moved from the Ontario Provincial Museum in Toronto to the anthropology division of the Geological Survey of Canada located in Ottawa's new Victoria Memorial Museum. That very year, William J. Wintemberg, Boyle's gifted young protégé, found temporary employment in the anthropology division. Before long he received a permanent appointment there as an assistant to Harlan I. Smith and went on to distinguish himself as Canada's premier archaeologist in the period between the two world wars.

David Boyle's contributions to the Ontario archaeological tradition were indeed impressive; considering that he was a self-educated man, they seem doubly so. Even more remarkably, during his years as a practising archaeologist-curator, he managed among other things to write a *History of Scarboro* (1896), the McSpurtle 'epistles' for the *Scottish American Journal*, and a teacher's handbook; he served as secretary of the Ontario Historical Society (1898–1907), undertook ethnological research, administered the provincial museum (1901–8), and produced a book of children's nursery rhymes. A common thread connects all these varied activities and accomplishments. They all reflect the unifying theme of Boyle's life – his commitment to self-culture and to the acquistion and imparting of knowledge. Intellectually, Boyle never ceased expanding his horizons or challenging conventional wisdom. He remained to the end the quintessential product of the British autodidact artisan culture out of which he sprang.

Abbreviations

AAAS	American Association for the Advancement of Science
ARO	*Archaeological Report for Ontario*
BAAS	British Association for the Advancement of Science
CHR	*Canadian Historical Review*
CJ	*Canadian Journal*
MTCL	Metropolitan Toronto Central Library
OA	Ontario Archives
OHS	Ontario Historical Society
OSP	Ontario, *Sessional Papers*
PAC	Public Archives of Canada
ROM, Archives	Royal Ontario Museum, Archives, David Boyle papers
ROM, Ethnology	Royal Ontario Museum, Department of Ethnology, David Boyle papers
UWO	University of Western Ontario

Notes

CHAPTER I

1 ROM, Ethnology, Boyle to the minister of the parish church, Sorn, Scotland, 26 April 1907
2 For most of the early Boyle genealogical and family history, I am indebted to Mrs Helen Boyd of Ottawa.
3 See E.P. Thompson, *The Making of the English Working Class* (London: Victor Gollancz 1965), 734–43; Zygmunt Bauman, *Between Class and Elite: The Evolution of the British Labour Movement. A Sociological Study* (Manchester: Manchester University Press 1972), 63–79; E.J. Hobsbawm, 'The Labouring Aristocracy in Nineteenth Century Britain,' in E.J. Hobsbawm, *Labouring Men: Studies in the History of Labour* (New York: Basic Books 1964), 272–315, for a discussion of the autodidact artisan culture.
4 John Borland (1818–82), David (1820–1910), James (1825–1908), Andrew (1827–?), Adam (1829–?), William (1833–?). The two girls were Agnes (1816–?) and Jane (1823–?).
5 See Angela Tuckett, *The Blacksmith's History: What Smithy Workers Gave Trade Unionism* (London: Lawrence and Wishart 1974), ch. 1; and Lloyd G. Reynolds, *The British Immigrant: His Social and Economic Adjustment* (Toronto: Oxford 1935), 159–63, for artisan attitudes and the apprenticeship system.
6 H.A. Moisley and A.G. Thain, eds, *The Third Statistical Account of Scotland: The County of Renfrew* (Glasgow: Collins 1962), 35–57 and 166–9
7 Michael S. Moss and John R. Hume, *Workshop of the British Empire: Engineering and Shipbuilding in the West of Scotland* (London: Heinemann 1977), 87–91
8 Moisley and Thain, *Third Statistical Account of Scotland*, 37
9 Moss and Hume, *Workshop of the British Empire*, passim. For a brief biographical sketch of John Boyle, see his obituary in the Elora *Express*, 1 June 1882.

10 This paragraph rests largely on Tuckett, *The Blacksmith's History*, ch. 1.

11 Hobsbawm, 'The Labouring Aristocracy,' 296. The Hobsbawm thesis on the labour aristocracy has come under critical attack. See Michael J. Piva, 'The Aristocracy of the English Working Class: Help for An Historical Debate in Difficulties,' *Histoire sociale – Social History* 7, no. 14 (November 1974), 270–92. The Boyle family experience tends to support the Hobsbawm interpretation.

12 Figures based on Tuckett, *The Blacksmith's History*, 70; Bauman, *Between Class and Elite*, 66; and W.H. Marwick, *Economic Developments in Victorian Scotland* (London: Geo. Allen and Unwin 1936), 148–9.

13 Moss and Hume, *Workshop of the British Empire*, 8

14 Thompson, *The Making of the English Working Class*, 327

15 Moisley and Thain, *Third Statistical Account of Scotland*, 38. Ninety-three per cent of the houses lacked indoor toilet facilities.

16 Quoted in J.H. Clapham, *An Economic History of Modern Britain: The Early Railway Age 1820–1850* (Cambridge: Cambridge University Press 1964), 540

17 Recollections of Greenock: Fifty Years Ago,' signed L.M., in *The Scottish American Journal*, 29 Jan. 1890

18 For considerable directory material pertaining to Greenock, I am indebted to Mr J.T. Hamilton, chief librarian, Central Library, Clyde Square, Greenock.

19 *The Scottish American Journal*, 26 June 1879

20 Toronto *Daily Star*, 10 June 1909

21 Bauman, *Between Class and Elite*, 70–4

22 Moisley and Thain, *Third Statistical Account of Scotland*, 194–5; and 'Recollections of Greenock,' *The Scottish American Journal*, 29 Jan. 1890

23 Information on the curriculum, fees, and location of the Mason's Hall School was provided by the Greenock Central Library.

24 Hobsbawm, 'The Labouring Aristocracy,' 274

25 *The Scottish American Journal*, 26 June 1879

26 Ibid., 6 May 1896. Boyle wrote under the pseudonym of Andrew McSpurtle.

27 Obituary in the *Annual Archaeological Report 1911: Including 1908-9-10. Being Part of Appendix to the Report of the Minister of Education, Ontario* (Toronto: L.K. Cameron 1911), 7

28 Glyn Daniel, *A Hundred and Fifty Years of Archaeology* (London: Duckworth 1975), 74. Layard published a new popular account of his work in 1853.

29 P.E. Razzell and R.W. Wainwright, eds, *The Victorian Working Class: Selections from Letters to the Morning Chronicle* (London: Frank Cass 1973), 142

30 Tuckett, *The Blacksmith's History*, 41

31 Alexander Wilson, *The Chartist Movement in Scotland* (Manchester: Manchester University Press 1970), ch. 10–12

32 Hobsbawm, 'The Labouring Aristocracy,' 278

33 *The Scottish American Journal*, 16 Dec. 1885
34 Adam Boyle to William Boyle, 6 April 1853. Original in possession of Mrs Helen Boyd, Ottawa.
35 Ibid.
36 Ibid.
37 UWO, Assessment rolls for the township of Sarnia, Lambton County, 1853 and 1855. David owned the west half of lot 3, concession 5. His three sons were situated on lots 3 and 4, concession 2.
38 William W. Mortimer, *History of the Hundred of Wirral* (Liverpool 1847); J. Hunter Robertson, *Birkenhead: Its Present Sanitary Condition* (1847); Philip Sulley, *History of Birkenhead* (1893); Francis E. Hyde, *Liverpool and the Mersey: An Economic History of a Port 1700–1970* (Newton Abbot, England: David and Charles 1971)
39 A.W. Currie, *The Grand Trunk Railway of Canada* (Toronto: University of Toronto Press 1957), 29; see also John Millar, *William Heap and His Company* (Rochdale, Lancashire: E. Wrigley and Sons 1976), 44–55.
40 Hilda Gamlin, *Memories or The Chronicles of Birkenhead: The Scenes and Peoples of its Early Days* (Liverpool: E. Howell 1892)
41 Mortimer, *History of the Hundred of Wirral*, 401. The log book of St Andrew's School begins in 1862. It can be reasonably assumed that the school was conducted around 1855 in much the same manner as in 1862. Mr W.R.S. McIntyre of Birkenhead, a retired headmaster and local historian, forwarded me excerpts from the log book. The research he so kindly undertook on my behalf is gratefully acknowledged.
42 This factor was typical of post-1850 emigrants. See Reynolds, *The British Immigrant*, 6–9; Rowland T. Berthoff, *British Immigrants in Industrial America, 1790–1950* (Cambridge: Harvard University Press 1953), 19; Helen I. Cowan, *British Immigrants to British North America: The First Hundred Years*, rev. enlarged ed. (Toronto: University of Toronto Press 1961), 201; Charlotte Erickson, *Invisible Immigrants: The Adaptation of English and Scottish Immigrants in Nineteenth Century America* (Coral Gables: University of Miami Press 1972), pt. II.
43 Cowan, *British Immigrants to British North America*, 174. See also Charlotte Erickson, 'The Encouragement of Emigration by British Trade Unions, 1850–1900,' *Population Studies* 3, pt. 3 (December 1949), 248–73.
44 David (1842–1911), John (1846–70), Mary Anne (1850–?), James (1852–1913), Agnes (1855–65). A fourth son, Andrew (1857–78), was born later in Canada West.
45 For the history of Salem, see J.R. Connon, 'The Village of Salem,' in Arthur W. Wright, ed., *Pioneer Days in Nichol* (1924); Elsie McLeod Murray, 'An Upper Canada "Bush Business" in the Fifties,' *Ontario Historical Society Papers and*

Records 36 (1944), 41–7; Ruth I. Mackenzie, 'Salem, Village of Peace,' *Western Ontario Historical Notes* 4, no. 2 (1946), 46–9.

46 J.M.S. Careless, *The Union of the Canadas: The Growth of Canadian Institutions 1841–1857* (Toronto: McClelland and Stewart 1967), 150–3

47 UWO, Wills, Middlesex County, vol. 10, no. 2353, John Boyle, d. 27 May 1882

48 Hazel Mack, *History of Eden Mills and Vicinity* (Eden Crest, Ont.: Eden Mills Women's Institute 1954)

49 *Census of the Canadas, 1860–61* (Montreal 1863). Scots by birth in Wellington, 6941. Huron County followed with 6204, Grey 5614, Middlesex 5545, Bruce 5916. There were 98,792 Scots in Canada West in a total population of 1,396,091.

50 On the process of assimilation of skilled immigrants see Erickson, *Invisible Immigrants*, pt. II.

51 John R. Connon, *The Early History of Elora, Ontario, and Vicinity* (Elora and Fergus: The Elora *Express* and the Fergus *News-Record* 1930), 161

52 Ibid., 162

53 *The National Cyclopaedia of American Biography* (Ann Arbor, Michigan, University microfilms 1967), VI

54 Connon, *Elora*, 162

55 Ibid.

CHAPTER 2

1 *Gazetteer and Directory of the County of Wellington for 1871–72: Giving the Names of Residents in the Towns, Villages, Post Offices, and Lists of Farmers in Each Township in the County.* A.O. Loomis and Co Publishers (Hamilton: Wm. Brown and Co. 1871), 90. Reprinted in 1976 by the Wellington County Museum.

2 ROM, Ethnology, memoirs of Anne Anderson Perry (ca. 1950). Anne A. Perry was the youngest daughter of David Boyle.

3 *Gazetteer and Directory of Wellington County, 1871–72*, 74–90; John R. Connon, *The Early History of Elora, Ontario and Vicinity* (Elora and Fergus: The Elora *Express* and Fergus *News-Record* 1930), passim

4 Connon, *Elora*, 156

5 Elora *Observer*, 1 July 1864

6 David Boyle, 'Our Own Blunders,' *Canada Educational Monthly and School Chronicle* 3 (1881), 4–5. All quotes in this paragraph are taken from this source.

7 Egerton Ryerson, 'Canadian Mechanics and Manufactures,' *Journal of Education for Upper Canada* 2 (February 1849), 17. Quoted in Alison Prentice, *The School Promoters: Education and Social Class in Mid-Nineteenth Century Upper Canada* (Toronto: McClelland and Stewart 1977), 77.

8 Alison Prentice, 'The Feminization of Teaching in British North America and

Canada 1845–1875,' *Histoire sociale – Social History* 8, no. 15 (May 1975), 5–20. See also James Love, 'The Professionalization of Teachers in Mid-Nineteenth-Century Upper Canada,' in Neil McDonald and Alf Chaiton, eds, *Egerton Ryerson and His Times* (Toronto: Macmillan of Canada 1978), 109–28, and J.D. Wilson, R.M. Stamp, L.-P. Audet, eds, *Canadian Education: A History* (Scarborough, Ont.: Prentice-Hall 1970), 316.

 9 MTCL, Baldwin Room, Boyle scrapbook 1866–70, *Journal of Education*, (November 1869). See also ROM, Ethnology, Boyle scrap-book 1870–2, Elora *Observer*, 4 Nov. 1870.

10 The theme of teaching as a skilled profession that had to be learned appeared repeatedly in the clippings contained in the Boyle scrapbooks for 1859–66. These scrapbooks are to be found in the Baldwin Room, MTCL, and the department of ethnology, ROM.

11 Michael Heafford, *Pestalozzi: His Thought and Its Relevance Today* (London: Methuen 1967), 47

12 Thomas A. Barlow, *Pestalozzi and American Education* (Boulder, Colo.: Este Es Press 1977), 158

13 Heafford, *Pestalozzi: His Thought*, 53; and Kate Silbur, *Pestalozzi: The Man and His Work* (New York: Schocken Books 1973), 126

14 Silbur, *Pestalozzi: The Man and His Work*, 126

15 Quoted in Heafford, *Pestalozzi: His Thought*, 66.

16 Ibid., 473

17 Margaret Gillet, *A History of Education: Thought and Practice* (Toronto: McGraw-Hill 1966), 219. Pestalozzi had a profound impact on education throughout Europe and North America; the tenets of his philosophy eventually became the basis of much of modern child-centred education. Pestalozzianism also promoted the concept of teaching as a skilled profession, one that required intelligent, humane people carefully trained in child psychology, teaching methods, and educational philosophy. It also helped spread the idea of schools as agencies of social reform.

18 Wilson, Stamp, and Audet, eds, *Canadian Education: A History*, 314–5

19 Silbur, *Pestalozzi: The Man and His Work*, 298–303. Prentice in *The School Promoters*, ch. 1, fails to indicate the extent to which Ryerson had been influenced by Pestalozzian concepts.

20 Quoted in Barlow, *Pestalozzi and American Education*, 92.

21 Ibid., 27, 94–5. Unfortunately, the 'Oswego Movement' by rigidly formalizing the object-lesson method became yet another process of 'verbalization and memorization' and lost touch with the essence of Pestalozzi's thought. See also Gerald Lee Gutek, *Pestalozzi and Education* (New York: Random House 1968), 163.

22 MTCL, Boyle scrapbooks 1859–63, 1863–6, passim. For Henry Barnard's influence see Barlow, *Pestalozzi and American Education*, ch. 5.

23 *Constitution and By-Laws of the Elora Mechanics' Institute and Library Association and Catalogue of Books in the Library* (Orangeville: Rastall and Brownell 1881), 112–3. The library was established in 1857, closed down in 1869, and reconstituted by Boyle and others in 1871. Some of the many Pestalozzian-inspired volumes would have been on the shelves in the 1860s. Boyle greatly expanded the collection in the 1870s.

24 [David Boyle], *The Ups and Downs of No. 7, Rexville, Being a Full, True and Correct Account of what happened in the said School Section during a Period of Twelve Months, more or less, and of some Things that were enacted beyond its Limits, with a few judicious Remarks on Religious Instruction in Public School: The Morality of Fresh Air, Teacher's 'Recommends,' and Bogus Certificates by an Old Maid, (who was 'Plucked.')* (n.p., [ca. 1884]), 100. This was a thinly veiled autobiographical and satirical novel of Boyle's experiences as a teacher in a rural school section.

25 MTCL, Baldwin Room, Boyle scrapbook 1863–6, Elora *Observer*, 1 Sept. 1865. The clipping is entitled 'Notes on Schools in Pilkington.' The figure of 38 per cent was the annual average during 1864–5 for the five township schools.

26 R.D. Gidney, 'Elementary Education in Upper Canada: A Reassessment,' *Ontario History* 65, no. 3 (September 1973), 181–2. Gidney argues that 'children too young to help with the family work and to cope with bad weather and the winter snow were usually sent to school only in the summer months; for older members of the family the pattern was reversed.'

27 OA, Education department, RG2, F3B, box 32, common schools, Pilkington Township, superintendent's report for the year ending 31 Dec. 1865

28 Ibid. No other male teacher in the township earned less than $300.

29 Charles Trick Currelly, *I Brought the Ages Home* (Toronto: Ryerson 1956), 294

30 Connon, *History of Elora*, 162. See also David Boyle, *Hints and Expedients: A Pocket Book for Young Teachers*, illustr. by J.W. Bengough (Toronto: Grip 1892), 65. Boyle argued that by appealing to the students' sense of honour, discipline could be maintained without force.

31 MTCL, Baldwin Room, Boyle scrapbook 1863–6, Elora *Observer*, 1 Sept. 1865

32 Elora *Observer*, 14 Dec. 1865

33 ROM, Ethnology, David Boyle, 'The Amenities of a Teacher's Life,' handwritten manuscript (n.d., [ca. 1868–80]), 2 (probably a paper read to the North Wellington Teachers' Association). These ideas likely came from the *Journal of Education for Upper Canada*. See, for example, 'Ornamenting School Grounds' and 'Love of Flowers,' 17 (April 1864), 57–8.

34 Boyle, *Ups and Downs of No. 7*, 100

35 ROM, Ethnology, David Boyle, 'The Natural History of Teachers,' handwritten

manuscript, 13 Oct. 1883, unpaginated (probably a paper read to the North Wellington Teachers' Association)

36 ROM, Ethnology, David Boyle, 'Teachers,' handwritten manuscript (n.d., [ca. 1868–80]), 2
37 Boyle, *Hints and Expedients*, 65
38 Prentice, *The School Promoters*, 33–5
39 Boyle, 'Amenities of a Teacher's Life,' 4
40 Boyle, *Hints and Expedients*, 65
41 Boyle, *Ups and Downs of No. 7*, 101
42 Boyle, 'Teachers,' 5
43 Elora *Observer*, 12 March 1869
44 Boyle, 'Natural History of Teachers,' unpaginated
45 See Boyle, *Ups and Downs of No. 7*, 101, and 'Teachers,' 5.
46 Boyle, *Hints and Expedients*, 58
47 Boyle, *Ups and Downs of No. 7*, 31
48 Ibid., 100
49 David Boyle, 'Teach Children to Observe,' *Canada Educational Monthly and School Chronicle* 5 (1883), 235
50 ROM, Ethnology, David Boyle, 'What is Civilization?,' handwritten manuscript (n.d., [ca. 1868–80]), 28–30
51 Boyle, 'Natural History of Teachers,' unpaginated
52 Boyle, 'What is Civilization?' 28–30
53 Susan E. Houston, 'Politics, Schools, and Social Change in Upper Canada,' *CHR* 53, no. 3 (September 1972), 249–71. This paragraph is based largely on this article.
54 Boyle, *Ups and Downs of No. 7*, 40–1
55 OA, Education department, RG2, F3B, box 32, common schools, Pilkington Township superintendent's reports for the years 1865–70
56 Boyle, *Ups and Downs of No. 7*, 41
57 Ibid.
58 Carl Berger, *The Sense of Power: Studies in the Ideas of Canadian Imperialism 1867–1914* (Toronto: University of Toronto Press 1970), ch. 2; David P. Gagan, 'The Relevance of "Canada First",' *Journal of Canadian Studies / Revue d'études canadiennes* 5, no. 4 (November 1970), 36–44
59 Boyle, 'Teachers,' 10
60 Boyle, *Ups and Downs of No. 7*, 101
61 OA, Education department, RG2, F3B, common schools, Pilkington Township, superintendent's report for 1870
62 Elora *Observer*, 3 May 1866
63 Elora *Lightning Express*, 3 June 1880. For details of the marriage relationship see ROM, Ethnology, memoirs of Anne Anderson Perry (ca. 1950).
64 ROM, Archives, T.A. Brough to Boyle, 24 Sept. 1898

65 MTCL, Baldwin Room, Boyle scrapbook 1866–70, unidentified clipping, 10 Sept. 1869. See also Fergus *News-Record*, 10 Dec. 1869.
66 OA, Charles Clarke diary, 15 Dec. 1870
67 *Canada Educational Monthly and School Chronicle* 4 (1882), 146. Letter signed 'Vindex.' Boyle's performance at this exam became a matter of public controversy during his years as a textbook editor from 1881 to 1883. See also the Elora *Express*, 16 March 1882.
68 Elora *Observer*, 25 Aug. 1871. At a subsequent exam in August 1871, a mere 14 of 90 candidates were certified.
69 Ibid., 11 Aug. 1871
70 ROM, Ethnology, Boyle scrapbook 1870–2, Elora *Observer*, 21 Dec. 1871
71 Elora *Observer*, 11 Aug. 1871
72 ROM, Ethnology, Boyle scrapbook 1870–2, Fergus *News-Record*, 19 Jan. 1872

CHAPTER 3

1 Clarke later represented East Wellington in the Ontario Legislature (1887–91), and served as speaker (1880–6) then clerk (1891–1907) of the Legislative Assembly.
2 OA, Charles Clarke diary, 3 Feb. 1867
3 OA, Charles Clarke papers, 'Inaugural Address' to the Elora Natural Science and Literary Society, 14 Nov. 1879
4 See Leo A. Johnson, *History of Guelph 1827–1927* (Guelph: Guelph Historical Society 1977), 215–7.
5 MTCL, Baldwin Room, Boyle scrapbook 1873–5, Elora *News*, 26 Dec. 1874; and unidentified clipping entitled 'School Report,' July 1873. 395 pupils were registered in 1873. Scrapbook 1875–7, unidentified clipping entitled 'School Statistics,' reports 421 students on the rolls in 1876.
6 Ibid. This attendance rate was probably higher than the provincial average which as late as 1886 was only 48 per cent. See OA, Ontario Education Association, Minute Book 1, Board of Directors and General Association, 1881–8, 12 Aug. 1886.
7 OA, Robert Cunningham papers, Boyle to Barbara Cunningham, 28 Feb. 1877
8 David Boyle, 'On the Local Geology of Elora,' in *Selected Papers from Proceedings of Elora Natural History Society 1874–5* (Elora: *Lightning Express* Office 1875), 5
9 *Archaeological Report 1899* (Toronto: Warwick Brothers and Rutter 1900), 22
10 OA, Mechanics' institute collection, [David Boyle], 'Mechanics' Institutes and the Best Means of Improving Them,' handwritten manuscript, signed 'Arole,' 27 March 1876

11 Elora *Observer*, 10 Nov. 1871

12 OA, Garron F. Wells, 'Mechanics' Institutes in Ontario, 1831–1895,' unpublished manuscript (December 1974), 11. The number of institutes receiving grants jumped from 13 in 1868 to 43 in 1871.

13 MTCL, Baldwin Room, Boyle scrapbook 1875–7, Elora *Observer*, 17 May 1877. For Boyle's involvement see Wellington County Museum Archives, minute book, Elora Mechanics' Institute, 1878–86.

14 OA. Education department, RG2, series R, reports of the mechanics' institutes. 186 people subscribed in the first year. See also Wellington County Museum Archives, library subscription book.

15 MTCL, Baldwin Room, Boyle scrapbook 1873–5, unidentified clipping, 10 Oct. 1873. The Toronto Mechanics' Institute listed a mere sixteen artisans on its rolls; see G.P. de T. Glazebrook *The Story of Toronto* (Toronto: University of Toronto Press 1971), 154. Most institutes seem to have been primarily used by the middle class according to Wells, 'Mechanics' Institutes in Ontario.'

16 Boyle, 'Mechanics' Institutes,' 27 March 1876, unpaginated

17 Ibid.

18 MTCL, Baldwin Room, Boyle scrapbook 1873–5, Elora *News*, 28 Nov. 1873

19 Boyle, 'Mechanics' Institutes,' 27 March 1876, unpaginated

20 Adam Boyle to William Boyle, 6 April 1853. Original in possession of Mrs Helen Boyd, Ottawa.

21 *Constitution and By-Laws of the Elora Mechanics' Institute and Library Association, and Catalogue of Books in the Library* (Orangeville: Rastall and Brownell 1881)

22 OA, Education department, RG2, series R, Elora Mechanics' Institute, report for 1878

23 MTCL, Baldwin Room, Boyle scrapbook 1875–7, Elora *Observer*, 17 May 1877. The figures for 1884 come from *OSP*, no. 5 (1885), 222.

24 *OSP*, no. 14 (1884), 211–2

25 MTCL, Baldwin Room, Boyle scrapbook 1875–7, Elora *Observer*, 17 May 1877. For the Toronto institute see Glazebrook, *Story of Toronto*, 154.

26 Quotes taken from Elora *Observer*, 10 Oct. 1873, 17 May 1877; and OA, Education department, RG2, series R, Elora Mechanics' Institute, reports for 1876 and 1877.

27 Boyle, 'Mechanics' Institutes,' 27 March 1876, unpaginated

28 Wells, 'Mechanics' Institutes in Ontario,' 16

29 For the impact of Darwinism in North America see Richard Hofstadter, *Social Darwinism in American Thought*, rev. ed. (New York: George Braziller 1959); and Cynthia Eagle Russett, *Darwin in America: The Intellectual Response 1865–1912* (San Francisco: W. H. Freeman 1976).

30 Glyn Daniel, *A Hundred and Fifty Years of Archaeology*, 2nd ed. (London: Duckworth 1975), ch. 1–3; Glyn Daniel, *The Idea of Prehistory* (Baltimore: Penguin 1964), ch. 2–3

31 *Transactions and Collections of the American Antiquarian Society* 1 (Worcester: Massachusets 1820), 105–267

32 Daniel Wilson, 'Supposed Evidence of the Existence of Inter-Glacial American Man,' *CJ*, new ser., 15 (1876–8), 557–73. Wilson was not convinced by Abbott's findings.

33 *Archaeological Report 1894–95* (Toronto: Warwick Bros. and Rutter 1896), 72

34 J.D. Wilson, R.M. Stamp, L.-P. Audet, eds, *Canadian Education: A History* (Scarborough, Ont.: Prentice-Hall 1970), 294

35 See, for example, the *Journal of Education* 17 (April 1864), 56; 18 (August 1865), 121–2; 21 (July 1868), 87; 22 (April 1869), 51; 22 (July 1869), 102; 22 (November 1869), 161–2; 23 (February 1870), 25.

36 ROM, Ethnology, Boyle scrapbook 1870–3, unidentified clipping entitled 'Draft of Bill,' 30 Nov. 1870

37 For an excellent overview of this issue see Wilson, Stamp, and Audet, eds, *Canadian Education: A History*, 292–6.

38 Elora *Observer*, 8 Sept. 1871

39 *Journal of Education* 22 (April 1869), 56 and (June 1869), 87

40 Archie F. Key, *Beyond Four Walls: The Origins and Development of Canadian Museums* (Toronto: McClelland and Stewart 1973), ch. 12

41 ROM, Ethnology, Boyle scrapbook 1870–3, Elora *News*, 10 April 1873

42 MTCL, Baldwin Room, Boyle scrapbook 1873–5, Elora *News*, 24 April 1873

43 Ibid., 15 Jan. 1874

44 OA, Byerly papers, circular, 'Elora School Museum,' September 1876

45 Key, *Beyond Four Walls*, 126. The National Museum had its origins in the 1840s through the work of William Edmund Logan for the Geological Survey.

46 Smithsonian Institution Archives RV26, office of the secretary (Joseph Henry, Spencer F. Baird), 1863–79, incoming correspondence, vol. 170, 110 (Boyle to Joseph Henry, 23 March 1878)

47 See ibid., vol. 120, 109 (Boyle to Mr Rhees, chief clerk [ca. 1878]); requests for publications, box 3, folder 25, 597, (Boyle to 'the Director,' 25 Feb. 1878); RV33, office of the secretary (Joseph Henry, Spencer F. Baird, Samuel P. Langley) 1865–91, outgoing correspondence, vol. 63, 383–5.

48 OA, Charles Clarke papers, Boyle to Clark, 23 Feb. 1874

49 For Barnett, see OA, RG18 BO, Royal Commission to Enquire into Alleged Abuses Occurring in the Vicinity of Niagara Falls, 17 Nov. 1873. See also Gerald Killan, 'Mowat and a Park Policy for Niagara Falls 1873–1887,' *Ontario History* 70, no. 2 (June 1978), 115–35; and Henry Scadding, 'On Mueseums and other Classified

Collections, Temporary and Permanent, as Instruments of Education in Natural Science,' *CJ*, new ser., 13 (1871–3), 24

50 MTCL, Baldwin Room, Boyle scrapbook 1873–5, unidentified clipping, 5 Dec. 1873

51 Elora *Observer*, 12 July 1874; copy of letter, Nicholson to Boyle, 25 May 1874.

52 MTCL, Baldwin Room, Boyle scrapbook 1873–5, Elora *Observer*, 24 Dec. 1874

53 Guelph *Weekly Mercury and Advertiser*, 3 Sept. 1874

54 Smithsonian Institution Archives, RV26, office of the secretary (Joseph Henry, Spencer F. Baird), 1863–79, incoming correspondence, vol. 170, 105–6 (Boyle to J.G. Macgregor, 7 March 1878)

55 Ibid.

56 Elora *Lightning Express*, 1 July 1880 and 25 August 1881

57 Boyle, 'On the Local Geology of Elora,' 6

58 OA, Charles Clarke papers, 'Inaugural Address' to the Elora Natural History, Scientific and Literary Society, 14 Nov. 1879

59 John R. Connon, *The Early History of Elora, Ontario and Vicinity* (Elora and Fergus: The Elora *Express* and Fergus *News-Record* 1930). See the picture of the cave between pp. 40 and 41.

60 ROM, Archives, M. Edith Day to Boyle, 10 Nov. 1898

61 ROM, Ethnology, A.A. Perry, 'David Boyle: An Original Mind,' unpaginated

62 Boyle, 'Mechanics' Institutes,' 27 March 1876, unpaginated

63 Daniel, *Idea of Prehistory*, 151–2

64 Boyle, 'On the Local Geology of Elora,' 6

65 Clarke, 'Inaugural Address,' 14 Nov. 1879

66 Ibid.

67 Boyle, *Ups and Downs of No. 7*, 98

68 Elora *Lightning Express*, 8 March 1883

69 Ibid., 18 Jan. 1883

70 Charles Darwin, *On the Origin of Species by Means of Natural Selection, Or the Preservation of Favoured Races in the Struggle for Life* (New York: Washington Square Press 1963), 469

71 Russett, *Darwin in America*, 27–8

72 ROM, Ethnology, David Boyle, 'Biology as a Factor in National Education,' handwritten manuscript (n.d.), 5. For the Natural History Society debate on Darwin's theory of evolution see Elora *Lightning Express*, 25 Dec. 1879.

73 ROM, Ethnology, David Boyle, 'Moot Points,' handwritten manuscript, 11 May 1884, unpaginated

74 Boyle, 'Biology as a Factor,' 4

75 David Boyle, 'Our Poor Relations,' *Canada Educational Monthly and School Chronicle* 4 (1882), 383

76 ROM, Archives, A. E. Ackerman to Boyle [ca. May 1898]. Boyle had discussed these matters with Ackerman.

77 MTCL, Baldwin Room, Boyle scrapbook 1873–5, Elora *Observer*, 5 Dec. 1873, 1 May 1874

78 Henry Alleyne Nicholson, *Report Upon the Palaeontology of the Province of Ontario* (Toronto: Hunter, Rose 1875), 63, in *OSP*, no. 8 (1874)

79 Elora *Lightning Express*, 30 Sept. 1880

80 David Boyle, 'School Museums,' *Canada Educational Monthly and School Chronicle* 1 (1879), 83–6

81 *Canada Educational Monthly*, 2 (1880), 584

82 Boyle, 'Biology as a Factor,' 10–11. Herbert Spencer advocated many of these ideas. See *Journal of Education* 17 (April 1864), 56; 18 (August 1865), 121–2.

83 Boyle, 'Biology as a Factor,' 16. See also ROM, Ethnology, David Boyle, 'Teachers,' handwritten manuscript, n.d.

84 Boyle, 'Biology as a Factor,' 17–18

85 Ibid., 13

86 Ibid., 13–14

87 OA, RG8, 17F2, petitions re game and fish

88 OA, Charles Clarke papers, C. Clarke, 'Our Local Ornithology,' read to the Elora Natural History Society, 1 Feb. 1875. See also 'An Act for the Protection in Ontario of Insectivorous and other Birds beneficial to Agriculture,' 1873 (36 Vic, c45). This legislation improved upon an 1864 act.

89 Boyle, 'Biology as a Factor,' 18–21. See also ROM, Ethnology, 'Misunderstood Friends,' handwritten manuscript read before the Elora Natural History Society, 1 Feb. 1875.

90 See the Boyle scrapbooks 1868–81, passim. For one of Boyle's strongest performances at a county convention see MTCL, Baldwin Room, Boyle scrapbook 1875–7, Elora *Observer*, 10 March 1876.

91 David Boyle, 'The Teachers' Superannuation Fund,' *Canada Educational Monthly and School Chronicle* 2 (1880), 445–9

92 'An Act to Consolidate and Amend the Public Schools Act, 1885' (48 Vic, c49). Many of the demands expressed by Boyle were conceded in the legislation.

93 OA, Ontario Educational Association, Minute Book 1, Board of Directors and General Association 1881–8, 9–11 Aug. 1881

94 David Boyle, 'Credentials,' *Canada Educational Monthly and School Chronicle* 4 (1882), 51–3

95 OA, Charles Clarke papers, Boyle to Clarke, 1 July 1890

96 The journal was owned and edited by Archibald M. Stewart for almost its entire span from 1857 to 1919.

97 *Scottish American Journal*, 26 Oct. 1882

98 James Morgan, *The Canadian Men and Women of the Times: A Handbook of Canadian Biography of Living Characters* (Toronto: William Briggs 1912), 132
99 Boyle, 'Moot Points,' unpaginated

CHAPTER 4

1 *Canada Educational Monthly* (Advertiser) 4 (1882), 7
2 Allan Smith, 'Old Ontario and the Emergence of a National Frame of Mind,' in F.H. Armstrong, H.A. Stevenson, and J.D. Wilson, eds, *Aspects of Nineteenth-Century Ontario: Essays Presented to James J. Talman* (Toronto: University of Toronto Press in association with the University of Western Ontario 1974), 194–217
3 Elora *Lightning Express*, 22 Dec. 1881
4 Ibid.
5 Ibid.
6 Wellington County Museum Archives, Elora Mechanics' Institute, minute book, 13 April 1882; Elora *Lightning Express*, 20 April and 12 Oct. 1882. See also *Canada Educational Monthly* 4 (1882), 312.
7 Elora *Lightning Express*, 5 Jan. 1882
8 Viola Elizabeth Parvin, *Authorization of Textbooks for the Schools of Ontario 1846–1950* (Toronto: University of Toronto Press in association with the Canadian Textbook Publishers' Institute 1965), 53
9 *Canada Educational Monthly* 4 (1882), 193–4
10 Elora *Lightning Express*, 16 March 1882. This source cites the March 1882 issue of the *Canada School Journal*. No copy of this issue is extant.
11 *Canada Educational Monthly* 4 (1882), 140. See also the editorial in defence of Boyle in the Elora *Lightning Express*, 16 March 1882.
12 See, for example, PAC, John A. Macdonald papers, MG26A, vol. 389, 184154–6. Boyle to Macdonald, 6 Oct. and 6 Nov. 1882. The biography was not written for the Canada Publishing Company; however, in 1891, Adam prepared a revised and expanded edition of the late Edmund Collins's *Life of Sir John A. Macdonald*.
13 *Canada Educational Monthly* 5 (1883), 308
14 Parvin, *Authorization of Textbooks*, 54–7
15 *Canada Educational Monthly* 5 (1883), 446, 498
16 Parvin, *Authorization of Textbooks*, 66–8. All three companies were given the right to print the series.
17 G.P. de T. Glazebrook, *The Story of Toronto* (Toronto: University of Toronto Press 1971), 196. In 1881 Toronto had a population of 96,196 people, which increased to 181,215 by 1891.
18 Peter G. Goheen, *Victorian Toronto, 1850 to 1900: Pattern and Process of Growth*

(University of Chicago, Department of Geography, Research paper no. 127, 1970), ch. 4. See also Jacob Spelt, *Urban Development in South Central Ontario* (Toronto: McClelland and Stewart, Carleton Library no. 57, 1972), ch. 5.

19 Glazebrook, *The Story of Toronto*, 169–70

20 For an overview of the kind of books stocked in the store, see MTCL, Baldwin Room, David Boyle account book, 1884–6.

21 *Canada Educational Monthly* (Advertiser) 5 (1883); 7 (1885), unpaginated

22 OA, Education department, RG2, series N, box 2, 'Minutes of Evidence Taken in an Enquiry under a Commission from the Minister of Education of Ontario into Charges Preferred against Dr. May, of the Department of Education, January 3 1882.'

23 MTCL, Baldwin Room, David Boyle account book, 1884–6, passim. The largest orders from the education department totalled $152.45 (April 1884) and $99.51 (December 1885).

24 *American Anthropologist*, new ser. 12 (1911), 160

25 *Scottish American Journal*, 7 May 1885

26 Ibid.

27 *Canada Educational Monthly*, 6 (1884), 405

28 OA, Education department, RG2, series P2, box 51, postcard re West Lambton Teachers' Association meeting, 21–22 Oct. 1886

29 David Boyle, 'Union is Strength,' *Canada Educational Monthly* 7 (1885), 216–18

30 OA, Mechanics' institute collection, 1835–97, minutes of the Association of Mechanics' Institutes of Ontario, 16 Oct. 1884

31 OA, Mechanics' institute collection, 1835–97, *The Seventeenth Annual Report of the Association of Mechanics' Institutes of Ontario, September 15, 1885*, 6–9

32 ROM, Ethnology, notes by Anne A. Perry, ca. 1950

33 MTCL, Baldwin Room, David Boyle account book. See enclosed letter, S. Phillips to Boyle, 16 Sept. 1886, for an example of the difficulties arising from his billing procedures. See entry for 12 March 1884 for the bill paid to the Toronto News Company for *The Ups and Downs of No. 7*.

34 Gordon R. Willey and Jeremy A. Sabloff, *A History of American Archaeology* (San Francisco: W.H. Freeman 1973), ch. 3

35 For a more complete analysis of this theme than is to be found here see Gerald Killan, 'The Canadian Institute and the Origins of the Ontario Archaeological Tradition 1851–1884,' *Ontario Archaeology*, no. 34 (1980), 3–16. See also Bruce G. Trigger, 'Giants and Pygmies: The Professionalization of Canadian Archaeology,' in Glyn Daniel, ed, *Towards a History of Archaeology* (London: Thames and Hudson 1981), ch. 6.

36 W. Stewart Wallace, ed, *The Royal Canadian Institute Centennial Volume 1849–1949* (Toronto: Royal Canadian Institute 1949), 131

37 The full title was *The Canadian Journal; A Repertory of Industry, Science and Art; and a Record of the Proceedings of the Canadian Institute.* In 1856, the title was shortened to *The Canadian Journal of Science, Literature, and History.* In 1879, the *Journal* was replaced by the *Proceedings of the Canadian Institute.* A fourth series of the periodical appeared in 1890 as the *Transactions of the Canadian Institute.*

38 See John Connolly, 'Archaeology in Nova Scotia and New Brunswick Between 1863 and 1914 and its Relationship to the Development of North American Archaeology,' *Man and the Northeast* 13 (spring 1977), 3–34; and William C. Noble, 'One Hundred and Twenty-Five Years of Archaeology in the Canadian Provinces,' *Canadian Archaeological Association Bulletin*, no. 4 (1972), 1–78.

39 Robert Silverberg, *Mound Builders of Ancient America: The Archaeology of a Myth* (Greenwich, Conn.: New York Graphic Society Ltd 1968), 6, 57. For a mid-nineteenth-century Canadian perspective on the Mound Builder issue see 'An Old Letter About the Origin of the Indians,' *Archaeological Report 1899.* (Toronto: Warwick Bros and Rutter 1900), 164–5.

40 See the *CJ* 1 (1852–3), 160, and Noble, 'One Hundred and Twenty-Five Years of Archaeology,' 15. What passed for field-work in this early period occurred on a random basis, often undertaken by antiquarian relic hunters who swooped down on sites accidentally unearthed by farmers or construction gangs.

41 The preceding paragraphs have drawn upon Glyn Daniel, *A Hundred and Fifty Years of Archaeology* (Trowbridge and Esher, England: Duckworth 1975), ch. 2 and 3, and Willey and Sabloff, *A History of American Archaeology*, ch. 2.

42 *CJ* 1 (1852–3), 25

43 *Annual Archaeological Report 1907* (Toronto: L.K. Cameron 1908), 12. Boyle states that Fleming admitted to being the author of the questionnaire.

44 *CJ* 1 (1852–3), 98

45 *Annual Archaeological Report and Canadian Institute (Session 1892–93)* (Toronto: Warwick Bros and Rutter 1893), 1

46 Bruce G. Trigger, 'Sir Daniel Wilson: Canada's First Anthropologist,' *Anthropologica* 8 (1966), 3–28

47 Daniel Wilson, 'Discovery of Indian Remains, County Norfolk, Canada West,' *CJ* new ser. 1 (1856), 519

48 Daniel Wilson, 'Hints for the Formation of a Canadian Collection of Ancient Crania.' *CJ* 3 (1854–5), 347. These instructions were repeated in 'Discovery of Indian Remains, County Norfolk, Canada West,' *CJ*, new ser. 1 (1856), 511–19.

49 *CJ*, new ser., 15 (1876), 177–230. See also Trigger, 'Daniel Wilson,' 17.

50 M.E. Lartet, 'On the Co-existence of Man with Certain Extinct Quadrupeds, Proved by Fossil Bones (from various Pleistocene Deposits), Bearing Incisions made by Sharp Instruments,' *CJ*, new ser., 6 (1861), 368–79. See also *CJ*,

new ser., 9 (1864), 262–9: article entitled 'Upon some new Observations of Messrs. Lartet and Christy, relative to the existence of Man in the centre of France at a period when that country was inhabited by ... animals which do not live there at the present time,' translated by M. Milne Edwards; A. Morlot, 'Introductory Lecture of a Course on Remote Antiquity,' *CJ*, new ser., 8 (1863), 249–67; M. de Vibraye, 'Note upon some new proofs of the Existence of Man in the Centre of France, at an epoch when certain animals were found there which do not inhabit that country at the present day,' *CJ*, new ser., 9 (1864), 270–7. See *CJ*, new ser., 8 (1863), 378–90, for reviews of Lyell's *Antiquity of Man* (1863) and Huxley's *On the Origin of Species, or the Causes of the Phenomena of Organic Nature: A Course of Lectures to Working Men* (1863). See also R. Ramsay Wright, 'Haeckel's "Anthropogenie",' *CJ*, new ser., 15 (1876–8), 231–48.

51 The great popularizer of archaeology, Sir John Lubbock, drew extensively from Wilson's work for a chapter on North American archaeology in his widely read *Prehistoric Times*, which went through seven editions between 1865 and 1913. Moreover, Wilson's *Prehistoric Annals of Scotland* and *Prehistoric Man* seem to have had a considerable influence on the development of American archaeology, since they were used as textbooks by many students in the United States. See Sir John Lubbock, *Prehistoric Times, As Illustrated by Ancient Remains, and the Manners and Customs of Modern Savages*, 2nd ed. (New York: D. Appleton and Co 1972), ch. 8. See also Frederick Starr, 'Anthropological Work in America,' *Popular Science Monthly*, July 1882, 307.

52 Peabody Museum of Archaeology and Ethnology, Archives, Boyle to F.W. Putnam, 22 Nov. 1886

53 Toronto *Globe*, 10 Nov. 1879. See comprehensive collection of clippings in ROM, Ethnology, Laidlaw scrapbooks, 1874–96.

54 Ibid., Laidlaw scrapbook I, Toronto *Globe*, 10 Dec. 1878

55 Ibid., Laidlaw scrapbook II, Toronto *Globe*, 3 Nov. 1879 and 9 March 1882

56 Ibid., Laidlaw scrapbook I. See editorials in *Canadian Illustrated News*, 20 Jan. 1877, and Walkerton *Telescope*, 4 Jan. 1878.

57 Elora *Lightning Express*, 25 Dec. 1879

58 Daniel, *A Hundred and Fifty Years of Archaeology*, 152. The term is attributed to Seton Lloyd.

59 Elora *Lightning Express*, 25 Dec. 1879

60 Daniel, *A Hundred and Fifty Years of Archaeology*, 160–4

61 Wallace, *The Royal Canadian Institute*, 150–4. See also *Proceedings of the Canadian Institute*, 3rd ser., 1 (1879–83), 236, 268, 351; and ibid., 3rd ser., 2 (1883–4), 246.

62 See his inaugural address, *Proceedings of the Canadian Institute*, 3rd ser., 5 (1886–7), 11.

63 ROM, Ethnology, David Boyle, 'Moot Points,' handwritten manuscript, 11 May 1884, unpaginated

64 OA, Robert Cunningham papers, Boyle to Barbara Cunningham, 28 Feb. 1877

65 *Proceedings of the Canadian Institute*, 3rd ser., 3 (1884–5), 121

66 Ibid., 3rd ser., 4 (1885–6), 208–9

67 *Annual Archaeological Report 1907* (Toronto: L.K. Cameron 1908), 12

68 'Archaeological Report,' in *Annual Report of the Canadian Institute, Session 1886–87.* (Toronto: Warwick 1888), 15

69 ROM, Ethnology, Laidlaw scrapbook II, Toronto *Mail*, 25 April and 30 Oct. 1885, and Toronto *Globe*, 25 April 1885

70 David Boyle, 'The Archaeological Outlook,' *Proceedings of the Canadian Institute*, 3rd ser., 4 (1885–6), 4, 208–9

71 ROM, Ethnology, Laidlaw scrapbook II, Toronto *Mail*, 14 Jan. 1886

72 Simcoe County Museum Archives, A.F. Hunter papers, Hunter to parents, 24 Nov. 1885

73 Boyle, 'Archaeological Outlook,' 5

74 ROM, Ethnology, Laidlaw scrapbook I, Toronto *Globe*, 5 Oct. 1885

75 Ibid., Laidlaw scrapbooks I and II, Toronto *Mail*, 4, 14, 21 Sept. and 4, 11 Nov. 1885: Toronto *Week*, 5 Nov. 1885

76 Ibid., Laidlaw scrapbook II, Toronto *Mail*, 4 Nov. 1885

77 Ibid., Laidlaw scrapbook I, 21 Sept. 1885

78 Ibid., Laidlaw scrapbook II, 4 Nov. 1885

79 Ibid., 11 Nov. 1885

80 Boyle, 'Archaeological Outlook,' 2–7

81 ROM, Ethnology, Laidlaw scrapbook II, Toronto *Globe*, 14 Jan. 1886. See also *Proceedings of the Canadian Institute*, 3rd ser., 4 (1885), 209.

82 Douglas Cole, 'The Origins of Canadian Anthropology, 1850–1910,' *Journal of Canadian Studies / Revue d'études canadiennes* 8, no. 1 (February 1973), 33–44

83 ROM, Ethnology, Laidlaw scrapbook I, Toronto *Mail*, 15 Feb. 1886

84 ROM, Ethnology, Boyle papers, 'Memorial to the Hon. Oliver Mowat, Att. Gen.,' n.d., handwritten manuscript

85 Desmond Morton, 'People and Politics in Ontario,' in Donald C. Macdonald, ed., *Government and Politics of Ontario* (Toronto: Macmillan 1975), 1–2. These figures are for 1893.

86 *Special Report of the Minister of Education on the Mechanics' Institutes* (Toronto: C. Blackett Robinson 1881), 40

87 OA, Charles Clarke papers, Harris to Clarke, 2 Oct. 1885

88 *Proceedings of the Canadian Institute*, 3rd ser., 4 (1885–6), 209–10
89 Peabody Museum of Archaeology and Ethnology, Archives, Boyle to Putnam, 22 Nov. 1886
90 ROM, Ethnology, Boyle papers, memorandum to George Ross entitled 'Re the Archaeology of Ontario,' n.d., handwritten
91 Boyle, 'Archaeological Outlook,' 3

CHAPTER 5

1 *Annual Report of the Canadian Institute, Session 1886–87.* (Toronto: Warwick and Sons 1888), 9–14. *The Archaeological Report* encompassed pp. 9–59. Cited hereafter as *ARO.*
2 D. Boyle, 'Our Poor Relations,' *Canada Educational Monthly* 4 (1882), 330
3 *ARO 1886–7*, 9
4 Ibid., 11
5 *ARO 1888–9*, 2
6 *ARO 1890–1*, 6
7 *ARO 1887–8*, 4. Boyle spent $235 on specimens in 1886–7.
8 *ARO 1886–7*, 14
9 Ibid., 15
10 *ARO 1890–1*, 7
11 *ARO 1886–7*, 16
12 Ibid.
13 *ARO 1888–9*, 53
14 Gordon R. Willey and Jeremy A. Sabloff, *A History of American Archaeology* (San Francisco: W. H. Freeman 1974), 83. See also Bruce G. Trigger, 'Major Concepts of Archaeology in Historical Perspective,' *Man*, new ser., 3, no. 4 (1968), 528.
15 *ARO 1887–8*, 24
16 Glyn Daniel, *The Idea of Prehistory* (Cleveland: World Publishing 1963), 157. Trigger, 'Major Concepts of Archaeology,' 528
17 *ARO 1886–7*, 42. The Lougheed site has been identified by Charles Garrad as a historic Petun village site, perhaps the capital town of Ehway in the *Jesuit Relations*. For a study of the red siltstone and slate bead manufacturing industry see William A. Fox, '*Miskwo Sinnée Munnidôminug*,' unpublished manuscript, 1979.
18 *ARO 1886–7*, 54–5
19 *ARO 1894–5*, 29, 33
20 D. Boyle, 'Archaeological Remains, A Factor in the Study of History,' *Transac-*

tions of the Canadian Institute, 4th ser., 1 (1889–90), 70–1. See also *ARO 1894–5*, 25.

21 *ARO 1888–9*, 47

22 *ARO 1887–8*, 14

23 Ibid. See also *ARO 1888–9*, 47–101, for the catalogue.

24 ROM, Ethnology, Laidlaw scrapbook II, Toronto *Mail*, 16 May 1887. See also 7 Nov. 1887.

25 Ibid., Toronto *Empire*, 12 Feb. 1889, and Toronto *World*, 13 March 1889

26 *ARO 1887–8*, 5. See also OA, Education department, RG2, series P2, box 29, code XIII, no. 20, Scadding to [the Rev. Francis Henry] Marling, 18 May 1887.

27 ROM, Ethnology, Laidlaw scrapbook II, Toronto *Mail*, 7 Nov. 1887

28 *ARO 1886–7*, 9

29 *ARO 1888–9*, 1

30 *ARO 1886–7*, 14; *ARO 1887–8*, 10; *ARO 1888–9*, 18; Boyle, 'Archaeological Remains,' 69

31 *ARO 1896–7*, 98–116; *ARO 1897–8*, 67–87; *ARO 1900*, 50–62

32 *ARO 1890–1*, 71–3

33 Ibid., 68–71

34 *ARO 1894–5*, 75–9

35 *ARO 1891*, 8–9

36 Ibid., 9. L.H. Morgan, *League of the Iroquois* (1851)

37 *Centennial Exposition of the Ohio Valley and Central States, Cincinnati, July 4 to October 27, 1888. Mineral Exhibit of the Province of Ontario: Descriptive Catalogue* (Cincinnati: Robt. Clark and Co. 1888), 8

38 OA, Charles Clarke papers, Boyle to Clarke, 18 Aug. 1888

39 *Scottish American Journal*, 3 Oct. 1888

40 OA, Charles Clarke papers, Boyle to Clarke, 18 Aug. 1888

41 *ARO 1887–8*, 9

42 Ibid., 10

43 Ibid., 11–12

44 Ibid., 37–8

45 *ARO 1888–9*, 15

46 Ibid., 15–18

47 William A. Fox (personal communication)

48 Wilfrid Jury, *Clearville Prehistoric Village Site, Orford Township, Kent County, Ontario*, University of Western Ontario, Museum of Indian Archaeology Bulletin no. 2 (1941)

49 *ARO 1888–9*, 9–11

50 Ibid., 2, 4–15

51 A.F. Hunter, 'French Relics from Village Sites of the Hurons. The Geographical Distribution of these Relics in the Counties of Simcoe, York, and Ontario,' *ARO 1888–9*, 42–6. In another paper, 'National Characteristics and Migrations of the Hurons as Indicated by Their Remains in North Simcoe,' (*Transactions of the Canadian Institute*, 4th ser., 3 [1891–2], 225–8), Hunter explained how he distinguished between Huron and Algonkian sites on the basis of location and burial practices. Hunter's use of the term Huron is now outdated. He refers to the Huron ethnohistorically as a single people or tribal group (so did Boyle), which they were not. Rather, the Huron were an 'agglomeration of different groups' (five tribes or nations) with linguistic and cultural similarities who lived in different parts of the vicinity of Georgian Bay and Lake Simcoe. See Peter George Ramsden, *A Refinement of Some Aspects of Huron Ceramic Analysis*, Archaeological Survey of Canada Paper no. 63 (Ottawa: National Museums of Canada 1977), 1–3, for a discussion of the term 'Huron' and its uses by archaeologists. See also Conrad Heidenreich, *Huronia: A History and Geography of the Huron Indians 1600–1650* (Toronto: McClelland and Stewart 1971) for a model of recent historical-geographical investigation.

52 For an excellent overview of the development of this theory see Ramsden, *Huron Ceramic Analysis*, ch. 1. J. Norman Emerson developed the south-to-north migration theory in 'The Archaeology of the Ontario Iroquois' (PHD diss., University of Chicago 1954).

53 *ARO 1888–9*, 18

54 ROM, Ethnology, register of the Canadian Institute Museum

55 *ARO 1891*, 57–101

56 Frederick Starr mentioned Boyle's efforts in 'Anthropological Work in America,' *Popular Science Monthly*, July 1892, 307. W.H. Holmes used Boyle's pottery studies (*ARO 1889* and *ARO 1890–1*) in his 'Aboriginal Pottery of the Eastern United States,' *Twentieth Annual Report of the Bureau of American Ethnology to the Secretary of the Smithsonian Institution 1898–99* (Washington 1903), 159, 170–1. Cyrus Thomas did likewise in his *Introduction to the Study of North American Archaeology* (Cincinnati 1908), republished with an introduction by Jeremy A. Sabloff (New York: AMS Press for the Peabody Museum of Archaeology 1973), 88, 102. Later, Stewart Culin drew heavily from the *AROs* for his 'Games of the North American Indians,' *Twenty-fourth Annual Report of the Bureau of American Ethnology to the Secretary of the Smithsonian Institution 1902–1903* (Washington 1907), 84, 116–17, 350–1, 534–5.

57 John Connolly, 'Archaeology in Nova Scotia and New Brunswick Between 1863 and 1914, and its Relationship to the Development of North American Archaeology,' *Man in the Northeast*, no. 13 (spring 1977), 3–34

58 OA, Charles Clarke papers, Boyle to Clarke, 1 July 1890

59 *Transactions of the Canadian Institute*, 4th ser., 1 (1889–90), 22

60 Simcoe County Museum Archives, A.F. Hunter papers, Boyle to Hunter, 6 March 1890

61 Neil M. Judd, *The Bureau of American Ethnology: A Partial History* (Norman: University of Oklahoma Press 1976), 13. The director received $3600; executive officer, $3000; chief clerk, $2100; photographer, $1800; linguist, $1500; letter clerk, $600; messenger, $480.

62 Smithsonian Institution Archives, RV189, assistant secretary in charge of the United States National Museum, 1860–1908, incoming correspondence, box 12, folder 6 (Boyle to G. Brown Goode, 28 July 1891)

63 *ARO 1890–1*, 8–9

64 Ibid., 11

65 Ibid., 21

66 Ibid., 22–3

67 Ibid., 5, 13, 25. The Coulter site was excavated in 1978 by Eric J. Demkjar of McMaster University (William C. Noble-Peter Ramsden, personal communication).

68 *ARO 1897–8*, 51

69 *ARO 1890–1*, 77

70 *ARO 1893–4*, 19

71 James F. Pendergast (personal communication). In 1954, on the basis of pottery studies, J. Norman Emerson in 'The Archaeology of the Ontario Iroquois' (PH D diss., University of Chicago 1954), 254, 261, followed Laidlaw in suggesting that certain sites in the Balsam Lake area were expressions of a migration from the St Lawrence River up the Trent Valley into the Huron country in late prehistoric or early contact times. He argued that the St Lawrence Iroquois fused with groups moving north from the Toronto area to form the historic Huron. Recently, Peter Ramsden revised this hypothesis and argued instead that Iroquoian-speaking peoples in Victoria County in the Balsam Lake area were involved in trade with the St Lawrence Iroquois, trade stimulated in the mid-sixteenth century by the European demand for furs long before the French ventured into the interior. The Balsam Lake people, who may have served as middlemen between Huron villages to the west and the St Lawrence Iroquois, are said to have migrated from the Toronto area to take advantage of better trade opportunities along the Trent River system. Ramsden also speculates that prior to Champlain, the Huron may have eliminated the St Lawrence Iroquois as middlemen, a theory supported by J.V. Wright who suggests that the capture of St Lawrence Iroquois women in battle would explain the appearance of considerable quantities of St Lawrence pottery at village sites around Balsam Lake and further west in the Huron country proper. See Ramsden, *Huron Ceramic Analysis*, 285–6; and J.V. Wright, *Ontario*

Prehistory: An Eleven-Thousand Year Archaeological Outline (Ottawa: National Museums of Canada 1972), 90. Bruce Trigger in *The Children of Aataentsic: A History of the Huron People to 1660*, 2 vol. (Montreal and London: McGill-Queen's University Press 1976), I, 227, thinks there is substance to the theory that the St Lawrence ceramic styles found along the Trent were the result of the absorption into Arendarhonon villages of groups of St Lawrence Iroquois refugees fleeing Mohawk attacks.

72 ROM, Ethnology, Laidlaw scrapbook II, clippings for August 1896

73 *ARO 1890–1*, 5

74 Ibid., 6, 24

75 *Transactions of the Canadian Institute*, 4th ser., 1 (1889–90), 4

76 *ARO 1890–1*, 18–19

77 Simcoe County Museum Archives, A.F. Hunter papers, Boyle to Hunter, 19, 20 Nov. 1890

78 Barrie *Examiner*, 4 Dec. 1890; 29 Jan. 1891; 21 May 1891. OA, minute book, Simcoe County Pioneer and Historical Society, 6 Nov. 1891. For the meeting of the Canadian Institute in Penetanguishene and on Christian Island, see *Transactions of the Canadian Institute*, 4th ser., 3 (1891–2), 2–4.

79 Ibid., 59. Part of the land was owned by the Jesuit Order, a group who for many years oversaw the site and played no small part in its long-term protection. See A.F. Hunter, 'The Site of the Mission of Ste Marie on the Wye; Its Possessors and Present Condition,' *Transactions of the Canadian Institute* 4 (1892–3), 230.

80 *ARO 1890–1*, 10

81 UWO, James Coyne papers, unidentified clipping, 'A New Society,' 30 April 1891

82 Toronto *Globe*, 19 Aug. 1930, reported that the official dedication of the site by the Historical Sites and Monuments Board would take place on 15 Sept. 1930. See also minute books, Elgin Historical and Scientific Institute, 1891–1930, for the record of that society's involvement with the earthwork. These books are in the possession of George Thorman, St Thomas.

83 *ARO 1890–1*, 14–15

84 A.F. Chamberlain, 'The Algonkian Indians of Baptiste Lake,' *ARO 1890–1*, 83–9

85 *ARO 1891*, 11. The Pound site was excavated by Dr Philleo Nash of the University of Toronto in 1938–9. The Dalby site has not been excavated to this day (William A. Fox, personal communication).

86 Ibid., 13. For the Beckstead site, see James F. Pendergast, *Three Prehistoric Iroquois Components in Eastern Ontario*, National Museums of Canada, Bulletin no. 208 (Ottawa 1966).

87 *ARO 1891*, 13–15

88 Ibid., 15. The Rideau Lake area is still 'an archaeological hiatus' (James F. Pendergast, personal communication).

89 Ibid., 5

90 David Boyle, *Hints and Expedients: A Pocket Book for Young Teachers*, illustr. by J.W. Bengough (Toronto: Grip 1892)
91 *ARO 1890–1*, 6, and *ARO 1891*, 5
92 *ARO 1890–1*, 6. See ROM, Ethnology, A.F. Hunter papers, the Hunter-Laidlaw correspondence, 1889-1912.
93 OA, Charles Clarke papers, Boyle to Clarke, 1 July 1890
94 Royal Commission on the Mineral Resources of Ontario, *Report* (Toronto 1890). See H.V. Nelles, *The Politics of Development: Forests, Mines and Hydro-Electric Power in Ontario 1849–1941* (Toronto: Macmillan 1974), 138–53.
95 *ARO 1887–8*, 13
96 OA, Alexander Fraser papers, Boyle to Fraser, 31 March 1896. See also *Transactions of the Canadian Institute*, 4th ser., 3 (1891–2), 48.
97 *ARO 1891*, 5–6; *ARO 1892–3*, 2
98 *Report of the Ontario Commissioner to the World's Columbian Exposition 1893* (Toronto: Warwick Bros and Rutter 1894), 27
99 Ibid., 29–30
100 Ibid., 11
101 Ibid., 36
102 PAC, MG24, D82 1250, William Loch papers, Boyle to W. Loch Stewart, 24 June 1893
103 ROM, Archives, Boyle papers, Haseltine to Boyle, 14 May 1900
104 *Report of World's Columbian Exposition*, 40
105 Ibid., 12, 42
106 Ibid., 41–2
107 *ARO 1893–4*, 6
108 Ibid., 7–14. Part of this collection of some 600 specimens were pictured in this report.
109 *American Anthropologist*, old ser., 6 (1893), 423–4
110 ROM, Archives, Boyle papers, Holmes to Boyle, 11 Dec. 1893
111 Holmes, 'Aboriginal Pottery of Eastern United States,' 159, 170–1
112 David Boyle, *Notes on the life of Dr. Joseph Workman* (Toronto: Arbuthnot Bros. and Co. 1894), 8
113 U of T Archives, Workman diary. The Boyle family is mentioned often during the period 1887–93.
114 OA, Education department, RG2, series P2, box 51, T.W. Beeman to George Ross, 21 Aug. 1894

CHAPTER 6

1 W. Stewart Wallace, ed., *The Royal Canadian Institute Centennial Volume 1849–1949* (Toronto: The Royal Canadian Institute 1949), 156–8

2 *Transactions of the Canadian Institute*, 4th ser., 2 (1890–1), 3–6
3 Ibid., 5–6
4 Simcoe County Museum Archives, A.F. Hunter papers, Boyle to Hunter, 10 July 1895. For an example of the new supervision over Boyle's work see OA, Education department, RG2, series P2, box 51, Boyle to Ross, 20 Nov. 1894.
5 *ARO 1895*, 4
6 Douglas Cole, 'The Origins of Canadian Anthropology, 1850–1910,' *Journal of Canadian Studies / Revue d'études canadiennes* 8, no. 1 (February 1973), 43
7 Boyle cited a host of authorities, including archaeologists, ethnologists, and geologists such as D.G. Brinton, W.H. Dall, Charles Darwin, John Fiske, James Geike, Horatio Hale, Rudolph Hoernes, O.T. Mason, Oscar Peschel, and Cyrus Thomas.
8 *ARO 1895*, 10. See also ROM, Ethnology, six lectures on ethnology, 5 (28 Oct. 1906), 11–16.
9 Ibid., 6–11
10 *ARO 1892–3*, 3–6
11 *ARO 1895*, 42
12 Gordon R. Willey and Jeremy A. Sabloff, *A History of American Archaeology* (San Francisco: W.H. Freeman 1974), 56–9
13 *ARO 1895*, 13–14
14 *ARO 1886–7*, 17
15 Ibid., 5
16 *ARO 1895*, 92
17 *ARO 1892–3*, 5
18 See, for example, William C. Noble, 'Van Beisen (Af Hd-2). A Study in Glen Meyer Development,' *Ontario Archaeology*, no. 24 (1975) and 'Corn and Villages in Southern Ontario,' *Ontario Archaeology*, no. 25 (1975), 37–46.
19 See Willey and Sabloff, *History of American Archaeology*, 86–9, and Marvin Harris, *The Rise of Anthropological Theory* (New York: Thos. Y. Crowell 1968), ch. 7
20 *ARO 1894–5*, 34–5
21 Ibid., 5
22 Ibid., 35–7
23 A thorough examination of this site was not made until 1939. See W.J. Wintemberg, *Lawson Prehistoric Village Site, Middlesex County, Ontario*, National Museum of Canada, Bulletin no. 94
24 *ARO 1894–5*, 38–40
25 Ibid., 33–4. See also Joseph Henry, 'Editorial Comment,' *Annual Report of the Smithsonian Institution for 1874* (Washngton, DC 1875), 335.

26 *ARO 1894–5*, 40. These pits may have been grave sites used prior to ossuary burial. (William C. Noble, personal communication).

27 *ARO 1894–5*, 42

28 Ibid., 41–2

29 Ibid., 52–3

30 Ibid., 51–2

31 Ibid., 47. Boyle quoted Mallery at length in this report. Only a few people had recorded rock art sites in Ontario prior to Boyle. For example, Henry Schoolcraft recorded the Agawa Site, now in Lake Superior Provincial Park, prior to 1850. Two sites were recorded by Lawson in 1885 in the Lake of the Woods area. See Selwyn Dewdney and Kenneth E. Kidd, *Indian Rock Paintings of the Great Lakes*, 2nd ed. (Toronto: University of Toronto Press 1973), 10.

32 Ibid., 96. In 1958 Dewdney counted 135 painted symbols scattered over 27 faces.

33 *ARO 1894–5*, 44

34 Ibid., 48

35 Dewdney and Kidd, *Indian Rock Paintings*, 161

36 *ARO 1894–5*, 46. Kenneth Kidd argues that such rock paintings were 'the work of a people of Woodland culture, probably the late Woodland of prehistoric and Eastern Woodland of early historic times.' Dewdney and Kidd, *Indian Rock Paintings*, 168

37 Ibid., 170

38 W.H.C. Phillips, 'Rock Paintings at Temagami District,' *ARO 1906*, 41–7

39 *ARO 1907*, 31–3

40 *ARO 1894–5*, 5–6

41 OA, Alexander Fraser papers, Boyle to Fraser, 3 March 1896. See also *ARO, 1894–5*, 5–6

42 OA, Alexander Fraser papers, Boyle to Fraser, 24 June 1896

43 Ibid., Boyle to Fraser, 3 March 1896

44 ROM, Archives, Culin to Boyle, 17 July 1896

45 David Boyle, *The Township of Scarboro 1796–1896* (Toronto: William Briggs 1896), preface

46 G.M. Wrong, 'The Beginnings of Historical Criticism in Canada: A Retroscpect 1896–1936; *CHR* 17, no. 1 (March 1936), 1–8

47 See Fritz Stern, ed. *The Varieties of History From Voltaire to the Present* (Cleveland and New York: Meridian Books 1966), intro. and ch. 3 on Leopold von Ranke.

48 Hans Meyerhoff, ed., *The Philosophy of History in Our Time* (Garden City, NY: Doubleday 1959), 21

49 David Boyle, 'The Philosophy of Folk Lore,' in Pioneer and Historical Association of the Province of Ontario, *Report 1896*, 49–55

50 The column ran from November 1897 to March 1898. See also ROM, Archives, J.S. Willison to Boyle, 21 March 1898.

51 See Gerald Killan, *Preserving Ontario's Heritage: A History of the Ontario Historical Society* (Ottawa: Love Printing 1976), ch. 2.

52 OA, William Canniff papers, pkg. no. 12. See William Canniff, 'A Review of Historical Work in Upper Canada,' presidential address to the historical section of the Canadian Institute, 9 Nov. 1893.

53 PAC, Department of Militia and Defence, deputy-minister's office records, RG9, II, A1, 358, file A12216

54 *Transactions of the Canadian Institute*, 4th ser., 2 (1890–1), 6, 13, 62, 75

55 Killan, *Preserving Ontario's Heritage*, ch. 1

56 Carl Berger, *The Sense of Power: Studies in the Ideas of Canadian Imperialism 1867–1914* (Toronto: University of Toronto Press 1970), ch. 3

57 *Journal and Transactions of the Wentworth Historical Society* 1 (1892), 16: address by F.W. Fearman, 5 June 1889

58 Killan, *Preserving Ontario's Heritage*, ch. 1

59 David Boyle, 'History Taught by Museums,' *Niagara Historical Society Publication no. 4* (Niagara-on-the-Lake: The Times 1899), 12

60 *Transactions of the Canadian Institute*, 4th ser., 1 (1889–90), 66

61 Pioneer and Historical Association, *Report 1896*, 33, 56–60

62 *The Scottish American Journal*, 17 June 1896

63 ROM, Ethnology, David Boyle, 'What is Civilization,' handwritten manuscript, n.d.

64 See J.R. Miller, *Equal Rights: The Jesuits' Estates Act Controversy* (Montreal: McGill-Queen's University Press 1979).

65 ROM, Ethnology, McCarthy to Boyle, 30 March 1889. McCarthy is quoting Boyle in this reference.

66 *The Scottish American Journal*, 3 April 1895

67 Rowland Tappen Berthoff, *British Immigrants in Industrial America 1790–1950* (Cambridge: Harvard University Press 1953), 138

68 *The Scottish American Journal*, 23 Nov. 1882

69 PAC, Laurier papers, MG26, G 176, 50267–69, Boyle to Laurier, 2 Nov. 1900

70 OA, Education department, RG2, series P2, box 51, Boyle to Ross, 21 Sept. 1896

71 Simcoe County Museum Archives, A.F. Hunter papers, Boyle to Hunter, 21 Sept. 1896

72 Richard B. Johnston, *The Archaeology of the Serpent Mounds Site*, Royal Ontario Museum, Art and Archaeology Occasional Paper no. 10 (Toronto: University of Toronto Press 1968), 16. Evidently Boyle failed to observe two smaller, inconspicuous mounds.

73 See *ARO 1896–7*, 19–26, for full description of the excavation and Boyle's conclusions.

74 Johnston, *Archaeology of Serpent Mounds.* Johnston suspects that Boyle confused intrusive and disturbed burials.

75 OA, Education department, RG2, series P2, box 51, Boyle to Ross, 6 Sept. 1896: 'Interim Report'

76 Ibid., Boyle to Ross, 15 Sept. 1896

77 *ARO 1896–7*, 26

78 OA, Education department, RG2, series P2, box 51, Boyle to Ross, 8 Oct. 1896

79 For the BAAS see ROM, Archives, G.M. Dawson to Boyle, 2, 13, 21 Oct. 1897; 17 Nov. 1897; 15 Jan. 1898. For the Town and County of Peterborough Historical Society see ROM, Archives, T.A.S. Hay to Boyle, 13 August, 17 Dec. 1897; J.M. Drummond, clerk-treasurer of Otonabee Township, to Boyle, 18 Dec. 1897; William Anderson, warden of Otonabee, to Boyle, 21 Dec. 1897.

80 See *ARO 1896–7*, 28–9, for the site report. The turtle effigy is figured on p. 56.

81 OA, Education department, RG2, series P2, box 51, Boyle to Ross, 6 Sept. 1896. Richard B. Johnston, *Archaeology of Rice Lake, Ontario*, National Museum of Canada, Anthropology Papers, no. 19 (August 1968), 13, suggests that this shell effigy pendant may have been intrusive, the product of a protohistoric or historic Iroquoian people.

82 *ARO 1896–7*, 33

83 See ibid., 30–3, for the site report.

84 See ibid., 33–5, for the site report.

85 Ibid., 35–6

86 Ibid., 38

87 The Le Vesconte site on the Trent River.

88 Johnston, *Archaeology of Rice Lake*, 26–30

89 Michael W. Spence and J. Russell Harper, *The Cameron's Point Site*, Royal Ontario Museum, Art and Archaeology Occasional Paper no. 12 (Toronto: University of Toronto Press 1968), 55

90 There is an extensive correspondence on this matter in the Simcoe County Museum Archives, A.F. Hunter papers.

91 *ARO 1896–7*, 76

92 Simcoe County Museum Archives, A.F. Hunter papers, Boyle to Hunter, 23 Dec. 1896

93 OA, Education department, RG2, series P2, box 46, order-in-council, 27 May 1897

94 Simcoe County Museum Archives, A.F. Hunter papers, Boyle to Hunter, 4 Nov. 1897

95 This is the breakdown of material provided by Boyle to G.M. Dawson. See PAC,

RG45, 16, file 17, no. 21: copy of 'Report of the "Ontario Archaeological Museum" March 5, 1897' for the *Report on the State of the Principal Museums in Canada and Newfoundland*, ed. by Henry M. Ami for the Geological Survey of Canada (Toronto: for the British Association for the Advancement of Science 1897).

96 *ARO 1897–8*, 15

97 ROM, Ethnology, Hunter papers, Laidlaw to Hunter, 2 Nov. 1897

98 *ARO 1900*, 1

99 Smithsonian Institution Archives, RV112, Assistant secretary in charge of the United States National Museum, 1879–1907, outgoing correspondence, vol. 109, 474–5, Goode to Boyle, 25 Nov. 1895

100 *ARO 1897–8*, 40–41

101 Ibid., 44

102 Toronto *Mail and Empire*, 19 Aug. 1897

103 *ARO 1897–8*, 1

104 *ARO 1891*, 7, from *Popular Science Monthly* (September 1891), 585–6

105 Harris, *The Rise of Anthropological Theory*, 164–9

106 *Proceedings of the Canadian Institute*, 3rd ser., 22 (1886), 129–31. Boyle recycled this manuscript as 'Some Mental and Social Inheritances,' read to the Hamilton Association on 13 April 1899. It appeared in the *Journal and Proceedings of the Hamilton Association* 15 (1899), 35–45.

107 Harris, *The Rise of Anthropological Theory*, 138–40

108 Boyle, 'The Philosophy of Folk Lore,' 53

109 ROM, Ethnology, David Boyle, six lectures on ethnology, no. 6 (29 Oct. 1906), 5–7, handwritten manuscript

110 ROM, Ethnology, David Boyle, 'Aphorisms,' handwritten manuscript, n.d., 8. See also *ARO 1898*, 167–8.

111 ROM, Ethnology, Laidlaw scrapbook III, Toronto *Mail and Empire*, 31 Dec. 1908. See also *ARO 1900*, 11–15.

112 ROM, Ethnology, Boyle to Willis J. Beecher, president of the Cayuga Historical Society, New York, 27 Jan. 1908

113 *ARO 1898*, 3

114 Ibid., 143–56

115 Ibid., 1

116 Charles M. Johnston, ed., *The Valley of the Six Nations. A Collection of Documents on the Indian Lands of the Grand River*, Champlain Society, Ontario Series 7 (Toronto: University of Toronto Press 1964), lxxxiii

117 See Annemarie Shimony, *Conservatism Among the Iroquois at the Six Nations' Reserve* (New Haven 1961), 203. Shimony also argued that Handsome Lake shared 'traits not only with the prophets of other nativist … Indian movements,

but also with the intellectual climate of northeastern America of his day.'

118 Johnston, *Valley of the Six Nations*, lxxxiii, argues that the Iroquois had always embraced a vague monotheism, but Beautiful Lake's 'conflict with Christianity served to throw it into sharper relief.'

119 David Boyle, 'On the Paganism of the Civilised Iroquois of Ontario,' *ARO 1901*, 124; read before the British Association in Bradford, England, 5 Sept. 1900, and reprinted from *The Journal of the Anthropological Institute* 30 (July-December 1900), 263–73

120 *ARO 1898*, 56

121 Boyle, 'Paganism of the Civilised Iroquois,' 125

122 Ibid., 124

123 *ARO 1898*, 190–4

124 Ibid., 194–5

125 Ibid., 196

126 OA, Education department, RG2, series P2, box 51, Evelyn C.H. Johnston to Richard Harcourt, 6 Jan. 1902

127 Ibid., Boyle to Harcourt, 9 Jan. 1902

128 *ARO 1898*, 4

129 ROM, Archives, Culin to Boyle, 31 Jan. 1898

130 Ibid., Cushing to Boyle, 29 March 1898. The list of those who encouraged Boyle was impressive, and included such worthies at Otis T. Mason, W.M. Beauchamp, General John S. Clark, Clarence B. Moore, Gerard Fowke, Frederick Starr, J.W. Powell, and F.W. Putnam.

131 For full documentation of this section see Killan, *Preserving Ontario's Heritage*, ch. 2.

132 *Pioneer and Historical Association of the Province of Ontario: Report of the Special Meeting, Toronto, March 30, 1898* (Toronto 1898), 4

133 Simcoe County Museum Archives, A.F. Hunter papers, Coyne to Hunter, 9 April 1898

CHAPTER 7

1 *ARO 1899*, 30–5

2 *ARO 1901*, 25–9

3 Ibid., 30–2

4 Thomas E. Lee, 'The Parker Earthwork, Corunna, Ontario,' reprint from *Pennsylvania Archaeologist, Bulletin of the Society for Pennsylvania Archaeology* 28, no. 1 (April 1958), 3–30

5 *ARO 1901*, 35

6 *ARO 1907*, 18–19

7 See, for example: F.W.Waugh, 'Notes on Canadian Pottery,' *ARO 1901*, 108–15, and 'Attiwandaron or Neutral Village Sites in Brant County,' *ARO 1902*, 70–9; R.T. Anderson, 'Malahide, Yarmouth and Bayham Townships,' *ARO 1902*, 79–91; L.D. Brown, 'Indian Occupation in Nissouri,' *ARO 1901*, 38–43; W. Brodie, 'Animal Remains Found on Indian Village Sites,' *ARO 1901*, 44–51.

8 ROM, Ethnology, A.F. Hunter papers, Hunter to Laidlaw, 4 Dec. 1898

9 OA, Education department, RG2, series P2, box 51, Hunter to Millar, 2 Dec. 1901

10 Ibid., D. Davidson to Harcourt, 20 Nov. 1901

11 Ibid., Boyle to John Millar, 26 Nov. 1901

12 Ibid., Hunter to Harcourt, 9 Dec. 1902

13 Ibid., Boyle to Harcourt, 12 Dec. 1902

14 See Toronto *News*, 17 Feb. 1908. ROM, Ethnology, A.F. Hunter papers, Hunter to Clark, 12 June 1903

15 See his ' " *8endake Ehan* " or Old Huronia,' *Fifth Report of the Bureau of Archives for the Province of Ontario* (Toronto 1908)

16 F. Birch, 'The Standing Rock,' *ARO 1903*, 98–101

17 W. Jury and S. Fox, in 'St Ignace, Canadian Altar of Martyrdom,' *Transactions of the Royal Society of Canada*, 3rd ser., 41, (1947), sect. II, 55–78, located the site along the Sturgeon River, a location that had already been rejected by W.J. Wintemberg. Conrad Heidenreich thinks their choice is dubious at best. See C.E. Heidenreich, 'Maps Relating to the First Half of the 17th Century and Their Use in Determining the Location of Jesuit Missions in Huronia,' *The Cartographer* 3 (1966), 103–26. More recently, Bruce G. Trigger, in *The Children of Aataentsic: A History of the Huron People to 1660* (Montreal and London: McGill-Queen's University Press 1976), II, 855, note 5, agrees with Frank Ridley that St Ignace II never existed. As for *Cahiagué*, in recent years it has been identified with the Warminster site, located north-west of Bass Lake in Medonte Township. See T.F. McIlwraith, 'On the Location of *Cahiagué*,' *Transactions of the Royal Society of Canada*, 3rd ser., 41 (1947), sect. II, 99–102, and J.N. Emerson, *Cahiagué 1961*, University of Toronto Archaeological Field School, Public Lecture Series (Orillia 1961). Trigger (*Children of Aataentsic*, I, 304) is not convinced that Warminster is *Cahiagué*.

18 OA, Education department, RG2, series P2, box 51, Hunter to Harcourt, 3 Feb. 1903

19 Ibid., Harcourt to Hunter, 5 Feb. 1903

20 Ibid., Boyle to John Millar, 4 March 1904

21 ROM, Archives, Wintemberg to Boyle, ca. January 1898

22 W.J. Wintemberg, 'Indian Village Sites in the Counties of Oxford and Waterloo,' *ARO 1899*, 83–92; *ARO 1900*, 37–40

23 ROM, Archives, Wintemberg to Boyle, 27 Feb. 1898

24 OA, Education department, RG2, series P2, box 51, Boyle to R.M. Wilkinson, acting deputy minister, 20 May 1903

25 *ARO 1905*, 33–56

26 *ARO 1907*, 38–90

27 *ARO 1904*, 39–42

28 David Boyle, 'Who Made the Effigy Stone Pipes,' *ARO 1903*, 27–35, 48–56. See also William C. Noble, 'Ontario Iroquois Effigy Pipes,' *Canadian Journal of Archaeology*, no. 3 (1979), 82.

29 *ARO 1903*, 36–43

30 Ibid., 80–6

31 *ARO 1904*, 36

32 See *ARO 1903*, 43–7, for McGuire's response, and 85–6 for Beauchamp's.

33 ROM, Archives, McGuire to Boyle, 14 Oct. 1903

34 *American Anthropologist*, new ser., 6 (1904), 160

35 ROM, Archives, McGuire to Boyle, 24 April 1904

36 Ibid., Beauchamp to Boyle, 21 May 1901

37 OA, Education department, RG2, series P2, box 51, Thomas to Richard Harcourt, 8 May 1903

38 Ibid., memorandum to Harcourt with translation of the review by Nadaillac in *L'Anthropologie* (1902), 677. Re the Anthropological Institute see ROM, Ethnology, J.L. Myres to Boyle, 28 June 1900

39 ROM, Archives, W.J. McGee to Boyle, 22 June 1903. For the founding of the AAA see *American Anthropologist*, new ser., 5 (1903), 178–92.

40 ROM, Archives, Wrong to Boyle, 14 June 1900

41 William C. Noble, 'Obituary: John Norman Emerson (1917–1978),' *Canadian Journal of Archaeology*, no. 3 (1979), 240–4

42 *ARO 1900*, 1–2

43 See lists of accessions and introductions to *ARO*s between 1900 and 1906.

44 OA, Burns Monument Committee papers, minute book, 2 Oct. 1902

45 OA, Education department. RG2, series P2, box 7, Boyle to Harcourt, 9 Nov. 1900

46 OA, OHS records, Victoria exhibition scrapbook. For a more extensive discussion of the exhibition see Gerald Killan, *Preserving Ontario's Heritage: A History of the Ontario Historical Society* (Toronto 1976), 106–13.

47 *Annual Report of the Ontario Historical Society 1900* (Toronto: William Briggs 1900), 16

48 Killan, *Preserving Ontario's Heritage*, 101–6

49 Simcoe County Museum Archives, Hunter papers, Hunter to Coyne, 5 Dec. 1900

50 Ibid., Boyle to Hunter, 22 April 1902

51 Frederic Barlow Cumberland, 'Canada's Heirlooms of Empire,' *Annual Report OHS 1910*, 33

52 ROM, Ethnology, see G.H. Hale to Boyle, 1 Aug., 18 Dec. 1900, for correspondence on imperial issues. For McSpurtle see *Scottish American Journal*, 21 Sept. 1898.

53 *The Centenary Celebration of the Battle of Lundy's Lane, July 25, 1914* (Niagara Falls: Lundy's Lane Historical Society 1919), 50

54 ROM, Ethnology, Boyle to Oliver, 24 April 1907

55 Ibid., Boyle to Bourassa, 3 May 1907

56 John Higham, *Strangers in the Land: Patterns of American Nativism 1860–1925*, 2nd ed. (New York: Atheneum 1972), ch. 4

57 OA, Education department, RG2, series P2, box 51, Boyle to John Millar, 22 Feb. 1901

58 Ibid. See the critical letter from Elizabeth J. Leston, director, Buffalo Society of Natural Science, to Richard Harcourt, 10 Oct. 1901.

59 Ibid., memoranda, Boyle to Harcourt, 15 Nov. 1901, and Boyle to John Millar, 20 Dec. 1901. For funding data see *OSP* 1901, no. 1, Public Accounts, 41–2.

60 OA, Education department, RG2, series P2, box 51, C.C. James to Boyle, 25 Feb. 1902; for Brodie and Robertson see Boyle to Harcourt, 3 March 1902.

61 Ibid., Walker to Harcourt, 22 July 1902

62 Ibid., Boyle to Harcourt, 17 Jan. 1903

63 Ibid., Boyle to Harcourt, 15 Nov. 1901

64 Ibid., Boyle to John Millar, 6 Jan. 1900

65 ROM, Archives, J.M. [Kingkentry?] to Boyle, 21 May 1902

66 *International Congress of Americanists: Thirteenth Session Held in New York in 1902* (Easton, Pa.: Eschenbach Printing 1905)

67 OA, Education department, RG2, series P2, box 51, Boyle to Harcourt, 10 Nov. 1902 (confidential)

68 Ibid.

69 Ibid., Harcourt to Boyle, 12 Nov. 1902 (confidential)

70 *OSP*, 1903, no. 1, Public Accounts, Estimates, 1903, 19. This figure does not include Boyle's salary of $1100.

71 ROM, Ethnology, George Pattullo to Boyle, 2 Jan. 1903; J.A. Gemmill to Boyle, 17 Aug. 1903; *ARO 1903*, 5

72 David Boyle, 'A Museum, or a Musée?' *ARO 1904*, 101

73 Ibid., 100–1

74 Ibid., 101–2

75 OA, Education department, RG2, series P2, box 51, Boyle to Harcourt, 4 Oct. 1904

76 Charles W. Humphries, 'The Sources of Ontario "Progressive" Conservatism, 1900–1914,' Canadian Historical Association *Historical Papers*, 1967, 122

77 OA, Education department, RG2, series D7, box 9, memorandum to Boyle, 17 April 1905. See also *ARO 1905*, 5, and *OSP*, 1906, no. 1, Public Accounts, 73.

CHAPTER 8

1 Based on data obtained from the Public Accounts in *Ontario Sessional Papers*, 1900–8
2 OA, Education department, RG2, series P2, box 51, James to Boyle, 25 Feb. 1902
3 Ibid., Boyle to John Millar, 19 Feb. 1904
4 ROM, Ethnology, Boyle to the Rev. T. Crosby, 4 Aug. 1906
5 *Uncle Jim's Canadian Nursery Rhymes for Family and Kindergarten Use*, illustr. by C.W. Jefferys (London and Toronto: Musson Book Co. Ltd. n.d.), 3
6 ROM, Ethnology, Boyle to N. McTavish, 28 Nov. 1908
7 Ibid. See these handwritten lectures on file.
8 ROM, Archives, Boas to Boyle, 5 and 15 June 1905
9 *ARO 1905*, 71
10 Ibid., 148–9. Boyle's southern hypothesis of Iroquoian origins was not original. It was posited by H.M. Lloyd in his 1904 edition of L.H. Morgan's *League of the Iroquois*. William Beauchamp also advanced the idea in the early 1890s (Bruce G. Trigger, personal communication). Boyle did not acknowledge either of these sources in his article.
11 Ibid., 146–55
12 *ARO 1903*, 126–38. See the companion piece 'The Killing of *Wa-sak-apee-quay* by *Pe-se-quan* and others,' *ARO 1907*, 91–121.
13 *ARO 1907*, 15
14 *ARO 1900*, 2
15 ROM, Ethnology, normal school papers, Dr Enrico H. Giglioli to Boyle, 17 Sept. 1907, 5 March 1908
16 The other recipients were John S. Clark and William H. Beauchamp. Two other Canadians have won this award: Kenneth E. Kidd in 1969 and Bruce G. Trigger in 1979.
17 ROM, Ethnology, Boyle to Beauchamp, 31 Jan. 1908; Beauchamp to Boyle, 7 Feb. 1908
18 *ARO 1907*, 31–3
19 *ARO 1911*, 9–11
20 ROM, Ethnology, Boyle to T.A. Brough, 27 Oct. 1908
21 Ibid., Boyle to Jean Barr, 14 Sept. 1908
22 Ibid., A.F. Hunter papers, Laidlaw to Boyle, 4 May 1909
23 Ibid., Laidlaw scrapbook II. See Toronto *Mail and Empire* and the Toronto *World* for 14 June 1909.
24 Ibid., A.F. Hunter papers
25 Gordon R. Willey and Jeremy A. Sabloff, *A History of American Archaeology* (San Francisco: W.H. Freeman and Co. 1974), 83

Index